STUDIES IN INTERNATIONAL SECURITY

*

I. Nato in the 1960s, by Alastair Buchan

II. The Control of the Arms Race, by Hedley Bull

III. Men in Uniform, by M. R. D. Foot

IV. World Order and New States, by Peter Calvocoressi

V. The Spread of Nuclear Weapons,
by Leonard Beaton and John Maddox

VI. Arms and Stability in Europe,
by Alastair Buchan and Philip Windsor

VII. Strategic Mobility, by Neville Brown

VIII. The Security of Southern Asia, by D. E. Kennedy

IX. China and the Peace of Asia, ed. Alastair Buchan

STUDIES IN INTERNATIONAL SECURITY: 8

THE SECURITY OF SOUTHERN ASIA

D. E. Kennedy

FREDERICK A. PRAEGER, *Publishers*
New York • Washington

BOOKS THAT MATTER

Published in the United States of America in 1965
by Frederick A. Praeger, Inc., Publishers
111 Fourth Avenue, New York 3, N.Y.

All rights reserved

Printed in the United States of America

CONTENTS

PREFACE   Page vii

CHAPTER

1. CHINA AND THE ASIAN BALANCE

I. The Shadow of China   1
II. The Limitations of Collective Security   12

2. THE EXTERNAL POWERS: NATIONAL INTERESTS IN SOUTHERN ASIA

I. The Development of National Interests, 1954 1964   28
II. The Communist Powers   30
III. The SEATO Powers   41
IV. Other European Countries   57

3. THE SOUTHERN ASIAN COUNTRIES: POLICIES AND POTENTIALS

I. The Indian Sub-continent   59
II. The Indochina Zone   71
III. The Maphilindo Area   98
IV. The Offshore Powers   113

4. THE THREAT OF COMMUNIST SUBVERSION

I. The Soviet Union, China and the Instrumentalities
   of Subversion   130
II. Techniques of Subversion: the Viet Cong in South
    Viet Nam   143

5. INTERNAL DEFENCE AND EXTERNAL ASSISTANCE

I. Aid and the Problem of Disequilibrium   159
II. Counterinsurgency in Asia: 166
    (a) The Philippine Experience   166
    (b) The Lessons of Malaya   175
    (c) The Problems of Viet Nam   183

CONTENTS

6. HIGH LEVEL VIOLENCE IN SOUTHERN
   ASIA
   I. Conventional War   200
   II. China and her Nuclear Capability   214

7. AN INDIGENOUS DEFENCE SYSTEM   234

Conclusion: The Security of Southern Asia   248

Appendix I: The Armed Forces of the External Powers
             and the Indigenous Countries   262
         II: Viet Cong Reports   294

Index   305

                              MAPS
   1. Southern Asia   xii
   2. The Indochina Zone   70

Preface

The idea for this book was conceived at the Institute for Strategic Studies, as one of a series of re-examinations of critical or controversial aspects of international security. The security of Southern Asia is at once a critical and controversial problem. The countries of this broad area are endangered by a wide range of threats to their stability and security, arising out of their own internal weaknesses and the external pressures of subversion and conventional attack. In the future, there will be the problem of confronting a nuclear armed China. It is controversial because of the serious disagreements about the best way to defend the area. The support of external powers in a front line and guarantor role is essential to the security of the indigenous countries, and will remain so for the foreseeable future, while the scale of probable threats may increase and the development of modern weapons systems will enhance the dependence of the Asian countries upon outside assistance.

The concept of defence arrangements through formal multilateral pacts has not widely taken root in Asia, where, after a millennium of conflict, there is no tradition of military cooperation between the states. The decolonialisation of Southern Asia allows fresh scope for historical conflicts which were held in check by the imperial powers. But their withdrawal left a vacuum of power and responsibility in the area, which has made it necessary for the Western nations to become once more militarily involved in Southern Asia (without the degree of political control over the countries which they previously had), in order to help build up a stable international society in a vulnerable subordinate state system. The manner of their involvement causes acute problems of disequilibrium in their relationships with the Southern Asian countries, for the exigencies of military relationships conflict with their desire to strengthen the economic basis of the new states and to respect their sovereign independence.

The withdrawal of European and American colonial rule from the Indian sub-continent and Southeast Asia has left the successor states with widely varying national traditions and interests, political structures and economic prospects. It forms the perimeter of a single large power, China, whose intentions towards all her neighbours are now suspect where they are not actively hostile, and whose long-term interests and attitudes arouse misgivings as her power and population grows. The problem of her true relationship with the Soviet Union serves to increase rather than decrease tensions and apprehensions in the area, since it robs Communist policy as a whole of the clarity which has been exhibited in Europe, and leads to a competitive diplomacy between the two powers in Southern Asia.

Since the early 1950s, most Communist challenges in Southern Asia have been met by direct Western intervention, American, British or French, and by the foundation of two collective and several bilateral security pacts. Thus, though the age of Western colonial rule has virtually passed, the Western powers have remained deeply entangled in the disputes and tensions of the area. This appears to have had two consequences. First, it has stultified the growth of a sense of collective responsibility for their own security amongst the new nations in Southern Asia. Second, it has made it difficult to re-examine how a more satisfactory relationship between China and the major Western powers might eventually be evolved. Some general problems of this relationship are examined in Chapter 1.

The national interests of the external powers and the policies of the indigenous countries are discussed in Chapters 2 and 3, with particular reference to the sources of conflict and instability in the area, and the problems of collective defence. For example, to what extent have developments since the Bandung Conference and the signing of the Manila Treaty in 1954 altered national attitudes and policies in the Southern Asian countries, including India and Japan? To what extent are they creating a greater sense of common responsibility for the security of the area? Some conclusions are drawn about the development of an indigenous defence system (Chapter 7) after a discussion of the threats of subversion (Chapter 4), the problems of internal defence and external assistance (Chapter 5), and the possibilities and implications of high level violence in Southern Asia (Chapter 6).

In the Conclusion, I have posed a question which is raised by the trend of the argument of this book. It is whether defence co-operation between external and indigenous countries for

the security of Southern Asia can most easily grow out of
formal political collaboration, or vice versa. Strong Asian
reluctance to join formal security pacts, such as SEATO,
gives this question a central significance. In some forms of
defence assistance, as in countering subversion, elaborate
organisations of the SEATO-type are not only militarily
ineffective, but also unnecessary: similar arguments may apply
to some extent to conventional hostilities in the area. Military
exigencies of the future, like the air defence of Southern Asia
as a whole against a sophisticated Chinese nuclear capability,
require long-term planning arrangements to be made on an
area basis, without respect to the political alignments of the
countries in the area. There is a strong case to be made that
military planning for the contingencies of future conflict (which
if it occurs will remove some of the Asian political inhibitions
on collaboration with the West, as the example of India has
recently shown), must precede the development of a political
climate in Asia in favour of formal commitments. This raises
the question whether formal multilateral and bilateral arrangements for the defence of Southern Asia are obsolete, or growing
irrelevant to major security problems.

Some comment is necessary about the sources and vocabulary of this book. References have been kept to a minimum;
many of the works cited have adequate bibliographies for
further reading, and footnotes have generally been restricted to
the more recent events. Some sources of information must
remain anonymous as a condition of the interviews which
I had with people in official positions; though I am sure that
Prince Souphanouvong will not mind my citing in Chapter 3
his account of the Laotian Government's prescriptions for the
economic future of the country. Some of the arguments discussed here could be reinforced by restricted information, but
the important thing is that they can be sustained without it. I
have tried to avoid the technical vocabularies and jargon which
are frequently employed in books about international problems,
believing them for the most part to be unnecessary and an
obstruction to the general reader. This is difficult, however, in
some cases, such as nuclear strategy and the capabilities of
modern weapons systems, where it has seemed best for the sake
of precision to use the language evolved for the special studies of
these matters.

More serious difficulties arise in connection with words in
common usage, such as 'aggression', and 'power' which has

particular connotations in the nuclear age. The Chinese attack upon India in 1962 was 'aggression' with what might be described as the classic objectives, to rectify a frontier and humiliate the adversary, like the German attack upon France in 1870. This is a serious matter in an era of nuclear weapons, and there have been few instances of it, despite the irredentist tendencies of some Asian governments: 'power' has exercised an effective restraint. Indonesia is potentially aggressive in her policy towards Malaysia, in that she is disposed to attack the Federation. But at the time of writing the aim of the policy of confrontation to crush Malaysia does not appear to have anything to do with borders; and if anyone is to be humiliated, it is the British 'neo-colonialists' rather than the peoples of Malaysia. Communist subversion is aggressive in intent, but it does not have the classic objectives or use orthodox methods. The North Vietnamese war of national liberation is designed to abolish a border which, when it was drawn, was not intended to have permanent political significance, and to reunite the Vietnamese people, not humiliate those in the south. Many of the conflicts between Southern Asian states and the attacks upon the *status quo* in the region are better perhaps described by other words than 'aggression'. Despite the Sino-Indian border war, there are substantial reasons for thinking that the threats which China poses to her southern neighbours will not lead to aggression and high level violence, though India must prepare for it. It is a paradox that classic grounds for aggression are to be found in the situation on China's north-west borders, between the two most powerful Communist states.[1]

The possibility that Western powers will commit aggression in the area should not be entirely ruled out. It seems probable at the time of writing that the United States may be tempted to bomb North Viet Nam in an effort to influence the course of the war in the south. If this happens, North Viet Nam could cease to pose a serious threat to its neighbours. Other developments, such as in the Sino-Indian conflict along the Himalayas and the Indonesian confrontation of Malaysia in Borneo and on the mainland, could lead to situations of high level violence in Southern Asia. Successful attempts at subversion might also change the balance of power in the area. For these reasons, it is necessary to add the caveat that many of the judgements expressed in this book must be regarded as provisional in the

[1] 'Where China and Russia Meet', *The Times*, 10 September 1963

context of the rapid march of events in Asia. As President
Sukarno said in his speech at Cairo in October 1964, 'the
problem of world peace itself now resides in the question of
the security of the developing nations. Persistent insecurity in
these new states can spark off the fire of local domestic conflict. This can spread at the edges, like a flame in the grass,
and develop into conflict with neighbours, and then into
conflict throughout a region. . . . And, once a conflict has
spread region-wide, it constitutes—if not before—a standing
invitation to involvement by the big power blocs.'[1]

*   *   *

I am grateful to the Trustees of the Rockefeller Foundation for
making it possible for me to travel through Southern Asia in
search of questions and answers; to the Institute for Strategic
Studies, and the librarian and administrative staff for facilities
and indispensable help, and for the invitations to present papers
at its conference on Southern Asia held at the California
Institute of Technology (financed by a generous grant from the
Ford Foundation), in August 1963, and at its Annual Conference
at Christ Church, Oxford, in September 1964, which enabled
me to hear the views of students of the problems of the region;
and to the Nuffield Foundation for the grant of a Fellowship
during my sabbatical year. The Institute for Strategic Studies
gave permission to print relevant sections of its publication,
The Military Balance 1964–65, as an Appendix. The American
Information Agency in Saigon made available copies of
documents captured from the Viet Cong, parts of which are also
printed in an Appendix. My thanks are due to the many
scholars, soldiers, diplomats, members of special agencies and
officials, in Southern Asia, Australia, the United States and
Europe, who generously gave me so much help: the errors I
have made in using information obtained from them are my
own. It is a pleasure to acknowledge my debts to these people,
and to Alastair Buchan, Director of the Institute for Strategic
Studies, for his stimulating assistance and encouragement
throughout; and to my wife for her support and patience, to
whom I dedicate my efforts.

London, December 1964   D. E. KENNEDY

[1] *The Guardian*, 20 November 1964

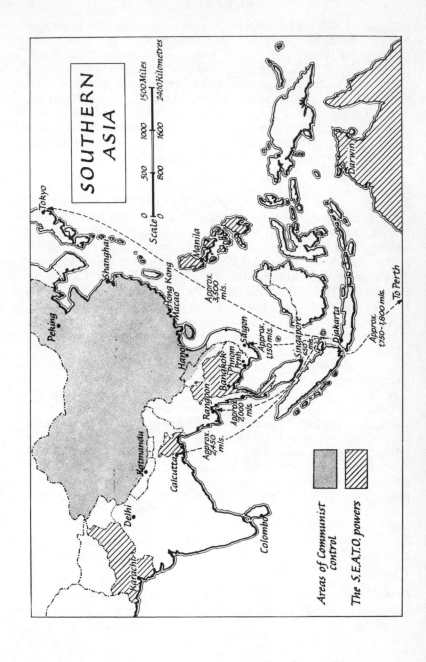

SOUTHERN ASIA

Scale

0   500   1000   1500 Miles
0   800   1600   2400 Kilometres

Tokyo
Shanghai
Peking
Hong Kong
Macao
Hanoi
Katmandu
Delhi
Calcutta
Karachi
Colombo
Rangoon
Bangkok
Phnom Penh
Saigon
Manila
Singapore
Djakarta
Darwin

Approx. 3,500 mls.
Approx. 650 mls.
Approx. 1,150 mls.
Approx. 2,000 mls.
Approx. 2,450 mls.
Approx. 1,750–1,800 mls.

To Perth

Areas of Communist control

The S.E.A.T.O. powers

Chapter 1

China and the Asian Balance

I. The Shadow of China

THE phrase 'Southern Asia' is a fairly recent addition to the vocabulary of politics. It has a broader compass than 'South-east Asia' and it is divested of the Western-centred assumptions of 'Far East': it represents a new preoccupation. The older phrases date from a period when European powers exercised a dominion over the area; a period described by an Indian historian as the Vasco da Gama epoch (1498–1945), when the superior naval power and armaments employed by the nation states of Europe enabled them to establish colonies in the region. These European possessions imposed new patterns upon the map which cut across the ethnic groupings and political boundaries of the older cultures. Political agglomerations were formed which represented the successful conquests by external powers, and the settlement imposed in the area was one which reflected the extensions of European conflicts. In so far as a balance of power existed in the area, it was maintained by the imperialist countries. The security of Southern Asia was a Western responsibility, interpreted primarily in terms of the current polities, national interests and alignments of European states. During the past twenty years, that European domination has been replaced by independence. There is now a new structure of power relations in the area, and 'Southern Asia' has come into usage as part of the analysis of the change.

The political independence of Southern Asia has introduced a new element into world politics, a new focus of policy. Southern Asia has ceased to be an appendage of Europe, with its alignments following those of European colonial powers. Substantial sections of Southern Asia are non-aligned, a position which represents a conscious rejection of European patterns of policy; and those states who through treaties are formally aligned with external powers have their own and not Western interests to further. In this sense, and from the viewpoint of the indigenous powers, the West has become their appendage—the reverse of colonialism. Perhaps the clearest illustration of this changed focus is the manifest intention of the Chinese Government in Taiwan to employ, if possible, Western backing to achieve its own political preoccupation, the return to the mainland of China.

In this study, the definition of 'Southern Asia' has been based upon strategic rather than geographical unity. For this purpose it is regarded as the area between the 65th and 180th parallels of longitude and south of the 25th parallel of latitude. This embraces the following non-Communist countries: Pakistan, India, Burma, Thailand, Cambodia, South Viet Nam, Laos, Malaysia, Indonesia, Taiwan, the Philippines, Australia and New Zealand. The two latter countries are included because for all strategic purposes their security is intimately connected with that of their Southern Asian neighbours. The Communist countries (or parts thereof) included in this area are China and North Viet Nam. Much of Southern Asia so defined falls within the boundaries of China as set out in the *China Yearbooks* published by the Republic of China in Taiwan, and in maps printed in China proper.

Southern Asia is dominated by the land mass of the People's Republic of China which is determined to assert its hegemony over those regions which traditionally paid tribute to imperial China, and whose ideology commits it to the furtherance of the Communist world revolution. The presence and the purposes of Communist China impose a certain unity on the whole area from Pakistan to Japan, which forms China's perimeter. Strategically it is a unit, though it has no natural unity. It is an area, writes Michael Brecher, in which 'the process of integration has barely begun', the 'most underdeveloped of all contemporary Subordinate State Systems'.[1] He argued that the configuration, the distribution and level, of power in the area was generally at a low level, and that its organisational integration was acutely underdeveloped. He recognised an important feature of this Subordinate State System to be the 'constant penetration by the Dominant System', that is, the pressure on the politics of the region by states outside it. This underdeveloped, unintegrated area is consequently thought to be particularly vulnerable to Communist pressures and penetration, while its capacity for

[1] 'International Relations and Asian Studies. The Subordinate State System of Southern Asia', *World Politics*, Vol. XV (January 1963), pp. 213–35

collective defence is low. After the Vasco da Gama epoch, direct Western control in Southern Asia has been replaced by an involvement based upon, and justified by, the fear of Chinese expansion and an estimate of the friable character of the indigenous state system.

The hostile confrontation that has arisen in Southern Asia between the aggressive countries, China, North Viet Nam and Indonesia, and the *status quo* powers and their Western allies differs in a number of respects from the hostile confrontation in Europe between the NATO and the Warsaw Pact countries. By contrast with the situation in Europe, in Southern Asia there is neither a 'balance of prudence' nor the beginnings of any political equilibrium between the Communist powers and the members of SEATO. There is, on the contrary, a much more open situation where on the flanks of China the two major powers, India and Japan, remain outside collective defence arrangements, and where on the Asian mainland the members of SEATO are enclaves in a neutral or hostile environment. This is the background for any discussion of the exact nature of the Chinese threat to the region.

The range of means at China's disposal for the manipulation of Chinese influence in this environment is now thought to have been extended by Peking's employment of military force against India in 1962. The problems which this poses for the security of Southern Asia are described in a Report to the Committee on Foreign Relations of the United States Senate, in 1963:

> Considerable Chinese Communist influence already is present, quite in addition to the large Chinese commercial communities which have long been established in Southeast Asia. Heretofore, however, Peking's influence has been diplomatic, ideological, economic, and only indirectly military, as in the case of aid to North Viet Nam. But the Sino-Indian clash makes clear that it is now necessary for the Southeast Asian nations to reckon with the enlargement of the Chinese role at any time to include the direct use of military power in a full modern revival of the classic pattern of Chinese imperial techniques in Southeast Asia.[1]

It is clear that defence planning must now take into consideration the possibility of further Chinese use of military

[1] *Viet Nam and Southeast Asia*, Report of Senator Mike Mansfield *et al.*, Washington 1963, pp. 1–2

force. At the same time, according to the Report, the West is if anything moving away from, rather than towards, a military balance which may lead in turn to a balance of prudence in Southern Asia. After pointing out that 'What transpires in Viet Nam inevitably colors the course of U.S. policy throughout Southeast Asia' Senator Mansfield wrote that the most disturbing feature there was that 'Viet Nam now appears to be, as it was then, [that is, on his previous visit] only at the beginning of a beginning in coping with its grave inner problems. All of the current difficulties existed in 1955, along with hope and energy to meet them. But it is seven years later and $2 billion of U.S. aid later. Yet, substantially the same difficulties remain if, indeed, they have not been compounded.'

The Report affirms two points which are important in the context of the argument from the Viet Nam case, that the United States has after the expenditure of so much effort and treasure made little progress in developing techniques for countering threats which are at once acceptable to an independent Asian ally, and effective even when the adversary receives little direct Chinese aid. The first is noted as obvious at the outset (page 2). It is that the American involvement in the area prevents further encroachments of Chinese power. Whatever the inadequacies of the multilateral and bilateral barriers, they do brace a door against China.

> Any sudden withdrawal [by the United States] from this position—as, for example, by the sudden termination of aid programs—would open the region to upheaval and chaos. What would eventually emerge is uncertain but there is little doubt that, in present circumstances, the Chinese shadow on the northern periphery would lengthen over Southeast Asia.

The second argument reaffirms a maxim of American policy that the threat to the area and to American security in the Pacific is predominantly the result of China's deep hostility. The conclusion of the Report states that

> This report does not deal with U.S.–Communist Chinese relations. Yet these relations are the basic factor in our present deep involvement in Southeast Asia. It was the hostility of China in Korea which first projected the United States in depth—via aid programs—into Indochina. It is Chinese hostility which evokes the continued flow of the

bulk of U.S. aid and other activity into Southeast Asia. It is Chinese hostility which underlies the U.S. treaty commitment to SEATO. In short, we are involved in Southeast Asia preponderantly because of the implications of a Chinese hostility to the whole structure of our own security in the Pacific—a hostility which at this time is of unfathomable depth and uncertain duration.[1]

Neither of these arguments is new; as the Mansfield Report indicates, they explain the American treaty commitment to SEATO in 1954. But American policy has been obsessed with them to the extent that until recently it has provided no constructive political suggestions about how to deal with the basic factor of Chinese hostility, whilst at the same time it has adopted postures which arguably have served to confirm that hostility. American-Chinese relations have been set in narrow military terms ever since China came out of her isolation with bared teeth.

In an address to a sub-committee of Congress on 26 January 1954, Mr. Walter Robertson, Assistant Secretary of State for Far Eastern Affairs, stated that 'the United States must dominate Asia for an indefinite period and pose a military threat to Communist China until it broke up internally'. This is one clear answer to the strategic question posed by the Communist victory in China. It assumes that China is and will be an enemy as long as she remains a Communist state. Corollaries of this attitude are the diplomatic efforts to isolate China internationally, to exclude China from the United Nations, and by military arrangements with Southern Asian states to contain China. At the time of Mr. Robertson's statement, Thailand, Japan, the Philippines, Australia, New Zealand and South Korea had made military assistance and security arrangements with the United States. Later that year, the Republic of China entered into a mutual defence treaty with the United States, and SEATO was established. It could, therefore, with some justice be claimed that both the objects of an American domination of Asia and an American military threat to China were being brought to pass by the end of 1954.

But ten years later, China, despite her internal difficulties, appears unlikely to break up internally; nor is it apparent that policies to isolate and threaten China will facilitate an internal dissolution and the destruction of Communist rule. It is unclear

[1] *Ibid*, p. 19

thinking to base or to justify a policy towards China on the hope that in due course her troubles will destroy the present government. The Communist Government of China shows every sign of enduring; indeed it may without much exaggeration be described as the most viable government in Asia. The Chinese claim that their national experiment provides a model for Asian development is taken seriously in Asia as well as the West; and this itself is a grudging tribute to the durability of the Communist régime, and to its achievements in face of great adversity. On the assumption, then, that China does not break up internally, and that she will continue to play an international role under Communist leadership, the question arises as to whether the policies advocated by Mr. Robertson are the best course to adopt 'for an indefinite period'. Can the security of Southern Asia be secured by an American domination of the region and by military threats to the national independence of China? If the question is put in this form the policy of domination and confrontation seems barren; what, after all, is the political objective of such a policy? If China remains under Communist leadership despite the policy, what will cause the internal break up of the régime? If the régime is not broken up, what are the benefits accruing to the policy?

There appear to be two grounds on which a policy based on the expectation that China will break up internally may be criticised; first, that it does not match the known facts, and second, that it is certain to create and to perpetuate hostilities which will render alternative policies unworkable. If China remains a Communist power, then policies of the type advocated by Mr. Robertson will require to be justified on grounds other than that they are interim holding devices until such time as the present régime in China collapses. They must be weighed against what such policies cannot achieve and against alternative policies. For example, such policies rule out of practical consideration any diplomatic interchange with China, even of the normal cold-war type as with the Soviet Union. Communication between the United States and China is restricted to a degree rare in peacetime international relations. A disadvantage of this situation is that when communication is thought desirable, when negotiations become necessary, there is little common ground between the areas of mutual suspicion and hostility. Laos is a case in point. By the Geneva agreements, China is a responsible party. Here is a situation where willynilly the United States and China are partners in a joint enterprise.

The nuclear power of the United States does pose a military threat to China, irrespective of the type of policy currently favoured by Washington, and threatening diplomacy in addition would appear to be superogatory. It merely confirms, in Chinese eyes, the Chinese image of America. There is a distinction between a diplomacy from strength directed towards constructive ends, and a diplomacy of strength directed towards destructive ends: the brand of diplomacy advocated by Mr. Robertson is of the latter type and is characterised by the narrowness of its political objective. A government is not likely to be co-operative with another government whose avowed aim is to seek its destruction, and since in Southern Asia there are already occasions for co-operation between the United States and China, there are grounds for rejecting policies towards China which serve only to perpetuate hostility and inhibit collaboration. This is not to take too sanguine a view of Peking's readiness to co-operate with the United States or to advocate a lack of firmness in the style of Washington's diplomacy. It is merely to point out that some intercourse between Peking and Washington is unavoidable and to recommend that the fact be recognised in future policy. For the extent of China's ambition does not appear to depend upon the Communist character of the government, but rather upon the strength of that government; Taipei's view of the proper boundaries between China and India is close to Peking's. If the Christian general Chiang Kai-shek were to replace the Communist general Mao Tse-tung in Peking would China prove less intractable?

Amongst the reasons which might be urged in support of this attitude is the view that inevitably some kind of Tordesillas line, as that between Spain and Portugal in 1494, will have to be drawn between American and Chinese spheres of influence in Southern Asia. Proposals for a neutral zone of security in Southern Asia accept this, as they acknowledge that such a political objective cannot be established without the consent of China. That consent may be difficult to obtain—in the present policy situation it is probably impossible—but it is in China's long term interests to consider the proposal and an object of Western diplomacy could be to make this clear to Peking. It is reasonable to believe that Peking can make realistic policy decisions concerning China's vital interests. The achievement of a neutral zone of security in Southern Asia requires, as well as consultation with China, the utilisation of the forces of non-alignment, and the policy of American domination of Asia seemed both to reject and to alienate those forces. The policy of an American domination of Asia is opposed not only by China as a threat to her national interests but also by the non-Communist Southern Asian states. Indian opinion reacted sharply and with hostile overtones against the prospect of American domination. Mr. Nehru described the United States as in its way as powerfully expansionist as the Soviet Union, and he commented as follows upon Mr. Robertson's remark 'Whatever the objective may be, the countries of Asia, and certainly India, do not propose to be dominated by any country for whatever purpose.'

Asian animosity was heightened by the belief that the United States disapproved of Asian neutralism and aspired to impose its own solutions to Southern Asian problems. Thus, the policy enunciated by Mr. Robertson in 1954 as a way of dealing with China restricted the openings for co-operation between those countries in and out of Southern Asia who were concerned to preserve the sovereign independence of the indigenous states. Her critics say that the United States' policy in the area has involved attitudes which have not failed to irritate the sensibilities both of her European allies and of the Asian powers. It has been marked by fervent anti-colonialism and anti-Communism, by suspicions of ex-imperial powers and neutrals alike. This calvinist approach to foreign policy was personified by Mr. Dulles during the years when Communists achieved notable successes in Southeast Asia. 'He that is not with us is against us' may be an admirable guide theologically, but in the fallen world of diplomacy it brings little credit upon its sponsor.

By 1964, Western co-operation with Southern Asian powers on the terms prescribed by their own sensibilities and values is seen to be an indispensable condition for the security of Southern Asia, and to be a proper objective of Western diplomacy. Policy is evolving within the framework of the barriers against the advance of Communism into Southern Asia which were set up in the apprehensive years of the 1950s, and in ways which make it possible to envisage something more than a barren military confrontation between the United States and China. The new trends offer some prospect that a balance of prudence leading towards a future political equilibrium may yet be established in Southern Asia. But enormous obstacles remain in the way of that development and policies designed to achieve it carry a high degree of uncertainty.

A decade after Mr. Robertson's speech on China, Mr. Roger Hilsman, one of his successors as Assistant Secretary of State for Far Eastern Affairs, stressed two of the planks of the earlier American-China policy. In a speech recorded in Australia in February 1964, he said that there must be firmness in the free world's determination to meet any aggression by China, and in its determination to maintain its strength in Asia and to help its allies and friends maintain their own military strength. His third point opened up new vistas for American policy, when he stressed that the free world must be willing to talk with the Chinese on such matters as a test-ban treaty and a renunciation of force in the Formosa Straits. In this reasoning there is still the assumption of the Mansfield Report that the military strength of the West and its allies does deter Chinese adventurism. But it admits the possibilities of a broadening area of discussion between the United States and China. By advocating a dialogue between the United States and China on a range of particular questions involving their respective national interests, it does not rule out the chance of a *détente* between the two countries on certain specific issues. This is a proposal for an American policy which allows more room than previous policies for political manoeuvres *vis-à-vis* China. We are in a trough between different American policies towards China, but Washington has relinquished the highly moral Dulles China policy for what without cynicism may be termed an amoral China policy.

Mr. Hilsman's speech of December 1963, which proclaimed a determination 'to keep the door open to the possibility of change' in Chinese policies,[1] elicited an interesting response in the Peking *People's Daily* two months later. The Chinese reply suggests that Peking is interested in exploring this issue and may indicate the beginning of a dialogue between the United States and China. As quoted, the reply states that although seven years ago Dulles arrogantly declared that Communist rule in China was 'a passing and not a perpetual phase', his disciple Hilsman had to admit recently that 'we have no reason to believe that there is at present any likelihood that the Communist régime will be overthrown'.[2] This

[1] Address to the Commonwealth Club, San Francisco, 13 December 1963, reprinted in *Survival*, March–April 1964
[2] *The Guardian*, 20 February 1964

rejection of some clearly stated assumptions of the Dulles policy is a welcome initiative in American diplomacy. If, as the quotation implies, Peking accepts that Washington no longer aspires to overthrow the present government of China, then some of the assumptions of Chinese policy about the American threat might be re-examined.

The question of American recognition of China is a crux of the development of more flexible American policies. The first point to be raised is how would American recognition be likely to affect the general Asian military situation, and the particular responses of Washington's Asian allies to the need to keep up their military preparedness? There is a danger that some Asian countries would interpret an American change of policy on this point as meaning that somehow American involvement in Southern Asia was diminished; that they would see it as a political defeat for the United States engineered by China, and orient their policy accordingly. In view of this contingency, any American recognition of China would need to be accompanied by reaffirmations of the American guarantees as well as a discreet political education of those countries who believed that recognition was a Chinese victory.

Apart from the effect of this policy upon Asian opinion, a second point concerns its effect upon China's actions in Southern Asia. Even if recognition of the Peking Government does meet a Chinese need for public acknowledgement of China's great power status, it is not likely to induce China's leaders to alter their ambitions or their policies in Southern Asia. Recognition is not a panacea. India, as China's sponsor in the international community, was nevertheless attacked on grounds which in themselves seem relatively insignificant. Conversely, it is difficult to find any concrete evidence that American recognition of China would stimulate Peking to take increased risks in Asia. A calculation of the military possibilities would have to take into account the range of China's present capabilities; where in fact China can apply varying degrees of power? what this power could be? and what would be the consequences of applying it? Such a calculation would most probably show that China's purely military options would not be increased by American recognition, only her broad political options. And here the problem of the consequences of American recognition, though still highly uncertain, can at least be thought of in terms of policy response. For it is possible to judge it in terms of Peking's capacity to influence those countries where she has diplomatic representation and those where she has not.

The case against American recognition of the People's Republic of China has strong arguments and stronger voices to uphold it. But it is a case which makes no provision for breaking out of the deadlock of mutual hostility. The Mansfield Report stressed that 'the basic stimulant to U.S. commitment in Southeast Asia is not to be found in the region at all. Rather, it is to be found in the hostility which characterises the relation with the Chinese mainland government and the dangerous implications of that continuing hostility to our long-range security'.[1] And if the hostility has dangerous implications for American security, a strong motive is provided for fresh attempts to reappraise its causes and conditions. That hostility is not all on the one side, and an objective view of the problem will recognise the justifiable elements in the Chinese reasoning. Peking has claimed in effect that Washington's hostility constitutes a threat to China's long-range security. The two giants are locked in Southern Asia by their incompatible foreign policies, but the resultant is not a balance as in Europe; it is a dangerous hostile imbalance. In this situation prudence suggests that ways of political manoeuvring be found, and there is a case to be examined that the recognition by the United States of the People's Republic of China is one of these ways.

The American intransigence towards the People's Republic of China is not shared by all the allies of the United States. Both the United Kingdom and France recognise China, and Australia, Canada and Japan have relations with China without recognising her. The United States will sell wheat to the Soviet Union, but resents it when Australia sells wheat to China. This kind of judgement suggests that there is an interesting distinction between the American view of the hostile confrontations in Europe with the Soviet Union and in Southern Asia with China. In seeking reasons for this, it may be a simplification, but not a distortion, of the truth to single out the emotional character of the American response to the People's Republic of China.[2] It contrasts with the matter-of-fact attitudes of the United Kingdom and France towards China, and has coloured the American approach to the

---

[1] Page 20

[2] In December 1963, Mr. Hilsman commented: 'There has perhaps been more emotion about our China policy than about our policy toward any single country since World War II'

security problems of Southern Asia, particularly since the Korean War. In part, too, the difference can be traced to the problems themselves, to the strategic situation of SEATO as contrasted with that of NATO.

II. The Limitations of Collective Security

Southern Asia today is frequently likened to nineteenth-century central Europe. It is described as a balkanised region subject to external threats from a powerful neighbour with expansionist tendencies and divided by a number of serious political ruptures. Whilst this is an apt description of the political sociology of Southern Asia, it is a less satisfactory concept when used to illustrate analogously the defence problems of the area. An analogy between the problems of European and Southern Asian security, and specifically between NATO and SEATO, is misleading. The differences between the defence requirements of the two regions which belie the analogy point up the peculiar difficulties in the path of a Southern Asian system of collective security. Both NATO and SEATO are dispersed maritime coalitions faced with a centralised land power as the major potential enemy, but the distribution and availability of military strength and the collective character—the corporate lives—of the two defence systems are markedly dissimilar. NATO consists of an alliance of 14 nations whose total mobilised manpower in 1963–64 exceeded that of the 8 Warsaw Pact countries.[1] SEATO, on the other hand, is a mixed alliance of developed and under-developed countries combined to defend a part of Southern Asia against an opponent with the largest manpower in the world. SEATO has often and unfavourably been contrasted with NATO as a system which had only to develop along NATO lines to achieve a comparable deterrent value. During the early days of the organisation, Mr. Dulles attempted to avoid the word 'SEATO' in an unsuccessful effort to prevent a NATO-type organisation being thereby implied. Whilst she supported the establishment of a Southeast Asia Treaty Organisation, the United States was not in favour of an Asian NATO with a unified command, joint forces specially earmarked for the purpose, and a common infrastructure and strategy.

[1] See *The Military Balance 1963–1964*, Table II, The Institute for Strategic Studies

There are differences between the character of NATO and SEATO as instruments embodying an American guarantee. The strong American guarantee to Southern Asia has not been formalised, as in Europe, for several reasons. First, the fact that private assurances did not oblige the Soviet Union to support the adversary power where public assurances might. Second, the preference of some Asian governments, because of domestic political circumstances, for private assurances instead of formal public commitments. And third, the disparity in the size and strength of the Asian countries which made it difficult to enter into treaty relationships with some of them and Washington's natural reluctance to give formal military guarantees to unstable governments, in case the tail should wag the dog. It has been claimed that SEATO had more flexibility than a NATO system, in that when the United States wished to act unilaterally, as it had in 1962, there was no veto power to frustrate her. The character of SEATO's response mechanism complicates Peking's risk and response calculus and gives the allies more ways of communicating with the Chinese without limiting their options for the deployment of forces and for escalating power. And there are virtues in having several strings to a bow which is not readily drawn.

Nevertheless, there are ambiguities about the way SEATO will respond to conventional and nuclear aggression. Despite SEATO's continuous planning and its *ad hoc* readiness and mobility exercises like *Seascape* in 1962, and *Sea Serpent* in 1963, its general strategy is not perhaps as clear as that of NATO. The symbolic rather than the combat function of the forces available has been stressed during the history of the organisation, and the net addition SEATO makes to the defence resources of Southern Asia remains a matter of argument. France, for example, maintains no forces in direct support of the SEATO alliance. A real question in the event of a conventional war involving SEATO is the degree to which the military forces of the Asian allies can usefully support the American and Commonwealth forces—the 7th Fleet based on the Philippines and Taiwan with ground and air units positioned in Okinawa and Guam, and the 28th Commonwealth Brigade of British, Australian and New Zealand forces plus air units and British naval forces based in Malaysia.

The American view of the function of NATO's ground forces has passed through several phases: conventional defence

(1952), as a trigger for the Strategic Air Command (1954), to ensure a delay before the use of tactical nuclear weapons (1957). More recently, the American Secretary of Defense, Mr. McNamara, has suggested that NATO strength on the ground is not adequate to repulse without nuclear weapons a surprise non-nuclear Communist attack. It is hard to determine exactly what is the proposed role of SEATO's ground forces in the event of high level violence. In the years when the doctrine of massive retaliation may have provided a key to United States' strategy, SEATO ground forces might have been intended to act as a trigger or to provide a delay as in NATO. Western strategic thinking in the recent years of nuclear stalemate has emphasised the role of conventional forces, particularly in limited wars, as 'usable power'. It is extremely unlikely that the ground forces at SEATO's disposal could fulfil the type of role assigned to NATO ground forces in 1952, and defend the Southern Asian mainland against a major attack, without a considerable drain upon the American and British general strategic reserves; and violence of this level is very likely to cause a general war, in which case those reserves may be required elsewhere, or invite a nuclear response.

In operations involving SEATO forces, the point at which nuclear weapons would be employed against an aggressor can only be inferred from the organisation's declaratory policy and the disposition of its forces. It appears likely that the obscurity surrounding SEATO's possible nuclear role may not be the result of a rational tactic of uncertainty designed to puzzle an enemy, but rather the product of a genuine uncertainty arising out of the disparate nature of the coalition and the conflict of views within it. Particularly during the period when China develops a nuclear weapon and a rudimentary delivery system, the nuclear ambiguities of SEATO are likely to bring about a transfer to Southern Asia of NATO-type anxieties, for example the political problems of sustaining confidence amongst allies, the sharing of the decision to use nuclear weapons, and the fears that the United States would be reluctant to use them if her own territory were threatened by the Soviet Union. Now that China has joined the nuclear club, even as a junior member, the powers allied with the United States will undoubtedly want information about the guide lines and ground rules of the nuclear force which may be employed by the instrumentality of SEATO. Some countries may demand an automatic nuclear SEATO response as a deterrent to China, a development which in turn could strengthen in other states the forces of neutralism and of accommodation with Peking.

Thus the transfer of NATO-type anxieties to the Southern Asian region will probably have long-term effects upon the collective defence structure if they develop pressures for more organisation of the power at SEATO's disposal. When this happens, Washington's attitudes will be of crucial importance. If the allies of the United States seek more clearly to define their nuclear umbrella, if they, for example, contemplate a wider participation in the formulation of nuclear doctrine and targeting, the United States can reasonably demand in return that the cost of a nuclear system be shared and more sites for nuclear missiles be made available. The demands which Washington could make on Australia in this situation would have profound internal consequences by forcing an Australian acceptance of the unhappy fact that in a nuclear age she might be a nuclear target. In any case, an overall organisation of the Southern Asian countries with a settled order of battle is not a feasible prospect: nor is it apparent that developments in the structure of SEATO[1] will meet the military and stability problems of the area with its chequerboard of neutral states, Overseas Chinese, and the complex internal dynamics, which are the best reasons for the analogy with the Balkans in the nineteenth century.

In Europe, the political and military confrontation of the NATO and Warsaw Pact powers constitutes what has been described as a balance of prudence which in the course of time is coming to possess some of the qualities of a political equilibrium. In order to understand how a balance of prudence was reached in Europe, one might inquire what kind of Soviet threat was there in Europe between 1945–49? Was there one after NATO was established? Is there one today? One could then investigate how the achievement through NATO of a military balance countered the Russian threat by inducing prudential attitudes. For two things commonly assumed about this European situation are, first, that whether the Soviet Union intended conquest or more limited ends, she recognises no concept of international stability and has therefore to be restrained; and, second, that the NATO build-up does exercise

[1]The function and organisation of SEATO is analysed by George Modelski in *SEATO Six studies*, edited by George Modelski, F. W. Cheshire for the Australian National University, 1962

a restraining influence on Russian policy. An alternative view is that there is not, and has not been, a serious threat in Europe, that there is so to speak a zero force instead of a zero resultant of forces in the NATO–Warsaw Pact equation. In other words, the massively armed NATO organisation is pushing against a possible threat, and if the treaty organisation were removed the result would show that it had all the time been bracing a door against which there was no force. On the other hand, a sharp diminution in defences and a large scale American withdrawal from Europe might create the threat which had not been there before.

To transfer this speculative example to Southern Asia, where the problems appear in a more dramatic form, the question is just how much more has to be done to hold the Chinese. Has Peking been pushing as hard as it is able against the multilateral and bilateral barriers erected by the West? Does a great deal more have to be done in the line of mutual defence and self-defence against Chinese power in Southern Asia? Is the Chinese pressure such that if South Viet Nam is communised, the remaining countries of Southeast Asia will fall like dominoes? One assumption that appears in NATO–SEATO comparisons is that the Chinese have not been doing all they can to spread their influence into Southern Asia, and that as a consequence it is necessary to develop SEATO along NATO lines to meet the potentials of Chinese expansionism. There has been a defensive psychology, 'a waiting for the other shoe to drop', in the discussions of how exactly the military strength available to the non-Communist countries involved in Southern Asia should be aligned in relation to the political factors and the threats to the security of the area. But the crucial point of the difference between the hostile confrontations in Europe and in Southern Asia is that in the latter region there is no indigenous tradition of co-operation on which to build a collective security system.

In sum, the achievement of a balance of prudence and something like the political equilibrium of Europe still lies in the future for Southern Asia. At present, a number of political difficulties remain in the way of an effective use of the military resources available to the Southern Asian states and their allies. A military build-up in the area may induce prudence on the part of would-be aggressors, but in Southern Asia such measures cannot be established in an overall NATO-type organisation which could then develop a useful political life of its own and create a balance with an opposing bloc. An equilibrium in Southern Asia between China and the SEATO powers, for example, is not possible in the European way and on the NATO–Warsaw Pact model. A general Southern Asian defence system will probably have to derive its corporate character from looser political and military bonds, from associations, understandings and guarantees, as well as from the existing military alliances. Political adjustments of the intramural conflicts in the area are a necessary condition for stability and for general co-operation between the indigenous and external nations. An object of Western policy might well be to attempt to develop the conditions for a balance of prudence in Southern Asia, so that in the long view the present military and political confrontation in the region is likely to acquire sufficient stability to develop some of the qualities of a political equilibrium—as in Europe.

There is a common denominator in the political interests of the SEATO powers concerned with Southern Asia, and that is agreement on the need to prevent a Chinese domination of the region. The political object of the interested external powers is to help the countries of Southern Asia create and sustain a balance of power *vis-à-vis* China in political and economic terms. Whilst China remains the dominant Asian military power, the West must provide the military strength required to match and if possible to restrain China's power, and at the same time help to build up the political and economic health of the region. A full-scale Chinese invasion of her neighbours is at present unlikely, but it is conceivable. When China develops even a modest nuclear strike capacity, her leaders may choose to employ it for purposes of outright aggression or the political blackmail of China's weaker neighbours. A more immediate contingency is that China will employ her superior military power in support of a policy of active subversion south of her border, as a means of extending Peking's control by a low risk policy. The external powers must be prepared to support the indigenous countries in the event of military pressure from whatever source and of any kind, and against subversion and military blackmail whether conventional or nuclear.

An elaborate system of defence alliances (which have been established since the Second World War) links various countries on the southern perimeter of the Asian heartland and the offshore nations with the European and Atlantic powers: its purpose is most succinctly expressed as the containment of the Communist powers in Southern Asia. Footholds are thereby acquired on the mainland rim and in the neighbouring islands for the deployment of American and European power against Communist expansion south from the heartland. The system of alliances comprises the Central Treaty Organisation, the South-East Asia Treaty Organisation, a number of bilateral defence treaties with the United States, and the ANZUS treaty. CENTO includes the United Kingdom, Turkey, Iran and Pakistan, at the western edge of Southern Asia. SEATO's members are the United Kingdom, France, Australia and New Zealand, the United States, Pakistan, Thailand and the Philippines. The signatories of the ANZUS treaty are the United States, Australia and New Zealand. The Philippines, Taiwan, South Korea and Japan all have bilateral defence agreements with the United States. The United Kingdom is pledged by formal agreement to help defend Malaysia. Viet Nam, Cambodia and Laos were offered protection by the terms of the Manila Pact which established SEATO.

Of the world powers involved in the system, the United Kingdom and France have accepted responsibilities in the area as far east as Australia and New Zealand, and the United States as far west as Pakistan. SEATO is, however, the sole element in the system—apart from CENTO which is not directed towards Southern Asia—which includes states on the Southern Asian mainland, providing access as well as military commitments in three areas, West and East Pakistan and Thailand. The gaps in the system designed to counter a Communist advance on the mainland are obvious. India and Burma, both with borders against China, refused to enter the system. Cambodia has moved into the Chinese-North Vietnamese orbit. Laos has disclaimed the protection of SEATO, and her decision was recognised by the parties to the Geneva Conference on Laos in July 1962. The island congeries of Indonesia lying athwart the SEATO area remains outside the defence system and opposed to it, whilst her leaders aspire to a dominant position in the region.

The existence of the system of alliances in Southern Asia has provided a framework for discussions about the security problems of the area, as well as establishing some procedures for dealing with the problems themselves. In particular, the alliances provide values for judgements about diplomatic and strategic problems, and the assumptions of the alliances have tended to become part of those values. The rapid evolution of the system can be traced in the measures from the mutual defence treaty between the United States and the Philippines (1951) to the South-East Asia Treaty Organisation (1954), 'which, in effect, pitted U.S. prestige against a Chinese advance into the region'.[1] The nature of the threat to be countered is progressively defined and made more inclusive, since the original definition as external armed attack is broadened into armed attack plus subversion. At the same time, the machinery for implementing the treaty arrangements has been elaborated. This aspect of the system should be stressed because the adverse comment directed in particular against SEATO has described it as rigid, inappropriate, obsolescent and even as stimulating the spread of Communist influence—a far cry from the belief of John Foster Dulles, enunciated in September 1954, that SEATO would 'make a substantial contribution to preserve free government in Southeast Asia and to prevent communism from rushing on into the Pacific area, where it would seriously threaten the defense of the United States'.

The system of collective security devised by the West and its Southern Asian allies during the 1950s exists now as part of the equation. It is believed to provide the force which holds shut the door against China, which otherwise would be wrenched open. It may be, as some critics have suggested, a political liability, but it cannot be summarily abolished; particularly in view of the lack of any clear or accepted notion of what would replace it to hold fast the door. It is useful, therefore, in discussing the characteristics and criticisms of the system to keep this in mind.

SEATO is the most ambitious essay in collective defence in Southern Asia, and it appears to represent the most that can be achieved there in the way of formal military alliances. There have been no additions to the organisation in ten years, and public support of it in Pakistan has fluctuated.[2] It excludes the major Asian powers, and its existence is seen by them as a threat to Asian independence. It exists in an adverse climate of opinion where there are powerful elements which hamper the development of a sense of collective responsibility for the defence of Southern Asia. One such element is the profound Asian suspicion of Western-sponsored security arrangements.

[1] *Viet Nam and Southeast Asia*, Report of Senator Mike Mansfield *et al.*, Washington 1963, p. 2
[2] *SEATO Six studies*, ed. George Modelski, p. 140

A study of *Defence and Security in the Indian Ocean Area*, issued under the auspices of the Indian Council of World Affairs as late as 1958, argued of SEATO that: 'It would appear that the U.S.A., believing fully as she does in collective security, has sponsored and secured the existing treaty as a *pis aller* and a means of exerting diplomatic coercion on India, Indonesia and other Powers of the region to discard their political scruples over foreign alliances and to abandon their strict neutrality for the alternative of wholesale military alliance with the U.S.A.'[1] It has been characteristic of much Indian comment to state the alternative as *either* wholesale military alliance with the United States *or* neutrality, whereas the real issue today is to find ways to expand formal and informal relationships between Asian countries and the West.

A second element is most simply described as a movement away from the conception of collective responsibility through formal alliances, on the grounds that even the non-aligned countries are offered Western assistance when, like India, they are attacked. A third element is the widespread preference for bilateral security pacts with the United States, rather than collective arrangements, as means of defending national interests in Southern Asia. There is little reason to expect any change in this situation and it seems, to judge from official announcements critical of SEATO, that some of the countries which are members of multilateral pacts would prefer more private arrangements.

From the standpoint of the United States, the second and third of these elements are probably the two least efficient approaches to defence problems, and there are similar military grounds for criticising them. In the first place, they are un-acceptable in so far as they diminish the allies' capacity and resolution for military self-help, and in the second, they make it difficult in a time of emergency to improvise all the necessary defence measures, which in general involve more than just the United States and the indigenous country. The proposals for a 'Maphilindo' association of Malaysia, the Philippines and Indonesia, have important implications as a model for co-operation amongst the Southern Asian countries. If it materialises (which seems improbable in the near future), it could become, according to an American report, 'an im-portant catalyst among Asian countries for their self-protection

[1] Asia Publishing House, London, p. 180

CHINA AND THE ASIAN BALANCE

and mutual aid'.[1] And second, Maphilindo could offer a convenient focus for Western assistance for the achievement of peaceful goals, and the consolidation of regional strength. In any case, Maphilindo is a test of the capacity of Southern Asian nations to associate for their mutual benefit, and such experiments are sadly needed.

The various elements in this adverse climate of opinion reveal the degree to which there is an apparent confusion of political objectives amongst those countries which share the same general interest in remaining free of Communist domination in Southern Asia. The responsibility for the security of Southern Asia is collective, even though the bulk of the conventional power for defence, and the nuclear *ultima ratio requm*, remain in few hands; and the problems of defending this divided and threatened region will not be resolved by a reliance upon either multilateral or bilateral pacts with external powers. The challenge now is to find ways of employing all available sources of political and military strength in an effort to protect not just certain areas but the region as a whole against hostile pressures and subversion. An essential requirement for the defence of the area is to devise some new and more effective means for transferring skills and knowledge —the techniques for external defence and internal security as well as for nation and community building—in order to develop the stability of Southern Asia and curtail its intramural tensions.

It can be seriously argued that the trend of developments in Southern Asia has, broadly speaking, favoured the pursuit of Russian and Chinese political objectives in the area rather than the West's aims. The argument is concerned with the character of Western and Communist strategy and responsibilities in the area, and with the extent and limits of their respective aims. Two assumptions are advanced about Communist strategy. First, that an intensification of Russian and Chinese activities can be expected in Southern Asia, at least as a result of the dispute between the two nations but also very probably as a continuation of initiatives taken by local Communist parties from Indochina to Indonesia. Second, that Communist activities will be directed to take advantage of the inherent weaknesses of the indigenous nations from without and from within; and that so long as those weaknesses remain

[1] *Report of the Special Study Mission to Southeast Asia of the Committee on Foreign Affairs*, 3 to 19 October 1963, Washington 1963, p. 24

they provide scope for Communist manipulation. The political
and economic structure of Southern Asia invites subversion.
If Communist strategy follows these lines, it will give its proponents certain advantages in Southern Asia where the Communist powers possess tactical opportunities and means of
manoeuvre denied to the West. The West's relations with
Southern Asian countries are in the form of political, military
and commercial links, exemplified by the treaty system, based
upon diplomacy not coercion, upon *élite* and not majority
decisions. Russia's and China's relations with Southern Asia
have the advantage of the opportunities afforded by the local
Communist parties and by the Overseas Chinese. They are, as
it were, far more deeply involved than the West in the internal
affairs of those countries. In some states, the Communist
parties are part of the government; in others, the dynamic of
development and national aspirations makes the governments
sympathetic to Communism or non-aligned towards Communist states. These are general conditions which facilitate Communist penetration in Southern Asia.

One strategic objective of the Western nations should be to
develop politically usable power in Southern Asia. Only in this
way can be established the conditions for an effective defence
against the political objectives and tactical operations of the
Communist nations with ambitions in Southern Asia. Neither
Russia nor China regard the situation in this or any other
part of the world as static. They both seek dynamic change in
the furtherance of their political objectives, and it is in their
interests to create and use instability in Southern Asia for
purposes of exploitation. In Communist doctrine, the internal
problems of the non-Communist nations are weapons to be
employed against the national bourgeois governments. It is
Communist strategy to manipulate the difficulties of the Southern Asian nations, to obtain a leverage in their affairs through
the dissensions and weaknesses which are their inheritance
from the era of colonial rule. Subject to Communist manipulation, the problems of the indigenous nations become threats to
the stability and hence to the security of Southern Asia.

In addition to the defence of their territorial integrity, the
problems include the development of political institutions of
their own choice in their own way, and of their economies,
essential for national existence. With the achievement of
independence, not all of the national entities inherited suitable
political institutions or viable economies; and they require time

and opportunity to overcome domestic problems and achieve national existence and stability in the fullest sense. Some of these countries, like Laos, with a thin crust of 'national' power at the top, are more appropriately described as communities or societies than as nation states. Units possess boundaries which have little to do with their ethnic or historical traces, and which have political significance in relation to previous disputes between the colonial powers. The shape of these units may prove to be the most abiding legacy of the European conquerors.

In a number of instances, the end of colonial rule has meant the removal of a central government which, however negligent, was at least capable of exercising its authority effectively within the territorial limits. In the post-colonial period, governmental authority has in more than one state weakened in the outlying provinces and become concentrated about the capital cities, and there has been a marked differentiation between the political life of the *élites* in the Europeanised capitals and the immemorial life of the peasant majorities. In a country subject to hostile pressure, like South Viet Nam, such differences become of strategic significance. They provide the conditions in which Communist propaganda flourishes and Communist agitation is effective. Western aid has been given to Southern Asia in order to end these differences, but Western political contact to a great extent is restricted to the *élites* in the capital cities. The agreements to join defensive alliances with the West are chosen by *élites* and not by the majority of the inhabitants in most Southern Asian states, who remain indifferent or ignorant of the alignments prescribed for their countries. These majorities are subject more to Communist influences than to Western contacts; and so far the West has devised no satisfactory means to broaden its relationships with Southern Asian countries in a way to match the range and intimacy of Communist influences. It is urgently necessary that this be achieved in some manner. Meanwhile, the whole structure of alignments with the West remains on a base only as secure as the *élites* who have negotiated the treaties.

There have been important changes in Southern Asia since the present free world institutional and ideological commitments were formed. Following the collapse of French rule in Indochina, the creation of SEATO, the Bandung Conference and the Chinese attack upon India, many of the standard assumptions made in the 1950s about the security of Southern Asia are questionable. SEATO was promoted in the year of

Dienbienphu, and in an atmosphere of concern which was summed up by President Eisenhower's remark in April 1954, that 'The loss of Indochina will cause the fall of Southeast Asia like a set of dominoes.' Some of the defence arguments then current have since been modified. The doctrine of massive retaliation was replaced several years ago by the more flexible orthodoxy of selective response and a multiple options strategy. The 'domino effect' of the consequences of the failure to prop a crumbling line of defence against Communist pressure is no longer regarded as axiomatic, though the importance to the United States of maintaining the integrity of South Viet Nam is still expressed in these or similar terms.[1] The belief that Chinese aggression anywhere in Asia would lead to a general war has been shown to be wrong by the Sino-Indian border conflict.

It was argued that a zone of neutral states in Southern Asia was a political structure which could be erected upon the foundation of non-alignment, which would derive its strength from a grouping of those nations who desired to remain free of cold war complications in the Bandung spirit, and which had value as a means of blunting the confrontation between Communist and anti-Communist powers. Much less faith is placed latterly on the viability of such structure. The situation in Laos during 1963 well illustrated the difficulties of setting up a viable buffer state with even nominal co-operation from Communists, and Chinese activities in the Himalayan hill states have shown the ease with which a buffer zone can be penetrated by measures short of war. Further developments in the post-Bandung period have revealed the vulnerability of India's non-aligned position and have demonstrated that in Indonesia non-alignment was quite compatible with an aggressive diplomacy and a disposition to employ force in international disputes.

The most striking rupture with the recent past in Southern Asia is the conflict between China and India, the two most powerful subscribers to the principles of peaceful co-existence. The dispute has had a profound influence on the image of Indian leadership of the Asian neutrals—a truth not readily admitted in Indian governmental circles—and smaller, more vulnerable Asian powers have drawn from it the lessons which the Chinese no doubt desired. It has shown China's disposition

[1] In his address to the Economic Club of New York, on 23 of April, 1963, Mr. Dean Rusk spoke of the strategic importance of South Viet Nam, adding that its loss 'would put the remaining states of South-East Asia in mortal danger.

to resort to force in a situation which did not seem to require it, as well as revealing, in the amoral world of power politics, the hollowness of reliance upon moral platitudes. India's limited military capability has been revealed and the reluctance of her government to proffer assurance to India's weak neighbours, the arguments that India is too preoccupied with her own difficulties at present, harm the prospects of an Indian leadership of the neutral states in mainland Southern Asia.

India's non-alignment still remains the official mystique, but its practice as distinct from its metaphysics has become much less mysterious. India has received substantial military aid from the West, if not entirely in the form desired, and a little from the Soviet Union. The Soviet Union's reluctance to accept China's justification of the aggression has added fuel to the ideological dispute between Moscow and Peking. Indian spokesmen are able to construe non-alignment policies as meaning closer *rapprochements* both with Russian and the West, that is, as diplomatic initiatives which cut across the general global alignments of the Great Powers. They have pointed out, however, that India is not non-aligned with China. Indian non-alignment now only remains ambiguous in relation to her friends. The hypothesis that Delhi was able to exercise a moderating influence on Peking has been revised.

A second important change is Indonesia's development into a substantial military power as a result of massive Russian and some American aid. Indonesia must now be circumspectly regarded as a potential threat to the security of Southern Asia, as well optimistically as a 'bastion against Communism'. The façade of Indonesian non-alignment stands incongrously against the background of revolution, confrontation and of economic irresponsibility that may conceivably drive her leaders into foreign adventures. Indonesia has disappointed her friends by joining China as an advocate of force in international relations, and her acquired military potential gives that advocacy some point. Malaysia, established as a device to ensure greater stability in Southern Asia, is interpreted officially in Indonesia as a disguised colonial measure which has to be opposed by force. Indonesian (and Filipino) opposition to the new state of Malaysia has jeopardised the Maphilindo projects. In all, Indonesia has made good her claim to be taken seriously in world counsels, but she has drawn attention to herself as a disruptive not a stabilising power. The schizoid nature of her politics is likely to continue to bedevil her neighbours, at least as long as the present régime lasts.

It is unfortunate that the assurances of her leaders, that Indonesia has no further territorial claims, carry so little conviction in view of the recent history of West Irian, and when they are part of a farrago of threats against colonialism, neo-colonialism, Malaysia and all those who stand (however obscurely) in Indonesia's revolutionary path. Her present ability to impose grave strains upon the economic life of the new Federation of Malaysia poses a serious threat to the stability of the region. Her publicised intention to destroy the Federation has initiated conflict and could start a war. An anti-Western régime in control of the Indonesian state would place a hostile government athwart the strategic sea lanes of the area, threatening the West's mobility by sea and its position in Malaysia and to the north.

The changed character of the Western presence in Southern Asia affects the strategic geography of the region, in particular with respect to the withdrawal of colonial rule and the consolidation of China's power. The Dutch empire has been dramatically wound up in the East Indies. France no longer possesses imperial interests in Southern Asia, though her cultural influence remains strong in Indochina, and as a member of SEATO she retains certain responsibilities towards her Asian allies. The United Kingdom has been divesting herself of her colonies, but not of her obligations; as a member of CENTO and SEATO, as a guarantor of Malaysia's integrity, and in the colony of Hong Kong, she has firm commitments and interests in Southern Asia. The general withdrawal of the colonial powers has led to an increasing American involvement in Southern Asia, in the practical form of alliances and guarantees against certain forms of aggression, and in the moral aspect of a deep sense of responsibility for the independence of the ex-colonies. Western power is still, therefore, of profound strategic significance in the region. It is based not on imperial responsibilities but on negotiated agreements with the independent nations of Southern Asia. It has a narrower foundation, as entry of that power into the region is through those agreements and at the desire of the allied independent nations, but it has a powerful structure.

In one respect Western power has been removed and not replaced in alternative forms. The trading rights and political privileges imposed on China by sea power and as a result of her own internal weaknesses have been destroyed with the Communist victory in China. China is in a position to assert her ancient rights over the eastern seaboard of Asia and along the mainland of Southern Asia. Western strategic thinking recognises the resurgence of China's power. But it opposes China's historical claim to dominate the land mass of Southern Asia and to reassert her influence in what were once her vassal states. Its political object is precisely to prevent the spread of Chinese influence and power into a region until recently dominated by colonial rule. This shift and regroupment of strategic interests focuses attention upon the Southern Asian perimeter of China, for it is along this perimeter that China has been most manifestly aggressive, where she has great scope for action, and where her national interests are most likely to prompt her to exert pressure to remove the influence of the Western powers.

Chapter 2

The External Powers:
National Interests in Southern Asia

I. The Development of National Interests, 1954–64

THE major Powers in the world today have all defined, in their several ways, the character of their national interests in Southern Asia. That the expression of Russian and Chinese policies has assumed an ideological content does not disguise the fact that they have national interests. Western commentators have come to emphasise this element, and some have seen it as the driving force of China's ambitions, as the resurgence of the Middle Kingdom outlook now that China is strong again. The United States has made clear the intensity and depth of its involvement in Southern Asia. No less deep, perhaps, is the commitment of the United Kingdom to defend Malaysia against Indonesia. France, in the person of General de Gaulle, has spoken of her cultural and intellectual intimacies with Southern Asian countries. India's policy has been to proffer her leadership based upon the moral strength of non-alignment. Lesser powers have joined in the chorus. Indonesia's irredentist ambitions have been stridently proclaimed. The Philippines has shown signs of a desire to throw off American diplomatic tutelage, and to mark out a more independent foreign policy, without shifting her ground from her anti-Communist position. The Australian concern with developments in her Near North is an increasingly significant factor in the shaping of her foreign policy. The wide variety of national interests which are held to be at stake in Southern Asia suggests an answer to the question: why has Southern Asia in such a comparatively brief time become a focus of international tensions?

In the first place, the colonial peace has come to an end since 1954, the year of Dienbienphu and of the Geneva Conference, releasing vigorous nationalist forces throughout the region. The years of the decline of the European empires in Southern Asia have been years of change in the national interests of the European powers themselves. The alliances previously adopted by those powers may no longer be regarded as providing an entirely accurate reflection of their current interests in Southern Asia; the more so as on a number of occasions since the Korean War, they have considered the policy of the United States to be at variance with their own interests. France's participation in SEATO is an example, since her interests in Southern Asia are professedly cultural and economic, and not military. She has no empire, except of the mind, to defend in Southern Asia. The achievement of independence by the Southern Asian colonies has provided opportunities for the assertion of national interests which owe something to the historical conflicts kept in check during the long European interregnum. The development of national interests by the Southern Asian countries has in several instances run parallel to the formation of a national and international identity moulded by the nationalist forces prominent in the liberation struggles. There have been as a consequence new images of power. China played a role on the international stage during the Korean War and at the Geneva Conference. Out of the Indochina War have emerged two Viet Nams, Laos and Cambodia, in the place of one colonial possession. And Indonesia has engaged in her first successful exercise in aggrandizement. Two significant features of the attitudes of Southern Asian governments during the last decade have been their suspicion of Great Power efforts to implement policy in the region, for example collective security measures, and their determination to frustrate such efforts if possible. On a first view, this suggests that it is becoming more difficult for external powers to maintain their interests in the area at a time when it is a focus of great power rivalry. Those Asian countries which adopt neutral or non-aligned positions thereby reject formal military involvement with external powers. Asian criticisms were made explicit at the Bandung Conference in April 1955. Though some of the sentiments expressed at the Conference appear chimerical in retrospect—as President Sukarno's 'live and let live' motto—a feature of Southern Asian diplomacy since 1955 has been the assertion of principles critical of Western interference in local affairs. The attitude is derived from the release of nationalist forces in Southern Asia, and is not confined to neutral or non-aligned countries.

In the second place, the American view of the United States' national interests in Southern Asia has been extended to include the belief that she now has territory to defend on the mainland, in South Viet Nam, Thailand and Pakistan. This is a signal change of policy. Before the Manila Treaty of 1954, Washington did not approve of Thailand's request for a military commitment, but offered American diplomatic support to Thailand as the only country in the area which had not been colonised. In 1962, the preservation of Thailand's national integrity was stated to be a vital national interest of the United States. After the Second World War, the defensive perimeter of the United States extended as far as the island groups, Japan, the Ryukus, the Philippines and the Aleutians, as when Dean Acheson defined it in 1950. The responsibilities of the ex-colonial powers on the Southern Asian mainland have been replaced by American commitments accepted as part of a world-wide anti-Communist policy. The 'real origins of SEATO and of U.S. military commitments in mainland Southeast Asia' are to be found in the changed American attitudes caused by the crisis in Indochina, wrote Russell H. Fifield in his study of *Southeast Asia in United States Policy*.[1] This involvement grew in response to a determination to prevent China from reasserting her traditional influence in the areas on her southern borders. It was expressed as a concept of salvation by Mr. Dulles in 1954, as 'to save all of Southeast Asia if it can be saved; if not, to save essential parts of it'. That Southern Asia is an area where certain countries have demonstrably incompatible national interests is one consequence of the extension of the American defensive perimeter. While Southern Asia is regarded as part of the American defensive perimeter, and while it is held to be part of China's historical sphere of interest, there will be a clash of interests between those two powers.

II. The Communist Powers

China

Discussions about China have been bedevilled by the fact that it is a Communist country. There has been a tendency to assume that the Chinese leaders, because they are Communist, have two standards—nationalist and ideological—and that one or the other of them predominates in the formulation of

---

[1] Published for the Council on Foreign Relations, Frederick A. Praeger, New York and London, 1963, p. 37

policy in certain definable areas. This is a curious development in the exegesis of Communist policy, for the argument has not been applied with the same conviction to other Communist régimes. It is one of the durable myths about the abnormality of Communist China, and it makes the remarkable claim that the separate elements in Chinese calculations of their national interests can be distinguished with sufficient precision for comparative judgement. There are two such propositions about China's national interests in Southern Asia. The first is that, at least since the Korean War, Chinese policy and *instinctive* behaviour towards those areas of Asia which are part of China's historical experience have been predominantly concerned with China's national interests, and that Communist ideology has taken second place in Peking's calculations. (The qualification might be made that, although China's desire is to restore her authority within what she regards as her proper borders, the Chinese themselves have not been clear about where they are; for example, in 1949 the Chinese Government apparently had no clearly defined policy towards the hill states of Bhutan and Sikkim.) The second is that, throughout the whole area of Southern Asia, China has major defensive concerns, expressed in the desire to see hostile powers withdrawn from any neighbouring territory from which Peking thinks that she can be threatened.

Professor C. P. Fitzgerald's study of 'The Chinese view of foreign relations' is a most forceful exposition of this general thesis.[1] He wrote that 'there is a sharp distinction between the Chinese policy which can be applied in neighbouring States and border regions and that which can be followed in the wider world. In her relations with the borderlands Chinese policy is manifestly traditional, national, strategic and only modified to a minor degree by the ideology of Communism. It is indeed very doubtful whether the policy and actions of an equally strong non-Communist China would be perceptibly different.' Burma, Cambodia, Laos and Thailand play the same role in Chinese policy today as they did in the past. 'It is no more essential to Chinese security that these countries be Communist than it was in former times that they should be subservient. What is important is they should not fall under the control of a hostile Power. So if Burma is strictly neutral, Cambodia and Laos should be the same, and Indonesia and Malaya, so long

[1] *The World Today*, The Royal Institute of International Affairs, January 1963. p.14, ss.

as they join no hostile combination, such as SEATO, can be left alone. .... But China has made her presence felt and her power feared; between the alternatives of SEATO and non-alignment, all but Thailand have chosen the second.' 'The Chinese empire in the height of its ancient power never looked much beyond this range', and Fitzgerald argued that today China acts within these limits like the old Middle Kingdom, not like the vanguard of Communism. It is only beyond the border-lands that ideology takes precedence *because* tradition provides no guide: 'In the lands beyond this ancient Chinese sphere of influence tradition gives no guidance. There was no Chinese foreign policy for western Asia, Europe, America, Africa or the Pacific region. Here therefore ideology takes precedence over national tradition and defence. The United States is a world-wide power and China's opponent; it is therefore clear that she must be opposed everywhere, if only to keep her in-volved as much as possible, and at as great a distance as possible from China.'

This argument maintains that China's objective in Southern Asia is to consolidate her borders, and that her security requirements are satisfied so long as states like Burma remain neutral. Accordingly, China has little reason to foment subver-sion in neutral countries and create the conditions for Commun-ists to achieve power in the borderlands. This certainly dismisses ideology and denies to Chinese Communism any missionary zeal near home. The importance of the security factor in Chinese thinking is not here at issue; what is arguable is the view that the Chinese Communist leaders do not pose the problem of security in terms of their ideology. They, in fact, assert that security is endangered by imperialist attempts to penetrate China's historical spheres of influence. In *Red Flag*, the Party theoretical journal, the Chinese Communists interpret security in the light of Communist theories of world conflict.[1] According to those theories, the borderlands are endangered by the imperialists who are driven by the contradictions of capitalist development to impose new and old colonialism on the territories near China. The 'intermediate zone' is an area of sharp conflict between capitalism and socialism.

In their polemic, 'More on the Differences Between Comrade Togliatti and Us', the Chinese Communists repeatedly refer to

[1] See the Editorial in *Renmin Ribao*, 31 December 1962, trans-lated and published as 'The Differences Between Comrade Tog-liati and Us,' *Peking Review*, No. 1, 4 January 1963

the need to continue the revolutionary struggle in Asia and elsewhere. Their missionary zeal is pronounced. 'The ever-mounting tide of revolution in these areas [Asia, Africa and Latin America] and the fight over them between the imperialist powers and between the new and old colonialists clearly show that these areas are the focus of all the contradictions of the capitalist world; it may also be said that they are the focus of world contradictions. These areas are the weakest link in the imperialist chain and the storm-centre of world revolution. . . . The peoples in these areas are still a long way from completing their struggle against imperialism.'[1] China has an interest in acquiring Communist states on her borders if only to keep the United States 'at as great a distance as possible from China'. A Communist satellite is better for Chinese security than a neutral neighbour. This explains the character of Chinese-backed subversion in Southern Asia more satisfactorily than the argument which excludes the Communist element from Chinese thinking about the area. Communist subversion in Thailand with its Western alliance is explicable in terms of the view that it is enough for China that the borderlands do not fall into hostile hands. But the subversion of neutrals raises another sort of problem about China's policy. It suggests that China regards them as future Communist satellites. Fitz-gerald recognises this possibility when he wrote that 'It may well be that China thinks that by being left alone they [that is, Burma, Cambodia, Laos, Thailand, Indonesia and Malaya] will make quicker progress towards Communism than if she interfered.' This seems to be an admission that China has a Communist policy for her borderlands.

The development of polycentric Communism made ideology a vital factor of the debate on Communist strategy, and the Chinese have directed their arguments specifically towards problems of the underdeveloped world, including Asia. China, reviving a policy at variance with the Soviet Union's, provided a theoretical defence of the change.[2] This conflict over texts

[1] *Peking Review*, No. 10 and 11, 15 March 1963, pp. 16–17
[2] Although Richard Lowenthal does not 'deal with the impact of the dispute on Chinese foreign policy, as distinct from Chinese ideology' in 'Diplomacy and Revolution: The Dialectics of a Dispute', his discussion clarifies the importance of ideological considerations in Communist Chinese thinking about policy. He wrote, 'To say that the 1960 Chinese challenge to Soviet ideological authority grew out of pragmatic disagreements over foreign policy

and doctrines can be regarded merely as a great power conflict over the Asian intermediate zone. But as China chose as an act of policy to defend her position by reference to Marxism–Leninism, the nature of the defence is significant as evidence, and the arguments worth taking seriously. They may illustrate the real character of the dispute in a way that explanations which dismiss the theoretical issues do not. They are part of the difference between Russian and Chinese policies, an additional factor in the broad dispute, and part of the explanation of Chinese practice. The Chinese ideological argument is, after all, a form of evidence. Alternative explanations about the motives of China's policy-makers inevitably involve speculation. We have no way of knowing whether the Chinese argument is itself a rationalisation of policy based on a different calculus. If it is a rationalisation, that is the form in which the Chinese Communists presented their decisions, and the truth as they wish it to be apprehended by a non-commited world as well as by a hostile bloc.

If ideology is important in Chinese foreign policy-making, then the sharp geographical distinction between the 'Communist' and 'Chinese' elements of her policy is arbitrary. The 'traditional', 'national' and 'strategic' factors shaping decisions are concepts more likely than not to be coloured by Communist presuppositions. For example, to say that Nationalist China is at one with Communist China in its view of the borders disputed with India is not a sufficient explanation of Communist China's actions; the inadequacy of such an argument is precisely that it ignores Communist influences. It is a question of the rationality of the Chinese Communist argument. In short, the hypothesis of a sharp distinction on a geographical basis in Chinese foreign policy minimises the role of Communist ideology, and quite literally prescribes the areas in which it is powerful enough effectively to modify policy, namely, away from China's neighbours and borders. An objection can be put in this way. Why should a creed which proposes establishing Communism everywhere only take precedence in China's foreign policy towards those remote states 'where tradition

---

is not to take the view that the varieties of Communist ideology are a mere cloak for conflicts of national interest'. See *The Sino-Soviet Dispute*, documented and analysed by G. F. Hudson, Richard Lowenthal and Roderick MacFarquhar, *The China Quarterly*, 1961, p. 9 ff.

gives no guidance'? Why does Communist China impose such a self-denying ordinance on its own dialetical tenets? The sharp distinction between traditional and Communist Chinese foreign policies blurs the real issue. In point of fact, China is Communist; let it be admitted that the foreign policy of Communist China and a hypothetical 'equally strong non-Communist China' may not be perceptibly different, though the assertion is not corrigible. The position surely is that policy is usually based on a number of considerations and, as China's policy-makers are Communist, it requires forcible arguments and firm evidence to relegate Communist thinking to a minor role amongst such considerations. The significance of the Communist element in China's formulation of policy is an abtruse but not an abstract question. It is a matter of establishing a criterion for judgements about China's diplomacy.

It is clear that however the Chinese leadership is influenced by ideological considerations, it is not blinkered by traditional conceptions. If history provides some definition of China's national interests in Asia, it does not set out tactics for the pursuit of those interests. Historical arguments throw little light upon the reasons for the Chinese conflict with the Soviet Union. On realistic considerations of China's national interests, Peking has every reason to compose the dispute with the Soviet Union. Russian aid would help China to cut a major figure in the world at large; and yet in a calculated fashion Peking decided to push matters close to a break with the Soviet Union, and to make a bid for the leadership of the non-white world. The motives for this decision may offer a clue to Peking's long-term appraisal of China's national interests. The priorities of China's diplomatic objectives can usefully be examined in terms of three balances; the local balance in Asia, the central world balance, and the foreseeable balance. The inference is that China is following the path of all great powers in her desire to be a dominant power rather than just the ascendant power in Asia, and that to achieve dominant power status she is developing techniques of manipulating the existing balances to her advantage. For example, it can be argued from recent Chinese policy, including the conflict with the Soviet Union, that China's objectives in the central balance—primarily the balance between the Soviet Union and the United States—are more important to her at the present time than her objectives in the local balance, and, furthermore, that China's policy in the local balance is largely governed by the objectives in the central balance. Peking is fast developing techniques of using the local balance as an element in the central balance, and these could be employed to effect in South Viet Nam. By putting pressure on South Viet Nam, China could involve the central balance very sharply; the Soviet Union against China or against the United States. China could even conceivably force the Russians to 'sell down the river' a movement of national liberation to their discredit and China's political advantage.[1] The result either way could be to bring China into negotiation with the central balance and make her an important contender in the forseeable balance between the nuclear oligarchs and the non-nuclear powers. There is inevitably a considerable amount of inference in this analysis, but it does offer a synthesis instead of an explanation of China's national interests in historical and ideological terms.

On 16 October 1964, China detonated a nuclear device near the marshy salt basin of Lop Nor, on the eastern edge of the Takla Makan desert of Sinkiang. The official statement on the explosion, as quoted by the New China News Agency, described the event as 'a major achievement of the Chinese people in their struggle to increase their national defence capability and oppose the United States imperialist policy of nuclear blackmail and nuclear threats'. The statement iterated Mao Tse-tung's dictum that the atom bomb is a paper tiger, and explained China's aim in developing nuclear weapons as 'to break the nuclear monopoly of the nuclear powers and to eliminate nuclear weapons'. The statement also contained the solemn declaration that 'China will never at any time and under any circumstances be the first to use nuclear weapons'.[2]

The Chinese device was of a more advanced kind than had been expected. But there is little evidence to suggest when or how she will become an operational nuclear power. Unless there is a significant change in Sino-Soviet relations, that would restore them to the intimacy of the mid-1950s, she must remain more dependent on her own efforts, almost totally divorced from any form of technological assistance, than any other significant power in the world. She has a missile range on which she may have tested high altitude rockets: she may have some short range missile prototypes left over from the period of Soviet military assistance. But there is no sign of a Chinese

[1] I owe these points to Dr. Coral Bell. Developments in Laos during 1963–64 lend weight to this hypothesis
[2] *The Times*, 17 October 1964

bomber programme, and the development of even a medium range striking capability that could penetrate the defence systems which the Western powers have made, or could easily make, available to her neighbours, belongs more probably to the 1970s than to the current decade. The development of a strategic striking power which would threaten either the United States or Western Russia is more likely to be a feature of the 1980s than of the 1970s.

Nevertheless, the possession of a token capability has certain immediate consequences. In purely military terms, it may expose China to increased risks, since if there were to be a direct clash with the United States or her allies there might be fewer American inhibitions on using nuclear weapons in Asia against China as a nuclear power than hitherto. The threat of unorthodox means of delivery, suitcases or merchant ships, may alarm the credulous, but are no real deterrent against serious military powers and their allies. But in political terms the Chinese bomb may be an asset long before it is a military reality. For example, China is expected to exploit proposals for a nuclear-free zone in Southern Asia with the object of mobilising Asian opinion 'in favour of a position that would both inhibit any effective local reaction to the detonation and intensify pressures for restrictions on U.S. military policies in the area'.[1] It is the expectation of American analysts that Chinese propaganda will invest the detonation with a false credibility in order to undermine Asian faith in the credibility of the American nuclear deterrent. It can be argued that China will try and convince the less sophisticated Asian governments and peoples that her nuclear capability has caused a decisive shift in the balance of power in Southern Asia; the grounds of the argument being that China's nuclear weapons cancel out the deterrent value of the United States nuclear force and that her conventional strength is greater than that of the United States and her allies in Southern Asia.

While neither India nor Japan will be convinced by this argument, both will be potentially threatened by China. India may have to reconsider Nehru's decision not to permit the manufacture of nuclear weapons in any circumstances. Japan will be under pressure to sever her ties with the Republic of China and the United States. Threats may be employed to persuade Pakistan to withdraw from SEATO. The Chinese

[1] Alice Langley Hsieh, *Communist China and Nuclear Force*, The Rand Corporation, 1963, p. 25

pressure on Taiwan will probably be increased but kept below the nuclear threshold, the point at which a nuclear counter blow becomes a likelihood. The political and psychological effects of a token Chinese nuclear capability are thought likely to be most pronounced in the Indochina zone, which is expected to be a target for increased propaganda and subversion. Burma, Thailand, Cambodia, Laos and South Viet Nam, may be subject to nuclear blackmail in a Chinese effort to reduce American influence and prestige in the zone, and as part of a more general plan to weaken the American military alliance system in Southern Asia, to neutralise the allies of the United States and to restrict American access to the region.

The Soviet Union

The Soviet Union has no vital national interests in Southeast Asia. But as a territorial power in Central Asia, she has a direct interest in developments in the region of Afghanistan and West Pakistan, and thus a less direct but still significant interest in the general affairs of the Indian sub-continent. As a Central Asian power, the Soviet Union also has interests to protect along her borders with China. Moscow is concerned in the Laos settlement, as co-chairman with the United Kingdom under the Geneva agreement on Indochina. The tentative proposals of Mr. Khrushchev's successors for a conference with the United Kingdom on Cambodia probably stem from a Russian desire to forestall Chinese penetration in Cambodia. The Soviet Union has long been established in Southern Asia as the organizer and educator of Communist movements, and although the Russian leadership within the Communist movement is challenged by China, Russian influence is not dead even in North Korea and North Viet Nam. Though on certain issues, like the test-ban treaty, the two Asian Communist governments have sided with China, this probably reflects their independence rather than a straightforward Chinese victory over the Soviet Union. Russian economic, political and military support for North Viet Nam has provided the Government with a useful counterweight to Chinese influence in Hanoi. The Soviet Union has declared its full support for Ho Chi Minh's national liberation war in South Viet Nam, and has denounced the American intervention. After the fall of Mr. Khrushchev in 1964, the critical Russian attitude to French policy in South-East Asia appeared to be changing. The fortieth anniversary of France's formal recognition of the Soviet Union, in 1924, was the occasion for statements from Moscow to the effect that Russian public opinion 'took a positive view of France's initiative aimed at restoring peace in Southeast Asia and insuring the neutrality of South Vietnam'.[1]

The Soviet Union is involved in Southern Asia as a true world power with a widespread aid programme, unliquidated commitments and formal responsibilities. Russian assistance to India includes the delivery of MiG jet fighters, transport and other aircraft. The Russian presence in Indonesia is represented by some 3,000 technicians and a billion dollar investment. The prestige of the Soviet Union is not committed publicly to success in any part of Southern Asia, unlike that of the United States in South Viet Nam, so that her malleable diplomacy is less vulnerable in the event of failures or political set-backs. The Soviet Union has consequently a great deal of room for manoeuvre in Southern Asia within the limits imposed by her doubtful obligation to China under the 1950 Sino-Soviet Treaty of alliance. In the circumstances, the question of her national interests in Southern Asia is fundamentally a question of the use the Soviet Union makes, or is capable of making, of her considerable political and military resources.

The Soviet Union's national interests in Southern Asia are now threatened by China. The grounds for this opinion are, first, that although Moscow pays lip service to the ideological goal of communising the world, she genuinely wishes to exercise a moderating influence in Asia, since her global interests require it, and, second, that in the polycentric Communism of today Moscow's influence over her Chinese ally and the Asian Communist Parties is generally on the decline. The Chinese challenge for the hegemony of Southern Asia threatens the interests of the Soviet Union in maintaining a *détente* with the United States and avoiding issues which could cause a nuclear confrontation of the two super-powers. In the Chinese view, the Soviet Union's great power interests predominate over her revolutionary ambitions; Peking has tried to employ this argument against Moscow, casting the Russians as fat European Communists who have lost the revolutionary ardour of the thin Asian Communists, and maintaining that selfish calculations of Russian national interests offset selfless Chinese considerations of international Communism. They find evidence for this contention in the words and actions of the Soviet Union.

[1] *The Christian Science Monitor*, 3 November 1964

The ideological dispute between China and the Soviet Union provides texts to show that the Soviet leaders have advocated more cautious tactics than the bellicose Chinese. Mr. Khrushchev justified moderation in his general arguments for the co-existence of countries with different social systems.[1] The Soviet Union's willingness to honour the Geneva agreements for a neutral Laos, her refusal to support in force Hanoi's revolutionary war for the reunification of Viet Nam, and her support for India, all suggest that in the present phase of her policy Moscow has repudiated Peking's forward strategy in Southern Asia.

The support offered by the Soviet Union to India has been to the Congress Government and has meant the discouragement of Communist revolutionary militancy in India. The Russian policy has split the Indian Communist Party, and though the majority of the Party has rallied to the Indian Government in response to the Chinese aggression, a substantial minority has broken away and would probably be ready to use Chinese support in a revolutionary uprising, for which conditions in India provide serious possibilities. Russian policy towards India, ever since the consolidation of the Communist régime in China, has very likely been decided with a view to strengthening India as a counterweight to China. If this hypothesis is correct, then Russian and Chinese attitudes towards India are diametrically opposed. This is a matter of politics irrespective of ideological camps, but it has given the Chinese a strong case for denouncing the Russian betrayal of Communist solidarity. The first demonstration of the Russian policy of friendship towards India under her Congress Government was the proposal in 1958, at the time of the Iraq–Lebanon crisis, for India, but not China, to take part in a Five-Power Summit Conference. It was followed by the Russian declaration of neutrality vis-à-vis the Sino-Indian border clash, and by the supply of fighter aircraft to India after the Indian military disaster in the eastern Himalayas.[2]

With regard to Indonesia, where the Communists are probably closer to power than in any other Southern Asian country not yet under Communist rule, the policy of the Soviet Union has been to support President Sukarno rather than the Communist Party of Indonesia, and the Communist Party of

[1] The Chinese accused him of 'Parliamentary cretinism'

[2] For these points, and for his assistance in this and the following chapter, I am grateful to Mr. G. F. Hudson

Indonesia has on the whole become pro-Chinese. It remains to be seen whether the new leadership in Moscow under Mr. Kosygin and Mr. Brezhnev, or whoever succeeds them, will be more ready to support the Communist Parties in Southern Asia than Mr. Khrushchev was. There is also a question of how far the concentration of Russian military assistance on Indonesia—a country remote from the Soviet Union—is to be regarded merely as an attempt by the Soviet Union to exert political influence there, and how far it has definite strategic aims. The possibility of using submarine and air bases in Indonesia, in the event of a war, would greatly increase the capacity of the Soviet Union to operate in the Pacific and Indian Oceans and disrupt the maritime communications of the West.

Russian military power in Asia is of profound strategic significance. Russian forces stationed in the Far East are composed of elements of the long-range strategic bomber force, 17 army divisions, and some 120 conventional submarines, including Z-class craft with a radius of action of more than 20,000 miles. A number of missile-carrying submarines have a strategic role with the Russian Far East Fleet. The use of Russian depot ships would facilitate the southward deployment of the naval forces into the Pacific Ocean from bases in the Kamchatka peninsula (at Petropavlovsk there is a submarine base with direct access to the high seas), the Kuriles, Sakhalin and Vladivostok.

III. The SEATO Powers

The United States

Since the Second World War, American interests in Southern Asia have developed in ways which would have been inconceivable in the years of isolationism. In 1945, the United States had a sound economy in a world broken by war and was the monopolist of nuclear weapons. She looked to the regional groupings as foreseen by the United Nations Charter as a way of settling Southern Asia. Soviet nuclear power, NATO and the Korean and Indochina Wars changed the American outlook. There was a tendency in Washington to leave security arrangements in the region to the United Kingdom, though there was no such understanding with the French and Dutch. By the time of the Geneva Conference of 1954, however, it was seen that some action was necessary to prevent the flow of Chinese influence into what the Mansfield Report described nine years later as the 'hiatus of power and responsibility' left in the region by the withdrawal of the colonial powers: 'It has been largely in compensation for this weakness that U.S. policies for Southeast Asia have formed over the past decade. From the most limited and casual interest scarcely a dozen years ago, we have plunged heavily into the affairs of that region. It would be more accurate to say, perhaps, that we have backed into the involvement. For it was the bitter conflict with the Chinese in Korea at the other end of Asia which directed our attention sharply to the southern flank of the continent. And it was largely out of the estimates of the military necessities of that conflict that we became immersed in Southeast Asia.[1]'

The American involvement in Southern Asia was undertaken in response to a threat, and the American responsibilities in the three zones of Southern Asia are calculated accordingly. The consensus of expert American opinion seems at present to be that although China has done all she can in Southern Asia in the furtherance of her political ambitions, her opportunities have so far been limited, but that when China obtains even a token nuclear capability Peking will seek further opportunities for pressure. It is concluded that the Chinese have a sophisticated conception of how over the long run they can exert their influence in the region, and that the real limits of China's ability to influence and manipulate situations to her own advantage are realised in Peking. Chinese writings on political military doctrine are taken as evidence that the government has made realistic estimates of the range of options that remains open to them on the basis of their assessments of their own capabilities, advantages and weaknesses, the military posture of the United States, the opportunities which they can exploit and the extent of help that they can expect from the Soviet Union. China is thought to be developing operations analysis to the point where she can accurately gauge what blows she can with impunity accept, or where she can calculate the political constraints upon the United States' use of nuclear weapons, so that she is likely to be prudent in exposing herself to a counter blow. The strong American nuclear position in the Pacific is a deterrent to activities against Taiwan. China has deliberately commited herself to a go-it-alone policy without assistance or support from the Soviet Union.

[1] *Viet Nam and Southeast Asia*, Report of Senator Mike Mansfield *et al.*, Washington, 1963, p. 2

All this, in the American view, leaves China with fairly low-level opportunities for the intimidation of governments in particular areas (as in Burma, Cambodia, the Himalayan hill states), for limited actions on the Indian frontier, and for subversive operations by proxy. China has a number of ways in which she can operate under cover; by friendship policies and economic assistance, through subversion financed by Chinese diplomats or by the Bank of China, as in India, through Overseas Chinese financial support for local Communist parties as in Indonesia, though moral support for national liberation movements as in Viet Nam. And the advantage of this type of operation is that the amount of countervailing military power that the United States and her allies can introduce is very restricted because of the political repercussions it might have upon local and world opinion.

Which of her national interests in Southern Asia does the United States consider to be fundamental? The answer seems to depend upon a time-factor. Between 1954 and 1959, there was the view that the Chinese were advancing rapidly in a world of falling dominoes and that this demanded vigorous American action. SEATO is the monument of this period. More recently there has been the view that time is on the side of the free countries and that longer-term aspirations for regional collaboration could be pursued. But the crisis in Laos, and developments of the war in South Viet Nam, have in some measure renewed the anxieties of the 1950s. The result has been a re-emphasis on SEATO and its utility; the joint statement issued in 1962 by Mr. Dean Rusk and the Thai Foreign Minister, Thanat Khoman, included *inter alia* the assurance 'that the United States regards the preservation of the independence and integrity of Thailand as vital to the national interests of the United States and to world peace'. It would be an oversimplification to state that the American commitment in the whole area hardens in response to Communist pressures, but a significant recent development has been the firmness with which the United States has asserted its national interests in the Indochina zone.

In South Viet Nam the commitment is virtually limitless—in spite of the vagaries of American politics, no Administration is likely to relinquish its obligation there—and the involvement of the United States has passed the point of no return, according to senior State Department officials. It is like Naboth's vineyard; the United States will do a great deal to secure it.

For a Viet Cong victory in South Viet Nam would mean that the whole of Viet Nam would be united under Communist control, even if, for the sake of appearances, a separate coalition government were established in South Viet Nam to disguise the takeover. A unified Viet Nam would have the largest population of any Southern Asian state, except Indonesia, and the existing army of North Viet Nam, which was built up in the war against France, is already probably the best indigenous military force in Southern Asia. Neither Laos nor Cambodia could offer any effective resistance to a unified Viet Nam. If the United States, after her deep commitment in South Viet Nam, were to withdraw her support, Thailand would no longer retain any confidence in American protection; she would hasten to come to terms with China, if only to obtain some cover against the dominant local power of Viet Nam. The American relationship with Thailand depends upon the United States securing her position in South Viet Nam.

Perhaps the basic question is how long the United States will remain in Southern Asia in pursuance of her national interests. The Asian powers have to take into consideration the fact that China is always present and the possibility that the United States could at any time withdraw. The ultimate withdrawal of American tactical power is indeed envisaged in the proposals for the local powers to assume more responsibility for their own defence in regional groupings. In the zone of the Indian subcontinent, however, there could be no permanent arrangements until India and Pakistan reach some agreement over the problems which divide them and which dissipate whatever potential for regional security is to be found in the combined military and economic strength of the two countries. In the Indochina zone, where there is insufficient strength and perhaps least opportunity for a viable regional defence agreement, the American commitment will remain as long as Thailand is threatened and until the North Vietnamese Communists—in American opinion the mainspring of the revolution in South Viet Nam—withdraw to North Viet Nam. At the same time, the United States, conscious of the danger of military operations close to the borders of China, is careful not to aggravate Peking into policy miscalculations. In his warning to those who control and supply the guerrilla war in South Viet Nam, President Johnson took care to avoid misunderstanding by naming North Viet Nam as the source of aid. Though Peking gives moral support to Hanoi, Washington does not believe that the Chinese are playing an important part in the conflict, or that Chinese assistance has made much difference to the North Vietnamese. This premise leaves the way open for the United States to accept a neutral and non-Communist South Viet Nam as perhaps the best solution that remains, if it proves to be practicable. Washington's objections to this solution do not reject the principle, but stress the practical difficulties of achieving a neutral North Viet Nam.

American decisions are still in the making in the Maphilindo zone, where a great deal will depend upon the attitude of Indonesia to Malaysia, and upon the balance of power within Indonesia between the Army, President Sukarno's Nationalist Party and the Communist Party. The economic decay of Indonesia is highly favourable to the Communist Party's prospects of gaining power. If the Communist Party won power in Java, there would be a chance of civil war between Java and the Outer Islands. Indonesia is one of the least cohesive of the Southern Asian countries, and both the personality of President Sukarno and the aggressive policies of confrontation are probably necessary to hold the state together. Indonesia cannot possibly be an element of stability in the area for a long time.

During the 1950s, American policy in Southern Asia was based upon the confident assumption that Southern Asian nationalism, supported by economic assistance and protected by American striking power, could become a force strong enough to prevent any extension of Chinese influence into the area. (Dulles once thought that the battle of Dienbienphu was a blessing in disguise, since it would enable the settlement of a firm basis of policy.) The phrase, 'backed into involvement', seems in retrospect to be particularly apt, for in approaching the security problems of Southern Asia in this manner, the United States was not able to see clearly where her policy was leading. While the American commitment has filled the hiatus of power in Southern Asia, which was its cause, the American presence is regarded by some non-Communist governments, as in Burma and Cambodia, as posing a threat to their own interests. American power and influence are so pervasive that they have a disturbing effect upon these governments and affect their relationships with China. Countries such as Burma and Cambodia which are fearful of China are in turn fearful of what they consider to be the American threat. This attitude has led them to sever certain of their relationships with the

United States, at some cost in aid, and to develop good relations with China.

These fears of American power hamper Washington's efforts to encourage regional groupings. The difficulty is that no such grouping would be a collaboration of equals; some power would be dominant. In the vacuum after the decolonising of Southern Asia, something like an American *imperium in imperio* has appeared as the United States became immersed in the area. This has placed strains upon American diplomacy, for while in possession of the strength, the United States does not possess wholly satisfactory means of persuasion to put her policies into effect without unproductive results. At worst, in the South Viet Nam of the Ngo dynasty, her interests and power were virtually placed in unfriendly hands; at best, as in Thailand, her policy is to a certain extent shaped by her commitment. As noted already, the American commitment is serious and durable, but it is neither limitless nor unconditional. It does not guarantee all the present frontiers in Southern Asia, and it depends upon the attitudes of Britain, France, and the governments of the area and their contributions to their own defence. The United States would be reluctant to commit herself if all the countries of the region were supine, and she had to occupy them in order to defend them. Thus, there is an element of bluff in the American commitment; if you do not do your share, we shall let you go down the drain. The problem of the hiatus of responsibility has not been solved by the commitment of American strength in Southern Asia to prevent a Chinese advance into the area.

The United Kingdom

During the first twelve years after the Second World War, British military policy was concentrated primarily on securing and encouraging a permanent system of defence, first in Europe, where the danger to the United Kingdom seemed most acute, and second in the Middle East, with a tendency to disengage in the Far East. The United Kingdom was an active promoter of NATO, but only entered SEATO with reluctance. There were three main elements in British policy in Southern Asia. First, for a brief period between approximately 1957 and 1961, the United Kingdom seriously considered the possibility of with-drawing from Southern Asia. This was intended only to be a partial withdrawal of the British presence, including a considerable reduction in the overseas garrisons wherever possible. But, as the 1957 White Paper on future defence policy made clear, it was not planned to relinquish certain responsibilities, such as in Hong Kong or the SEATO commitment.[1] (The Commonwealth Brigade in Malaya was established for SEATO purposes in 1955.) The British desire was that, at the end of the 1957 five-year defence plan, her 'allies—especially those in the Commonwealth—do rather more than they do now in the various collective defence organisations. That, at least, is the hope, fortified by the Australian decision to make America rather than Britain its arsenal.'[2]

Second, the United Kingdom recognised a need to reorganise her military presence in Southern Asia. The development of these policies, however, was attended by a number of difficulties. For example, the conditions of the retention of the British base rights in Singapore remained uncertain until Singapore could be persuaded to join Malaya on terms acceptable to the Malays. In October 1961, Tunku Abdul Rahman, the Prime Minister of Malaya, announced that he would seek agreement on the continued use of the base, but not for SEATO purposes. Since early in 1962, the British Government has been aware that the attempt to include Brunei and Sarawak in a Federation of Malaysia would incur Indonesian hostility and create an endemic security problem in the area for a number of years.

Third, a preoccupation of British policy in Southern Asia since the 1950s has been to induce the United States to take over some of the responsibilities for the defence of the area. For a while this policy seemed to be succeeding brilliantly, and it began to appear that its success would enable the United Kingdom to withdraw from the area and to devote her attention to the more immediate problems of the community of Europe. To many people in the United Kingdom, and particularly to the Labour Party, it was obvious that the United Kingdom could not continue to devote one quarter of her defence budget to the region East of Suez, and maintain eleven infantry battalions with supporting air and naval units there, if she were to develop a more flexible military posture and exercise more influence in Europe. NATO seemed to require more attention than SEATO. Southern Asia was once more the 'Far East'. The

[1] *Defence. Outline of Future Policy*, Presented by the Minister of Defence to Parliament, April 1957. Cmnd. 124, p. 5
[2] *The Daily Telegraph*, 5 April 1957

danger from China seemed remote; and the mood in England was that her national interests in Southern Asia had narrowed in the wake of the imperial retreat to a residual economic stake.

While this policy had its advantages as far as the United Kingdom was concerned, to her allies it was a source of irritation and even concern. The State Department wanted to see the British presence removed from the area, but there was a tendency in the United States to view the British policy with suspicion as an attempt to get the United States to accept further responsibilities for the defence of the area and for the protection of other than American interests. There were unfriendly reactions in the American press to the 1957 White Paper on defence. In the headquarters of SEATO, there were strong feelings that the British (as well as the French) interest in the Organisation had lagged behind that of the Americans and the Australians, who had continually to prod their reluctant allies into action. These feelings were matched by British irritation at what was thought to be the myopic Australian attitude towards Indonesia. The British and the French Governments were described to me at SEATO headquarters as 'apathetic' and even 'obstructionist'. Australian government officials were probably more understanding of the British opinion than were their American counterparts, whose views they shared. But a sense of a British withdrawal remained a source of concern for Australia, and, as Australian thinking about foreign policy became more articulate, it helped to confirm the wartime belief that Australia's safety depended upon Uncle Sam, and not John Bull.

Her critics assumed that the United Kingdom's policy was symptomatic of a genuine withdrawal of interest from Asia, and a desire to avoid further responsibilities in the area. Does the 'British withdrawal' really mean this? During the last few years, the threat from the Soviet Union in Europe has appeared to recede, whereas the Chinese attack upon India has emphasised the danger from China, and the Indonesian 'confrontation' with Malaysia has brought out a remarkable degree of determination in the United Kingdom to defend the new state. (The Labour Party has changed its former position, as Malaysia is considered to be no longer colonial, but a genuine democratic creation which deserves protection, morally and legally.)

The British responsibility for Malaysia is not included in her SEATO charges. The new Federation is protected under the

Anglo-Malaysian Defence Agreement, embodying the 1957 agreement between Malaya and the United Kingdom, which makes provision for the future establishment of British forces in Malaya and the constituent states. When the British Government talked of withdrawal, it was perhaps thinking in terms of a change from the recent past, when military commitment to Southern Asia seemed to be a matter of the allocation of major forces to the area, like the American Seventh Fleet, or of expensive and apparently endless wars on the ground, as in Indochina and Malaya. Before Indonesia's threatening attitude to Malaysia, the dangers to the area seemed to be less urgent or immediate, and the maintenance of British interests was believed to require alternative forms for her military presence on a smaller scale, perhaps, but commensurate with her reduced responsibilities in the skeleton of an empire. It was argued, for example, that in the long run the main problem in Malaysia was how to integrate the races, a task for which British forces were unfitted. The belief proved to be too sanguine. The United Kingdom has undertaken new defence arrangements with India, and Australia and New Zealand have agreed to accede to the Anglo-Malaysian defence agreements. Thus, it is now likely that there will be a continuous British interest in the Indian Ocean area for some time to come.

British estimates of the United Kingdom's commitments in Southern Asia have changed since the Sino-Soviet dispute and the Indian border crisis. There has been much more sympathy for the view that China might become the most serious long-term menace to world security. With the failure of her attempt to enter the European Common Market, there has been less reason for the United Kingdom urgently to reinforce her military presence in Europe. The arguments for the United Kingdom to increase her military commitments in Europe and to decrease her military power in Southern Asia have lost ground. The United States places emphasis upon the British military contribution in SEATO and in Southern Asia, as well as in Europe. In the changed circumstances, the logistical basis of the United Kingdom's military presence in Southern Asia will have to be adjusted. There are technical problems of where to locate the British forces necessary for the United Kingdom to fulfil her military commitments in Southern Asia. The Singapore base which is used by the Royal Navy and the Seventh Fleet is no longer under British sovereignty. The deployment of forces at the base can be affected by the political decisions of the Malaysian Government, by the subversion of the Chinese work force, by sabotage mines placed in the shallow Straits of Johore, and by the proximity of the base to Indonesia.

But while the United Kingdom's commitments have been revised in this direction, the future of her presence in Southern Asia has not been settled. It is still a subject of inquiry and of some scepticism. There was little definition, for example, in the election debates of 1964 about the United Kingdom's future in Southern Asia as a whole; the weight of the discussions fell upon her Atlantic role and her place at the high table of the nuclear college. The arguments about the narrowed range of British interests in Southern Asia still carry validity, limitations remain on the amount of conventional force the United Kingdom can deploy, or afford to deploy, in the region, and the same doubts persist about the durability of her commitment or will to be committed there. Despite the historical and technical reasons that may be used to explain the change, the decision to abolish the position of Commissioner General for Southeast Asia may have a symbolic significance.

One of the crucial factors in the eventual British decision will be the security and expense of her lines of communication with Southern Asia, so it will be governed by developments in Africa and the Middle East, by the tacit bargain that is struck between London and Washington on burden sharing East of Suez, as well as by developments in Southern Asia itself.

The United Kingdom's military presence in Southern Asia could take on a different aspect if Britain decided to enact a nuclear part in the area. There has been little discussion of this possibility, but much argument to justify or condemn an independent British nuclear deterrent in Europe. If the arguments are about the best way to employ the existing British nuclear power, the conjectural advantages of a British deterrent in Southern Asia can at least be raised here. For example, if in the future India were to require a guarantee of nuclear weapons for her defence against a threatened or actual Chinese nuclear attack—a not entirely remote possibility—it might be more appropriate for the United Kingdom to undertake the responsibility, rather than the United States. The present British medium bomber force—if it could operate from Indian air bases—would be fully adequate against China during the period when China is developing more than a rudimentary nuclear capability, and an air defence system might be a useful counter to Chinese threats of nuclear blackmail against the

Asian and Antipodian members of SEATO. While the United Kingdom's Polaris submarines cannot at present be employed outside the Atlantic region for communications reasons, the British V-Bomber force could be used against China for another ten or more years. These weapons may not deter the Soviet Union from an adventure in Europe, but they might well deter China. The advantage of a British nuclear deterrent employed in this manner is that there is less chance of it reactivating the Sino-Soviet treaty alliance than an American nuclear deterrent.

France

France has acquired a fund of ill will in Southern Asia. There has been ill will between France and Thailand over Cambodia, and the Thais have informally accused France of supporting Kong Le's coup in Vientiane and the abortive 1960 coup against Ngo Dinh Diem in Saigon. More recently, General de Gaulle's proposals for a unified and neutral Viet Nam have been firmly rejected by Washington and by Saigon's ruling junta who regarded them as untimely and unfriendly. France's attitudes towards Southern Asia have been the subject of persistent criticism by her European and Asian allies in SEATO. The criticisms have a wide scope, for France is accused of being both too interfering and too uninterested in Southern Asia. There have seemed to be anomalies in the French position, a general lack of interest in Southern Asia, and a marked unwillingness to commit even token French forces there for symbolic purposes. Pote Sarasin, the then Secretary General of SEATO, was reported early in 1963 as stating that 'Depuis quelques années la France semble se pencher beaucoup moins sur la partie du monde dont s'occupe l'*O.T.A.S.E.*'[1]

Much of this type of criticism flourished, particularly in Bangkok, as a result of the situation in Laos during 1962. The Thai Government, uneasy at the deterioration of the situation in Laos and fearful for its own territorial integrity, appealed to its SEATO partners for assistance. The United States promptly sent 4,000 combat troops and tactical air support to reinforce the existing American troops in Thailand. The United Kingdom, Australia and New Zealand dispatched small forces for their symbolic value in underwriting the alliance. France did not send troops, believing that the threat to Thailand's integrity was exaggerated. As *Le Monde* wrily commented, 'Le

[1] *Le Monde*, 5 April 1963

fait qu'en fin de compte la façon de voir de la France ait été con-
firmée n'a d'ailleurs pas apaisé les réactions défavorables. Il ne
suffit pas en effet d'avoir raison. Il faut encore—c'est du moins
ce qu'estiment certains autres membres du pacte—que les
interventions d'un partenaire, aussi avisé soit-il, ne se manifes-
tent pas seulement d'une façon négative.'[1] There is indeed
little likelihood that in the future France will intervene in
Southern Asia in a positive, that is, a military fashion. For
France has no direct strategic involvement in the region; she has
no military presence there, and it is not very credible that any
French government would support a military expedition in
Southern Asia and employ the land component of the French
strategic reserve, the *force d'intervention*, for the purpose. France
can best protect her prestige, her cultural and economic
interests in Southern Asia, by exercising a political influence.
France, say her critics, may have the power but does not seem
to have the will to undertake military commitments in Southern
Asia. It has been said that France demands a consultative
voice in the councils of SEATO without being prepared to incur
the cost of consultation in military commitments, and that
France is a sleeping partner in SEATO. How just is this criticism?

The symbols of SEATO's corporate military life have been
the series of military exercises held for the purpose of acquiring
experience of combined operations in conventional war. The
SEATO Report for 1962–3 stated that twenty-five of these
exercises have been held since 1956; and France has manifested an interest in them throughout the programme. The
largest exercise for the training year 1962–63 was a combined
ground and air tactical exercise, entitled *Dhanarajata*, held in
Thailand in June 1963, in which all the member nations took
part. It is noteworthy that this interest has been maintained
despite the fact that in the French viewpoint SEATO is too
much aimed against a conventional military threat and not
sufficiently organised to meet the threat of political subversion.
According to French estimates, the security of Southern Asia
is not threatened by any direct, military aggressive intentions
by China, but rather by subversion; and it is in line with this
thinking, and with the lessons of the French experience in
Southern Asia, to recommend political measures.

Nevertheless, France has demonstrated her solidarity with
SEATO by taking part in what in her own terms must have

[1] *Le Monde*, 6 April 1963

seemed to her to be military measures designed to meet an improbable menace; and her inaction in the face of Thailand's request for help in 1962 is hardly evidence to the contrary. The Manila Pact obliges its members to consult immediately if in the opinion of any of the parties there is a threat; it does not oblige them to take their allies' estimates of the threat at face value. The French have placed emphasis on those aspects of the Pact which require its members to strengthen the ability of the parties 'to maintain and develop their individual and collective capacity to resist armed attack and to prevent and counter subversive activities directed from without against their territorial integrity and political stability' (Article 11). It is believed in France that this obligation extends also to neutral states, and French policy has been directed towards the strengthening of neutrals in preference to the increasing of Western commitments. It is also the French belief that their experience and sources of intelligence in Southern Asia—France has a strong diplomatic representation in Asia, which has been enhanced by the exchange of ambassadors with Peking—can be useful to the United States, and confers a right to be consulted.

It is perhaps more accurate to describe France's attitudes towards Southern Asia as independent rather than indifferent. The independence of French policy has been demonstrated by General de Gaulle's initiative in recognising the People's Republic of China and by his proposals for a neutralised Viet Nam. The French proposals for strengthening and developing the neutral states have special significance for the Indochina zone. It was suggested in France that General de Gaulle may have had the recent history of Indochina very much in mind when he formulated his neutralisation policy. Since Washington sources described these proposals as inconvenient to the United States, and as a grievance, it is as well to recall that France too has a grievance concerning American policy in Indochina.

It is the French thesis that the replacement of French authority in Saigon in 1955 by American influence was effected in circumstances which were often humiliating to those who had suffered defeat at Dienbienphu. President Roosevelt had decided upon this substitution of authority in Indochina before the end of the Second World War. As early as 1943 the President had conceived the idea of a joint American, British and Chinese trusteeship for Indochina. Between the Moscow, Teheran and

Yalta conferences the trusteeship concept went through several changes, but the exclusion of French authority from Indochina remained a prime object of the policy. After tracing this historical background, Bernard Fall concluded that 'it strikes at the root cause of why there is not (and cannot be) any Western "united front" in Southeast Asia today, and why de Gaulle proves difficult today. France has no reason whatever to trust American actions on the basis of past performance . . .'[1]

Some scholars are inclined to explain French policy in terms of the treatment of the French in Indochina by the United States from the period of the Second World War until 1955, and of General de Gaulle's long memory for past injuries. The view is gaining ground in both the United Kingdom and the United States that vindictiveness is a major element in current French policy, that the French are out to wreck the American position in Southeast Asia because they do not wish to see the United States succeed where France failed. It is believed that France does not greatly care whether Southeast Asia goes Communist or falls under Chinese domination, as there is no French territory, base or military presence there. The main French interest is the cultural one in the French language and culture of Indochina, and this is not an anti-Communist interest. The threat to French culture in Indochina comes rather from the English-speaking Americans and their influence. It is doubtful whether France really believes that her formula for neutralisation is anything but a euphemism for permitting the Communists to have their way throughout the region. If it is to be understood as implying a balance between Communists and anti-Communists inside a state, it clearly could not work in Viet Nam, with North Viet Nam fully under Communist control and the Viet Cong strong in South Viet Nam. In sum, the French attitude appears to be basically incompatible with the policy of the United States, even though some American politicians are attracted by the neutrality formula.

After nearly a decade of American influence in Indochina, the United States has, in the French judgement, expended millions of dollars of aid without either removing the Communist threat from South Viet Nam or rallying the population, whose *élites* remain profoundly attached to the French culture. The Mansfield Report summed up the situation in South Viet Nam in 1963 in similar terms. Subsequently, Senator Mansfield has

[1] *The Two Viet Nams. A Political and Military Analysis*, Pall Mall Press, 1963, p. 71

commended the Gaullist plan for a neutral Viet Nam. At the root of the French concept is the belief that a neutral zone in Indochina, maintained in an equilibrium, is politically feasible and best meets the needs and interests of the indigenous peoples.

Although Laos offers less prospect than Cambodia for this kind of equilibrium, it is regarded in France as a significant if fragile instance, the first case of an explicit accord between the United States and China to establish a neutral state in the zone. Cambodia ardently desires to remain in a neutral equilibrium. The French presence in Cambodia is perhaps the clearest illustration of the role France is prepared to play in the Indochina zone in the future, and of the way in which French influences can be maintained in the process of strengthening the indigenous countries. In 1963 there were three French missions in Cambodia. The economic aid mission consisted of experts engaged in various agricultural pursuits—cotton, sugar palm, mining and administrative and technical training. The officers and *sous-officiers* of the French Army, Navy and Air Force, constituted the Military Mission entrusted with the training of the Cambodian forces. The largest mission was the Cultural Mission: 400 teachers in the principal Cambodian lycées, the lycée Descartes in Phnom Penh, and at the University.

The Gaullist plan for a unified Viet Nam recalls that the accords signed in Geneva in 1954 did envisage the reunification of the country; a clause pigeon-holed in Washington and forgotten in Saigon, according to *Le Figaro*.[1] French writers, adopting a legalistic viewpoint, point out that the armistice agreement of 20 July 1954 has been infringed by the American as well as the North Vietnamese intervention in South Viet Nam. The proposals for a neutral Viet Nam are part of a coherent French policy and, if the French assumptions about the Communist threat to Southern Asia are granted, one that has some prospects of success. There has been, however, little clarification from Paris about how the policy would work in detail. How, for example, are the neutral states to be protected from subversion?

The United Kingdom and the United States support Laotian neutrality, but they are aware that the cease-fire established in Laos in 1962 is recurrently violated by the Pathet Lao whose intransigence has prevented the government by three factions from functioning as a coalition. The Premier, Prince Souvanna

[1] 1 September 1963

Phouma, has condemned the Pathet Lao attacks without being able to prevent them, and he has stated that the Pathet Lao have received considerable assistance from North Viet Nam. The United Kingdom and the United States have no objection to Cambodian neutrality—the principle is fully supported by the British Government—but both governments responded coldly to Prince Sihanouk's ultimatum over a conference to guarantee that neutrality. The neutral policy advocated by France would affect Thailand's position and change the status of South Viet Nam; and the considerations which Paris sweeps aside remain uppermost in London and Washington, where the threats to Southern Asia are differently appraised. Neither Thailand nor South Viet Nam have any interest in attending the conference called for by Cambodia because, apart from their differences with Cambodia, they believe that at such a conference the Communist representatives could mount a propaganda attack upon them and demand the removal of American and Allied troops and the neutralisation of South Viet Nam.

A stumbling block to the French proposals for Viet Nam is the belief held in the other Western capitals that the timetable of the Communist attempts to advance into Southern Asia depends upon the outcome of the struggle in South Viet Nam. This is not quite the same thing as the domino thesis; it is the belief that the West's determination to resist Communist-inspired attacks is on trial in South Viet Nam, and that if resistance falters there the tempo of Communist attacks elsewhere will be accelerated. There is considerable evidence in the Indochina zone to support this belief; all the countries in the mainland part of the zone are subject in various ways to Communist pressures. Already Thailand is a target for Communist subversion, particularly in the Northeast region where Communist cadres are attempting to subvert the local population as well as the numerous Vietnamese refugees settled there. Although the belief in the general significance of the war in South Viet Nam remains an hypothesis, it poses the key question of the justification of the West's participation in the struggle. One writer, setting out the arguments in favour of General de Gaulle's policy of unifying Viet Nam, recognised this: 'The war can only be justified on the ground that the Vietnamese must suffer for some larger end: perhaps the preservation of independent governments elsewhere on the continent. Is the war making this long-term objective more attainable'?[1] In Bangkok, Canberra, London and Washington, the answer would be 'yes'. That Paris would probably answer 'No', reveals the strong possibility of a conflict of policy between France and her partners in SEATO.

IV. Other European Countries

There is little evidence to suggest that either the European Community or the individual countries of Western Europe, except Britain, would develop other than economic interests in Southern Asia. Only Portugal has a colonial nexus with its little backwater of Timor. The ex-colonial powers have maintained economic ties with their former colonies, for example, the United Kingdom's investment in India and Malaysia, the French interests in Indochina, and the revived Dutch economic relations with Indonesia. Some agreements for an experimental joint venture to market Indonesian exports with the co-operation of foreign capital were signed in Djakarta in 1964 with Dutch and West German interests. The Indonesians have devised a production-sharing formula by which a foreign investor supplies foreign credit and technical knowledge to Indonesian private or state concerns. The Indonesian Government is considering proposals whose object is to attract Dutch investment and divert Dutch aid to underdeveloped countries towards Indonesia. A Dutch trade mission visited Indonesia in 1963 and reported favourably on the prospects of investment in the development of Indonesia's rich natural resources. But after the stinging humiliation of West Irian, the Netherlands has no intention of becoming strategically involved in the area.

The Federal Republic of Germany takes part in a number of multilateral programmes of economic aid. There is considerable West German investment in India, an increasing stake in Indonesia, and an interest in Nepal, Burma, the Philippines and Australia. Germany lies third amongst the foreign investors in India, after the United Kingdom and the United States, and before Japan and Switzerland. The steel plant at Rourkela in Orissa, built with German aid, has a rated capacity of one million tons yearly. In March 1964, Bonn announced that the German credit of 55 million marks granted to Indonesia was to be extended by an additional 30 million marks, to enable the Indonesian Government to buy 35 Diesel locomotives from Germany. It has pledged credits worth 200 million marks

[1] 'Reunifying Vietnam' in *The New Republic*, 14 September 1963

to Nepal. Like Japan, Germany is preparing to expand its trade with the Philippines, particularly after 1974 when the cheap tariff agreement between Manila and Washington lapses, and is looking towards the markets of mainland China. Encouraged by Chinese officials to set up a trade mission to China, German industry wants to plan an economic strategy to open up the Chinese consumer market.

As the situation in South Viet Nam deteriorated in 1964, an object of American policy was to obtain a firm commitment of the members of NATO, and specifically of Germany, to help maintain the struggle in Asia. In May, Mr. McNamara visited Bonn in an unsuccessful attempt to enlist German co-operation. The communiqué issued after three days of talks merely noted the 'United States hope for the support of other NATO partners, for instance, in South Vietnam against the Communist threat'.[1] Mr. Rusk, in private discussions with Dr. Luns, the Netherlands Foreign Minister, also in May, found him reluctant to commit Dutch support so far afield. It is doubtful whether the United States will secure any such commitment from the NATO powers in the near future.

[1] *The Times*, 12 May 1964

Chapter 3

The Southern Asian Countries:
Policies and Potentials

THE national interests of the external powers in Southern Asia have embroiled them in the conflicts which divide the indigenous countries into hostile groupings. Those conflicts have so far been localised in the several areas of Southern Asia, and can be most conveniently discussed in these terms, although the problems of security which they cause may require broader regional solutions in the future. The local character of the Asian conflicts arises from the nature of the Southern Asian state system. Most countries fear their immediate neighbours more than any of the external powers, and their various territorial claims provide grounds for suspicion and enmity. Thus, in the Indian sub-continent, India and Pakistan have been politically divided since partition. Each group of countries has its own particular problems and potentials. The security of Burma and Thailand, both of whom have borders with parts of Laos under Communist control, is connected with the situation in the Indochina group of states. In the Maphilindo area, Indonesia has determined to crush Malaysia, and the Philippines have laid claim to part of her territory. The fourth group, the Offshore Powers, includes the continent of Australia and the islands of New Zealand, Japan and Taiwan, which are as it were on the circumference of the Asian land mass; these countries in their different fashions all regard their security as affected by developments on the mainland.

I. The Indian Sub-continent
India

India entered a period of difficulty, and perhaps even of crisis, in her domestic and foreign affairs after the Chinese attack in 1962 and the death of Nehru in 1964. Mr. Shastri, Nehru's successor as Prime Minister of India, has described India's two great problems as poverty and hunger. India's economic development has traditionally been planned on the basis of

Indian unity, yet the forces of disunity show signs of gaining strength and the authority of the Centre has weakened. Even during Nehru's lifetime, the Indian states were asserting themselves against New Delhi. Support for the extended use of the Hindu language has been growing. And there are serious problems of sub-nationalism in the country, particularly the Tamil separatism in the South, which are factors weakening the federal system and likely to be dangerous now that the charismatic figure of Jawaharlal Nehru is no longer there. As the *Spectator* commented on 5 June 1964, 'With Nehru gone, New Delhi becomes a less important place, at least for a time. His being there made it an almost automatic stopping-place for world leaders travelling East or West, for Asian consultations, Commonwealth exchanges or for plotting the strategy of non-alignment. Now, however, the danger is that it might, slide down even on the Indian scale, let alone internationally.'

Much of Nehru's foreign policy lay in ruins at the time of his death. India's relations with her neighbours were bad; China was an enemy, Pakistan hostile and Burma unfriendly. The influence which New Delhi had been accustomed to exercise in the Himalayan hill states was in danger of passing to China who rejected India's jurisdictional claims there. The border dispute with China remained unsettled, in glaring contrast to the arrangements with China made by Burma and Pakistan. The Kashmir problem continued to poison relationships with Pakistan, and affected Indian attitudes towards the United Kingdom and the United States. New Delhi rejected as unwarranted intrusions the efforts by London and Washington to find solutions, and the failure of communication between the capitals stimulated the belief in India that she had been misunderstood and even betrayed by her Western friends. In sum, the West has been irritated by India's policy of being 'friendly to neutrals, neutral to enemies, hostile to friends'. India's tie with the Commonwealth could possibly weaken after the death of its architect, Mr. Nehru. After fourteen years of Independence under Nehru's leadership, when New Delhi acted as a moulder of Asian opinion, India found herself more isolated in Asia than ever before.

China has enforced on India a preoccupation with defence matters which signifies a new departure in India's diplomacy. Hitherto, India has sought to protect and even extend her interests in Asia by the exercise of a moral influence, engaging in a maximum of political activity without a corresponding military power. Indian explanations of the Chinese attack in 1962 accept that Peking intended to reduce India's stature in Asia, expose her military weakness and inflict economic damage by disrupting the Third Five-Year Plan. There can be little doubt that China did regard India as a rival for influence in Asia, since India was trying to build a modern economy on a democratic basis, and her success would have refuted the Chinese claim that it could only be done with a totalitarian system. At the beginning of China's 'Great Leap Forward', it looked as though India was being left behind, but when the Great Leap failed, India's economic performance showed well in comparison. The desire to humiliate and deflate India—over and above the genuine conflict about the frontier—was probably the main motive for the Chinese offensive in the eastern Himalayas in the autumn of 1962. By attacking India, China sought to demonstrate that in military terms there is now only one great power in continental Asia, apart from the Soviet Union, which both the Chinese and the Japanese insist is a European power.

China's plan to do harm to the Indian economic programme met with some immediate success. New Delhi was obliged to divert economic resources from peaceful development projects to defence requirements. The Third Five-Year Plan, as a consequence, was adversely affected. But the Plan had in any case lagged behind its industrial and agricultural targets. An increase of 11 per cent a year was planned for industrial production, but the figure actually reached during the first two and a half years of the plan was an 8 per cent annual increase. Agricultural growth lagged even farther behind, and it was barely sufficient to keep pace with the increase of population. The planned target growth rate of 5 per cent a year was double the real increase. Rice and wheat production in 1962–63 fell below the low levels of the previous year, and the Planning Commission requested the state governments to devote special attention to agriculture during the remaining years of the Plan.

India has undertaken a rearmament programme in the expectation of further hostilities with China. According to the budget proposals presented to Parliament by Mr. T. T. Krishnamachari, the Minister of Finance, the sum spent on defence during the financial year beginning on April 1964, would increase by £34,543,000 over the last year's expenditure, to reach a total of £434,357,000. In 1964–65, an estimated 41.8

per cent of Indian central government expenditure was devoted to the armed forces, the Army receiving 76 per cent of the total.[1]

The Army suffered from a serious shortage of modern equipment, and the variety of equipment which India had acquired from a number of sources posed logistical, spare-part and replacement problems. A major difficulty for the General Staff was the provision of an adequate supply of trained officers for the expanded Army. The Navy was centred round India's single aircraft carrier and, lacking either cruisers or destroyers, was weak in comparison with the Indonesian Navy. The defence of India's cities and industrial centres against a Chinese conventional or nuclear air attack sets grave problems, which might not be solved without fundamental changes in Indian planning and policy, and a willingness on the part of the Indian Government to allow foreign bases on Indian soil.

The defence of India against a future Chinese attack is hindered by the strategic consequences of the quarrel with Pakistan. It was the concentration of the Indian forces in the west against Pakistan which rendered India incapable of successfully opposing China in 1962. If there should be further hostilities in the eastern Himalayan region, the neutrality of Pakistan would make it possible for the Chinese forces to cut off Assam (and its oil) completely by a thrust through Darjeeling to the East Pakistan border. A genuine reconciliation between India and Pakistan would, on the other hand, make it possible to provide a proper joint defence for the sub-continent; and a combination of the two countries could be a Great Power, as India by herself cannot be. But some Indian officials speak of Pakistan's 'collusion and collaboration' with China,[2] and affirm that there is evidence that China is training Pakistani guerrillas. Their thinking is geared to the contingency that India might have to fight on two fronts, against Pakistan in the west and China in the east. That this view is not shared by senior Indian army officers illustrates the extent of the disagreements within India over basic questions of security.

[1] *The Military Balance 1964–65*, p. 40
[2] Rebutting this charge in an address to the United Nations General Assembly, on 11 October 1963, Pakistan's Foreign Minister pointed out that 'When India was in conflict with China and had to withdraw the bulk of its armed forces for the first time for the Chinese front, Pakistan did nothing at all, did not lift a finger, did not move a single soldier, did not fire a single bullet'

The Indian Government considers it likely that Chinese pressure on the northern borders will increase in 1966 or thereafter, when China is expected to have completed her communications system in Tibet, including the railway to Lhasa and the road from Lhasa to Katmandu. There has also been a conflicting tendency in India to regard the Chinese attack upon India as concerned with specific limited aims, and related to the problems of China's control of Tibet, and not as part of a general Chinese forward strategy in Asia. This is to take a limited perspective. It is perfectly consistent with a long-term Chinese plan to extend Peking's influence in Asia that India should be given a sharp lesson in the politics of power. The military risks were low and the political gains potentially high, in humbling the largest non-Communist power in Southern Asia.

Arising out of the conflict, there has been military collaboration with the United States and the United Kingdom, especially on problems of the air defence of Indian cities. The Soviet Union has supplied military aid, but there has been no collaboration between Moscow and New Delhi on defence. India has moved closer to the West as a result of the joint discussions of India's defence problems, though there have been no discussions between them about the defence problems of the region as a whole. There is a distinct reluctance in Indian government circles to regard the problem of defence against Chinese attacks as part of a broader series of problems affecting the several strategic zones of Southern Asia, and the crisis of Indo-Chinese relations has not led to any systematic planning for a co-ordination of common defence efforts in the region.

This is a situation which poses a number of serious questions about India's *post bellum* role in Southern Asia. India's prestige has been lowered by defeat. Her confidence in the diplomacy of the Panch Shila has been shaken. She has been forced to rearm. Is the damage done to India's leadership potential more apparent than real? Or does her voice command less than its previous authority in Asian councils? It is significant in this context that the Afro-Asian countries failed conspicuously to rally behind India during and after the border crisis. A group of non-aligned countries, following the initiative taken by Ceylon, offered to mediate between India and China, and drew up proposals to form the basis of negotiation; but they carefully refrained from expressing sympathy for India or condemning China's aggression.

India's ability to influence Asian and world affairs rested upon her diplomatic position as a major power amongst the non-aligned countries. India has chosen to remain non-aligned, and is thus able to receive military and economic assistance from the West as well as the Communist bloc. In India itself Nehru was accused of deserting India's traditional policies of non-alignment by accepting military aid from the United States; but those on the left in Indian politics who raise this criticism seem not to be aware that non-alignment no longer occupies a clearly defined position in the spectrum of political attitudes. The Indian Government is more realistic about the changing forms of non-alignment in an atmosphere of peaceful co-existence between Moscow and the West, and of hostility between Moscow and Peking. India's status as a major non-aligned power has been damaged by the Chinese attack, which revealed India as a feeble Goliath, and by the propaganda from Peking designed to demonstrate New Delhi's obduracy.

India's military defeat has probably been given more weight in Asia than it deserved, but it is an uncomfortable fact that there was covert jubilation in a number of Asian capitals at India's discomfiture in the border war. It is clear that various Asian governments wished to see India discomfited. Anti-Indian sentiments are quite widespread in Southern Asia, and one cause appears to be resentment at India's prominence in regional affairs. The holier-than-thou attitudes expressed with such conviction by Mr. V. K. Krishna Menon at the United Nations not unexpectedly proved to be a political liability. It seems to be true that the style of Indian diplomacy has little at present to offer other Southern Asian countries either as a guide to their own foreign relations or as a focus for the practice of the Bandung spirit. India's position as a mediator has been seriously damaged, and her retention of the doctrine of non-alignment makes it difficult for her to join forces with her few Asian sympathisers, like Malaysia, which has been India's only unequivocal Asian supporter, or with anti-Communist countries like Thailand and the Philippines. India's relationship with Japan is only formally cordial—there is room here for an Indian diplomatic initiative—and her attitude towards Indonesia is cool and tinged with suspicion.

It is clear that India's Government must give a fresh direction to India's policy in Asia, but less certain how her policy will develop or which of her previous positions she will abandon. The non-aligned position appears to have more value to

India with regard to her relations with the Soviet Union than with her Southern Asian neighbours. The non-aligned countries of Southern Asia have cast themselves loose from India's influence, and the mantle of leadership of the 'newly-emerging forces' has passed from Nehru to Sukarno. A new basis of policy, and one which accepts the relevance to Indian security of regional groupings, is in India's long-term interests in Southern Asia, since she is surrounded by overtly or covertly hostile countries. Her security along her extended and vulnerable coastline rests not in Indian naval strength, but in British and American power. To the north, the land threat to India is restricted by geography: there are a limited number of passes and access routes into India; but the possibility of a Chinese thrust at India across north Burma is not excluded by Indian officials. The major threat to India's security during the next ten years might not be against her frontiers, but against her cities, either by airborne strikes from the north or conceivably by seaborne attacks from the south.

Pakistan

Pakistan is probably the least concerned of all the SEATO countries with the defence problems of the Indochina and Maphilindo areas. There are two main reasons for this. First, Pakistan has no vital interests throughout the whole of the treaty area. Pakistan's most serious concerns for her security relate to the threats from her unfriendly neighbours, India and Afghanistan, and to the possibility of a hostile combination of Afghanistan and the Soviet Union. Though Pakistan's representative at the SEATO discussions in Manila in 1954 spoke of Pakistan's vital interests and responsibilities in Southeast Asia as well as the Middle East, Pakistan's geographical remoteness from the trouble-spots of Southeast Asia has given her a detached view of the problems which concern her SEATO allies. The war in South Viet Nam is a long way from Rawalpindi. The only country in Southeast Asia with a common border with Pakistan is Burma, and despite incidents relations between the two countries are correct, if not cordial. The common tie of the Islamic religion (despite its local variations) has not formed a political bond between Malaysia, Indonesia and Pakistan; nor is it likely to do so. Second, although Pakistan has not repudiated her membership of, or her obligations to, SEATO, she argues that her military value to the alliance has been diminished by the continuance of the Kashmir dispute, and by the Western arms supply to India which has placed her security in a precarious balance. Pakistan believes, rightly or wrongly, that the Western arms supplied to India have contributed to India's intransigence on Kashmir. Whatever she may think of the situation in Southeast Asia, Pakistan does not dare to move a single soldier out of her territories for fear of Indian aggression.

Pakistan's *raison d'être* is to be distinct from India. This is a major preoccupation of Pakistan's foreign policy, which affects her attitude towards China, Southeast Asia and her alliances with the West. Pakistan's army of 230,000 men is less than half the size of India's, and her air force is small in comparison with the Indian air force. To Pakistan, India is a strong aggressive neighbour, the main threat to her security (just as Pakistan appears to her weaker neighbour, Afghanistan); and the Kashmir problem keeps their antagonism alive. What Pakistanis regard as the 'massive' provision of British and American military assistance to India, after she had been attacked by China in 1962, served to exacerbate Pakistan's feelings against her military allies and provided fresh arguments for the development of her *rapprochement* with China and the Soviet Union.[1] Pakistan has impressed upon Washington her opinion that the joint defence of the Indian sub-continent is an impossibility in view of Pakistan's fears of India. India is regarded as a more dangerous and less tractable neighbour than China. Relations between India and Pakistan have rarely been worse than they were during the early months of 1964. In January, the outbreaks of violence in Calcutta and in East Bengal shocked both governments, but Pakistan rejected India's appeal for a joint declaration.

The long debate in the Security Council on Kashmir was adjourned indefinitely on 17 February 1964, though the question of Kashmir remained on the Council's agenda. Pakistan had been unable to persuade any member of the Council to move a resolution against India, and the discussions revealed little sign of a new spirit on either side. Pakistan's Foreign Minister, Mr. Zulfikar Ali Bhutto, indicated before the adjournment that the proposed consensus favoured by most members of the Council did not satisfy his country. The

[1] See, for example, Zubeida Hasan, 'Western Arms Aid to India', *Pakistan Horizon*, Fourth Quarter 1963, Pakistan Institute of International Affairs

absence of any resolution which reaffirmed the United Nations' previous decisions on the principle of self-determination for Kashmir was also regretted in Pakistan.

The United Kingdom's support for Pakistan during the debate aroused a strong and intemperate reaction in India. At a meeting of the Congress Parliamentary Party in February 1964 there were voices raised against British 'treachery' and in favour of breaking the tie with the Commonwealth. However inconclusive this stage of the long debate on Kashmir appeared to be, it did serve as a reminder that in future discussions in the Security Council the Indian position rests, in the final count, upon the Russian veto. Some form of open test of public opinion remains desirable for Kashmir, in spite of New Delhi's rather curious case that the victory of the pro-Indian National Conference Party in the elections in Indian-held Kashmir has made a plebiscite unnecessary. The intense feeling in Kashmir against the National Conference Party has been projected against New Delhi as well. Observers have reported that the state of public opinion in Kashmir early in 1964 was that, given a choice between India and Pakistan, the inhabitants would choose in favour of Pakistan. But if a plebiscite were held, what effect would it have upon relations between India and Pakistan?

Even in the unlikely instance that Indian objections to the plebiscite could be overcome, Indian opinion has been fixed too long in the belief that Kashmir is an integral part of India for her to accept the consequences of relinquishing Kashmir to Pakistan without violent internal reactions. These reactions would more probably increase Indian hostility to Pakistan, rather than decrease it, by inflaming the forces of Indian nationalism. Indian nationalism has been disguised by the policies of non-alignment and the Panch Shila, but its strength can be estimated in relation to the Kashmir and Naga issues and the response to the Chinese attack. Pakistan might have reason to fear Indian irredentism if she were to obtain Kashmir as a result of a test of public opinion in the Valley. On the other hand, if India were to retain Kashmir by means of such a test, the Pakistan Government would be unlikely to remain satisfied with the decision, and the reaction of government and people would probably be one of increased hostility towards India and disenchantment with the Western Alliance which provided so little practical support for her claims to Kashmir territory. It is too readily assumed that a settlement of the

Kashmir problem would suffice to remove the tensions between Rawalpindi and New Delhi. A settlement would not necessarily guarantee good relations in the future; for Pakistan fears the size and strength of her neighbour, mistrusts her intentions and her assurances. The question of Kashmir is a symptom and confirmation of those fears, not a cause.

Pakistan's relations with China have come nearly full circle since Pakistan joined SEATO in 1954, and CENTO (then the Bagdad Pact). Pakistan was one of the first countries to recognise the People's Republic of China, as Mr. Shoaib, the Minister of Finance, reminded Mr. Chou En-lai on the occasion of the Chinese Prime Minister's second visit to Pakistan in February 1964. Mr. Shoaib noted that 'the past years have seen a further development of friendly and good relations between our two countries'. When Mr. Chou En-lai first visited Pakistan in 1956, Pakistan was volubly anti-Communist, describing herself as a bulwark against Communism. In December 1961, in the course of the United Nations debate on the admission of Communist China, Pakistan strongly supported Peking's right to occupy the Republic of China's place in the Security Council. In May 1962 Pakistan agreed to negotiate with China a demarcation of the China–Kashmir border.

Conflicts with India gave Pakistan an incentive to develop closer and more friendly ties with China. Cultural and trade exchanges have been undertaken. An arrangement with Peking enabled Pakistan to pioneer commercial airline routes into China. In September 1963 Pakistan and China announced their agreement on measures to delineate their common frontier. China has expressed its solidarity with Pakistan on the Kashmir question, by advocating a settlement by reference to the will of the people—a stand denounced as 'patently unprincipled' by the Communist Party of India. It is clear, however, that Chou En-lai did not promise Chinese assistance to Pakistan in the event of any military action over Kashmir. Pakistan has gained some political and economic advantages from her friendship with China. She has gained a friendly neighbour to the north to balance the unfriendly neighbour to the east, and she seeks to press the advantages while India remains in a threatened and isolated position in Asia.

But there are limits to the advantages to be gained for Pakistan from China's sympathy and friendship. Whether sincerely or otherwise, China has throughout her quarrel with

India maintained a desire for friendship, seeking to negotiate their differences in accordance with the five principles. There is little reason for China to go beyond her present expressions of sympathy with Pakistan and to involve herself deeply or militarily in the divisions of the sub-continent. Pakistan's policy of friendship with China has to be carefully weighed against the possibility of American displeasure. It is still hoped in Pakistan that Washington will come to take a more sympathetic view of her case in Kashmir. Pakistan continues to remain dependent upon American economic and military assistance. The United States has been supplying non-military aid to Pakistan, at the rate of approximately $1 million a day, in addition to substantial military assistance, and has given Pakistan assurance over the supply of arms to India. The visit of Mr. George Ball, Under Secretary of State, to Rawalpindi in September 1963, came at a critical time and probably cleared up misunderstandings; but it did not deter Pakistan from her policy of friendship with China. The State Department has described Pakistan's relations with China as a pressure tactic against India, and an embarrassment to the United States.

The *entente* with China is in spirit, though not perhaps in the letter, incompatible with Pakistan's alignment with the Western powers under the CENTO and SEATO pacts. Despite the pro-Chinese policy in Rawalpindi, the United States continues to provide aid to Pakistan, which hovers uncertainly between the two camps. The feeling that Pakistan has been betrayed by her Western allies, who attach more importance to strengthening India, has caused a profound alienation of national sympathy from the West. As long as the Soviet Union continues to follow Mr. Khrushchev's policy of downright support for Afghanistan and India, Pakistan cannot but be anti-Russian.[1] But if this Russian policy were to be modified under the new Soviet leadership, and the Russian pro-Indian policy were to be dropped (which would be a condition for a reconciliation between the Soviet Union and China), it is possible that Pakistan might be won for a united Sino-Soviet bloc and the CENTO and SEATO alliances repudiated. Unless there is a radical change of Indian policy, Pakistan will be more afraid of India than of the Soviet Union or of China, and this fear must ultimately determine her international position and choice of alignment.

[1] Before the fall of Mr. Khrushchev, there were signs of a thaw in the relations between Pakistan and the Soviet Union

Indochina Zone

II. The Indochina Zone

North Viet Nam

The reunification of North and South Viet Nam is a major political objective of the Hanoi Government. The Geneva Conference Declaration of July 1954 proposed a political settlement in Viet Nam 'on the basis of respect for the principles of independence, unity, and territorial integrity'. Ho Chi Minh referred to this nationalist solution when he described his country's policies in 1963. He said that 'Conditions must be created in which the people of South Vietnam can freely elect a government of their own choice. Between such a government and that of [North Vietnam] agreements could be negotiated to abolish some of the dangerous abnormalities of the present situation and to abolish the existing trade, communications and cultural barriers between the North and South. But future governments of the South must engage to respect strictly the Geneva agreements as [North Vietnam] has done, and not enter any military blocs or permit the establishment of any foreign military bases on its territories.'[1] This is a lucid statement of Ho's policy and of Ho's dilemma, for his government has chosen to try and abolish the abnormalities of the partition of Viet Nam by means of war, and a war might threaten the independence of North Viet Nam.

Hanoi's policy has been to attempt to create in South Viet Nam the political conditions for the elections Ho desired, by supporting insurgency in the south on a substantial scale. French writers have argued that the increasing American commitment in South Viet Nam from 1956 onwards, in response to this insurgent pressure, appears to the North Vietnamese and Chinese Communists as a breach of the Geneva agreements and a further justification for Hanoi's policy of armed intervention in South Viet Nam. With one of the most battle-hardened armies in Asia at its disposal, North Viet Nam can draw on a reservoir of power for its war of national liberation in the south. Hanoi's conscript army apparently still received in 1964 the active support of both the Soviet Union and China, though the most modern Russian and

[1] Interview reported in *The Christian Science Monitor*, 10 February 1964

Chinese weapons have not been supplied. The Viet Cong forces operating in South Viet Nam were estimated in 1964 to number as many as 30,000 men, in spite of claims by American military sources in Saigon that 20,000 guerrillas were killed during 1963. One of the strengths of the Viet Cong, and of its sponsors in Hanoi, is that they appear to many Vietnamese as Nationalists and not as puppets of any foreign power, including China. Diem's régime and the military juntas which followed it may seem more like clients of an alien power. Ho Chi Minh has carefully sustained his image as a Vietnamese nationalist first and a Vietnamese Communist second.

Hanoi has expressed its determination to fight a long war in the south if necessary, but the political victory it seeks depends on two developments. The first is a grave deterioration of the situation inside South Viet Nam, and the second is a favourable international situation. The first of these developments is being achieved by the guerrilla successes which are isolating Saigon and by the failure of the successive governments in Saigon to protect, and win the support of, the peasant majority. Nevertheless, the North Vietnamese Government has to calculate very carefully the amount of military pressure it exercises in the south. In a major foreign policy speech at Los Angeles, in February 1964, President Johnson admonished 'those engaged in the external direction and supply' of the guerrillas in South Viet Nam that they were engaged in a 'deeply dangerous game'. The warning was directed to Hanoi, as the President's observations made clear. There are those in the United States who advocate carrying the war to North Viet Nam by means of the special forces trained for the purpose, but employed by the late President Diem as a praetorian guard, and by blockade or bombing the Viet Cong supply routes from the north. The economy of North Viet Nam is highly vulnerable to conventional air attack. The American involvement in South Viet Nam is so strong that pronounced Viet Cong successes might increase the American participation in the conflict and lead the Chinese to intervene directly in the war. (At present, China has no formal understanding to go to war in defence of North Viet Nam if the latter were to be subjected to armed retaliation by American and South Viet Nam forces.) In this eventuality, Hanoi would lose the political fruits of victory.

The second development also involves the central balance

and emphasises North Viet Nam's difficulties *vis-à-vis* the Soviet Union and China. Ho Chi Minh stubbornly avoided giving outright support to China in the Sino-Soviet dispute, and in this attitude he was supported by the Premier, Pham Van Dong, and the Defence Minister, Vo Nguyen Giap, against the pro-Chinese faction around Truong Chinh and Nguyen Chi Thanh. A formal commitment to Peking would make Ho's Government seem a client of China and rob it of its nationalist appeal. It is therefore in Hanoi's interests to maintain a certain autonomy, while depending upon China for support; its difficulty is that Peking is unlikely to encourage North Viet Nam to play this part. The Soviet Union, on the other hand, might find the role acceptable as a way of restricting Chinese influence, and of maintaining something of her own influence in Viet Nam.

But during 1964 it did not appear that Hanoi was holding a neutral balance in the great schism between Moscow and Peking. The exact nature of the pressure exercised by Peking on North Viet Nam's leaders not to sign the Moscow test-ban treaty remains obscure. This serious breach of Communist discipline could cause the Soviet Union and Czechoslovakia to withhold their assistance from North Viet Nam, with the paradoxical result, one French writer noted, that Hanoi might enlarge her relations with the West, and particularly with France, 'qui reste au sein de la "clique impérialiste" l'interlocuteur le plus abordable'.[1] Fears of China probably explain the discreet suggestions by North Vietnamese leaders to French diplomats in Hanoi that a unified Viet Nam, which met her food requirements from the rice-growing South, could then reduce her political and economic dependence upon China. It is believed that these approaches helped to inspire General de Gaulle's announcement that Viet Nam (as well as Laos and Cambodia) should adopt neutrality as the only situation compatible with the peaceful existence of the peoples concerned.[2] North Viet Nam's leaders probably agree with this Gaullist analysis, for they are reported to have estimated that the best way to obtain their national interests is to achieve with China a position comparable to the Polish relationship with the Soviet Union; but the United States will not accept their methods any more than China will recognise that status.

[1] Georges Chaffard in *Le Monde*, 4 September 1963
[2] *The Observer*, 1 September 1963

South Viet Nam

Before the Geneva Conference of 1954 put an end to the Indo-china war, the United States advocated a 'united action' policy with France, the United Kingdom and friendly Asian powers to oppose the Communist forces on the ground. The Secretary of State, John Foster Dulles, with the concurrence of President Eisenhower, urged that the risks of Chinese intervention be accepted and, if necessary, countered by air strikes against staging bases in South China. In the face of strong British opposition the plan for united action had to be dropped, and President Eisenhower agreed on 26 April 1954, that the conference should be given the opportunity to reach a satisfactory *modus vivendi*. The United States participated reluctantly in the conference. John Foster Dulles withdrew from the discussions before a settlement was reached, and the American delegation which returned to the conference was led by the Under Secretary of State, General Walter Bedell Smith.

The United States did not sign—it merely noted in a unilateral declaration—the agreements on the future of Indochina concluded at Geneva in July 1954, which provided *inter alia* for the temporary division of Viet Nam into two zones pending the establishment of peace and the holding of national elections in two years. The anti-Communist Vietnamese delegation to the Conference protested against the summary rejection of its proposal that provisional control by the United Nations be established before the elections were held. The protest was noted in the American declaration with the comment that the United States would not join in arrangements which hindered the Vietnamese people from determining their own future. No national elections were held within the stated period and none have been held since. The successive governments of the state of South Viet Nam have opposed national elections on the grounds that the population of the North outnumbers that of the South and that elections would therefore result in a Communist victory.

The state of South Viet Nam was named in the Protocol appended to the Manila Pact as one of the three Indochina states eligible for the economic measures contemplated under article III of the treaty and, on requesting it, eligible for the protection of SEATO. South Viet Nam has not claimed that protection (though the question has been considered); instead it has been taken under the special protection of the United States. The relationship between the two countries has not been defined in a formal treaty. The United States has unilaterally assumed the responsibility for assisting the successive governments of South Viet Nam in their war against Communist-directed insurgency.

The American commitment in South Viet Nam is very deep. It is measured not simply by the statistics of American aid to South Viet Nam, but also by the statements of Washington's determination to give practical support in the field as long as the embattled country is threatened by Communist insurgency. Officials no longer estimate that the war will be won by the end of 1965; they talk in terms of a period of five to ten years before the armed Communists are brought under control. On 26 March 1964 Mr. McNamara announced the purposes of the American intervention in South Viet Nam in the course of a policy speech at Washington. His statements underlined the moral and strategic assumptions of the Administration's thinking so far as they could be made public. The Secretary said that the United States acted to fufil her promise to the Vietnamese to help South Viet Nam preserve its independence, and to prevent an area of strategic significance in the forward defence of the United States from falling under Communist control. He described South Viet Nam as a test case of the new Communist strategy of wars of national liberation as enunciated by Mr. Khrushchev in 1961. The fall of the state of South Viet Nam would leave the Hanoi Government in control of all Viet Nam and, possibly, of Laos also, and would be the first step towards the Chinese hegemony in the region. Mr. McNamara firmly rejected any proposals for the neutralisation of Viet Nam: 'Under the shadow of Communist power neutralisation would in reality be an interim device to permit Communist consolidation and eventual take-over.' The speech was an authoritative statement of the aims and principles of American policy in South Viet Nam, but it did not break any new ground. Despite changes of administration, the United States is following essentially the same kind of policy in South Viet Nam as that stated in 1954 by John Foster Dulles.

There have been severe strains within the partnership, particularly in the years of Diem rule, when Washington and

Saigon did not agree on ways to conduct affairs against the Viet Cong and their sympathisers, when Diem refused to liberalise his government, and when at all levels there was friction between the Vietnamese and their American advisers. Under the government of General Nguyen Khanh, American-Vietnamese relationships appeared to improve; there was general agreement between Saigon and Washington on the objectives and priorities of the war. It was a product of a shift of Vietnamese rather than of American attitudes. General Khanh demonstrated that he was more amenable than the late President Diem to American advice and instruction, and the United States announced its full support for his government. The political and social reforms in the countryside that Washington had tried unsuccessfully to persuade Ngo Dinh Diem to adopt were accepted with enthusiasm by General Khanh. Mr. McNamara endorsed the plan for training more efficient district chiefs and government administrators, and the then American Ambassador, Mr. Henry Cabot Lodge, addressed the first group of district chiefs attending a training course. There has been a new and sharpened sense of partnership in the reports of the present relationship between Washington and Saigon, and on the surface a greater mutual trust than existed with the earlier régime. Outside American circles there was a disposition to wait and see whether General Khanh's Government could fulfil Mr. McNamara's confident prediction and carry the war to a successful conclusion.

As the situation in South Viet Nam deteriorated, more draconian measures were proposed, including the possibility of carrying the war into North Viet Nam. It has been commonly assumed that the insurgency in the south is maintained by trained cadres and supplies from the north; but disquieting reports have been made that during the current phase of the revolutionary war the insurgents equip themselves with captured weapons, rely upon local recruiting, and receive little material support from North Viet Nam. It is difficult to obtain accurate information on this matter, but early in 1964 Mr. McNamara spoke of 'the large indigenous support that the Viet Cong receives'. The stereotype of the war in South Viet Nam that has appeared in the Western press is of an insurrection directed from outside the state, with the implication that cutting off the supply lines or attacking the source of supply would strike the decisive blow against the guerrillas. If, however, the insurrection sustains itself within the state, the situation is more serious than has been publicly admitted. American military assistance staves off the defeat of the Saigon Government, but arms without ideas cannot achieve a political victory. The Communist guerrilla struggle is aimed at men's minds and the Saigon governments have so far conspicuously failed to rally the suffering peasantry of South Viet Nam to their support.

After Diem, the Government recognised that it must employ civil weapons and wage a political warfare against the Viet Cong terrorists. Premier Khanh launched a revitalised strategic hamlet programme—the ambitious nationwide 'pacification plan'—with Dr. Nguyen Ton Hoan as Vice-Premier in Charge of Pacification, in an all-out effort to win the allegiance of the rural population, whose will to resist the Viet Cong was eroded by Communist propaganda and terror and by the autocratic methods of the Diem Government. Reaffirming American support for South Viet Nam in January 1964, immediately after the Khanh coup, the State Department expressed confidence that the anti-guerrilla struggle could be won provided that the Vietnamese people were assured of security and that there was popular support for the Government. These remain the essential desiderata for victory. The fundamental war effort has to made in the south.

South Viet Nam returned to civilian rule in November 1964, with the apointment of Tran Van Huong, a former mayor of Saigon, as Premier. However, General Khanh retained his post as commander-in-chief, and doubts remained whether the South Viet Nam army would effectively relinquish its power to the civilian government. It remains to be seen what effect civilian rule will have upon the struggle in the countryside, in the areas still under the control of the government in Saigon, and whether the government will take initiatives to improve relations with neighbouring Cambodia.

Cambodia

In a paradoxical effort to ensure his country's neutrality Prince Norodom Sihanouk, the Cambodian Head of State, has threatened in effect to abandon a neutral position and make an alliance with China. In February 1964 the Prince indicated that he was prepared to begin negotiations with China for the construction of air bases in Cambodia. In March a Cambodian military delegation left for Peking. General Lon

Nol, Commander-in-chief of the Royal Khmer Army, led the group which had been authorised to purchase arms; the delegation visited Hanoi before travelling to Peking, and proposed to visit the Soviet Union. Western diplomats in Asia, who were already apprehensive of the increasing Communist alignment of Cambodian diplomacy, viewed these moves with alarm. The Prince's initiative is a further development of that 'extreme neutralism' which was noted in the Mansfield Report of 1963. It reflects the mounting disillusionment of Prince Norodom Sihanouk's erratic opinion of the Western world. In October 1963 he expressed his view that Western blunders in Asia had caused the Communist advances in the region. Commenting upon Cambodia's years of independence he wrote: 'Le communisme exerce une attirance indiscutable sur tous les jeunes des pays afro-asiatiques. Mais au Cambodge infiniment moins qu'ailleurs. La raison principale de cette avance communiste dans tout le "tiers monde" est la somme des erreurs accumulées par le monde libre, en particulier par les Etats-Unis d'Amérique, depuis la fin de la seconde guerre mondiale'.[1]

It is apparent from the Prince's attitude that the sums of more than $300 million of American assistance to Cambodia between 1955 and 1962 have not served to build up a friendly or understanding atmosphere between the two countries. The close American ties with Laos, South Viet Nam and Thailand have linked the United States with Cambodia's historic enemies. To Cambodians, therefore, the United States is not disinterested in her relationships with Cambodia, not genuinely concerned with Cambodia's neutral position; and this impression has been unfortunately heightened by the note of distrust of neutrals that has previously been struck in American diplomacy in Asia. The outcome, at least in the mind of the Cambodian head of state, has been the perfervid suspicions of American intentions which mark his utterances on Cambodian policy. He now apparently believes that the United States, as an ally of Thailand and of South Viet Nam, poses an actual threat to his country.

In December 1963 Prince Norodom Sihanouk made public his complaint that the United States gave its support from Thailand and South Viet Nam to the Free Cambodia (Khmer Serai) Movement; and he proposed the creation of a neutralised confederation consisting of Cambodia and South Viet Nam, stipulating that in the first place the Saigon Government

[1] *Le Monde*, 8 October 1963

pass a statute of neutrality.[1] In February 1964, the Prince proposed a four-nation conference of Cambodia, South Viet Nam, Thailand and the United States, and then rejected the proposal in March. During March, the Prince broadcast in the presence of a Council of Notables at Phnom Penh his remarkable charge that the United States, in complicity with Laos, South Viet Nam and Thailand, plotted to partition Cambodia. American attempts to help settle the border problems with South Viet Nam and Thailand are seen in the sinister light of policies designed to enforce Thai and Vietnamese solutions upon Cambodia. On receipt of Chinese military aid in March 1964, Prince Sihanouk announced that: 'It is certain that if China, the Soviet Union, France, and Yugoslavia had not hastened to help us militarily without conditions after the rejection of American aid, our enemies would already have struck out offensively against Cambodia.'[2]

It is hardly necessary to point out that the public record of American activities in Southern Asia does not give credence to these allegations. The problem is to understand why the charges have been made at all, whether or not they are believed in Phnom Penh; and the body of Prince Sihanouk's criticisms of American policy does not provide much explicit guidance. What is clear, in the first place, is that Cambodia now requires a specific declaration from the powers, including the United Kingdom and the United States, affirming Cambodian neutrality against Thailand and South Viet Nam. This demand for a modern international settlement of historic enmities is made irrespective of the difficulties to which it might give rise in the relationships between Thailand and her SEATO allies. The arrangement would benefit Cambodia by obliging the United States to stop her alleged plotting against Cambodia and to restrain Thailand and South Viet Nam in the event of any future border hostilities or other crises between the Indochina states. In other words, Cambodia believes that her national interests will be best served by an international arrangement to make substantive the Locarno-like aspiration of the 1954 Conference on the settlement of Indochina. With this object in view the Cambodian Foreign Minister, Mr. Huot Sambath, sent similar requests in November 1963 for a 9-nation conference on Cambodia's neutrality to the United

[1] *Daily Telegraph*, 2 December 1963; *New York Herald Tribune*, 4 December 1963
[2] *Christian Science Monitor*, 17 March 1964

Kingdom and the Soviet Union as co-chairmen of the 1954 Geneva Conference.

Secondly, it is also clear that the Cambodian authorities quite rightly do not regard the pious hopes of the conference at Geneva in 1954 as providing any sort of effective guarantee for Cambodia which protects her against her more powerful neighbours South Viet Nam and Thailand. The 9-nation conference at Geneva in 1954 (Thailand was not a participant) noted 'the declarations of the governments of Cambodia and Laos to the effect that they will not join in any agreement with other states if this agreement includes the obligation to partici-pate in a military alliance not in conformity with the principles of the Charter of the United Nations ... or, so long as their security is not threatened, the obligation to establish bases on Cambodian or Laotian territory for the military forces of foreign powers'. The chief American delegate, General Bedell Smith, added a separate declaration, to the effect that his government shared 'the hope that the agreements will permit Cambodia, Laos and Viet Nam to play their part, in full independence and sovereignty, in the peaceful community of nations, and will enable the peoples of that area to determine their own future'.

The settlement at Geneva in 1954 evidently does not satisfy Cambodia, if only for the reason that the dangers that she fears have continued to occur after the settlement. In the words of General Lon Nol: 'Le départ du corps expéditionnaire a sonné la fin de l'internationalisation de l'Indochine. Les mouvements agressifs continuateurs des mouvements Issarak et vietminh menacent l'existence du Cambodge'; he instanced 'L'incursion vietnamienne de Bokeo à l'automne 1958, le complot de Siem-Reap au printemps 1959'.[1] It appears that Cambodia, as a prime mover in the 1962 settlement which recognises the neutrality of Laos, will be satisfied by nothing less than a similar international recognition of her own neutrality. Prince Sihanouk has given the United Kingdom and the United States until May 1964 (later amended to earlier dates in March and April) to agree to take part in such a conference, before he enters into an alliance with China. On 11 March 1964, the American and British embassies in Phnom Penh were attacked and ransacked; the Prince accused the two countries of a lack of zeal for the conference.[2] The third clear

[1] *Le Monde*, 8 October 1963
[2] *The Guardian*, 12 March 1964

feature of Prince Nordom Sihanouk's search for an international affirmation of Cambodia's neutrality is his desire to achieve a diplomatic balance between China and the United States as interested powers. The expectation of this policy is that just as the United States would be obliged by her affirmation to restrain her Thai and Vietnamese allies, so China would be obliged to restrain the Communist Vietnamese and pro-Communist Pathet Lao from any attacks upon Cambodia. Prince Sihanouk has cried wolf too often, and by employing an ultimatum he is playing a dangerous game of diplomacy. The more his charming and relatively defenceless country falls within the Chinese sphere of influence, the greater the danger that Cambodia might lose her autonomy as well as her neutrality.

As his ultimatum suggests, the Prince is in a hurry to secure an international agreement on Cambodia. For he has estimated that the balance of power in Southern Asia is swinging in China's favour. He has described the North Vietnamese and the pro-Communist Pathet Lao as the future masters of Viet Nam and of Laos, and he threatened in March 1964 to negotiate with them for a guarantee of Cambodia's neutrality. He therefore needs an international settlement of Cambodian neutrality before Cambodia falls too much under the influence of China and whilst the United States is still in a powerful bargaining position in the area. He must persuade the United States to act by the threat of a Cambodian alliance with China, for if the United States cannot be persuaded to bargain with China for Cambodia's neutrality there is no pressure he can put on Peking, and his whole political defence of Cambodia fails. It is a pity therefore that he has so much debased his bargaining currency.

Laos

Laos is what was left on the map after the provinces of French Indochina were divided up, and it is part of the sophistry of the Geneva Agreement on Laos to have treated it as a nation. The sense of Laotian nationality is not developed amongst the 2.5 million inhabitants of Laos, approximately half of whom belong to minority groups. Until a decade ago there was no tradition of political leadership on a national level. National politics emerged in the form of factions, and only one leader, Prince Souvanna Phouma, the first Prime Minister of an independent Laos, has a stature which rises above faction. The size of their respective armies during 1964 provided an approximate index of the strengths of the three factions which taken together constitute the political life of the Buddhist kingdom.

The right-wing army of General Phoumi Nosavan was estimated to contain as many as 70,000 troops before demobilisation was commenced. More recent estimates give the number as 50,000 men (including the neutralist forces) controlling the area along the Mekong River valley and roads and agricultural plains in the south of Laos. The use of the word 'controlling' in this context may give an incorrect impression of the degree to which the right-wing forces exercise a jurisdiction within the area described. For example, in January 1964 it was reported that 4 North Vietnamese and 6 Pathet Lao battalions had launched an attack which took them within 9 miles of Thakhek in southern Laos.[1] Thakhek lies within a few miles of the Thai border, opposite Muang Nakhon Phanom; it is the only town on the Thai border between the rightist stronghold of Savannakhet in the south and Vientiane, a distance of some 300 miles, from which a road runs into Thailand. The strategic significance of Thakhek is that it is the junction of a road system which runs from North Viet Nam above the 1954 cease-fire line across into Thailand. From Muang Nakhon Phanom a road runs roughly due west to Udon Thani, and another road runs south to Ubol (Muang Ubon or Ubon Ratchathani). Udon Thani and Ubol are two main air fields in north-eastern Thailand.

The size of the left-wing Pathet Lao forces can only be guessed at. They were said in 1964 to have grown from 20,000 to 26,000 troops occupying northern Laos from the frontier of China and extending south to the frontiers of South Viet Nam and Cambodia, including the area traversed by the Ho Chi Minh trail (the Viet Cong's supply route from North Viet Nam to the South). General Kong Le's neutralist forces, which shrank from 10,000 to 3,000 to 5,000 men, were confined to enclaves in the north of Laos, for example, in Xieng Khouang province, but were pushed off the Plaine des Jarres. The right wing faction is the 'party of privilege', the Pathet Lao faction is the 'underdog party' and the neutral faction is the 'party of protest'. An interesting generalisation about the political life of Laos is suggested by a comparison of the ethnic map with the territories controlled by the three factions. The

[1] *Christian Science Monitor*, 31 January 1964

areas controlled by the right-wing army are virtually the same as the Lao ethnic areas, and the minority areas correspond broadly with the area of Pathet Lao control. There is no similar correspondence with respect to the neutral forces.

Kong Le, a member of a minority family from Tchepone, in Savannakhet province in the south, who is partly Kha (aboriginal) on his mother's side, emerged in August 1960 as the leader of the protest movement. His movement had no social base like the other factions and no party organisation, and was held together by the zeal for strict neutrality. Lacking social roots, the neutral faction has tended to polarise to right and left, a process which has been encouraged by the Pathet Lao, and reportedly by agents from Hanoi and Peking.[1] Yet ideally, the neutral position was, by the Geneva arrangements, to be the linch-pin of the settlement of Laos. 'Cette solution', a French correspondent wrote, 'tendait à consolider les forces du centre laotien, à en faire "l'épine dorsale" de l'Etat, flanquée des deux extremes: la droite pro-américaine du général Phoumi and la gauche procommuniste du Pathet-Lao, dirigée par le prince Souphannouvong et le général Singkapo.'[2]

Of the three major tasks which faced the provisional government after the 1962 Agreement, the first was the implementation of the cease fire. This has been substantially achieved, though a precarious balance remains, and there have been reports of continued Pathet Lao attacks upon neutralist and right wing positions. Moreover, the alignment of forces within this balance has changed since 1960, when right-wing attacks on neutral positions caused Kong Le to join forces with the Pathet Lao. In more recent developments, the Pathet Lao attacked Kong Le's troops and General Phoumi Nosavan's Meo guerrillas moved down from the mountains to provide a protective screen for the neutralist positions. The right wing and neutralist forces merged under an 11-man command staff in May 1964.[3] Both the right and left wings have continually exchanged territory as a result of their attacks and counter-attacks, without so far destroying the general balance of forces within Laos.

The second and third tasks were the unification of the army and the administration. As the proposed integrated army of

[1] *Neue Zürcher Zeitung*, 16 April 1963
[2] Jean Lacouture in *Le Monde*, 16 April 1963. By 1964, General Phoumi was apparently in eclipse
[3] *The Times*, 14 May 1964

Laos was to number 30,000 men, consisting of 10,000 from each faction, the unification of the armies required that the surplus forces of the right and left factions be demobilised; that is, about 40,000 of the right-wing soldiers and 16,000 Pathet Lao troops. Diplomats in Vientiane believed that General Phoumi Nosavan, whose position is likely to be weakened by the demobilisation, was nevertheless prepared to demobilise his army, provided that he had assurances that the Pathet Lao did likewise. During 1963 some 6,000 to 8,000 right-wing troops were in process of demobilisation as a token of the general's good faith. Despite some publicised spectacles of Pathet Lao demobilisation, it is clear that the left-wing forces have not been properly demobilised; in any case, de-mobilisation means different things to an army organised along conventional lines and to a guerrilla force. Thus it was difficult to give Phoumi Nosavan the assurances he required, and the rate of the general demobilisation in Laos continues to depend upon the actions of the Pathet Lao.

Prince Souphanouvong outlined to the author a plan to achieve the demobilisation of the 50,000 right- and left-wing troops in three stages, so that they could be absorbed into civilian life and by the under developed economy of Laos. Troops were first to be formed into construction corps and employed on public works. Second, those troops who desired to return to their villages and resume agricultural pursuits were to be permitted to do so. And, third, new villages were to be established to absorb the demobilised soldiers. Diplomats agreed that the average Laotian soldier would return without trouble to his village, particularly as in many cases troops have been serving in their own localities. But a political problem might be caused by the demobilisation of officers. Unless these men find positions in civilian life with rewards commensurate with their military standards, they are expected to form a core of discontent. This is a problem which pre-dominantly concerns the right-wing army with its abundance of officers. According to a diplomatic source in Vientiane, some of the officers remained on the French reserve and were paid by France. The plan to redraw the provincial boundaries of Laos and form smaller administrative units is already being put into practice and will create jobs for officers trained in administrative skills. The United States has offered to provide brief training courses for officers and other ranks, so that the technical skills acquired in the armed forces may be adapted to civilian life in a society desperately short of even such elementary skills as reading and writing.

The government's third task, to unify the three factions into one administration, cannot be completed until the demobilisation question is settled. In the circumstances, only a speculative answer can be given to the question; can Laos be settled on the basis of internal unification and international neutralisation?

There are those who regard the Geneva settlement as having failed, seeing it as a kind of Asian Munich which gained time in Southern Asia. It is too soon to make such a firm judgement, though there is a tendency in the West to write off Laos. The available evidence indicates that the major powers concerned in the Laotian settlement have respected the accord and withdrawn their forces from the country. But the persistent reports of the presence of Viet Minh forces amongst the Pathet Lao cannot be adequately checked as long as the work of the International Control Commission, which has the responsibility of determining whether all foreign forces have been withdrawn, is impeded by dissentions amongst its members and the intransigence of the left-wing forces. According to American officials in Vientiane, for example, there were 11 battalions of North Vietnamese troops inside Laos in May 1963. The settlement is also threatened by the Viet Cong use of a supply route in eastern Laos from North to South Viet Nam. However, the present distribution of forces in Laos is strategically significant, for the anti-communist Laotian Army so far remains in precarious command of the vital artery of the Mekong River through Laos and along the Thai frontier.

In spite of the uneasy military and political balance in Laos, the coalition government has agreed on a plan for the economic development of the country. Prince Souphanouvong has opined that a change of government would not alter the essentials of the plan. An economy has to be built virtually from scratch; the kingdom is mostly covered by jungle. The economic plan calls for the utilisation of the country's manpower and agricultural and forest resources jointly with the assistance of foreign aid. The United Kingdom and France have agreed to contribute to the programmes of economic reconstruction. The Soviet Union gives assistance largely through a commercial payments agreement. American aid, which was cut to about $40 million in 1963, continues to provide the main external support for Laos. In its later stages, the plan envisages the development of an export trade to cut down the national deficit: handicrafts, mineral resources and ultimately light and heavy industries. Railway and river transportation are to be developed and proposals have been made for negotiations with the neighbouring countries to provide land-locked Laos with outlets to the sea for her exports at the ports of Rangoon, Bangkok, Sihanoukville and Haiphong in North Viet Nam. It is an ambitious programme which emphasise just how much has to be done to make Laos an economically independent and viable unit.

Thailand

Thailand has been the pampered member of SEATO. Owing to the establishment of SEATO headquarters in Bangkok, which has tended to make Thailand a showpiece of the Organisation, and to the co-operation of the Thai Government, Thailand has received most of the civil aid benefits granted by SEATO. In some of the SEATO aid programmes in Thailand, Bangkok has provided as much as 40 per cent of the cost of the projects. The Thai Government made available land, buildings, fixtures, transport and staff for the Military Technical Training School in Bangkok, which is a joint venture with Australia, whose contribution is equipment, training aids and instructors. The civilian element of this SEATO skilled labour project in Thailand included 19 vocational schools in provincial towns, 77 workshops (17 more were to be added), and more than 5,000 students in 1962–63. Together, the two projects offered 46 per cent of the technical training facilities then available in Thailand.

In November 1962, the Government of Thailand opened its first Regional Community Development Technical Assistance Centre at Ubol in the north-east, with a broad programme of training, research and co-ordination of community development projects. A proposal to improve the telecommunications system for the purpose of acquiring aeronautical and meteorological information in Thailand and the Philippines was approved in 1961–62, and the United States allocated $800,000 to the project. Australia and Thailand have established a medium-wave radio network in north-east Thailand. The need for such a network was noted by a SEATO committee, and the Australian Government made a grant out of its military aid vote towards the cost of erecting three radio

stations at Ubol, Khorat and Khon Kaen. The United States
lent Thailand a radio station to be used for local broadcasts
from Khon Kaen. Australia has provided personnel, vehicles
and equipment for the community development centre and
for the Provincial Police. New Zealand sent a doctor and
mobile medical unit to Thailand's north-east. France supplied
an agricultural expert to the community development centre,
and the United Kingdom provided an agricultural economist
and equipment.

In spite of these numerous benefits, the Thai alignment
with the West has needed to be continually re-confirmed.
Thailand has been a most vociferous critic of SEATO's role
as a military pact in the defence of the treaty area and of its
supine inactivity in the recurrent Laotian crises since 1955.
For their part, some of Thailand's allies have taken pains to
sooth Thai sensibilities, turn away criticisms and proffer
renewed assurances. Developments in Laos and Pathet Lao
approaches to Thailand's sensitive north-eastern border have
been the cause of Thai concern. Field Marshal Sarit Thanarat,
the late Prime Minister, described Thailand's security as
depending upon a friendly Laos, and the graph of Bangkok's
criticisms of SEATO fluctuated with the fortunes of the right-
wing government of Prince Boon Oum and General Phoumi
Nosavan.

At the beginning of 1961 SEATO members, apart from the
United States and Thailand, were slow to respond to the
overtures of the Laotian Ambassador to Thailand in exploring
the possibility of a SEATO inquiry into Communist activity
in Laos. The United Kingdom and France opposed the plan,
which was subsequently dropped. This failure to act inflamed
Thai sensibilities already smarting under the reduction of the
amount of United States economic aid in the fiscal year 1960–
61; the $24.4 million grant in 1959–60 was reduced by $0.6
million in the following year. Thai enthusiasm for the Western
alliance waned, although it was officially denied that Thailand
had any intention of withdrawing from SEATO. Vice-President
Johnson's visit to Bangkok in May 1961 did not long satisfy
Thailand's need for assurances, particularly for guarantees of
the security of Laos in face of the agreement at Vienna in
June between the Soviet Union and the United States on a
coalition government in Laos led by neutrals; and some
sharp comments were made in Bangkok about 'our great
friend'. Marshal Sarit Thanarat announced his willingness to

support moves to refashion SEATO into a more useful instrument, and the Thai press severely criticised the United Kingdom, France and SEATO.

The Dean Rusk–Thanat Khoman joint Statement at Washington in March 1962 gave Thailand a specific American guarantee and added a significant new element to the United States' interpretation of the Manila Treaty. These assurances were probably necessary if Bangkok were to acquiesce in the policy of a neutral Laos withdrawn from the protection of SEATO. Mr. Dean Acheson pleaded the Cambodian case for possession of the disputed and ruined Preah Vihear temple before the International Court, whose decision in 1962 in favour of the Khmer state led to renewed Thai criticisms of the United States. American–Thai relations were further exacerbated when, in August, it was reported that American assistance had been granted to Cambodia, Thailand's traditional enemy, to be employed against the Viet Cong operating from bases in Cambodian territory. The government in Bangkok was partly appeased when, before the SEATO Council meeting in Paris in April 1963, President Kennedy publicly commended Thailand's contribution to the security of the region. At the Paris meeting one of the objects of Thai diplomacy was achieved, when the unanimity rule of the Organisation was modified so that the Council of Representatives would decide on a proposal after a stated period if five members approve, three members do not indicate their viewpoints, and no member objects.

The fundamental difficulty with Thailand as a member of SEATO is the existence of Laos as an independent state. Laos was under Siamese control at the time of the French conquest of Indochina, and it would have been much better if it had been returned to Thailand after the dissolution of French Indochina. The bulk of the Lao people live in Thailand; only a minority of them are in Laos, and a Laos unfriendly to Thailand must be a base for Lao irredentism in Thailand and a threat to Thailand's existence as a state. Thai policy has therefore always been to keep a pro-Thai government in power in Laos. Bangkok has been committed to the support of the Boon Oum—Nosavan faction in Laos. The United States formerly endorsed this policy, but when the Laos situation became critical she switched to the neutralist formula for Laos, which has, as the Thais foresaw, led to a strengthening of the Pathet Lao, who are directed from Hanoi. Thailand is more afraid of a Vietnamese–Lao combination, which would be much too strong for her, than she is of China. If the Thais cannot obtain what they regard as adequate American support against such a combination, they will try to reinsure with China. This is what Thais mean by a policy of neutrality. If the Thais were not too much entangled in the American alliance, they could jump on the Chinese bandwagon just as they jumped on the Japanese bandwagon in 1941.

Thailand's internal problems do not seem to constitute an immediately serious threat to the stability of the kingdom, except in the north-east. The question of the succession to Marshal Sarit Thanarat did not disrupt the governing military oligarchy. As the government in Bangkok acquires more knowledge of Communist organisation and learns from SEATO sources more about the techniques of counter-subversion, it is better able to deal with the problems of the political sympathies of the Overseas Chinese and of Communist agitation amongst the volatile student bodies. But Communist subversive activities have been intensified in the remote rural areas of Thailand and in the protocol states along her extended eastern and northern borders.[1] The border between Thailand and Burma is relatively secure, since it has been the policy of the Thai Government to maintain excellent relations with Burma, and to regard the question of the Shan states (two of which were obtained by Thailand during the Second World War) as a strictly internal Burmese affair. Irredentism is unlikely to be an important source of conflict between Bangkok and Rangoon in the immediate future.

But the borders with Cambodia and Laos are unstable. During recent years the threat of subversion by Communist infiltration from Laos across the Mekong River has been taken seriously in Bangkok. Mr. Kenneth Young, the United States Ambassador to Thailand, was quoted in February 1963 as affirming that in the remote areas of Thailand Communist activity 'was on the brink of emerging from infiltration to subversion' as large but unknown numbers of Communist cadres entered the country from Laos.'[2] There is evidence of subversive activity through Laos from North Viet Nam and

[1] The Communist threat to north-east Thailand is described in five articles, 'The Battle for the North-East', published during May 1963 in the *Bangkok Post*, and republished as a SEATO press release (Bangkok, June 1963)

[2] *The Guardian* (Rangoon), 8 February 1963

China on a 'ladder principle', according to the Ambassador, though it is difficult to identify the sources and stages of the process farther back. The evidence is lacking for any Russian participation in this subversive activity. The Chinese would face great logistical difficulties in mounting a full-scale invasion in this region; but they have plenty of people, and agents are being sent in to the remote Thai provinces to win the stomachs, eyes and minds of the aboriginal inhabitants. American sources in Bangkok report that the Chinese efforts at subversion are more advanced than the West's counter-efforts. They advance the thesis that the Chinese, taking advantage of the historical hill and valley opposition of the inhabitants (exemplified in the *montagnard* and plains people rivalry in Viet Nam) are infiltrating the mountain peoples in the great belt from China to Burma, in an attempt to win them away from their nominal governments. Some of these peoples are incredibly remote; the 'Yellow Leaves' tribe, first discovered some thirty-five years ago, has only recently been re-discovered. It is also suggested that the Chinese anthropological–political work amongst these peoples is quite advanced to obtain control over the aboriginals and the mountains they inhabit. Control of the mountains will give the Chinese control of the passes leading south to the sea.

The Thai Government, supported by its SEATO allies, is working to counter this threat by the community development schemes in an effort to build up amongst the peoples of the remote provinces a sense of identity with Bangkok. Pictures of the Thai King and Queen have been distributed. Plenty of scope remains for Communist activity in these provinces where several million of the region's 8 million inhabitants speak Lao. Amongst the non-Thai aboriginal tribes in the north-east, there is little knowledge of Bangkok, and that little knowledge is often accompanied by a sense of resentment at the Government's neglect of them. An estimated 50,000 to 80,000 pro-Communist refugees from Viet Nam have settled in the area since the Second World War. Viet Minh agents have been active amongst these people, some of whom have crossed the Mekong River to help the Pathet Lao. They have resisted the attempts of the Thai Government to resettle them in the south, and the scheme to repatriate them to Viet Nam will take an anticipated 6 years at least to complete. The absence of law and order in the north-east, and the lack of economic development, make it difficult to defend the area politically, and the lack of logistical roads increases the difficulties of defending it militarily. On the other side of the Mekong River, the Pathet Lao are extending their road system from China to the corners of Thailand.

The responsibility for controlling the extended Thai border, which rests for some 800 miles against Laos, was given to the Border Police, not the army. The strength of this force in 1962 was estimated to be about 5,000 men. The Provincial Police, a separate body from the Border Police, have been the forgotten element in the Thai armed forces. Australia and the United States are building up this internal security force by providing training and wireless facilities, and vehicles to increase its mobility. The American Aid Mission has established four training centres, two in the north-east, for the instruction of the Provincial Police in counterinsurgency jungle tactics. Approximately 2,200 policemen graduated from the first courses in 1963.[1] Early in 1963, a military attaché in Bangkok gave the author a startling picture of the Thai Army, describing it as an over-officered force with more generals than companies, small proficiency in jungle operations, as centred on Bangkok, and with a complicated control and command structure designed by Marshal Sarit Thanarat to seal up those avenues in the army which he used for promotion and to prevent coups against the Government. It was alleged that the signatures of five generals were required before a tank could be moved.

A significant attempt was made by the Thai Government and the United States at the beginning of 1962 to remedy this situation. The American plan was to provide training and generally to lead the Thai Army from behind, as had been attempted in South Viet Nam. At first, the American advisers on the ground made little impact; the four or five thousand advisers were thinly spread with one officer and two non-commissioned officers to a regimental battle group. Much yet remains to be done to increase the operational efficiency of the Thai Army and to transform it according to the new concept of mobile hard-hitting small forces to encounter, combat and destroy terrorists. Political inhibitions may stand in the way of realising this concept, for it would give more power to subordinate commanders than Marshal Sarit Thanarat thought advisable and would create just the kind of army that could undertake a coup efficiently in the Thai tradition.

Some encouraging lessons were drawn from the training exercise *Dhanarajata* held in Thailand in June, 1963. More than 24,000 officers and men of the armed services of all the

[1] *New York Times*, 2 January 1964

SEATO members took part in the exercise which was described in the Secretary-General's Report for 1962–3 as consisting of '(a) a command post exercise involving the deployment of combined and national headquarters and token logistics administrative forces, and (b) a two-sided field manoeuvre exercise with emphasis on delaying, defensive, and counter-offensive operations'. The problems of supplying forces operating in northern Thailand have been studied on the ground by experts of the RAND Corporation, and some of their conclusions were ratified by Exercise *Dhanarajata*. From the United States long-range military transport aircraft reached Thailand 'within hours', the SEATO report continued. Troops and some 200,000 lbs. of equipment were parachuted into a small drop zone in north-east Thailand, in a defensive action conducted from Clark Field in the Philippines. The armed forces participating in the exercise also assisted the civilian population in various ways by providing medical services and water tanks, constructing a school and dams, and repairing roads, bridges and dams.

Thailand's position in SEATO appeared to be consolidated during 1963–64. But an uneasy balance has been reached and a new crisis in Laos, where the Pathet Lao have renewed their attacks on the neutral government, could stimulate another outburst of Thai criticism of SEATO and lead to weakening dissentions within the Organisation. In the previous periods of dissatisfaction with SEATO, Thai leaders have openly speculated about the possibility of their government breaking away from the United States and regaining the traditional Thai policy of neutrality; a policy, declared the Minister of the Interior, General Praphas Charusathien, 'that is all our own, peculiarly Thai—a Thai-ist policy'. This is an argument which retains a strong emotional appeal in Bangkok. Western officials in Bangkok report that reflective Thais are concerned that their country is being 'locked to the Western orbit'—one described it as an American colony—which makes it increasingly difficult to retain a supple and Thai-ist policy.

Anti-Americanism has been a feature of Thailand's internal politics, as statesmen have used it as a weapon against their opponents in order to cast themselves as Thai patriots. Marshal Sarit employed it against Marshal Pibulsonggram; and General Praphat Charusathien, who was mentioned as Sarit's successor, stood in favour of traditional Thai neutrality and displayed small concern for an alliance with the West. The present Prime Minister, General Thanom Kittakachorn, does not dominate the military junta as completely as his predecessor did. Power had gravitated towards General Phaphas Charusathien, who has a stronger following than his two rivals, Generals Chitti Navisathira and Kris Srivara. The urge to assert Thai independence can be expected to recur. Thai arguments in favour of non-alignment have for a time been curtailed by the lessons drawn from the Chinese attack upon India, but the tradition of neutral or non-aligned policies will be held up whenever the members of SEATO do not act in the manner desired by Bangkok. These arguments, used to put pressure on Thailand's allies, remain a touchstone of policy.

Burma

The energies of the Government of Burma are directed towards the creation of a Burmese nation. Burma is a non-aligned and neutral country bent on following its own path to socialism. It is in the process of defining that path. In January 1963 the ruling Burma Socialist Programme Party published its philosophy in a manifesto entitled 'The System of Correlation of Man and His Environment'.[1] The doctrine is an individual blend of Buddhist, Marxist and metaphysical principles. To Westerners this Burmese *Weltanschauung* may seem a confusing document, but it is clearly an expression of the Government's determination to construct a Burmese national synthesis. On the practical level General Ne Win's Government is reconstructing the economy on socialist principles, and the general leftwards trend in Burma reflects developments within the ruling military *élite*.

Two powerful brigadiers in General Ne Win's administration, Aung Gyi and Tin Pe, have been building up separate fiefdoms within the Army and Government; a prominent Burmese politician compared the situation to the Fourth French Republic. Aung Gyi, regarded as the number two in the heirarchy, had links with the Anti-Fascist People's Freedom League and as a moderate pragmatic Socialist was never wholly committed to the régime's policies, which he served with reservations. He opposed the severe repressive measures against the Rangoon University students in July 1962, and disagreed with

[1] See *The Guardian* (Rangoon), 18 January 1963; also 21 January for Party Rule 1, and 23 January for a critical review of the philosophy by Dr. Ba Maw, an ex-Prime Minister of Burma

the other members of the Revolutionary Council over the extent of the socialisation programme. In particular he had opposed the proposals for the abolition of private industry and the nationalisation of the banks. A shift in power within the Government removed Aung Gyi from the inner circles and replaced him by Brigadier Tin Pe, a doctrinaire socialist and a more intransigent personality. On the 8 Feburary 1963 the Revolutionary Council accepted Aung Gyi's resignation from his offices as Vice-Chief of the Army, Minister for Trade Development and Industry, and chairman of the Burma Oil Company Ltd. The change, which is said to have confirmed General Ne Win's overall control, apparently consolidated Tin Pe's position as number two in the Revolutionary Council amongst the pro-Soviet and pro-Chinese counsellors who are the general's closest confidants.

The achievement of a Burmese national synthesis has been impeded by the years of internal disorder. Ever since the attainment of independence in 1948, the Union Government has been struggling to assert its control in the face of Communist insurgency, separatist movements and banditry.[1] The Government adopted a policy of conciliation in 1963. In April, an amnesty was announced and at the end of June the time limit was indefinitely extended, as few insurgents had surrendered. The peace talks which began hopefully in September were broken off in November, as the government discovered that the insurgents had been extending their influence under cover of the talks. The amnesty finally expired at the end of January 1964. In Mandalay on Union Day, 12 February 1964, General Ne Win declared his thesis of an undivided Burma on the basis of the fraternity and solidarity of all the indigenous races; but later that month there were 10,000 to 20,000 insurgents in arms.[2]

The Union forces have made significant progress in their protracted campaign against the Trotskyist Red Flag and White Flag Communists since their setbacks in 1949. They have confined Communist operations to specific areas, and a measure of their success is that the Communists have sued for peace. The Trotskyist Communists in the Arakan Hills no longer pose a serious threat. The left is led by the White Flag Communists

[1] See *Burma and the Insurrections*, Government of the Union of Burma publication, September 1949 (1st reprint, 1957)

[2] *The Times*, 13 February 1964, 14 March 1964; *New York Times*, 25 February 1964

based in the Prome-Toungoo area in the west, who are allied with the left-wing Karens in the Irrawaddy delta.

The separatist movements remain a major preoccupation. There is a social and economic revolution among Burma's several million Karens who demand a separate state, independent of the central government. The Karen organisation has an estimated 10,000 men under arms, and is active in the delta east of the Sittang River and around Moulmein. The right-wing Karens, under the leadership of Saw Hunter Tha Hmwe and the Karen Revolutionary Council, have been engaged in peace talks with the Government since 28 October 1963. On 12 March 1964 an agreement was reached which committed the Burma Revolutionary Council to call a national convention of the indigenous races to adopt a new constitution on the basis of the Burmese way to socialism. The Karens agreed to drop their demands for independence in return for an enlarged Karen State—to be called Kawthoolei—and a tribal veto over the decisions of the central government. Their delegation accepted General Ne Win's definition of the rights and duties of the states as set out in his Union Day address. The future of Kawthoolei remains to be discussed at a future convention; meanwhile the 15-year war between the Karens and the Government has ended.

The Shan insurgents, who are ethnically close to the Thais, have in the past received assistance from Thailand. The Burmese authorities concerned with the suppression of the narcotics trade believe that the Shans exchange opium for Thai arms of American origin. The Kachins in the extreme north control most of the country north and east of Myitkyina as far as the China border. The distance of their area of operations from Rangoon has increased the difficulties of the Union Army in putting down their revolt. The Kachin Independence Army was very active in mid 1962 and again in 1963. The Mon National Defence Organisation, based on an ethnic group near Moulmein, resorts to outright banditry.

The Army has been employed for more than a decade against these threats to internal security. Its operations have been adversely affected by the preoccupation of senior officers with the civilian tasks allocated to them by the Government. The Army has an estimated 100,000 men organised on a counterinsurgency basis. It has been fully extended by its duties and was unable to make much headway against Kuomintang troops under General Li Mi, consisting of the remnant of the defeated

Nationalist 93rd division which trepassed into Burma in 1950. In its years of fighting the Burmese Army has been slowly improving its organisation, administration and equipment, though it still remains an inadequate force for national defence. Unlike the Indian Army, the Burmese Army is not a British creation; it developed from the Burma National Army of the late General Aung San which was raised during the Japanese occupation and built on the Japanese model, it was consciously part of the Burmese revolution. General Ne Win was one of the officers who received their training in Japan. The mentality of the army permeates the government and civil life of Burma. It is a reasonably well-disciplined force which justified its assumption of authority on the usual grounds of its efficiency, incorruptibility and ability to govern. The military socialists have claimed that they will hand the government back to civilian rule in several years time. But in March 1964, General Ne Win promulgated a law dissolving all political organisations in Burma.[1]

In its drive towards socialism, the Government has followed a policy of nationalisation and is taking over business and the press. Since March 1962, when General Ne Win seized power for the second time, some 70 per cent of all trading in Burma has been taken out of private hands and established in state agencies which have yet to demonstrate their competence. Systematic pressure is placed on the remaining private enterprises and taxes absorb 95 per cent of earnings after the first £4,600 of net profit. Few senior representatives of important British firms remain in the country. Government control is spreading over the press; there is a nationalised press agency and the editor of the *Nation*, the last liberal newspaper, was reported to have been arrested. The army in effect manages the country which lacks sufficient trained administrators, and officers on special duty control all levels of the government departments and supervise the work of the country's 300,000 civil servants. The measures to be adopted in the Burmese way to socialism were announced in Rangoon on 15 February 1963 by General Ne Win. The Government proposed to take over all enterprises in the country relating to the procurement, production, distribution, import and export of goods. The buying of rice was to be the monopoly of the State Agricultural Marketing Board, which during an interim period would employ private rice mills for milling the rice before the mills

[1] *The Times*, 30 March 1964

were in due course taken over by the Government. The Government had ceased issuing permits for setting up new private industries, since the socialist programme required state ownership of all means of production. Further steps were taken on 23 February, when the Government nationalised the ten local Burmese banks, and the fourteen foreign banks, and on the 28th, when the timber trade was taken over. Businesses in Rangoon were nationalised in March 1964.

In its foreign relations, the Revolutionary Council has adopted a policy of cautious friendship with China. It has signed a border agreement with Peking which has demarcated the 1,200-mile common frontier along the McCarthy line; this curiously enough is an eastward extension of the concept of the McMahon line. China probably exercises more influence in Rangoon than the Soviet Union, which has provided more technicians. In 1961 Peking granted Burma a long-term loan of some $80 million for economic and technical assistance. China's imports from Burma amounted in 1960 to $6·4 million, but in the first three quarters of 1961 the value of the imports increased to $49·2 million. General Ne Win has, however, refused Chinese offers of troops to help put down the various national separatist revolts; he has also arrested Burmese Communists and their sympathisers and broken off negotiations with both the Red Flag and White Flag insurgent groups, including delegates from the latter sent from Peking.

The Government keeps a distant attitude towards the West. Its officials cannot accept invitations from Western diplomats without special permission, and are said to be required to write reports on any meetings. There is little warmth in the formal diplomatic relationships and a minimum of contact. The Revolutionary Council has terminated the private assistance programmes sponsored by the Asia and the Ford Foundations, stopped the educational exchanges of the Fulbright programme, and permits American aid only on the basis of specific limited undertakings which do not require any American administrative structure in the country. There is no permanent aid mission in Burma; but the Agency for International Development had financed the work which has begun on highway construction between Rangoon and Mandalay. $28 million in private credits has been granted by West Germany to Burma. Relations with Israel are quietly developing and Burma makes use of Israeli experts particularly in the field of agriculture.

In two years the foreign exchange reserves have doubled to $513 million, and in 1963 foreign trade increased by $40 million. The exportable surplus of rice was estimated in 1964 to be 1·8 million tons, the highest figure for several years.

The Burmese Government's application of its strict concept of Burmanisation is not likely to be in Burma's best interests. The nearly 700,000 Indians in Burma have been a main target of the campaign, which has led to an exodus of thousands of Indians and caused tension with India; it has also put pressure upon the Chinese in Burma. Since from 70 to 80 per cent of Burma's foreign exchange earnings come from the sales of rice, her economy is particularly subject to market fluctuations. Thus Burma attaches great importance of obtaining from the developed countries compensatory finance and long-term commodity agreements. But Burma's determination to reject all foreign influences may have political repercussions detrimental to her economic hopes. 'The trouble is that Burma, in pursuing such a nationalist policy at home, is in danger of rebuffing the wider world beyond.'[1]

III. The Maphilindo Area

Indonesia

One of the problems in analysing Indonesia's policies in Southern Asia is the great gap in rationality between the Indonesian explanations of policy and the policies actually adopted. Even when rational criteria can be adduced for Indonesian decisions, it is sometimes difficult to determine how much the decisions rest upon them and how much upon more obscure and less respectable reasons. Indonesia's national interests seem to take second place to her leaders' nationalist ambitions. Her national interests would seem urgently to require peace; a peaceful environment for an internal development freed from the burden of a swollen defence establishment, and the maintenance of international confidence in her economy to attract foreign loan capital and to restore normal trade relations with her neighbours. But the Nasakom Government of President Sukarno has adopted aggressive foreign policies, a development which has suggested that the régime needs an external irritant in order to focus nationalist hostilities and maintain the fervour of the revolution. *Kemerdekaan hadiah*—

[1] *The Times*, 29 May 1964

freedom won without struggle—is a demeaning thing according to the nationalist ideology.

It was only at the time of the Brunei revolt, which began on 8 December 1962, that overt hostility to the Malaysia project appeared in Indonesia. Less than a month after the outbreak of the revolt, the long struggle against the Dutch for West Irian ended in victory. Subsequently, Malaysia became the focus for Indonesian hostility, replacing the Dutch as the external enemy; and a major theme in Indonesia's foreign policy after 1962 has been the opposition to Malaysia. Since the 16 September 1963, the date of the inauguration of Malaysia, Indonesian opposition has hardened into the rigid and dangerous policy of 'confrontation'. This policy has been maintained at some cost to Indonesia's interests. It has strained relations with the West and with some of the Afro–Asian powers; it has meant the loss of valuable Western assistance, including American military aid, and the cessation of legitimate trade with Malaysia; and it is reported to have had a disastrous effect upon the liberalising economic regulations promulgated in May 1963, to execute President Sukarno's Economic Declaration of the previous March. Indonesia's attitude towards Malaysia raises the questions; why did Indonesia oppose the Federation? and why did her opposition develop into 'confrontation' in defiance of Indonesia's real interests?

If the Indonesian answers to these questions are considered, it will be seen that the assertions about Indonesia's national interests constitute a weak part of the explanation and do not adequately reveal why an aggressive and risky policy was chosen. To answer the second question we need to consider the Indonesian nationalist ideology and the struggle for power within the state. Indonesian objections to Malaysia reveal how it is thought to be a threat to her national interests by controlling sections of Indonesia's foreign trade, encouraging separatism within Indonesia and encircling her. Something more than their face value is implicated in these claims. For example, it is not clear how Malaysia, with a population of 10 million people, and which in 1963 spent 17 per cent of the united national budgets on defence, could in any literal sense encircle Indonesia with her population of 100 million spread over 3,000 islands and thousands of miles, where 70 per cent of the budget was devoted to defence. The objections gain force in the context of Indonesia's nationalist and radical ideology. In this context Malaysia is a 'neo-colonialist' device, and the conflict with her appears as part of a world-wide struggle between the old imperialist nations, which never relinquish their powers until beaten, and the new emerging forces which President Sukarno aspires to lead.

President Sukarno's strong stand on Malaysia has the powerful support of the Army and the Indonesian Communist Party. These two organisations may support this stand for different reasons, but the rivalry between them incontestably stimulates the national revolutionary ardour since neither organisation wishes to lag behind the other in appealing to radical nationalist sentiments. The Indonesian Communist Party has adopted a stronger line on Malaysia than the President or the Army.[1] It consistently supported 'confrontation' when, during May and June of 1963, the Government appeared to move towards a peaceful settlement along 'Maphilindo' lines. Indonesian Communists oppose Maphilindo. Anti-Communists in the Army favour a form of it as an instrument of Malay nationalism to bring Malaya under Indonesian influence. There may be in addition nationalist ambitions in all this. When Malaysia was first discussed in 1961, Indonesia approved of the proposals. The timing of her subsequent objections has prompted the view that Indonesia had long-term plans to absorb Malaya and Borneo into Greater Indonesia after West Irian had been assimilated, but that while she was engaged in the struggle over West Irian she concealed her ambitions.

There is another objection to Malaysia which probably exercises Indonesian leaders far more than the 'neo-colonialist' myths about the Federation. In Indonesia there is a firm belief that China poses a long-term threat to Southern Asia and to Indonesia's national interests in the area. This is an awkward belief to hold in conjunction with the official nationalist ideology which includes both nationalist and Communist elements amongst those new emerging forces building the future. It is therefore very difficult to discuss this fear with Indonesians in official positions, but its existence can hardly be doubted. The fear of China is coupled with the assumption that the West cannot be expected in the future to maintain its commitment of resources in Asia against China. Indonesians are very conscious that the United States might enter into another phase of isolationism and that Asians will be called upon to man their own defences. The Overseas Chinese and the local Com-

[1] See, for example, the report of an interview with the chairman of the Communist Party in *Christian Science Monitor*, 14 March 1964

munist parties form weak points in those defences. Indonesians estimate the potentials of Chinese influence in the region in terms of the local Communist parties and the leverage of the Overseas Chinese, and express concern that more than 40 per cent of the population of Malaysia is Chinese. The Indonesian Communist Party draws much of its financial support from the local Chinese communities. A minority of the population provide the financial sinews which make the Indonesian Communist Party economically the strongest in the country. By a parity of reasoning, Indonesians regard Malaysia as a state through which China's influence will be extended by the large Chinese minority. Their 'confrontation' of Malaysia needs to be understood in relation to this preoccupation with China and Chinese influence. Indonesians believe that Malaysia as it is constituted, is an inadequate way of absorbing the Overseas Chinese in Singapore and in Borneo. The criticism reflects Djakarta's fear that the Federation of Malaysia will inevitably be dominated by the Chinese Malaysians, and in time will develop affiliations with China. This in turn would open the way for the establishment of Chinese influence in the area right up to the borders of Indonesia, a development which Indonesian policy is concerned to prevent.

It is, of course, a paradox that the Indonesian Communists, who are pro-Chinese, should be backing a policy towards Malaysia which has an anti-Chinese motivation among Indonesian nationalists. But the Indonesian Communists probably consider that their party line pays good political dividends, since it embroils Sukarno more and more with the West and increases his dependence upon Communist arms supplies; these are mainly from the Soviet Union, and Russian policy is apparently to support Sukarno rather than the Indonesian Communist Party (which is aligned with China in the Sino-Soviet dispute). But if there is to be a Sino-Soviet *rapprochement* following the eclipse of Mr. Khrushchev, both the Soviet Union and China might support a Communist take-over in Djakarta. The Indonesian Communist Party is the strongest in Asia and is the nearest to power, at least in Java, outside those countries actually under Communist rule. Over-population in Java is probably worse than anywhere else in Asia, and the resentment of the Outer Islands—which produce most of Indonesia's foreign exchange—at being exploited for the benefit of Java is a permanently divisive factor. Indonesia is an inherently unstable state, with a run-down economy, an inadequate national cohesion and a top-heavy military apparatus; 'confrontation' together with pan-Malayan agitation are probably indispensable to keep it going. If Sukarno fails to obtain any satisfactory results from 'confrontation', his régime may collapse altogether and the Communists could take over power in Java; but this would probably be met by a counter-revolution in the Outer Islands and a prolonged civil war in which the West and the Communist powers might get involved.

Indonesia's Malaysian policy has created a number of international problems. The members of the Commonwealth which are committed to defend Malaysia find themselves in a position where they must contemplate a future conflict with Indonesia. Relations between the United Kingdom and Indonesia have sharply deteriorated since the Malaysia crisis, and Australia's post-war policy of friendly relations with Indonesia is in jeopardy. American policy towards Indonesia is also faced with difficult decisions. If the United States (which continues to hope that Indonesia will prove to be a strong anti-Communist influence in the region) supports Malaysia, it could lead President Sukarno to move closer to the Communists. If the United States does not support its Commonwealth allies over Malaysia, her policy would encourage those forces of Javanese imperialism which have the backing of the Indonesian and Chinese Communists. American efforts to bring pressure to bear on Indonesia by curtailing aid have had little political effect beyond provoking President Sukarno into verbal defiance. The Malaysia dispute poses one of the critical problems in the SEATO area, but unlike the case of South Viet Nam it is not readily translated into the terms of a Communist versus anti-Communist struggle. The ambivalence of Indonesia's non-alignment illustrates the complexities of the situation. Indonesia could possibly develop into an anti-Communist 'bastion' in Southern Asia, or it conceivably could become a major Communist power. Western policy must balance these long-range contingencies against the immediate threat to Malaysia and, whilst taking adequate precautions to defend Malaysia, leave open the way to encourage the anti-Communist elements within Indonesia. The problem is complicated by the fact that the anti-Communist elements, including the Army, are numbered amongst the supporters of 'confrontation'. The Army in Indonesia as well as the Communist Party has a vested interest in aggressive policies, and the amount of leverage that the United Kingdom and the United States can exercise on the forces of

Indonesian nationalism is strictly limited. It is important, however, that a common Western policy be evolved, if only for the
reasons that the spectacle of Western disunity over the Malaysia
crisis would discourage the West's Asian allies and provide
further opportunities for Indonesian 'divide and rule' tactics.
The political structure of Southeast Asia would be reconstituted if Indonesia succeeded in crushing Malaysia and
forming satellite states.

Malaysia

The Federation of Malaysia, consisting of the eleven states
of Malaya, which had been independent since 1957, and the
three British colonies of Singapore, Sarawak and Sabah, came
into being on 16 September 1963. The sultanate of Brunei
(which was not a colony) was offered membership but declined
to join Malaysia. Several motives lay behind the establishment
of the Federation. The problem was to provide a way of securing
the independent future of the constituent states after direct
British rule was ended in the colonies. Federation of the colonies
with Malaya enabled the United Kingdom to relinquish control
over her dependencies in Southeast Asia, except Brunei,
whilst it created what was hoped would prove to be a viable
economic and political entity within the Commonwealth. It
was expected that Malaysia would, in the long run, develop
sufficient strength and stability to become a firm anti-Communist state.

The multiracial state of Malaysia has yet to acquire nation-
hood, and not the least of the strains within the Federation has
been the opposition to Malaysia itself among the political
parties in the Federation. In Malaya, the Pan-Malayan
Islamic Party, an embodiment of Malay communalism which
appears to be declining in significance, feared that the position
of the Malays would be endangered. The People's Progressive
Party, like the Socialist Front and the left-wing groups of
Sarawak, pressed for the independence of Singapore before the
merger with Malaya. In Singapore the most vocal opposition to
Malaysia was a breakaway group of the People's Action Party,
the Barisan Socialis, who gave moral support to the Brunei
revolt by Azahari, a participant in the Indonesian revolution
against the Dutch. Although there was a popular majority
in favour of Malaysia, there are important elements on the
level of national politics which do not accept it. Both the

Pan-Malayan Islamic Party and the Socialist Front have been pro-Indonesian in sympathy. Amongst the objections of the opposition parties to Malaysia were the arguments that federation was intended by the British to maintain 'neo-colonial' influences, and that the territories (as well as Indonesia) had not been sufficiently consulted: arguments employed by the Indonesians themselves to justify their policy of 'confrontation'.

These are unscrupulous arguments. The Prime Minister of Singapore, Mr. Lee Kuan Yew, had urged Tunku Abdul Rahman to negotiate Singapore's entrance into the Federation of Malaya for months before the Tunku's speech on 27 May 1961, which led to open discussions of an early merger of Singapore and the Borneo territories with the Federation of Malaya. Direct negotiations between the Government of Singapore and the Federation were undertaken from September 1961. In September 1962 the Singapore electors signified by a large majority their approval of a merger. (In the referendum, it should be noted, the electorate was invited to vote only on alternative forms of a merger, not for and against a merger. The Barisan Socialis, who opposed the proposed alternatives, advised electors to submit blank votes in protest.) The result of the referendum was that 71 per cent of the votes favoured the Government's proposal, and just over 25 per cent of the votes cast were blank. These results were admitted by the Barisan Socialis, who added the disclaimer that the voters decided, 'in the great majority of cases, not because they supported the first [Malaysia] alternative, but because they feared the Government's threat that they would lose their citizenship if they supported our call to cast "blank" votes'.[1] The People's Action Party maintained that their election platform, on which they were voted to power in 1959, contained proposals for a merger and that, therefore, they had a mandate to proceed with the proposals. The People's Action Party argued in a policy statement of 1960 that if Singapore achieved independence before a merger with the Federation of Malaya, 'the logical consequence would be that the Chinese chauvinist sentiments which are at present being muted and slowly dissolved because of the

[1] 1. *Memorandum of the Barisan Socialis Party of Singapore on Malaysia*, 11 March 1963 (mimeo), cited in T. E. Smith, *The Background to Malaysia*, Chatham House Memoranda, September 1963, p. 19. The allegation about loss of citizenship is an exaggeration. In this, and the following two paragraphs, I have drawn on T. E. Smith's detailed study

objective of independence through merger, will openly and aggressively come to the fore'.[1]

Brunei's voluntary exclusion from Malaysia, which may not prove to be permanent, is a result of the Sultan exercising his right to negotiate the terms of entry. It should clear the government of the United Kingdom of the 'colonialist' charge that Malaysia was imposed upon governments and peoples who were reluctant to participate in the merger. Early in 1962 the Sultan of Brunei appointed a commission whose task it was to ascertain the feelings of the Brunei peoples on the question of joining Malaysia. The report of the commission was not published but its findings are said to have revealed that the vocal elements of the population, including the main political party, the Partai Rakyat, opposed the early creation of Malaysia and instead favoured an independent federation of the three Borneo territories. The Indonesian Government has ignored the evidence of widespread internal support for Malaysia within the Borneo member states, where the alternative course of incorporation into Indonesia evidently is not desired by the majority of the Bornean peoples. Many of the indigenous peoples of Sabah and Sarawak, and in particular the tribes of the interior, would have found the continuance of British rule to be quite acceptable, had not the climate of world opinion against colonialism prevented such a course.

The views of the population of British Borneo were assessed between February and April 1962 by a Commission of Enquiry under the chairmanship of Lord Cobbold. The report of the Commission, submitted in June 1962 (Cmnd. 1794), estimated that about one-third of the population in each of North Borneo and Sarawak supported the 'early realisation of Malaysia without too much concern about terms and conditions', that one-third required 'conditions and safeguards varying in nature and extent' before joining Malaysia, and that a final third was divided between supporters of independence before Malaysia was considered and those who desired to see British rule continued for some years. The Report of the Inter-Governmental Committee on Malaysia, known as the Lansdowne Committee, which was published in February 1963 (Cmnd. 1954), recommended safeguards for North Borneo and Sarawak. The constitutional arrangements for the two terri-

[1] 2. Lee Kuan Yew, *The Battle for Merger*, Singapore, Government Printing Office, 1963, app. 6, pp. 169–70, cited in T. E. Smith, *op. cit.*, p. 16

tories within the Federation of Malaysia stem from the Committee's recommendations. The 'special interests' of the Borneo territories are specifically safeguarded in the Malaysia Agreement.[1] The Cobbold Commission estimated that the 'hard core . . . which will oppose Malaysia on any terms unless it is preceded by independence and self-government' might amount to about 20 per cent of the population of Sarawak and somewhat less than that percentage in North Borneo (para. 144). A United Nations survey in August 1963, of the views of the inhabitants of the Borneo territories (which Indonesia and the Soviet Union regarded as inadequate) also found evidence of widespread support for Malaysia.

Threats to Malaysia's future have been posed by the opposition of her two most powerful neighbours, Indonesia (supported by the Soviet Union) and China. The Indonesian policy of 'confrontation' is a clearly expressed determination to destroy Malaysia by force. Indonesian guerrilla activity within the Borneo territories of Malaysia, if it were continued for several years, could be a heavy drain upon Malaysia's resources for peaceful development. China has in practice been more circumspect in her opposition; but both Indonesia and China have encouraged subversion within the Federation. There is a danger that the threat to her security will accentuate Malaysia's internal difficulties, as the subversion has a broader social base than the Chinese revolt during the Malayan Emergency. The pro-Indonesian parties in Malaya, the Communist-controlled Barisan Socialis Party in Singapore[2] (which is approved by Peking), some Chinese elements in Sarawak, and the more than 30,000 Indonesian workers in Sabah, provide bases for subversive activities directed against Malaysia. Early in 1963 the Malaysian Government detained Che Boestamam, a Malay leader of the Socialist Front, alleging that he had been implicated in the Azahari revolt in Brunei, and in contact with Indonesia. The operations of Indonesian terrorists and the subversive activities of the Clandestine Communist Organisations set grave security problems in Sarawak. About a thousand members of the Clandestine Communist Organisations have

[1] For example, See Title VI, chapter 2, of *Malaysia. Agreement concluded between the United Kingdom of Great Britain and Northern Ireland, the Federation of Malaya, North Borneo, Sarawak and Singapore,* 1963, Cmnd. 2094

[2] 'Internal Security Measures in Singapore,' *Colonial Office Information Department,* 2 February 1963

been trained in Kalimantan (Indonesian Borneo) and numbers of them are reported to be hidden in the Sarawak jungles. The Organisations have an estimated armed potential of 3,500 agents and 20,000 armed supporters. The Sarawak People's Party is a constitutional front for the Clandestine Communist Organisations.

The most unequivocal external support for Malaysia has come from Commonwealth countries. The United Kingdom has large economic interests in Malaysia and retains close ties with the Federal Government and the defence forces. Under the Federal Constitution, the United Kingdom retains the use of bases in Malaysia, including the base facilities of Singapore: and the Anglo-Malaysian Defence Agreement provides for British forces to be kept in the constituent states of the Federation. It is this relationship which has given some little credibility to the argument about British 'neo-colonialism' in Malaysia. Both Australian and New Zealand support Malaysia and are developing broader and more intimate relations with her, based on common interests in the area. Malaysia is not a member of SEATO, or of any collective defence arrangement with the United States, and the burden of the responsibility for her defence against external threats has been assumed by the United Kingdom, closely supported by Australia and New Zealand. 'Britain, Australia and New Zealand are the countries chiefly concerned with us on the Borneo situation', announced Tunku Abdul Rahman, the Prime Minister of Malaysia, in March 1964, welcoming a proposal for a meeting of the Commonwealth Prime Ministers to discuss the crisis between Malaysia and Indonesia.

The Malaysian leaders have been concerned to expound their position in the crisis and to counter the 'neo-colonial' arguments employed by their opponents, but their efforts have not been very successful on the international scene. The Commonwealth Prime Ministers' Conference in London, in 1964, disappointed Malaysian expectations. Malaysia was not invited to the second Bandung Conference which was to be held in 1965. Early in 1964 Mr. Lee Kuan Yew, the Prime Minister of Singapore, led a mission to Africa to present Malaysia's case. On his return, he received a sympathetic hearing in New Delhi. Mr. Lee proposed also to lead a similar mission to the United States. The attitude of the United States towards Malaysia was initially equivocal, apparently because Washington placed some weight on the 'neo-colonial' arguments against Malaysia and, moreover, did not wish to incur Indonesian displeasure by expressing support for Malaysia. In the early months of Malaysia's existence, American policy, on balance, seemed to favour the Indonesian position, though not, of course, the policy of 'confrontation'. It appeared that Washington doubted Malaysia's ability to survive and preferred to regard Indonesia as a more suitable barrier against Communism in Southeast Asia. The mission of Mr. Robert Kennedy, the American Attorney General, to the area early in 1964 appeared to confirm these impressions in Commonwealth capitals. After his Toyko meeting with President Sukarno, it was concluded in London that the United Kingdom was 'in danger of becoming embarrassingly isolated in its support of the Federation of Malaysia.'[1] It was not until February 1964 that the United States openly supported Malaysia. On 13 February a joint communiqué issued after the Washington meeting of Sir Alec Douglas-Home, the British Prime Minister, and President Johnson, affirmed American support for the peaceful independence of Malaysia. The Washington talks were interpreted as an exploration of the possibilities of a common Anglo-American policy in Southeast Asia, with Malaysia and South Viet Nam as central issues.

Malaysia must improve her already efficient internal security forces to cope with a wide range of subversive activities, and strengthen her armed services in readiness for war with Indonesia. In view of the magnitude of her defence problems, and her own weakness, Malaysia must continue to rely upon the support of the United Kingdom and other members of the Commonwealth. Mr. Lee Kuan Yew stated early in 1964 that Malaysia would accept aid from every source in the struggle against Indonesia, but the sources of aid seem restricted to the Western camp because of Malaysia's resolute anti-Communism. The United States has offered to assist her to buy American military equipment, but there is no American commitment to defend Malaysia; and Washington has taken the view that Malaysia is a British and Commonwealth responsibility. Nevertheless, a clear assumption of Malaysian policy is that the United States would not let the Federation be 'swallowed up by the Communists'.[2] The United Kingdom is determined to continue her support, but the strain upon British resources imposed by a protracted guerilla war in Southern Asia might

[1] *The Times*, 20 January 1964
[2] Tunku Abdul Rahman, as reported in *Christian Science Monitor*, 20 July 1964

cause the British Government to reconsider its position. Although Tunku Abdul Rahman has been reluctant to bring Malaysia into SEATO, his successor eventually may consider it in Malaysia's interests to do so in order to obtain American protection, particularly if the situation in Southeast Asia deteriorates. If Indonesia goes Communist, Malaysia might join a regional security pact.

The internal dangers to Malaysia are great. The state is based upon a form of anti-Chinese discrimination in favour of Malays, and this must breed dissatisfaction amongst the large and economically powerful Chinese minority; whilst the Malays are themselves divided on basic issues of policy. The political cohesion of Malaysia needs to be developed, and to some extent the Indonesian 'confrontation' has helped in this respect. But there is little in common between the life of the rural communities in the northern parts of Malaya, in Borneo and in the Singapore entrepôt. The Malaysian economy is built upon rubber, tin and other exports. The formation of a single economic unit with uniform trade practices will probably yield economic advantages, but it can also lead to renewed political difficulties about the distribution of the national income. The divisive tendencies within the Federation have been stimulated by Kuala Lumpur's apparent neglect of, and indifference to, the economic and political problems of Sarawak and Sabah, and within a year of the foundation of Malaysia enthusiasm for the Federation has diminished in parts of North Borneo, even amongst its erstwhile supporters who continue to oppose Indonesia. The political stability of Malaysia will in large measure depend upon her continued prosperity and relatively high standard of living; for a weakened economy would provide a situation which the presently ineffectual Malaysian Communist movement could exploit. But more than this is necessary. No one of Malaysia's four parts is a nation, and vigorous national leadership is required if Malaysia is to triumph over her internal weaknesses and survive as an independent country.

The Philippines

The Philippines is a country which has overcome a Communist revolutionary movement without eradicating the conditions in which protest movements develop. What President Johnson has called 'the grim recruiting sergeants of communism'—poverty and ignorance—can be found in the Philippines, particularly in the areas where the Hukbalahap rebellion flourished. There are certain democratic forces at work in the society; universal education, wide literacy and great social mobility. The state and private institutions make money available for education. Despite inequalities of wealth, the poor have some vested interest in the *status quo* through the Church and the widespread 'compadre' system of wealthy sponsors. But there is an underdeveloped social conscience and basic social misery. In the Philippines as a whole there is no shortage of land, but in central Luzon there is land hunger and a feudal land tenure. The policy of land resettlement in the south was not properly thought out or implemented. In 1960, in the Huk leader Luis Taroc's village of San Luis, Pampanga, 40 per cent of the land requisitioned for the peasants was in their possession. The remaining 60 per cent was left in the hands of a landlord who, as a judge, was able to block the requisition. President Magsaysay's policy of offering land to the landless rebels effectively countered Communist propaganda during the Hukbalahap rebellion. After his death, from 1957 to 1961, there was extreme social stagnation in the Philippines. With the election of the Macapagal administration, 1962 was an important year of change in domestic matters as in foreign affairs.[1]

President Ramon Magsaysay (elected 1953) and his Liberal predecessor Elpidio Quirino (elected 1949) both supported proposals for broad security arrangements in the Philippines area. The Philippines formed a mutual defence treaty with the United States in 1951 and became a member of SEATO in 1954. The country has remained firmly in the Western camp, impelled there by fears of China, and by attachment to democracy and the Church. There persists a strong sense of a special Philippine relationship with the United States based on history, gratitude and the particular benefits of American aid and educational opportunities. To a considerable extent, and even on an official level, the Filipinos are ill-informed about Asia and ignorant of Australia and New Zealand; they underestimate Europe (though West Germany is beginning to make

[1] Commenting on the progress made under Macapagal's administration, an American Mission stated that 'The major economic problem lies in the agricultural sector upon which more than 60 per cent of the population depends for its livelihood.' *Report of the Special Study Mission to Southeast Asia of the Committee on Foreign Affairs*, 3 to 19 October 1963, Washington 1963, p. 23

an impact there), and see the world through American spectacles. The armed services of the republic are sufficiently strong and efficient to deal with internal security and the remaining embers of rebellion, but they possess small capacity for offensive actions. The Philippines have not contributed a great deal to SEATO. The Philippine press has nevertheless been critical of the alliance and belligerent, urging other members on from the sidelines in the cases of Laos and South Viet Nam. It has been especially critical of Malaya for not joining collective security arrangements. The pro-Indonesian *Manila Chronicle* has adopted a strong nationalist outlook with regard to the Philippine claim to part of Sabah. The recent developments of Philippine attitudes should be measured against this background of commitment, ignorance and belligerence.

Since the election of President Macapagal, the Government has looked at the pattern of world power in local terms and has become involved uncomfortably in the forces of co-operation and division at work in the region. Manila has been receptive to proposals for regional co-operation. In Bangkok, in 1961, the Philippines joined with Malaya and Thailand to inaugurate the Association of Southeast Asia, sponsored by Tunku Abdul Rahman to promote the social and economic advance of the region. A 'Maphilindo' association of Malaysia, the Philippines and Indonesia was suggested for similar broadly-defined beneficent purposes. Manila's enthusiasm for these ventures was modified by the apprehension that there was some danger of the Philippines being dominated by a larger neighbour within such flexible groupings. The opposition of the Philippines and of Indonesia to Malaysia has for the time being at least set back hopes of fruitful regional cooperation along Maphilindo lines. The Philippines laid claim to a part of Sabah which has been incorporated into Malaysia. Relations between Malaysia and the Philippines deteriorated and were finally broken off as the Philippines were swept along by the unscrupulous force of the Indonesian opposition to Malaysia.

Indonesian attempts to bring about a *rapprochement* between Djakarta and Manila in their opposition to Malaysia met with limited success in political circles in the Philippines. Some Philippine politicians regarded the development of ties with Indonesia as a useful way to put pressure on the West and to declare their independent stature to other Asian governments and peoples. The Indonesian approach flattered the susceptibilities of Philippine nationalism. Philippine military authorities

were more circumspect in their reactions. They hold the view
that Indonesia is an expansionist power and, having noted
the techniques of infiltration practised by Indonesians in New
Guinea and Borneo, regard with concern the possibility of
Indonesian subversion amongst the large Muslim minority in
the south of the Philippines. In their effort to embroil the
Philippines in their 'struggle' against Malaysia, the Indonesian
Government offered the bribe that it would not stand in the way
of Manila's claim to Sabah. It has also been the practice of the
Indonesian Government to seek deliberately to confuse the
Philippine claim to Sabah with their own less simple reasons
for opposing Malaysia, to suggest falsely to the world that there
is an identity of interests on this question between Djakarta and
Manila. Philippine sources have officially corrected Indonesian
misrepresentations of their position in the dispute. In March
1964 the Philippine Acting Secretary of State denied the truth
of a report from Antara, the official Indonesian news agency,
that 'President Sukarno and President Macapagal expressed
the common conviction that the neo-colonialist project of
Malaysia should be continually crushed'.[1]

The *rapprochement* claimed by Indonesia has proved to be an
embarrassment to the Philippines. The Philippines have not,
like Indonesia, officially opposed Malaysia as a neo-colonialist
trick; they do not reject the concept of the Federation; and they
have neither appealed to force nor sent guerrilla forces into
the former British colonies of Sabah and Sarawak. President
Macapagal's policy is simply to obtain Malaysian recognition
of the right of the Philippines to make a legal claim before the
World Court to a part of Sabah. The Indonesian determination to destroy Malaysia is clearly not the posture that
the Philippine Government, which sought arbitration not
confrontation, wished to adopt. The Philippines have been
disengaging from the Indonesian embrace by denying false
Indonesian intelligence about their position and by adopting
a conciliatory role in the discussions with Malaysia. Mr.
Salvador Lopez, the then Philippines Foreign Minister, played
a prominent role in the talks at Bangkok during February and
March 1964 in the search for a formula of compromise between
Malaysia and Indonesia.[2] In the reports of the negotiations,

[1] *The Times*, 6 March 1964
[2] Mr. Lopez gave up his post as Foreign Minister in 1964 to
become Ambassador to the United Nations and envoy extra-
ordinary for setting up Maphilindo

there has been little reference to the Philippine claim to Sabah. It is apparent from the temper of Philippine diplomacy that Manila does not wish its claim to Sabah to be a divisive factor impairing Philippine relations with Malaysia.

Initially, the Philippines may have regarded the 'Maphilindo' concept as a useful way of guiding Indonesia on a pro-Western path. But she has become suspicious of Djakarta's friendships with Communist Powers, and fearful of the possibility of a Communist dominated Indonesia. This has had the effect of curbing some of the eagerness in Manila for a more independent position in Southeast Asia. As there seems to be little opportunity for a regional grouping of Southeast Asian states, including Indonesia, that would not be dominated by Indonesia, the Philippines have become concerned to mend their relations with Malaysia and strengthen their bonds with Thailand and their other SEATO partners. There is a saying that after three hundred years in a convent and fifty years in Hollywood, the Philippines have woken up in Asia. Her nationalist awakening has aroused fewer disruptive forces than in other Asian countries; and the peacemaking role of Manila in the talks during 1964 at Bangkok and elsewhere is marking out the type of quiet diplomatic activity by which the Philippines can make the most useful contribution to the stability of the region.

IV. The Offshore Powers

Australia and New Zealand

The statement that Australia may be the last colonial power in the world, because of her responsibility for the Trust Territory of New Guinea, offends some Australian officials since it illustrates a paradox in Australia's foreign policy. A premise of that policy is that since Australia's past is untainted by colonialism, her own colonial history will strike sympathetic echoes in Asia. It is an article of belief that the honesty of Australia's intentions is plain to see and that, consequently, she has a fund of goodwill readily usable in Southern Asia. This general argument may be naïve, but it is advanced in all seriousness. It is expressed by the statement that Australia has a special relationship with her Asian neighbours, unmarred by historical conflicts, so that in her diplomatic intercourse with those countries she can act the honest broker. Indonesians have been quick to exploit this position. They have argued that Australia

ceased to be impartial by supporting Malaysia, which prevented
Indonesia from calling upon her services as a mediator. The
criticism neatly illustrates the weakness of the middleman
theory of Australian foreign policy. If the broker's role depends
on that kind of impartiality, then Australia is unfitted for the
part. Australia is attempting to develop a more independent
foreign policy than the role of a broker implies. And Australia
is not neutral. She has specific interests to safeguard as an
ethnically European power in an Asian environment.

Goodwill certainly exists—Indonesians remember with
gratitude Australia's advocacy of their independence: Indonesia nominated Australia on the Good Offices Committee set
up under United Nations auspices—but the degree to which a
policy may be founded on it remains a matter of debate in
Australia. Goodwill is at most the concomitant of a policy;
it does not define a policy. A noteworthy feature of Australian
foreign policy is that it is passing through a new phase of
defining its objectives and calculating Australia's national
interests. The newness, indeed the rawness, of Australian foreign
policy strikes the observer. The two main political parties agree
on this development. The Minister for External Affairs spoke
in 1962 of the 'rising public interest ... in foreign policy',
which he attributed 'in no small part to the fact that we have
been steadily approaching the point where we not only have,
but also realise that we have, distinctly Australian interests to
pursue'. The Deputy Leader of the Opposition said in 1963
that 'an Australian foreign policy is gradually emerging. Its
pattern and principles are still in the process of definition.'[1]

The development of an informed public opinion is hampered
by the lack of a sustained debate on foreign policy either within
Parliament or outside it, and by the reluctance of those in
official positions to discuss problems with academic and other
experts. The remark of the Minister for External Affairs, in
1962, that public interest in foreign policy 'may not yet have
reached the point in Australia where foreign policy alone can
change the electoral fate of a political party, but I think that
we are continuing to approach it', was confirmed during the
federal elections in 1963. Both parties acted as if foreign policy
was a central issue, and deliberately brought it as such before

[1] Sir Garfield Barwick, *Australian Foreign Policy 1962*, The Australian Institute of International Affairs (1962); E. G. Whitlam, *Australian Foreign Policy 1963*, The Australian Institute of International
Affairs (1963)

the electorate. Despite the Labor Party criticisms of the Government's foreign policy, there was a measure of agreement between the parties on the need to increase the striking power of the armed services by the purchase of reconnaissance-strike bombers. There was a brisk controversy about the type of aircraft most suitable for Australian defence, and had the Labor Party won the election it was expected to reverse the Liberal Government's decision to buy American TFX aircraft in preference to the British TSR-2 aircraft. The desirability of a strategic strike force was not unconnected in people's minds with the proximity of Indonesia, her strength and her intentions.

Within Australia there is a broader consensus between the political parties about the general aims of foreign policy and the priorities of national interest than is perhaps realised abroad. But Labor attitudes towards the Government's defence policies have been criticised as inconsistent, irresponsible and partisan, despite its formal support on fundamental questions; the limits of Labor criticisms have not been clearly defined, and in effect Labor's role has been to make piecemeal attacks rather than the insistent criticism which helps in the shaping of alternative policies.[1]

The major change in Australia's defence policies since the Second World War has been the decision that Southeast Asia, rather than the Middle East, would be the area of Australia's prime military concern. The Labor Prime Minister, Mr. Curtin, appealing for American military help in 1941, stated: 'I make it clear that Australia looks to America free from any pangs about our traditional links of kinship to Britain'; and the sentiment has grown into a commonplace of Australian defence thinking over the following years. Hence, Australia places great emphasis upon the ANZUS pact: it is 'the most important' of Australia's collective security arrangements, declared the Deputy Leader of the Opposition, echoing a statement by the Federal Conference of the Labor Party in 1963 that 'co-operation with the United States in the areas of the South Pacific and Indian Oceans is of crucial importance and must be maintained'. The Australian Army has been reorganised in terms of this concept. In 1960 the American pentomic' division (which has since been abandoned by the United States Army), was adopted as a model for the Australian 'pentropic' division,

[1] See B. D. Beddie, 'Some Internal Political Problems', *Australia's Defence and Foreign Policy*, ed. John Wilkes, Australian Institute of Political Science 1964, pp. 144–49

which was designed to provide a flexible, self-contained force capable of fighting under conventional or nuclear conditions in a tropical area. Early in 1964, the Australian Army had two pentropic divisions, one consisting of two regular and three territorial battle groups, the other of five territorial battle groups with regular cadres. The only forces outside Australia, the battalion in Malaya with the Commonwealth Strategic Reserve and the battalion in New Guinea, were not organised on a pentropic basis. Without conscription, the Australian Government had difficulty in expanding this force, and a policy of selective conscription was announced in November 1964, to enable Australia to fulfil her obligations.

As a member of the Western anti-Communist alliances, of ANZUS and SEATO, as a Commonwealth supporter of Malaysia, Australia had adopted a position which defines her likeliest enemies as Asian. The decision to support Malaysia was based upon the Government's conclusion that the creation of the Federation was in the interests of regional security and stability and that it was desired by the majority of the inhabitants of Sabah and Sarawak. The prospect of conflict with Indonesia over Malaysia has caused some rethinking of Australia's defence requirements. Indonesia's reported intention of building an air base and port in Timor, some 500 miles and a half-hour's jet flight from Australia, may oblige Australia to station operational aircraft permanently at Darwin, the northernmost airbase within Australia. West Irian (Indonesian New Guinea) is thought to be a potential base for subversive influences in Papua and New Guinea, Australia's most important dependent territories. Australia has been preparing these territories for self-government and, in 1964, the Government supervised elections for the House of Assembly, the first representative Parliament in the history of the territory, whilst retaining control over the territory's finances and foreign relations. The United Nations Trusteeship Council has passed a resolution urging Australia to make greater efforts towards the self-determination of the New Guinea peoples, many of whom still live in the Stone Age. Australia is apprehensive that Afro-Asian nations seeking new 'colonial' targets, and possibly led in this endeavour by Indonesia, will try and force the pace in New Guinea, with the result that a régime hostile to Australia might in the long run be established there.

Australia's policy with regard to nuclear weapons is that she will neither be the first country to introduce them into

Southern Asia nor will she manufacture them in the foreseeable future. However, the Australian Foreign Minister was not able to give the Secretary-General of the United Nations in March 1962 any unilateral or unconditional guarantee that Australia would at all times refrain from manufacturing or acquiring nuclear weapons. Australia has reserved the right to arm her forces with nuclear weapons if it becomes necessary in the future. The Australian Government has also recognised the right of her major allies to conclude agreements for the stationing of their nuclear weapons wherever military exigencies require it. In 1963, in support of the more effective deployment of American naval forces, including Polaris submarines, Australia completed an agreement for the establishment of an American radio-relay station, the North-West Cape Radio Communication Station, on Australian soil.

The arrangements have given rise to the fear that thereby Australia is somehow involved in the nuclear world. This fear is not groundless.[1] There is apprehension that the powers threatened by the nuclear weapons system of which the station is part may retaliate against the station and its host country. These fears are likely to have political consequences. The speculation that Australia is now involved in nuclear affairs causes profound unease, particularly amongst those people who advocate that Southern Asia be made a nuclear-free zone. There is no developed nuclear disarmament movement at present in Australia, but it is from fears like this that such movements draw support. At the same time there is generally a willingness to acknowledge the protection afforded Australia by the nuclear and conventional strength of the United States: though it is by no means clear to Australians how this protection would be made available in specific crises in the area which involved Australian national interests.

American and Australian policies in Southern Asia share the same basic objectives, but on particular matters, such as the question of trade with China, the two governments differ.

---

[1] I understand that in Washington there is serious talk of asking Australia to take ICBMs if it becomes necessary to have a strategic nuclear confrontation of China. (Minutemen in the United States cannot reach China without overflying Russian territory). American nuclear strategists have pointed out to me the benefits of this proposal: for example, it would enable the United States to threaten China with missiles sited in Australia, without directly threatening the Soviet Union

Australia has economic relations with most of her Asian neighbours. Her imports and exports to many individual countries
in the region are small, within a range of one to three per cent.
The exceptions are Japan and China, with whom Australia
has developed an important trade. In 1961–62 Australia's
exports to those two countries comprised nearly 25 per cent of
all her exports (Japan 17·5 per cent, China 6·17 per cent).
In the same period, the proportion of Australia's exports to
Japan was second only to her exports to the United Kingdom
(19·27 per cent). Imports from Japan and China in 1961–62
totalled 6·04 per cent.[1] The expanding trade with Japan is
helping to break down Australia's anti-Japanese prejudices.
In spite of her trade with China, Australia regards China as the
main long-term threat to the security of her Near North.

The concept of Australian national interests is informed by
fears. There is a fear of Indonesian aggrandisement, a fear of
involvement in wars on the Asian mainland through ill-defined
treaty obligations, a fear of being left isolated in a hostile
environment, with inadequate defence forces, a small population
and an enviably high standard of living. These fears lie behind
Australia's lively search for alliances with what Sir Robert
Menzies calls 'our powerful friends'. There is a tendency for
her powerful friends to be critical of the efforts Australia makes
to defend herself—to point for example to the 'derisory portion'
of the national product devoted to defence expenditure (less
than 3 per cent until 1964 in comparison with 10 per cent in the
United States, 7 per cent in the United Kingdom, and 4½ per
cent in Western Europe generally),[2] and to question with some
acerbity just what Australia is prepared to do within such
alliances.

In terms of sheer power, she can do relatively little; her critics,
aware of this, are concerned however with her willingness to
act, to 'stand up and be counted' as one of them puts it. And
in this respect, both the platitudes of official commitment and
the hesitations in the past of Australia's *ex post facto* diplomacy
are unimpressive. Some critics have gained the impression that
Australian Governments have wished others to defend her
national interests; for there has been a disparity between the
words and deeds of Australian defence policies. In spite of firm
ministerial statements that Australia must secure her alliances

[1] *Official Year Book of the Commonwealth of Australia*, 1963, p. 551
[2] See R. I. Downing, 'The Cost of Defence', in *Australia's Defence
and Foreign Policy*

by increasing her contribution to collective defence, between 1952 and 1962 defence expenditure dropped from £203 million (1952–53) to sums between £170 million and £200 million. While seeking to strengthen her voice within her alliances Australia relaxed her defence effort.

The trend of Australian thinking about her national interests is towards clearer recognition of Southern Asian problems as of most immediate concern. With this goes the recognition that to her powerful allies who have world-wide responsibilities these problems may not have similarly high priorities. In this aspect, Australian attitudes have much in common with the style of Asian thinking and share common apprehensions, particularly concerning policies adopted for Southern Asia by external powers without appropriate consultation with the indigenous countries. The knowledge that little can be done to prevent such developments understandably provokes the strains of criticism which mark the Australian debate about foreign affairs, and which reflect an 'emerging country' sensibility about her prestige and influence with her allies.

A similar judgement can be made about New Zealand's sensibilities. Despite her remoteness from Southeast Asia, New Zealand shares with Australia the same type of preoccupations and policies in the region. New Zealand considers the area of Southeast Asia to be her first line of defence, where she can make the most significant individual contribution to collective security. 'New Zealand's defence policy has never been purely or even predominantly local in character.'[1] The object of her defence policy is to ensure that the country makes the best possible contribution to the defence of her own national interests and the interests regarded as vital by the three countries on whom she principally relies: Australia, the United Kingdom and the United States. New Zealand is a member of ANZUS, SEATO, and ANZAM, an arrangement with Australia and the United Kingdom for the co-ordination of the defence of their territories in Southeast Asia and the South-West Pacific area (where New Zealand has dependencies) in the event of war. The Prime Minister, Mr. Keith Holyoake, reaffirmed in 1963 that New Zealand's defensive arrangements did indeed centre upon Southeast Asia. His National Government has continued to place emphasis upon the preparation of 'forces in being' for use at short notice in Southeast Asia. But the task of providing

[1] *Review of Defence Policy 1961. Presented to the House of Representatives* A19, p. 3

them, together with adequate back up forces, has been the crux
of the problems of New Zealand's defence planning since the
Second World War. (New Zealand has a population somewhat
larger than Laos.)

The country's original post-war commitment was to provide
a division for service as required in the Middle East. In order to
provide an adequate reserve of trained manpower, the Government introduced compulsory military service in 1950. When, in
1955, the decision was taken to transfer this commitment of a
division to Southeast Asia, the Government realised that the
concept of providing a division of 23,000 men within a certain
period after the outbreak of war was outdated. Compulsory
military service was abolished in 1958, in favour of a better
equipped professional army. The abolition of compulsory
service made it in any case impossible to provide promptly
a force as large as 23,000 men. In 1961, the Government introduced a plan to fill the gaps in the armed services by a system
of selective military service. The 1961 White Paper on Defence
noted that the greatest need was for increased ground forces,
and it outlined a five-year programme (1961–66) for a build-up
of the armed forces with particular emphasis upon the Army.
The proposed arrangements would allow the rapid deployment
of 13,000 men in support of operations in Southeast Asia. The
Air Force and Navy were allotted a supporting role consistent
with their limited capabilities, and this concept has remained
unaltered throughout the changes in defence policy.

The anticipated costs of the five-year plan were £30·6
million in the 1961 financial year, rising to £38·8 million in
1965–66, an increase of 32 per cent on the amount spent on
defence in 1960–61. The total cost was estimated to be £174·7
million. Owing to financial stringency, less was to be achieved
with the re-equipment of the air and sea forces than with the
ground forces. In retrospect, the 1961 arrangements were not
entirely satisfactory, and in the following two years three
separate types of proposals were put forward. Firstly, during
1962, when New Zealand spent 2·3 per cent of the gross national product on defence, anxieties about the state of the country's
defence preparations prompted the suggestion that the Australian and New Zealand forces should be integrated. At the
September meeting of the Australian and New Zealand air
force Chiefs of Staff, the New Zealand representatives proposed
that the services be partially integrated and that a common
procurement programme be adopted. Secondly, in June 1963,

the Prime Minister, Mr. Holyoake, announced an expanded programme of defence expenditure. The additional sum of £21 million was to be spent over five years to allow an increased capital expenditure on army equipment and for the purchase of transport aircraft. Finally, in December 1963, it was announced that the army was to be reorganised early in 1964. The plan called for a combat brigade group of some 6,000 men accompanied by a logistical force of 3,000 men, a combat reserve group of 3,000 men and a static support force also of 3,000 men. This was the fourth major change in New Zealand's defence policy since the Second World War.

New Zealand, like Australia, has had to balance her policy of friendship towards Indonesia with her responsibilities to Malaysia. New Zealand was reluctant to commit forces to operations in the Borneo states of Malaysia because of the effect this would have upon her amicable relations with Indonesia. But in 1964 the New Zealand Government informed Indonesia of its vital interest in the security of Malaysia, and pointed out that Malaysia's armed forces could not possibly be a threat to Indonesia. In the event of any armed attack upon Malaysia, New Zealand would promptly consult with Malaysia and other members of the Commonwealth on measures to be taken. New Zealand gave priority to aid to Malaysia, as a member of the Commonwealth and her first commitment. In July 1964 New Zealand's Prime Minister announced that he could not at that time envisage any circumstances in which his country might become militarily involved in South Viet Nam.[1]

Japan

Japan has embarked upon a programme which is designed to promote closer ties with Asia and which has interesting implications for her political future. Despite her remarkable post-war recovery and her economic qualification as a great power, Japan has not attempted to play a dominant part in regional affairs since 1945. The Japanese governments have been cautious and restrained, following policies primarily concerned with expanding trade relationships and developing political good will. As a result, Japan has a large economic investment in Southern Asia in the form of trade, loans, credits, reparations payments, joint enterprises and the exchange and training of technicians. The Japanese have been

[1] *The Times*, 24 July 1964

somewhat inhibited in their relations with the countries of Southern Asia by the memories of the 'co-prosperity sphere' and Japanese imperialism, and by the strength of the anti-Japanese sentiments still found amongst her wartime victims in the region. Hatred (it is not too strong a word) of Japan is a feature of the public life of the Philippines, for example, and the increase of Japanese trade there over the past decade continues to build up political disapprobation.

Japan is not interested in undertaking political commitments or responsibilities in Southern Asia, even if it were possible for her to do so in the face of internal opposition and external mistrust. The image of Japan that is sedulously cultivated by the ruling Liberal Democratic Party is of a highly developed Asian country which could pioneer the techniques of co-operation between the West and the underdeveloped countries of Southern Asia. This reads very much like a revised version of the 'co-prosperity sphere' built up and sustained by economic interdependence undertaken as a result of Japanese initiatives, and not, as before, by Japanese military and political power. There is a tendency in Japan to view Asian countries, including China, as a natural market outlet for Japanese industry. Japan sees herself as eventually providing leadership in an Asian economic environment by virtue of her Westernised industrial capacity, and as achieving prominence in this field without undertaking onerous political responsibilities. This vision of Japan's future in Asia cuts across existing political alignments. Japan is prepared to trade with committed and uncommitted countries alike including Australia, China, Taiwan (with whom at present Japan has more trade than with Communist China), India, Indonesia and the United States, who took 28 per cent of Japanese exports in 1963.

Japan has thus marked out for herself an economic future in Asia unencumbered by the political obligations which are usually associated with Great Power status. This may prove, in practice, to be an unrealistic aspiration, since, for example, China does not separate trade from politics and the United States discourages trade with China on political grounds. As a model for Asian development, capitalist Japan is a serious rival to Communist China, and Japan's pursuit of a more political diplomacy in Southern Asia could possibly bring her into conflict with China's ambitions in the region. Trade between the two countries has grown steadily, though in 1964 it was less than one per cent of the total Japanese trade.

The Liberal Democratic Party is divided into pro-Taiwan and pro-China groups; and some Japanese businessmen are reluctant to become too involved in trade with China, as Peking has displayed a cavalier attitude towards contracts, and abruptly suspended trade six years ago after a flag burning incident at Nagasaki. Trade with China is still largely regulated by a five-year agreement negotiated in 1958.

A problem for the West in providing Japan with alternative markets is that Japanese competition affects those Western industries least capable of withstanding it. The Bank of Japan announced in March 1964 that the deficit of Japan's balance of international payments had more than doubled in a month, largely owing to rising imports, and the Federation of Economic Organisations (Keidanren) claimed that a big export drive was necessary to solve Japan's balance of payments problem.[1] Her American trade is of importance to Japan, and the Government cannot afford to ignore Washington's displeasure at her trade with China. In January 1964 Japan gave the United States what was taken to be an undertaking not to grant credit terms to China that went beyond the bounds of ordinary trade. But this type of understanding can cause misunderstandings, and it is difficult to see how Japan can avoid the political implications of her economic programme and continue to follow an uncomplicated diplomatic path between the two world blocs.

In a statement of Japanese policy contained in a speech in Tokyo in January 1964 the then Premier, Mr. Hayato Ikeda, announced that his government's objective was to develop relations with Asia as close as those between Japan and the United States.[2] On examination this superficially clear statement is puzzling, for in a number of obvious ways the relationship between the United States and Japan can hardly be duplicated in Japan's relations with the rest of Asia. Japan's position *vis-à-vis* the United States has, for example, been one of dependence in the post-war years. (Mr. Ikeda spoke of freeing Japan of the embarrassment of dependence on the United States.) The treaty arrangements between the United States and Japan have ensured American responsibility for the protection of Japan and accorded the United States the use of base facilities in Japan. The United States assumed a large share of the cost of Japan's defence after the Korean war

[1] *The Times*, 31 March 1964
[2] *The Times*, 28 January 1964

served as a catalyst for Japanese rearmament. Between 1952 and 1961, the United States paid approximately one third of Japan's defence costs. With this substantial assistance, Japan has been able to develop her Self-Defence Forces to their present pitch of efficiency without spending more than an insignificant proportion of her national product on defence; 1.2 per cent in 1953, 1.7 per cent in 1958 and 1959, and 1.4 per cent in 1961 (that is, the same percentage as Luxembourg spent in 1963 and less than one half of the percentage of national income spent on defence by Australia and Denmark). But this tie with the United States is precisely the type of responsibility to which Japan is unwilling to commit herself in Southern Asia.

Japan's relations with China have been a sensitive issue between Tokyo and Washington. Japan sees no immediate threat to herself from China and does not share the American viewpoint that as a matter of principle Peking should be isolated and as far as possible ignored. On the contrary, the Japanese stress their historical, cultural and economic ties with China, for even though the historical relations have been hostile, the cultural relations derivative, and the economic relations an embarrassment, there is a strong emotional feeling of solidarity with China and a potential complementary economic relation between a technologically advanced Japan and a still underdeveloped China. A desire to become more independent of American economic support appears to underline Japan's efforts to expand her economic penetration of Asian markets from India to the Philippines, with China as the largest potential market of all, which Japan cannot afford to lose, according to the director general of the Economic Planning Agency. Japan has been evolving an independent policy towards Asia, and she can no longer be expected to place her own interests below those of the United States in accordance with a foreign policy that is not her own. The Japanese urge to develop a diplomatic position untrammelled by Western ties will probably be strengthened as China increases her industrial power and acquires a nuclear capability. An independent Japanese diplomacy was clearly outlined in Mr. Ikeda's speech in January 1964. The then Prime Minister's statement could be taken to imply that he meant more than close trading relations with China, and this is the central issue of the development of Japan's relationships with Asia. The speech suggested that the Government of Japan admits the possibility of recognising the People's Republic of China when it is in Japan's interests to do so, though at present the question of developing trade has priority over that of diplomatic recognition. In November 1964 Mr. Eisaku Sato was nominated as Prime Minister to succeed Mr. Ikeda. He had been a stern critic of the lack of independence of Mr. Ikeda's foreign policy, and announced that he would press for the return of the Ryuku Islands (which include the Okinawa base used by the Americans).

The Liberal Democratic Government of Japan is under two kinds of pressure to move closer to Peking in its foreign policy: from the Right which expresses the hopes of businessmen for a great expansion of trade if satisfactory political relations can be established, and from the Left which is ideologically sympathetic to Communist China. The Government has to make gestures to appease these converging forces even though its leaders know that Japan's relations with Asia (and with Communist China in the first place) cannot be as close as with the United States as long as Japan has a defensive military alliance with the United States. Since there is no bipartisan foreign policy in Japan (the Socialists reject the American alliance), and since the Socialists might possibly win power in the next general election, the future international alignment of Japan is uncertain. In a longer term, a Sino-Japanese bloc is not out of the question. If Japan were to move out of the American orbit, it would be towards China and not towards the Soviet Union.

Taiwan

Japan's relations with Communist China are watched with concern by the Government of the Republic of China on Taiwan. The development of close ties between Japan and the Chinese People's Republic would pose Taiwan the choice of breaking off relations with Japan, the more likely alternative, or of admitting a kind of Two-Chinas status which she has hitherto rejected as unacceptable. Japan's recognition of the Republic of China makes a significant contribution to Taiwan's diplomatic strength, for the Republic is comparatively isolated diplomatically in Southern Asia.[1] Despite this, there is a certain

[1] In 1952 Japan recognised the government of Chiang Kaishek in Taiwan, the Pescadores, and in any other territories which it might acquire. The Japanese Government stated in March 1964 that it wished to maintain diplomatic relations with Nationalist China while maintaining *de facto* contacts with Peking

suspicion of Japan in Taiwan, where it is believed that Japan's hidden motive is to vie with India for the control of Asia. Taiwan has diplomatic ties with Australia, Malaysia (where a consulate was established in November 1964, with a view to strengthening trade ties), the Philippines and South Viet Nam, for example, as well as with Japan; but for the most part the Republic derives its international stature from American recognition and support.

With American backing, Nationalist China possesses one of the most powerful military establishments of all the countries on the periphery of China. With a population of 12 million, *festung Formosa* in 1964 had an army of 400,000 men, a navy of 5,000 men plus 27,000 marines, who constitute one of the finest bodies of fighting men in the region, and an air force of 82,000 men. This substantial armed strength backed by American power enables the Taiwan Government to fulfil adequately the strategic role of controlling the Formosa Straits section of the American defensive perimeter against China. Nationalist officials stress the strategic importance of their contribution which is to maintain the only position in the West's perimeter towards China where an aggressive concept is upheld. In their view, Nationalist forces tie down about $1\frac{1}{2}$ million of China's $2\frac{1}{2}$ million men under arms and prevent them from being employed elsewhere on the mainland of Asia.

It is extremely unlikely that the powerful Nationalist forces would be used anywhere else in Southern Asia, except in the remote contingency of their participation in United Nations operations. For the Nationalist Government has no interest in regional arrangements for the security of Southern Asia, despite its efforts in the late 1940s to develop an anti-Communist alliance in Asia. Its own security guaranteed by the United States, the prime concern of the régime is one day to return triumphantly to the mainland as the uncontested Government of China. While hopes of returning thus by invasion fade, the Nationalists wait for the internal dissolution of China to provide opportunities for their reinstatement in Nanking. Their intelligence sources report that numerous anti-Communist revolts take place on the mainland. Nationalist agents are sent to China by a number of routes (including Hong Kong, where the British authorities are said to detect and deport as many as 100 agents a week.) Nationalist sources claim that only a small percentage of their cadres on the mainland are caught by the Communists, and they argue that the large numbers still at liberty bear witness to the massive discontent of the Chinese people with the Peking régime. Since the actual numbers of the cadres sent to China are not released, this is a difficult argument to controvert, and it remains the official faith in Taiwan that the Chinese people are ripe for revolt. This view is not held as strongly outside Taiwan as it was ten years ago, when it was also an assumption of American planning. The years since 1949 are held to have been the Chu phase of the experience of the Republic of China. The apocalyptic vision of the return to the mainland is sustained by the historical analogy with the state of Ch'i, when all was lost save Chu, before the eventual re-conquest of the state. It is a noble dream and a bad analogy.

The idea of a return to the mainland covers a number of possibilities. The official one is that there will be a popular uprising against the Communists and the Kuomintang Army will then land on the Fukien coast and lead it to victory. But this is the least likely outcome of the existing situation. What is considerably more likely—though not very likely—is that after Mao's death there might be a struggle for power within the Chinese Communist Party in which the army would be divided, and the faction on the right of the Party would seek to make a pact with the Kuomintang in Taiwan, who would represent a substantial military force, offering them a subsidiary place in a political coalition in return for their support. Chiang Kai-shek would probably not accept this arrangement, but amongst the younger Kuomintang generals and politicians there might be future leaders who would.

There are really two political factors concerned in the question of Taiwan's future relations with Communist China, the Kuomintang mainlanders, both civilian and military, who have taken refuge there, and the Taiwan provincials. The former cherish the idea of a victorious return to the mainland, but it is amongst them also that a move for accommodation with Peking might be promoted if the hope of reconquest finally fades. On the other hand, it is amongst the Taiwanese that a Two-Chinas formula might be acceptable. The Taiwanese do not wish to return to the mainland, they were never there; but they have so long been detached from China, so differently conditioned, first by Japanese and then by American influences, and are so well aware that they have a much higher standard of living than the people on the mainland, that they would probably opt for an independent Taiwan if they could have it. As time goes on, the Taiwanese element becomes more and more important in the Taipei Government and Army. As the soldiers of Chiang Kai-shek's former army grow too old for active service, they are replaced by Taiwanese conscripts whose real attachment is almost certainly to their own island. Taiwan has a bigger population than one third of the member states of the United Nations—it has more people than Australia, twice as many inhabitants as Cambodia, and more than twenty times the population of Cyprus—and could well be a viable independent state.

*   *   *

In sum, there are a series of conflicts between the national interests of the South Asian states, and this local pattern of national politics has superimposed upon it the international rivalries of external powers with interests in the cockpit of Southern Asia. Major external powers conceive it in their interests to prevent certain developments in the local balance of power. Today, the main local clashes of interest are between China and Taiwan, China and India, Pakistan and India, Indonesia and Malaysia and, within Indochina, between North and South Viet Nam. There is an element of irredentism in all these cases. They are key points in the local balance of power. If the forces constituting that local balance were free to develop without external interference, there is little doubt about the shape of the outcome. China would absorb Taiwan as she has absorbed part of the territory claimed by India, Pakistan would not be able to assert her interests in Kashmir and any attempt to do so by force would be defeated by India, Indonesia could well destroy Malaysia or make her a satellite, and North Viet Nam could liberate South Viet Nam.

But the Western powers have been determined that the process of change in Asia shall be gradual, and therefore to inhibit the unrestrained pursuit of national interests. Individually, they have guaranteed the integrity of Taiwan, Malaysia and South Viet Nam, and have sought by peaceful means to resolve the conflict of interests between India and Pakistan. Their strategy has been to preserve a post-colonial balance of power in Southern Asia by inhibiting the forces that would destroy it, above all by containing China, or by attempting to control developments which could disturb it. Thus, in granting military aid to India for her defence against China, the West gave assurances to Pakistan to explain that the balance of power between India and Pakistan was not affected as a result—an argument that Pakistan finds unconvincing. On the other hand, it has been the policy of China and the Soviet Union to disturb the local balance by substantial military assistance to Indonesia, by encouraging North Viet Nam's assault upon South Viet Nam, by attacking India, and by the processes of subversion.

Chapter 4

The Threat of Communist Subversion

I. The Soviet Union, China: the Instrumentalities of Subversion

THE United States and the United Kingdom aspire to prevent any one power from dominating the land mass of Southern Asia and the adjoining islands. In effect, this means attempting to prevent China from acting in the normal way of great powers and asserting her strength outside her borders. By a series of defence arrangements, they have involved the Southern Asian states in this endeavour: they have involved the local balance in their world strategy. The local balance has consequently been rendered more sensitive to developments outside it, even to developments in the conflict of national interests between China and the Soviet Union. The alignment of forces brought to bear in this manner has little relation to the strength and capabilities of the Southern Asian states. Collectively, the Southern Asian states do not constitute a *balance* of power against China, the region's centre of gravity. A balance is maintained by the reserves of Western power, and, in China's view, that balance threatens her national interests. Peking has made it clear that she wishes to see Western power removed from Southern Asia; in other words, she is seeking to bring about a condition in which the local balance can operate in her favour, enabling China to exercise hegemony in Southern Asia. The main anti-Western strategy she has so far employed to this end is not to strike overtly at the structure of Western power in the region, but covertly at its base, by the subversion of the governments which are supported by the West.

Both China and the Soviet Union have made efforts to disturb the local balance of power in Southern Asia, but their policies have reached a point where they are no longer in accord. Mr. Khrushchev's suggestion that the Soviet Union and China could 'sychronize their watches' by reference to their common ideology was rejected by the Chinese who said: 'Now there are two watches. . . . Which is to be the master watch?'[1] The interests of the two Communist powers in fact clash on the northern and the southern flanks of Asia. To the north-west and the north-east, China disputes with the Soviet Union for the lands lost to Czarist imperialism during the nineteenth century; to the south, the conflict between their interests is mixed up with the ideology and pace of revolution. China's position is that she will brook no rivals in Southern Asia, where vital national interests of defence and security are concerned, and in the course of the Sino-Soviet dispute the Soviet Union has come to appear as a rival by breaching the solidarity of the world Communist movement, by withdrawing aid, by criticising a fraternal party for its part in the Indian border war, and in general by revealing a disregard for China's preoccupations on her southern border. China has denounced Khrushchevian co-existence as well as American 'imperialism'. In the circumstances, the consolidation of Chinese influence in the area can only be at the expense of Russian as well as American influences.

These developments have given rise to consideration of how the West could employ the divergence of Chinese and Russian interests to good effect in Southern Asia. The belief that Russian diplomacy would be thrown in the balance against China found acceptance in New Delhi after the Chinese attack. The Russian reaction to developments in Laos has been taken by the United States to be a kind of yardstick of the Soviet Union's willingness to co-operate with the West, or of her ability to do so. For example, in April 1963 President Kennedy described the purpose of Mr. Harriman's visit to Mr. Khrushchev as to determine whether the Russians were in control of the Communist-led Pathet Lao forces, whether they still had a desire to maintain their influence in Laos, and whether that influence would be used to preserve the frail peace. This was an assumption which was tested by the American policy on which it was based. That is to say, an expectation has arisen in Western capitals that the Soviet Union may now see it to her advantage to help preserve the local balance in Southern Asia and maintain the *status quo* for two reasons; first, to preserve her influence in the area against Chinese encroachments, and second, to maintain the *détente* with the United States in other areas. But it remains doubtful if this type of reasoning will affect Russian policy with respect to subversion, where in order to maintain her influence in the area she might have to struggle

[1] *Peking Review*, No. 10 and 11, 15 March 1963, p. 50

with China for control of the Communist instrumentalities of subversion, keeping in time with their revolutionary aspirations.

As suggested in Chapter 1, a Communist threat is built-in to Southern Asia. The political structure and social fabric of the indigenous countries invite the use of the tested Communist techniques of manipulation and externally inspired subversion, and offer good prospects for the success of such techniques. But what kind of threat to the Southern Asian countries does this imply? Or, perhaps, what kinds of threats, since the development of relations between China and the Soviet Union suggests the probability that in the future a competition will develop between them for influence in Southern Asia?

(It needs to be emphasised, in any case, that the dispute between Moscow and Peking is about means, not ends. Both powers are concerned to advance Communism by the most appropriate measures. The Chinese have challenged the Russian prescription of the most appropriate measures for Asia and the rest of the underdeveloped world. In doing so, they have deliberately challenged the Russian leadership of the world Communist movement, and offered their own prescription, their own orthodoxy, in specifically Asian terms. But, for our present purposes, the dispute is about the best way to wage an offensive, the best way to maintain pressures designed in the long run to consolidate Southern Asia under Communist control—whether that control is exercised from Moscow or Peking, or jointly by them.) Consequently, the question may be re-phrased in these terms: how will the Sino-Soviet dispute, in so far as it is concerned about Communist strategy towards the non-Communist world, affect Russian and Chinese political manipulation and subversion in Southern Asia? We are primarily concerned here to investigate the threat of Communist subversion in Southern Asia, with a view towards identifying those aspects of the Communist forward movement which are likely to be most effective, and those sectors where the West must contrive the most effective counter measures.

One claim about the future effects of the Communist split, with respect to subversion, can reasonably be made at the outset. It is that, whatever the respective roles of the Soviet Union and China in Southern Asia, in the future, any competition between them will more probably lead to an increase of subversive activities in the area than to a decrease. For the competition for Communist allegiances is likely to ensure that the power which advocates caution will be at a disadvantage *vis-à-vis* the more revolutionary power. China, in adopting a more revolutionary viewpoint than the Soviet Union, has cast her argument in the form that revolution itself becomes the mark of Communist orthodoxy; and the racialist connotations of the Chinese position, against which Moscow has raised its voice, underline the point.[1] The attractive effects of this argument in Asia are difficult to estimate at this juncture, but they may be powerful, in that the Chinese are suggesting Asian solutions to Asian problems and affirming that the Soviet Union is not an Asian power. Caution, compromise, co-existence are being cast as white Communist deviations from the true path. As Chen Yi said: 'The Chinese people see their yesterday in all the oppressed nations.' According to Chinese Communist doctrine, the area of Southern Asia is part of that underdeveloped intermediate zone where there is a head-on conflict with the forces of imperialism, led by the United States. It is also the region where the Khrushchev arguments about co-existence, peaceful economic co-operation, and the parliamentary method of acquiring power, are weakest in their application. In making this point, China has implied that the Russian arguments are themselves 'subversive' of Communism in Southern Asia. The logical extension of the Chinese arguments against Russian Communist deviations and racialism reaches a position not far removed from the Chinese reasoning against the United States. Both the Soviet Union and the United States are 'external' powers concerned to maintain their intrusive influence and presence in Southern Asia against the real interests of the indigenous peoples.

A competition between Moscow and Peking for influence in Southern Asia—that is, assuming that the Soviet Union does not relinquish its remaining authority there without a struggle —will include a contest to control the existing Communist instrumentalities in Southern Asia, and a struggle to exercise power through those instrumentalities against non-Communist states and even, foreseeably, against rival Communist forces.

[1] In opposing Russian participation in the Afro-Asian conference to be held in March 1965, China has stated: 'The Asian-African conference is a conference of heads of Asian and African countries. Since the Soviet Union is a European country, it of course should not take part in such a conference. This is a matter of principle, and we abide by principle.' The Soviet Union has rejoined by describing China's racial theories as nothing but a screen for her hegemonistic aims for the Afro-Asian countries

Although the Soviet Union may ideally advocate a more cautious approach than China, she cannot afford, in a region where subversive methods are likely to bring success, to lag far behind China in supporting those methods. Depending upon the number and strength of the instrumentalities which she controls, the Soviet Union may be able to exercise some degree of restraint; but wherever China's writ runs that restraint will not be obeyed, unless extrinsic reasons require it.

There is a further point to consider. Subversion is undertaken by Communists to undermine a government and to create the conditions for a bid for power. Both Moscow and Peking, despite their ideological clash, seem to retain a measure of agreement about the role of subversion in preparing for Communist takeovers and of its significance in the Communist armoury. The point at which they are likely to fall out is, I think, precisely that point at which the decision has to be taken whether or not subversion has created a ripe opportunity for the next stage: the acceleration of effort by insurgency. At this point, it can be argued (though tentatively, since it depends upon Moscow and Peking maintaining their present postures) that the Soviet Union will in the event be more circumspect than China; and when that stage of developments has arisen the Soviet Union might not be able to exercise any effective restraint at all. Thus, one might risk the working generalisation that the nearer a revolutionary situation approaches in a Southern Asian country, the greater will be China's influence, unless, in an effort to offset that influence, the Soviet Union also backs the revolutionary forces. The suggestion arising from this is that, at least on the level of externally inspired subversion, there is not likely to be much difference between the kinds of activity regarded as suitable by the Soviet Union and China, but that China will probably make the running. Such differences as may be expected to arise will in all likelihood concern tactics, and not the strategy to be employed. If this suggestion is correct, then on the operational level of subversion too much can be made of the effects of the Sino-Soviet split in Southern Asia.

The main instrumentalities of subversion, over which a struggle between the Soviet Union and China is already taking place, are the indigenous Communist parties and their various front organisations. Many of these parties have taken clear enough positions in the dispute to enable them to be placed approximately *vis-à-vis* the Soviet Union and China; and although the political arithmetic for this calculation is fairly imprecise, a useful general conclusion can be made about the fields of Russian and Chinese influence. For example, most of the Communist parties in Southern Asia have, during recent years, supported in varying degrees the Chinese case against the Soviet Union. The pro-Chinese parties included those in Cambodia, Indonesia, Japan, Malaysia, New Zealand, North Korea, North Viet Nam and Thailand. Several of the indigenous parties have split on this issue: they are the Communist parties of Australia (where the dominant element is pro-Russian), Burma and Ceylon. The Indian Communist Party is the outstanding example of a pro-Russian Asian Communist Party, though within it there is a strong pro-Chinese faction. The Soviet Union at the time of writing could still apparently bring diplomatic pressure to bear upon the Communists of Laos despite the pervasive Chinese and North Vietnamese influence there.

Before much practical significance can be attached to these alignments, it is necessary to consider what the pro-Chinese sentiments or expressions of the Communist parties mean. For it does not necessarily follow that the parties concerned would be prepared to adopt a Chinese 'line' in all respects of internal and external policy. A possible result could be, on the analogy with the Eastern European Communist Parties, that the Asian parties will achieve more independence from both the Soviet Union and China, obtaining more room for manoeuvre between the giants and enhanced opportunities to frame their own policies in terms of their local aspirations and priorities. Moreover, while the publicised policy statements of the pro-Chinese parties (which commonly have been taken as evidence for their position in the spectrum) give the impression that their stance has been taken on ideological grounds, the actual decisions may have been more pragmatic. For example, Mr. Aidit, the leader of the powerful pro-Chinese Indonesian Communist Party, was quoted as explaining his party's position in these terms: 'China is in Asia. Indonesia is in Asia. We face a common enemy,' (that is, American imperialism).[1] It is quite conceivable that in some circumstances mutual interests could be a stronger tie than a purely ideological connection. Those Communist leaders who reason like Aidit accept the premises of the Chinese view of the Asian situation. Like Aidit, however, they have to apply those general premises to their particular national environments. In the case of

[1] *Newsweek*, 27 April 1964

Indonesia, this has had the somewhat paradoxical result that the Communist Party, which does not oppose the Nasakom Government and the leader, Sukarno, follows what is essentially a 'Khrushchevian line' on the peaceful acquisition of power in the state. The instructive point here is that the Indonesian Communist leader has interpreted the mutual interests of his country and China in terms of *foreign* affairs, and a practical illustration of this is the common attempts by Indonesia and China to sabotage Malaysia.

In several of the countries where there is a pro-Chinese Communist Party, there are also strongly developed national antipathies to Chinese of any political beliefs or of none. In Indonesia, for example, it is difficult and even dangerous for the local Communists openly to co-operate with the Chinese. (Owing to this need for caution, the Indonesian Communists, I understand, have never permitted an Indonesian Chinese to become even a branch official of the party.) Elsewhere, there are similar inhibitions. Thai hostility to local Chinese political influence of any kind has been pronounced. In the Philippines, the orientation of the Communist Party was influenced by the strong Filipino antipathy towards Communist China, and the pro-Chinese Communist element in the islands is held to be insignificant. Anti-Chinese sentiments in India, however, are a comparatively recent phenomena. The Chinese attack upon India placed the Indian Communist Party in a difficult position, and it is not perhaps surprising that (in 1964) more than two-thirds of the party's national council were pro-Soviet. The ground swell of Indian hostility towards China has not eradicated pro-Chinese sympathies in the lower ranks of the party; such sentiments are pronounced in West Bengal. The Indian Communist Party, of some 150,000 members, is splitting into two factions, and the party leader, S. A. Dange, has predicted a war between them—which presumably attests the strength of the pro-Chinese attitudes amongst the Indian Communists. The pro-Chinese section has planned to assert itself as a quite separate organisation from the pro-Russian element, and by the end of 1963 it was already functioning as a parallel organisation.

These are the sort of factors which qualify the generalisation that the support of the various Southern Asian Communist parties thereby offers China a number of bases from which subversion and insurgency can spread. The estimates of the Chinese 'success' against Moscow in these matters have to be made with them in mind. The quality of the leverage which China has obtained in the countries where the Communist parties are ostensibly pro-Chinese depends upon the strength and position (both legal and social) of the parties, and upon their capacity to influence events. Whether or not the Communist parties can work openly in China's interests is a matter, for example, of their legal status. In North Viet Nam the party forms the government. Communist parties are legal in Laos and Cambodia, India and Indonesia; but they have been banned in Malaysia, the Philippines, South Viet Nam and Thailand. In Burma, the situation in this, as in other respects of the country's political life, is confused. After the failure of the attempt to compromise with the Communist insurgents, General Ne Win had, by early 1964, arrested more than 1,000 known Communists and left-wing suspects, including the leaders of the fellow-travelling National United Front—the 'above ground' Communists—and a number of the stalwarts of the old Anti-Fascist People's Freedom League.[1] The rump of the League members gives a grudging support to the military junta, but the Burma Communist Party maintains an underground organisation in opposition to the Government. The relationships of the Burmese Communists with China remain obscure, in spite of the fact that they are generally accepted to be Chinese in sympathy. The White Flag Communist insurgents are known to have contacts with Peking, but, in the opinion of some Western observers in Rangoon, neither the Red nor the White Flag Communists are actually *directed* from outside Burma. Certainly, Peking has not given the Burmese Communists substantial aid during the years of insurgency, and has been remarkably circumspect and restrained in its relations with the Government, even when the régime has acted harshly towards the local Communists.

North Viet Nam is a major source of subversion and insurgency on the mainland. Hanoi supports the war in South Viet Nam and through its connections with the Pathet Lao can exercise an influence in Laos as far as the Thai border (and possibly beyond). Communist and pro-Communist forces form part of the troika government of the kingdom of Laos, and act like an independent government. The Pathet Lao controls a large section of the country, and its political arm, the Neo Lao Hak Xat, has shown considerable strength at the polls. The Communist Party of Laos is an important link in the chain

[1] *The Times*, 13 February 1964

of subversion forged from China and North Viet Nam towards Burma and Thailand. In Cambodian politics, the Pracheachon or Nationalist Party serves as a legal political front for the Communists, and it is said to reflect Viet Minh influence. It has a small membership—Prince Sihanouk frowns on Communists in his own country—and has had a diminishing effect in the three elections since 1955. In 1955 the Pracheachon Party polled 3 per cent of the votes and in 1958 it received 1 per cent. In 1962 all the candidates of the Prince's Sangkum Reastr Niyum, the People's Socialist Community, were returned unopposed, gaining all the seats in the national assembly.[1] While the Communists in Cambodia appear to have little direct influence upon the Government, their indirect influence might be increased the more the country develops its relations with China and North Viet Nam. Indonesia has the largest Communist Party outside the Communist bloc. The party has been estimated to have as many as 3 million members, with several million more supporters. More than 7 million people voted for the party in the 1957 local elections. Although the party has no place in the cabinet, it is represented on two of President Sukarno's instruments of Guided Democracy, the Supreme Advisory Council and the National Planning Council. The party is believed to be effectively infiltrating its members into the lower echelons of the army, a significant consideration in view of the often-postulated conflict, after Sukarno, between the Communist Party and the Army.

The pro-Chinese Communist parties of Thailand and Malaysia fall into a distinct category, for in both of those countries the Communist parties have substantially been identified with the local Overseas Chinese. Since the obscure activities of the Siam Communist Party in the 1920s, Communism in Thailand has been manifested chiefly amongst the Chinese community and has hardly touched the Thais themselves.[2]

According to a recent estimate, the Thai Communist Party is said to have a mere 200 members, whereas the Chinese Communist Party in Thailand has a membership of about 5,000.[3] The estimated membership of the Chinese Communist

[1] Norodom Sihanouk, Le Cambodge dix années d'indépendance', Le Monde, 8 October 1963

[2] J. H. Brimmell, Communism in South East Asia. A Political Analysis, Oxford University Press 1959, pp. 111–16

[3] Russell H. Fifield, Southeast Asia in United States Policy, Frederick A. Praeger 1963, p. 55

Party is an insignificant proportion (one-sixth per cent) of the Chinese population of Thailand, which numbered in 1964 about three million of Thailand's 26 million people. The weak underground Chinese Communist Party of Thailand could have a great accession of strength amongst the Thai Chinese if, and when, the Government of Thailand, convinced that the tide was running against the West in Southern Asia, made overtures to Peking in a spirit of *sauve qui peut*. Meanwhile, the problem of subversion in Thailand seems to be most pressing in the north-eastern provinces amongst the pro-Communist Vietnamese refugees along the Laotian border.

In contrast with neighbouring Burma, Malaya and Indonesia, where Communist revolts broke out in 1948, Thailand remained free of Communist-inspired insurgency. The Malayan experience of Chinese-dominated Communism has differed greatly from that of the Thais, and has been an important factor in the considerations for a union with Singapore. In Malaya, the Emergency lasted from June 1948 until July 1960. The number of Communist guerrillas at the height of the Emergency was estimated to have been about six thousand effectives, who were in turn supported by as many as one hundred thousand Chinese squatters. The Federation of Malaya achieved its independence during the Emergency, and the prospects of Union with Singapore immediately after 1957 were remote, not least because of the belief in Malaya that it was necessary to protect the Federation from Singapore Chinese Communism. Since the early years of the Comintern, Singapore has been a base from which Communist activities have been organized, particularly in order to mobilise the Overseas Chinese throughout the region. The colony of Singapore was granted internal self-government in 1959; in the following year, which saw the end of the Emergency, the Malayan authorities were still not prepared to consider a merger. There were two main reasons for their attitude. The $1\frac{1}{4}$ million Singapore Chinese would, if included in the Federation, upset the Malayan racial balance; and the left-wing Singapore parties, including Mr. Lee's People's Action Party, were regarded with suspicion by the Alliance leaders. But by 1960, as already mentioned, the People's Action Party believed that independence plus a merger with the Federation was a way to dissolve the 'Chinese chauvinism' in Singapore.

The figures for the population of the Federation of Malaya

and of Singapore in 1960 reveal the sociological basis for the Malay fears. The figures for the Malay and Chinese populations (in thousands, and excluding other ethnic groups) were: the Federation of Malaya, 3,641 Malays and 2,552 Chinese; Singapore, 227 Malays and 1,231 Chinese.[1] Throughout the Federation of Malaysia, the Chinese are a major element in every area. The approximate proportions in 1963 were: in Malaya (population 7 million) 40 per cent Chinese; in Singapore (population 1,700,000) 75 per cent Chinese; in Sarawak (population 750,000) 31 per cent Chinese; in Sabah (population 500,000) 23 per cent Chinese.[2] (More than one half of Brunei's 84,000 people are Malay. If the sultanate entered Malaysia the racial balance of the Federation would not be substantially changed.) In his study of the problem, T. E. Smith stated that 'in Malaysia as a whole, there will be rather more than two Chinese in every five of the population'.[3] This proportion of over 40 per cent makes Malaysia more of a 'Chinese' state than its neighbours. Singapore remains a focal point for the dangerous combination of 'Chinese chauvinism' and organised Communism. Throughout the region, the Overseas Chinese appear to be a second instrumentality which can be employed for Communist, and specifically Chinese, subversive activities. The links between the Overseas Chinese and the local Communist parties are firm and obvious in both Thailand and Malaysia; they are rather more covert elsewhere in Southern Asia, but are nevertheless of manifest potential. There is a belief current in the West which likens the durable and economically significant Chinese communities in the area to political barometers, responsive to pressures from the Chinese mainland.

Even if this belief were true, as it may well prove to be, the results of the responsiveness of the Chinese communities to pressures from China, or to China's increased international stature (and, by inference, the decline of the Kuomintang's), would of themselves be significant only in a limited area of the Nan Yang (South Seas). For the density of the more than 12 million Overseas Chinese is socially significant only in Malaysia in the first instance (before its incorporation into the Federation, Singapore was the only Chinese state outside China, apart

[1] T. E. Smith, *The Background to Malaysia*, p. 3. The figures for 'Malays' include people of Indonesian origin.
[2] *The Observer*, 15 September 1963
[3] Op. cit., p. 3

from Taiwan), and perhaps in Thailand, where the local Chinese community numbers over 11 per cent of the population. According to the following estimate, no other state in the area has a Chinese minority approaching the proportions of these two: 'South Viet-Nam (6·2 per cent), Cambodia (5·5 per cent), Indonesia (2·7 per cent), Burma (1·6 per cent), the Philippines (1·2 per cent), Laos (0·6 per cent), and North Viet-Nam (0·4 per cent).'[1] The Overseas Chinese in the Philippines and South Viet Nam still favour Nationalist rather than Communist China. In the Philippines, Communism has not been strong among the Chinese community, and there is less of a problem of assimilating them than there is in Moslem countries. In South Viet Nam, the million Chinese, who are mostly concentrated in the city of Cho-lon, were ordered by the Diem Government to 'vietnamise' themselves and adopt Vietnamese surnames, and they seem to have accepted this situation.[2] Those with extensive experience of recent conditions in South Viet Nam can find no evidence that any of the insurgents had been Chinese or that there was any direct local Chinese intervention in the insurgency. This may be regarded as an instance of China's flexibility, probably deriving from a consciousness of the extreme unpopularity of the Chinese in Viet Nam, and from the assessment that if the Communist movement for 'national liberation' was known to be Chinese-influenced then many Vietnamese would swing away from it.

But if Peking is flexible in its attitudes towards the Overseas Chinese, it is necessarily so: it has to be particularly circumspect in the use it makes, or attempts to make, of them to further its own policies. The Overseas Chinese form a minority in the various countries of Southern Asia, and in most cases they encounter a hostile majority. The more these minorities display

[1] Russell H. Fifield, op. cit., p. 49. Fifield cites no source for these precise figures; but they are the same as those quoted from a 1959 study by A. Doak Barnett in his illuminating chapter on the Overseas Chinese, in *Communist China and Asia. Challenge to American Policy*, published for the Council on Foreign Relations, Harper 1960, p. 176. Fifield estimated the Chinese minority in Thailand as 11·3 per cent of the population: British sources place the figure at 20 per cent. British sources also estimate that about one fifth of the population of Cambodia is Chinese

[2] An ordinance dated 21 August 1956 made all Chinese born in Viet Nam Vietnamese citizens. Initially there was some resistance, and in 1957 about ½ per cent of the Chinese affected had complied with the law

their unity and separateness, the more they alienate the governments and peoples about them. And while the Overseas Chinese may look to China for protection, protection has not always been forthcoming. The constitution of the People's Republic expressly states that 'The People's Republic of China protects the well-earned rights and interests of the overseas Chinese' (article 98), but this has remained a dead letter. In a number of ways the People's Republic has attempted to take advantage of this attitude, and to organise it for political purposes. For example, a special party—the Chih Kung Party—was set up for the Overseas Chinese; offers were made to some 10,000 Overseas Chinese intellectuals to induce them to return to China,[1] and Chinese embassies maintain contacts with the Overseas Chinese in Cambodia, Burma, Indonesia and Laos.

But China has been unsuccessful, for example in Indonesia, in her attempts to protect her overseas 'citizens', and has had to modify her attitude that the Overseas Chinese remain citizens of the homeland. (Places for the Overseas Chinese in the National People's Congress are reserved by article 23 of the constitution.) Although the great majority of the Overseas Chinese have been born outside China, since the migrations have virtually ceased, there exists amongst them a strong sense of kinship and cultural affinity with China that forms a bond which may transcend self-interest, but which is not blind to self-interest. Manifestations of this sense are the large sums of money remitted by the Overseas Chinese to remote families in China, and the desire of many of them to be buried in China. However, this is a patriotic and nostalgic rather than a political attitude, and would persist even if the Kuomintang ruled a strong China.

If it is a professed object of Chinese policy to remove Western power from mainland Southern Asia, then those countries in the area which are supported by the West are the likely targets of subversion sponsored by China. The subversion of neutrals, Burma and Cambodia, for instance, while weakening the overall strategic position of the West, poses different problems. In countries where there is a treaty involvement, as through SEATO, or an assumed responsibility, as in Laos and South Viet Nam, subversion is a form of warfare directed against the West as well as against the governments it supports.

[1] Klaus Mehnert, *Peking and Moscow*, Weidenfeld and Nicolson, 1963, pp. 159, 184

The Western presence, that is, provides a *raison d'être* for Chinese-sponsored subversion, for it interposes an alien source of power between China and the local governments in an area which China regards as her own sphere of influence. Hence Peking's insistence that Western-supported governments are puppet régimes and cliques backed by the imperialists to pervert the course of Asian revolutionary development. The French ex-colony of Indochina is the clearest and most urgent example of this problem. Subversion in South Viet Nam threatens the American position in the area. If the Saigon Government collapses under Communist pressures, the United States will have little choice but to withdraw from the country and pin her hopes for preventing a Communist hegemony in the area upon her ally Thailand.

II. Techniques of Subversion:
The Viet Cong in South Viet Nam

It is on the level of subversion, at the immemorial grass roots of rural society, that a vital battle against Communism is fought in Southern Asia. The tactics of that battle, as exemplified by the activities of the Viet Cong in South Viet Nam, can illustrate the difficulties of the West in its supporting role. There is truth in the often-quoted American contention that the war in South Viet Nam is a Vietnamese war: a corollary is that it is precisely at the lowest levels of this warfare that the effects of Western assistance have so far been most limited. American and allied assistance to the successive Saigon governments has not *per se* rallied the Vietnamese peasantry against the Viet Cong; nor is it likely to do so in the future. The point with which George Tanham concluded his study of Communist revolutionary warfare in Indochina is pertinent for today and for the difficult period ahead. Writing in 1961, he stated that 'Until his [Diem's] government has the active and continuing support of the Vietnamese masses and the troops, all the economic and military aid in the world, though it may delay it, will not halt the Communist advance.'[1]

That is still the underlying problem, for on the deepest levels of the war in South Viet Nam the Viet Cong techniques are not being adequately matched by those who would halt the Communist advance. The Viet Cong continue to employ

[1] George K. Tanham, *Communist Revolutionary Warfare. The Vietminh in Indochina*, Frederick A. Praeger, 1961, p. 157

coercion and terror to erode the popular base of the Government in Saigon (and it is a moot point how much the successive governments ever had a popular base) in their 'revolution from the bottom'.[1] Further, in order to confirm the authority won by terror, the Viet Cong establish their own covert systems of government to administer districts wholly or partially under their jurisdiction, even if they control those districts merely during the night hours. These techniques are combined with a broad political offensive which is designed to win to their side the minorities in the strategic highlands of South Viet Nam and the majorities in the vulnerable lowlands, and which is conducted with a zeal borne of a conviction of ultimate victory. These points can be illustrated for the most part from documents captured from the Viet Cong themselves. By these methods the zealots conducting the national liberation war in the south have aimed with a great deal of success to isolate the Saigon Government by creating the populous 'sea' for the guerrilla 'fishes', according to the tenets of the Chinese master.

For the convenient purposes of analysis, four different techniques of subversion in South Viet Nam can be distinguished. On the one hand, they are the *erosion of the government* (i) by destroying its authority at the grass roots, and (ii) by erecting substitute authorities, shadow administrations possessing all the ultimate sanctions and powers of the overt government. On the other hand, they are the *art of seduction* (i) of the minorities in South Viet Nam which have not been adequately broken to the will of the central government in Saigon, and (ii) of the majority by the strenuous expedient of living amongst them and leading them painfully to the level of ideological commitment, towards an awareness that 'their interests are tied to the general struggle and that the glorious revolution is theirs'.[2] In practice, of course, these methods are not isolated but are used in conjunction: all is grist to the revolutionary mill where flexibility of tactics is a great virtue. As one Viet Cong cadre wrote presciently in 1962, in his survey of the general situation in the south:

[1] The phrase is used in Andrew R. Molnar *et al.*, *Undergrounds in Insurgent, Revolutionary, and Resistance Warfare*, Special Operations Research Office, American University, Washington, 1963, p. 36 ff

[2] Viet Cong, *Experiences in Turning XB Village in Kien Phong Province into a Combattant Village*, 1961, (Mimeo) Courtesy of the U.S. Information Agency, Saigon

In any event, we will win, but we should know how to win gradually, we should make transitional steps in our way towards complete victory. The world situation and the status of our struggle in the North and in the South at present are providing many potentialities for the revolution to make such steps and to progress; and these potentialities will increase when our forces grow stronger, and our struggle is intensified, and when the enemy suffers many defeats. With regard to leadership, we should orient the revolution in that direction. The transitional steps may take many different forms, sometimes complicated ones; the present situation in Laos is a very important transitional step for the Lao revolution. A transitional step, whether it be a major or a minor one, will represent a stride in the revolution, will have a very profound revolutionary meaning, and will be an important advantage gained by the revolutionary forces in SVN. A very minor transitional step may sometimes have a major meaning and effect. Now we are fighting and at the same time demanding the formation of a coalition government, demanding peace and neutrality, in order to institute transitional steps for the movement to progress more easily, to further the isolation of bellicose elements and to persuade peace-seekers in the very ranks of the enemy.[1]

The erosion of the Government

The first step is the destruction of the Government's authority by murder and terrorism. The rural officials of the Government of South Viet Nam, the provincial and village leaders, youth leaders, teachers, together with known and locally prominent government sympathisers, are the objects of a sustained terrorist campaign by the Viet Cong. These officials have been kidnapped and brain-washed, tortured and murdered, in a deliberate effort by the Communist terrorists to destroy the Government's authority in rural areas and to consolidate a rival authority. In 1964, Australian sources estimated that within the previous three years 2,500 Vietnamese civilians had been kidnapped and almost 3,000 civilians assassinated by the terrorists.[2] The discriminating employment of violence and terror for psychological and political ends is placed on an organised basis by the Viet Cong, like the Viet Minh before

[1] Viet Cong, *Report on the Revolutionary Movement in the South*, 1962 (Mimeo) Courtesy of the U.S. Information Agency, Saigon

[2] *Christian Science Monitor*, 13 May 1964

them,[1] and is entrusted to special cadres. These cadres are the Dich-Van armed propaganda units who operate in small groups: 'it was a DV operation that, on January 10, 1962, captured 100 youth-group leaders in South Viet-Nam, brainwashed them for several weeks, and then released them. Seven "incorrigibles" were held back and probably murdered.'[2] It is by such operations as this, wrote Bernard Fall, that the Dich-Van teams 'make themselves felt at a specifically "Vietnamese" level of fighting upon which the foreigner simply has no effect'.

The second step is the substitution of authority in rural areas. The Viet Cong *Report on the Revolutionary Movement in the South* (1962) placed special emphasis upon the task of establishing a government in the 'liberated' areas to mobilise manpower and strengthen the revolutionary forces.[3] 'Between one-half and three-fourths of the rural areas in SVN have been liberated or relieved from enemy pressures and our responsibility is to gather the people and rule them. . . .' Party cadres were to provide the leadership for the rural administration while, at the same time, involving the peasantry as much as possible in the organisational tasks and in the life of the shadow governments. Policies were specifically designed for the different areas of South Viet Nam. In the mountain and forest regions special committee members were assigned to this task by the Autonomous People's Committee, and a number of Communists were directed to assist the work of the cell leaders amongst the people. A similar pattern of leadership was to be developed and strengthened in the delta area. There, the rural administration was the responsibility of the Front Committees, or of the village Farmers' Association if there were no Front Committee in the area. Party members formed the cadres, 'the cell is responsible for leadership; the specialist comrades in the cell guide the people's organisations in carrying out the administration'.

The rural organisations were to remain flexible and osten-

---

[1] The Viet Minh employed Dich-Van groups 'to coerce the recalcitrants into supporting, or at least accepting, the Vietminh movement'. Bert Cooper *et al.*, *Case Studies in Insurgency and Revolutionary Warfare: Vietnam 1941–54*, Special Operations Research Office, American University, Washington, 1964, p. 95

[2] Bernard B. Fall, *The Two Viet-Nams. A Political and Military Analysis*, Pall Mall Press, 1963, p. 137

[3] See part IV, sections 3, 5, 7, cited in Appendix II

sibly democratic under the guidance of party members. An obvious monopolisation of power, and 'Situations such as cadres holding all the jobs, or the creation of unrealistic organisations', were to be avoided. As a general rule, 'The people will administer themselves in hamlets and villages (no official form of administration will be used) and this is the most suitable form of administration in our prolonged political and military struggle "without delimited boundaries" against the enemy.' The Report on XB village provides an instance of the process of establishing Communist authority against great initial odds (see below). In those areas where there is not what the Report calls a 'face to face' struggle with the Saigon Government's forces, where the Government's armed intrusions were spasmodic efforts, the main concern of the Viet Cong 'is to assign the people to practical activities, to set up combat villages, to administer the community, to improve the people's living conditions'. In other words, in those areas the Communist-led administration can fulfil the functions of a *de facto* government, relatively undisturbed by the government whose powers it has successfully usurped. In the rural areas for which the Viet Cong is still contending, and in urban areas, the 'face to face' struggle was to be intensified and extended. The basic principle for these activities was laid down in the slogan: 'a struggle should be justified, profitable and kept within bounds'.

By establishing an effective *de facto* government in rural areas, the Viet Cong develop the bases which form an integral element in the strategy of revolutionary warfare.[1] The Report already cited stressed the great importance in this form of warfare of the setting up and preservation of 'covert structures' of Communist rule, and warned that 'our structures in weak and contended areas are still inadequate and overt . . .' The bases taken together constitute a state within a state, the foundation of the Communist strength; their existence testifies to the degree to which the Government in Saigon is being eroded. Ultimately power is to be achieved by the consolidation and extension of these base areas where the Government's writ does not run.

In their development of 'covert structures', the Viet Cong are following the precedents of the Viet Minh in their war against the French forces. The French have studied the significance of these structures, which they have termed *hiérarchies*

[1] Cf. George K. Tanham, *op. cit.*, p. 25

parallèles, and 'parallel inventories'.[1] Bernard Fall described
the parallel hierarchies as the 'true innovation of the Indochina war'. In his judgement, Hanoi's major success in that
war lay 'in the effective control of much of the countryside—
despite its occupation by a large Western army—through the establishment of small but effective administrative units that
duplicated the existing Franco-Vietnamese administration'.[2]
For example, 'In some areas which were administered by pro-
French officials and under nominal French control, the Vietminh was able to set up a parallel administration ready to take
over the functions of government any time and exercising considerable control over the inhabitants. On the surface, many a
village may have appeared safe, but as soon as the military
situation permitted it, the secret Vietminh administration
would emerge and assume open control.'[3]

The procedures employed in the second Indochina War are
similar to those tested in the first Indochina War; and some of
the areas in South Viet Nam under Viet Cong control, like
parts of the Camau Peninsula, the Plain of Reeds and 'Zone
D', have remained under the jurisdiction of the Communists
for a number of years. Similar procedures are used in Laos. In
mid-1964, Radio Pathet Lao claimed that Communist govern-
ors were in power in twelve of the sixteen provinces of Laos.[4]

The art of seduction

The first step is the courtship of minorities and a good example can be found in the Rhade of South Viet Nam. The exact
number of the *montagnards,* the highland tribes of South Viet
Nam, is unknown. But there are an estimated 500,000 to 700,000
highlanders distributed over a territory which is about half
the size of the Republic; their number has even been estimated
to be as high as one million people. One of the most important
of the *montagnard* groups is the Rhade, consisting of approxi-

---

[1] Paul A. Jureidini *et al., Casebook on Insurgency and Revolutionary
Warfare: 23 Summary Accounts,* Special Operations Research Office,
American University, Washington, 1962, pp. 35–6: 'These organisations . . . ranged from male and female youth groups, farmers'
and trade unions to groups as specialised as a flute players' association.' All were used for the purposes of indoctrination

[2] Op. cit., p. 133 ff.

[3] *Casebook on Insurgency and Revolutionary Warfare: 23 Summary
Accounts,* p. 36

[4] *Sunday Times,* 7 June 1964

mately 115,000 people who occupy the extended province of Darlac in the central highlands, south of the Laotian border but contiguous to Cambodia. The Communist supply lines from North Viet Nam and through Cambodia to the south run through the strategically situated Darlac province. The highland provinces, like Darlac, are a focal point in the struggle for South Viet Nam; they are the areas which by the techniques of subversion, infiltration and terror the Communists have attempted to control, and which the government in Saigon must deny to the Viet Cong. There is a slogan, based upon historical experience, that whoever controls the highlands threatens the security of Viet Nam. During the first Indochina War, the Viet Minh used bases in the highlands for launching guerrilla attacks upon the French forces. Under French rule the *montagnard* regions were administered separately from lowland Viet Nam. After 1954, Communist agents, left behind after the Viet Minh armies withdrew, capitalised on the misery and backwardness of the *montagnards* and their suspicions of the Vietnamese.

Amongst the Rhade there was traditionally no political integration outside the local hamlet. Since the formation of the Republic of South Viet Nam, the Government has in various ways attempted to absorb the semi-nomadic Rhade and other highlanders into the national system.[1] Many of the hamlets have been incorporated into villages, the village is the smallest administrative unit, the headmen being chosen by the district chiefs and the provincial authorities. By means of a 'pilot village' scheme the Government set out to provide leadership, training and land redistribution for the Rhade. By the end of 1958, there were some forty pilot villages for a tribal population of 40,000. A special school at Hue was set up, where selected tribesmen could be taught to read and write and develop manual skills for use in the villages on their return. A programme of road building, including a road from Saigon to Banmethuot in Darlac, was planned to open up the plateau. At the same time, the Government encouraged migration into the high plateau from the lowlands. A government resettlement programme was inaugurated in 1957, and two years later some 44,000 lowland Vietnamese had been resettled.

[1] See, e.g., Joseph Buttinger, 'The Ethnic Minorities in the Republic of Vietnam', in *Problems of Freedom. South Vietnam Since Independence*, ed. Wesley R. Fishel, Free Press of Glencoe, 1961, pp. 105–8

In the event, it proved less difficult to resettle lowland Vietnamese than highland tribesmen. (Only three large, and some small, regroupment centres for the *montagnards* were operating by 1961.) The methods used by the Government to absorb the Rhade into a Vietnamese way of life were not uniformly well chosen and suitable, and in some instances have increased Rhade hostility. Government officials who observed the apathy of the Rhade were inclined to blame it on Communist propaganda. But an observer at one of the Land Development Centres noted that 'people lived in small, poorly-constructed, dark hovels. From the warmth, gaiety, companionship, and social cohesion of the extended family in the long-house, the people had been forced into isolation, uncertainty, and rootlessness.'[1] With the assistance of the U.S. Military Assistance Advisory Group and the Operations Mission in South Viet Nam, efforts have been made to win over the Rhade and to prevent the tribespeople from defecting to the Viet Cong.

But, despite the Government's activities, it was apparent, by 1961, that the Viet Cong had made serious inroads into the *montagnard* areas, where subversion, and terrorism, including the murder of government officials, were quite widespread. This extension of Communist harassment added to the already considerable burdens of the Government in the implementation of its assimilation policies. The Communist seduction of the *montagnard* population of South Viet Nam starts at the very roots of that primitive society. The personnel allotted to the task of subverting these people include some of the thousands of Viet Minh troops recruited from the tribes during the first Indochina War, and who were taken north after the partition, as well as later recruits from the same areas. Unlike the government officials undertaking work amongst the tribes, the Communist cadres set out to penetrate the village society: 'These cadres adopt the dress of the highlanders, break their teeth in the traditional manner, and marry into highland families in an attempt to convert the highlanders to their point of view.'[2]

As well as exploiting the discontents of the tribes, the Viet Cong offer them the prospect of autonomous states. This movement for autonomous states has the support of North Viet Nam, and Radio Hanoi broadcasts propaganda in several of the tribal dialects. (There are some 27 language groups in the

[1] John D. Donoghue, 'The Rhade of South Viet Nam: a Preliminary Report', *Current Anthropology*, Vol. 4, October 1963, p. 384
[2] John D. Donoghue, op. cit., p. 384

South Viet Nam highlands, and they are mutually unintelligible.) Hanoi formulated a policy for the northern *montagnards* as early as 1953. In 1955, the Thai-Meo Autonomous Zone was founded and a second zone set up in 1956; a third zone was abolished in 1959. These examples have had a profound effect amongst the highland peoples of the south. In September 1964, Rhade tribesmen who were armed and trained by American Special Forces rose against the Saigon Government, demanding regional autonomy. The revolt raised serious doubts about the effectiveness of the American programme for winning over the *montagnards*.[1] Hanoi conducts special schools for southerners, and a southern Rhade tribesman who was sent to the Soviet Union has held a seat in the legislature of the Democratic Republic of Viet Nam. In addition to these approaches, the Viet Cong apparently adopted a policy of terrorism in the highlands about 1958, the year that the government's schemes for the *montagnards* were under way. Since then, government officials in the highlands have been the special targets for the Communist murder teams, as in the lowland areas.

The final step is winning the masses. The subversion of XB village in Kien Phong Province (1959–61) provides a clear example of this technique. Kien Phong Province forms part of the Plain of Reeds. It lies west of Saigon, on the Mekong River, where it issues into South Viet Nam, and contiguous to Cambodia. It is in an area where the Viet Cong have maintained a relatively high degree of stable political control for a number of years, with parallel hierarchies to govern the people. The illuminating story of the subversion of XB village is set out in a captured Viet Cong report which throws light on the methods employed by the Communists to establish their control in this and other rural areas of South Viet Nam. The American editor of the translation of the document wrote:

We know nothing about the document's author, except that he is a southerner, probably a native of Kien Phong Province and most likely a Cao Daiist. Although he has picked up much of the jargon he is not a doctrinaire communist; much of what he says would be considered highly heretical in orthodox communist circles. He appears to be a man of the people—simple, direct, dedicated, and probably very effective.

[1] *The Observer*, 27 September 1964; *The New York Times*, 30 September 1964

The Report is a lucid document in four sections: (i) 'Situation facing us when we began'; (ii) 'Means and methods of our success'—the crux of the matter; and two sections of critical analysis of the shortcomings of this highly successful essay in subversion, (iii) 'Lessons to be learned from XB', and (iv) 'Situation at other villages as compared with XB.' The example of XB village illustrates on a small scale the general techniques employed by Vietnamese revolutionary groups since the first Viet Minh cadres were organised in 1941–42. Those techniques have been summarised as follows: 'first it [the Viet Minh] propagandised and organised the people under its control; then it affiliated these organisations with larger national liberation front groups; and finally it formed an armed force under its control'.[1]

The village of XB is entirely surrounded by water. It is a new village, founded in the late 1940s, during the first Indochina War, and has a population of 6,000. The land was originally held by one large landholder and fifty smaller landholders, though during the war the land was used by the peasants for their own purposes, since the landlords had fled. With peace, the landlords returned to occupy the land, so that the peasants were 'greatly motivated to struggle against the land lords'.

During the first years of the peace, the Viet Cong made several efforts to increase their activities to take advantage of the peasants' attitudes, but their task was not easy. Civil Guards and mobile troops of the South Vietnamese Army were active in the area. In the village there was a government administrative office, a security section and a militia post. The government forces were initially able to control the Viet Cong in XB village. The party organisation was thrice destroyed. Three party members were killed, two secretaries and more than 100 cadres and members were arrested. Finally, only one party member remained, and he was driven away and received no help from the villagers. This was the low point of the Communist movement in XB village, and in 1959 higher level cadres were sent into the area to rally the movement. By October 1961, the date of the Viet Cong Report, XB village had been transformed from a Diem strongpoint into a Communist combatant village. The Communist Party in the village consisted of 26 members, the Lao Dong Youth of 30 members, the Farmers' Association of 274 members, with other youth and

[1] *Case Studies in Insurgency and Revolutionary Warfare: Vietnam 1941–54*, p. 95

women's organisations. Altogether, 2,000 people took part in the activities guided by the Communist Party. On a number of occasions the village people were strong and determined enough to repulse incursions by the government troops, including an operation against the village by 600 soldiers in motor boats.

The means and methods by which this wholesale subversion was achieved included the elimination of the authority of 'the American-Diem clique' in the village councils, and the establishment of a village security system to prevent any pro-government activities among the people. Finally, it became impossible for the Diem Government to assert its influence in the village by maintaining a village council in the face of the collective opposition of the villagers. Then the support of the villagers was enlisted by the struggle for land. The party 'always used the subject of land as a means of propagandising the people and indoctrinating the masses'. A mass movement was built up by making use of the farmers' desire for land. All the public and private land of the village was distributed, the villagers being urged on by such slogans as 'Kill the Land Robbers', a slogan which 'was welcomed and used by the local people'. Thereafter, the party assumed the governmental functions of education, public health, sanitation and provided maternity facilities. A Pupil-Parent Association was founded and two schools built. 'The people pay for these services and they also have a voice in the management of them.' In the economic field, the party helped the farmers to market their produce, and through their organisation avoided merchant speculators. When the time came, in December 1960, to cele-brate the foundation of the National Liberation Front, the villagers enthusiastically prepared for the communal functions; though, as the criticisms in the Report suggest, the *political* significance of this may be overrated.

As regards the defence of the village, the villagers were, at first, unco-operative and apprehensive of government reprisals, and the Communist self-defence forces had to assume the responsibility for the defence of XB village. The peasants were gradually involved in the production of rudimentary weapons in order to defend their land; they built weapons such as 'naily boards'.[1] After some initial successes in repulsing government

[1] i.e. bamboo or metal spikes set so that they can pierce the foot, cf. the refrain of the American military song, 'Viet Cong Blues':
'I've got the Viet Cong Blues
Got bamboo spikes in my tennis shoes'

patrols by placing these weapons in the swamps and reeds, the villagers overcame their hesitations and helped to set up 'combat gates' or barricades covering the entrances to the village. The village Farmers' Association was put in charge of the eleven combat gates: 'Each sub-cell of the Farmers' association is in charge of one combat gate—and closes the gate when the enemy comes and gives the alarm by means of tocsin.' In addition, the villagers were exhorted to attempt to subvert the government troops, particularly those of local origin. Some small arms were acquired in this way from deserters. After each of the Government's mopping up operations, the villagers reviewed the success or failure of their resistance. 'A meeting is held and each hamlet makes a report, in the presence of a cadre, who then points out the experience gained. At this meeting the hamlet which showed initiative or which achieved some outstanding victory in fighting with rudimentary weapons occupies a place of honour in the front ranks.'

For the process of political indoctrination, the party's techniques ranged from mass meetings to individual exhortation and instruction. The cadres 'not only learned how to use the interests of each class, group and circle, but also learned to study carefully the interests of each individual so they could better influence him'. An essential feature of the process was the continuous, party-supervised mutual criticism of collective and individual actions. 'This,' the Report states, 'serves to increase devotion, bring out the strong points and the shortcomings of the effort. This enables the people *to convert experience into an improved organisation*' [italics added]. The use of slogans illustrates this point. In drawing the lessons from the experience of XB village, the author of the Report stressed the central importance of the political propaganda programme in the struggle to achieve mass support: it had to be very simple and concrete, 'made to fit the feelings of the people', for 'if one fails to base propaganda on the practical interests of the people, one cannot expect the people to stand up and face the struggle'.

The Report drew attention to a number of shortcomings at XB village due to the party's failure 'to make a full three-prong attack' on the several fronts of political struggle, armed struggle, and the struggle to proselytise in the government forces. The efforts to proselytise were regarded as the weakest, while the best progress was made in the armed struggle. But both the armed and political struggles were criticised stringently.

The party had not given sufficient attention to infiltrating agents into the army or establishing 'political bases in local military units'. The armed struggle had remained on the defensive: 'From a practical standpoint the whole effort was not aimed at destruction of the enemy, only injuring him.' The combat village XB still lacked many of the conditions which would have enabled the Viet Cong to go on the offensive. The party had achieved a limited success; it had 'only led the people to the point where they passively opposed our enemies and were content if the latter did not terrorise the village'. The political struggle was also described as weak, and not sufficiently bound to the armed struggle. The main complaint made about the political struggle was that it did not expand the horizons of the villagers from their local interests to the national obligations of the revolution. 'The political struggle is on a low level, consisting only of simple demands and denunciations ... Demands relating to economic and political rights have not yet reached the proper level.' This is to set a very high standard for the political education of illiterate peasants.

The conclusion is, in effect, that the people of XB village had been induced to withdraw their allegiance from the Government in Saigon and to support the local cadres; nevertheless, they had not reached the point where, on a more general level, they understood or were prepared to submit to 'the validity of the Revolution's policies'. The proper objective was that 'the poor people must learn how to advance the revolution through political means thus avoiding the risks of regrettable losses which hurt the revolution and discourage the people. Above all, we must keep the masses from becoming passive.' Moreover, the masses had not been sufficiently broken to Communist rule, had not comprehended 'that their rights and interests must be subordinated to the national interests of Independence, Peace and Reunification'. As a result, once the people's immediate needs (like land) had been satisfied, there was a tendency for the movement to degenerate, and 'This does not fit in with the Party's objective of mobilising the strength of the entire people for the day of the general uprising.'

In all of Southern Asia, the Southeast Asian peninsula is at present the area where Communist-supported subversion raises the most acute difficulties for maintaining internal security. For some of the non-Communist governments the threat of internal war is greater than the threat of overt aggression.

Dissident groups engaged in subversive activities pose varying threats to the governments of South Viet Nam, Laos, Thailand, Burma and Malaysia. Certain of the problems in this area may be grouped together for geographical and even strategic reasons. The Viet Cong guerrillas employ a land route from North Viet Nam through Laos to the south. They find a privileged sanctuary in Cambodia where, according to the Saigon Government, guerrilla rest camps, training bases and armouries are established. North Vietnamese units are continually reported to be present with the Pathet Lao forces in northern and central Laos. The Pathet Lao control of areas near the Thai border provides bases for the extension of subversion into north-eastern Thailand. These factors have suggested the hypothesis that there is a degree of co-ordination from Hanoi of the efforts of the liberation army in the south and the Laotian insurgents in the west, that there is in effect an overall plan for the subversion of the successor states of French Indochina. This hypothesis is not at all improbable; a similar co-ordination of efforts was effected in the strategy of the war against the French Union forces and by substantially the same group of North Vietnamese leaders.

But if the subversive groups can move fairly freely across the national boundaries, the various government troops opposing them cannot do so. As far as the governments of South Viet Nam, Laos and Cambodia are concerned, they are so divided by their historical disputes and antagonisms that they are unable to co-ordinate their several efforts to maintain internal security. Their response to a general threat is piecemeal and it is inhibited by jealousies over frontiers which they cannot adequately police. The ethnic confusions of the peninsula facilitate the movement of subversive groups across national frontiers. The divisive tendencies of some ethnic minorities are encouraged by China and North Viet Nam who support autonomous movements and 'Free Thai' and other forces in order to focus and develop these tendencies in their own interests.

The internal security problems of Burma and Malaysia are not closely related to the Indochina situation, though, of course, a Communist victory in Indochina would have repercussions in those countries. The various Burmese dissident groups do not appear to receive material support from outside the country, as do the Pathet Lao and Viet Cong forces. It is not suggested that even those groups who, like the Peking-oriented Burmese

Communists, look outside Burma for their inspiration, consciously determine their activities in the light of external directives. And while there is evidence of outside influence upon some of the Burmese Communists, there is little to indicate that the trend of dissident activity in Burma is in any manner related to developments in Indochina, or is designed to influence them, or is governed by the same strategy. Thailand occupies a vulnerable central position in the peninsula, with a long border against Laos; she is more exposed to hostile influences along this border to the east than she is along the Burmese frontier. The Thai and Burmese authorities are developing co-operative measures to ensure the internal security of their joint border regions. On the border of Thailand and Malaysia, several hundred hard core terrorists survive as a relic of the Emergency, and in October 1964, an agreement between the two countries was announced on joint action to eliminate the guerrillas.[1] These survivors must at present be regarded as one of the less significant threats to the Government of Malaysia. Far more threatening is the subversion on the mainland and in Borneo supported by the Indonesian Government as part of its 'confrontation' policy. The subversive groups in Malaysian Borneo operate from the privileged sanctuary of the Indonesian side of the frontier. Malaysia's internal security is also endangered by the inter-racial tensions of the Federation. In Singapore these tensions lead to repeated outbreaks of communal violence.

The non-Communist states of Southeast Asia are not likely to be free of the threats to their internal security in the immediate future. In a number of cases, it is most probable that the threats will increase. The continued existence of the coalition government in Laos and the régime in South Viet Nam is a matter of grave doubt; and in both instances it is apparent that the existing governments are not capable of withstanding the threat of subversion without assistance from those Western powers who see it as in their own interests to proffer support. Malaysia, also, remains in need of assistance from the interested Commonwealth members in order to defend herself against Indonesian subversion. Thus, in two of the crucial areas in Southeast Asia, the continuance of the struggle against subversion depends upon the assistance of external powers whose views of their own strategic interests in the area could well be modified in the stress of events. Much in the future will depend

[1] *Daily Telegraph*, 3 October 1964

upon the success or failure of the American attempts to bolster the faltering Government of South Viet Nam.

The argument that a military victory against the insurgents in South Viet Nam is not feasible has much to support it, and it is gaining ground both in South Viet Nam and beyond. Some proponents of the argument, however, have been inclined to overlook the point that a negotiated settlement between North and South Viet Nam that is acceptable to Western interests can only be made if the Government of South Viet Nam can maintain its position, in the first place by military means. As long as the Viet Cong appear to be within sight of victory in the countryside, their leaders are not likely to sit down at a conference table, except to confirm their victory. On this view, military successes by the Government of South Viet Nam and its American supporters are essential as one means of dealing with the threat of subversion in the general area, as well as in South Viet Nam itself.

A Viet Cong victory in South Viet Nam, achieved perhaps by the collapse of the Government under pressure rather than by military defeat, would expose Cambodia and Thailand to an increased range of Communist threats. In such a circumstance, the two governments might seek an accommodation with China and North Viet Nam, along the lines already adopted by the Cambodian leader. The anti-Communist Government of Malaysia would in turn be faced by hostile powers to the north as well as the south, and the entire Western presence on the mainland be constricted and threatened.

Chapter 5

Internal Defence and External Assistance

I. Aid and the Problem of Disequilibrium

VARIOUS external powers have assumed responsibilities to assist some of the Southern Asian countries in their efforts to counter subversion. Apart from the SEATO arrangements, the process has taken place by means of a number of particular understandings between specific countries varying from firm legal agreements for military assistance to offers of non-military help. SEATO provides *inter alia* that Pakistan, the Philippines and Thailand can claim assistance from the other signatories. In practice, Thailand is placed closer to the central problems of subversion from China or North Viet Nam than Pakistan or the Philippines. China apparently has no immediate interest in fomenting subversion in Pakistan; her policy is rather to consolidate the good relations which she has already developed. Chinese subversion against Pakistan remains a future possibility. The Philippines are protected from the Chinese and Vietnamese centres of contagion by her comparative isolation from the mainland across the South China Sea. Previously, of course, this isolation did not prevent the growth of a Communist-inspired revolutionary movement in Luzon; but then as now the difficulties of providing clandestine support to rebels in the Philippines from the mainland are considerable.[1]

In 1954, SEATO extended its protection to the Protocol states of Cambodia, Laos and South Viet Nam, whose governments were in favour of the protocol but were not asked to be signatories. Cambodia has since been hostile to SEATO and different régimes in Laos have varied between support and hostility towards it. South Viet Nam receives American support for the war against the Viet Cong by a direct arrangement with the United States. The United Kingdom has provided aid to South Viet Nam and made available the services of counter-insurgency experts. Malaysia and the United Kingdom have signed the Anglo-Malaysian Defence Agreement, as a result

[1] During the Communist revolution in the Philippines, the Filipino Communist Party received funds from China

of which British forces are committed to operations against the Indonesian guerrillas. Australia provides assistance to Malaysia by informal agreement, and to South Viet Nam where she maintains a team of Australian Army advisers. New Zealand agreed to commit forces to operations in the Borneo States of Malaysia after her Government decided in 1963 to associate the country with the Anglo-Malaysian Defence Agreement. The documents of association, which transferred to Malaysia the military obligations which New Zealand previously had with Malaya, impose no legal obligation upon New Zealand to maintain her forces in Malaysia or to follow specific courses of action for the external defence of Malaysia. In addition, New Zealand maintains a small non-combatant group of Army engineers in South Viet Nam. If the Government of South Viet Nam requested SEATO for assistance, and if the situation in South Viet Nam deteriorates it might consider doing so,[1] then New Zealand like the other signatories of the Manila Pact would be obliged to consider giving direct military help. Japan and other countries have considered granting non-military aid to South Viet Nam without being under any legal obligation to do so; Japan has sent an ambulance unit.

The purpose of the Manila Treaty, as stated in the second article, was to provide the means whereby the eight signatories could develop 'their individual and collective capacity to resist armed attack and to prevent and counter subversive activities directed from without'. In 1954, the probability of armed attacks in the treaty area was rated high, and the preoccupations of individual members of the organisation reflected this concern. The then Thai Minister of Foreign Affairs, Prince Wan Waithayakon, urged that SEATO provide a military commitment as near as possible to that of NATO. Since 1954, an increased emphasis has been placed upon the dangers from subversion directed from without, and this change has affected SEATO planning and organisation. The communiqué issued after the first meeting of the Treaty Council, in Bangkok, in February 1955, noted that 'subversion and infiltration constitute a serious threat to the peace and security of the area, and that this demands special efforts in all aspects of the national life'.

After the second meeting of the Council, in Karachi, in March 1956, it was announced that 'there had been useful pro-

---

[1] *The Christian Science Monitor*, 18 April 1964, reporting a comment by the then Foreign Minister, Phan Huy Quat, on his return from the April 1964 meeting of the Southeast Asia Treaty Organisation

gress in co-operation among member Governments in assisting each other to combat subversive activities'. SEATO seminars on subversion were held in 1957 and 1960. 'Subversion, infiltration, and local wars remain the principal tools of the Communists in the Treaty Area,' stated the SEATO Report for 1962–63, 'militant activities have been and will continue to be employed whenever a vulnerable spot is detected.' There are vulnerable spots throughout the treaty area which are constantly being detected and exploited (and, one can add, created) by the Communists in the interests of subversion. But the development of a SEATO doctrine of counter subversion was slow, and it needed American and Australian concern for a more active policy to provide the initiative for changes.

The Manila Treaty referred to the task of preventing subversion directed from without, as well as countering it. But how can subversion from without be prevented? This is a question about the source of subversion and the soil in which it grows. Experience does not suggest that a simple answer is to be found by threatening those governments, like the Soviet Union, China and North Viet Nam, which export subversion. North Viet Nam continues to wage war by proxy in South Viet Nam despite the fact that it means throwing down a gauntlet to a super power. The revolutionary war in Indochina may have reached, in 1964, the stage where the Viet Cong could sustain their momentum even if North Viet Nam ceased to provide support. The arguments that the United States, by air strikes or other forms of direct military pressure, could coerce the Government of North Viet Nam into stopping its support for the insurgents in the south encounter this possibility. By deliberately choosing a policy of escalation the United States would not end the struggle, she would merely transform and broaden the war. Subversion directed from without cannot be turned off at the source, like a tap.

Military pressure is without doubt an important factor in containing the forces of subversion and ultimately of cutting them out of the body politic. But social as well as military surgery is of paramount importance. To achieve success in countering subversion directed from without, a government is required to learn much about itself. It must ask what are the sources of guerrilla strength? what grievances do the guerrillas seek to exploit? what social problems cry out for remedy? When guerrillas establish a political base, to what extent is the fact of subversive warfare a sympton of a failure in government?

Setting one's own house in order is an essential feature of counterinsurgency operations, to prevent the guerrillas widening their political base at the expense of the Government. In Saigon, it is sometimes argued that wartime is no time for reforms. President Diem's 'Open Arms' policy, an inspiration which owed much to the example of President Magsaysay, was hailed as the beginning of a process of reform, but neither the Diem régime nor those which followed it carried out the social engineering required to overcome the failure of government in South Viet Nam.

This suggests one of the most intractable problems for those external powers who support the efforts of Southern Asian governments to counter subversion directed from without. Subversion flourishes in those countries where manifold injustices warp the social fabric and provide patterns for the growth of protest movements. The Philippines showed a classic modern instance, but the social order of most of the other Southern Asian countries displays symptoms of the same maladies. The successful counterinsurgency effort of the Philippine Government in the years 1946–54 is one of the most instructive examples of how a Southern Asian country can deal with a subversive threat to its own security, and valuable lessons can be learned from it. The Philippine effort was exceptional in a number of ways, as is seen when it is compared with the counterinsurgency programme in South Viet Nam, and particularly with respect to the emphasis given to social reform. In the same year that the Philippine counterinsurgency effort was reaching a successful conclusion, the French in Indochina were on the road to Dienbienphu. France had belatedly accepted the need for reform. The United Kingdom, the other colonial power similarly engaged at the same period in a major counterinsurgency programme in Malaya, offered reforms to the colony in time, and first promised and then granted it independence.

Experience in Southeast Asia over the past ten years throws light on the wider problems involved in the transfer of resources from external powers to Southern Asian governments in order to build up their collective capacity to resist hostile pressures. As Southern Asia has virtually been decolonialised, a consequence is that none of the external powers helping Southern Asian governments to counter subversion can directly initiate the social, economic or political reforms which it might regard as essential to the success of the counterinsurgency operations.

The colonial relationship offered particular advantages to an external power countering subversion in Southern Asia. The United Kingdom could not have defeated the Communist terrorists in Malaya during the Emergency if she had been, as at present, merely an ally and not in charge of operations. The peak of the Emergency was over before even nominal control of the operations against the terrorists passed from London to Kuala Lumpur. Relinquishing the colonial relationship has meant depriving the external power of control over police and intelligence that was of inestimable value in counter-insurgency operations. To return to a colonial relationship (which China and North Viet Nam accuse the United States of doing in South Viet Nam) may make the counterinsurgency operations more effective, but it also deprives the local population of one incentive to resist the insurgents. The French and the American experience in the first and second Indochina wars illustrates this problem.

The shift of political control from the external powers to the indigenous countries has had important effects which are felt most acutely by the United States in its Asian policies. Not having a colonial relationship with South Viet Nam, the United States has no authority to change or improve by direct means the society which she is committed to defend. Against the mandarin Diem and his military successors, the United States was unable to carry all her arguments for reform in the interests of widening the basis of popular support for the Government; and it remains to be seen whether the emergence of a civilian government will basically alter this situation. This is a problem of disequilibrium between the political and the military pressure which external powers can bring to bear in a region of particular concern to them. The situation in South Viet Nam is perhaps the clearest illustration of a problem which affects in some degree the relations of all the external aid giving powers with the governments of Southern Asia, and which has critical consequences for the whole practice of defence assistance.

Defence assistance (which has been broadly defined as 'to assist friendly nations to maintain military forces, to make other provisions for ensuring their internal stability, to help them deter foreign aggression, and to help them meet it if necessary')[1] is a large and complicating factor in the American relations with Southern Asia. Two-thirds of the $1,000 million requested

[1] Amos A. Jordan, Jr., *Foreign Aid and the Defense of Southeast Asia*, Frederick A. Praeger, 1962, p. 7

by President Johnson in 1964 for military assistance was to be expended in eleven countries along the periphery of the Sino-Soviet world, and four-fifths of the sum the President wanted for supporting assistance (which is given primarily to countries facing defence or security emergencies) was earmarked for South Viet Nam, Laos, South Korea and Jordan. Recent examinations of the problems of defence assistance in Southern Asia have focused attention upon South Viet Nam and Laos, where the threat of subversion is most advanced and the need to counter it most urgent. In those two countries, as elsewhere in the area, the main burden of defence assistance has been shouldered by the United States. American aid of all kinds to Viet Nam for the period 1955–62 reached a total of more than $2 billion; for the same period aid of all kinds to Laos totalled over $450 million. Yet, from the American viewpoint, the situation in both of these countries had deteriorated under subversive pressures. Aid was not preventing subversion from occurring, and it began to be questioned whether the forms of aid in use were particularly effective in countering subversion. Moreover, counterinsurgency cost far more than insurgency: compare the Vietnamese estimate of the cost per year to North Viet Nam to support the Viet Cong offensive ($12 million) with the value of American aid to South Viet Nam (about $500 million).[1] Was aid costing too much for too little?

Apropos of South Viet Nam, the Mansfield Report on the situation in Viet Nam and Southeast Asia in 1963 disgnosed that 'The pressures of the Vietcong guerrillas do not entirely explain this [deteriorating] situation. In retrospect, the Government of Viet Nam and our policies, particularly in the design and administration of aid, must bear a substantial, a very substantial, share of the responsibility.'[2] This diagnosis illustrates something of the frustrations and difficulties of American defence assistance policies. The charge that some of the blame for the situation in Viet Nam lay nearer home echoed earlier criticisms. In 1957, a Senate Report on Foreign Aid stated that aid had come to be regarded as a single policy device which was capable of achieving many objectives, and argued that this attitude impaired the usefulness of foreign aid. The need was for a narrower formulation of the objectives of defence assistance, in order to connect them in a measurable fashion with the costs. This approach to the fundamental

[1] *The Times*, 6 February 1964
[2] p. 8

problems of relating the financial costs of defence assistance with the political results, the basis of any fruitful analysis, is a comparatively new element in the process of evaluation. A recent study claimed that there had been no consistent effort by American officials to glean the lessons of the United States' experience of defence assistance during more than ten years and in more than 50 countries.[1]

Although no satisfactory solutions to a number of these problems are in sight, some conclusions are being drawn. First, that problems of disequilibrium relate to an area of intergovernmental relations where the United Nations can play no major role: United Nations' programs cannot fill the need met by the military and political operations conducted under American programs designated as "defense support" and "special assistance".[2] Second, that the political leverage which an external power gains through grants of aid is limited and likely to remain so, as the United States has discovered in South Viet Nam and Laos, and the Soviet Union found in Indonesia. Third, that successful efforts to counter subversion involve more than defence assistance and military operations. South Vietnamese forces, with American advisers, may capture or recapture a village like XB in the jungles of Viet Nam, but unless they also win the loyalty of the inhabitants the victory is hollow. The most vulnerable spots in Southern Asia are located in the minds of the Asian masses, and the political conquest of XB village by the Viet Cong exemplifies the real dangers of subversion from below against the independent governments of Southern Asia. Mao Tse-tung's dictum that it is man and not material that counts has value at the grass roots. The great difficulty is to bring the weight of the defence assistance granted by the external powers to bear on the problems of the lowest levels of Southern Asian society.

The efficient use of defence assistance to enable it to be felt at the XB village level is the ultimate responsibility of the sovereign Asian governments. While the material factors to counter subversion from without can and, in countries like South Viet Nam and Laos, must be supplied also from without, the moral factors must come from within the country itself. Responsibility for the conduct of operations against subversion remains in the hands of the Asian governments and their

[1] Amos A. Jordan, Jr., op. cit., p. 215
[2] John D. Montgomery, *The Politics of Foreign Aid. American Experience in Southeast Asia*, Frederick A. Praeger, 1962, pp. 275-76

local authorities from province chiefs to village headmen who constitute the vital connection between the central power and the people, which the insurgents attempt to break. Only the indigenous leaders can provide the essential non-material sources of strength, the qualities of will, resource, leadership and morale, which were so amply demonstrated by President Ramón Magsaysay of the Philippines. His policy of 'All-Out Friendship or All-Out Force' was designed to wrest the political and military initiative from the insurgents, to steal their thunder by vigorous and combative leadership. Magsaysay has been described as 'Probably the first to use twentieth-century knowledge and techniques in a deliberate, rigorous exploitation of this approach to counterguerrilla warfare',[1] and he was probably the first Asian leader to do so.

II. Counterinsurgency in Asia

The Philippine Experience, 1946-54

The interest of the Philippine experience lies in the fact that it was the first occasion that an Asian government had to deal, and dealt successfully, with a Communist-inspired insurrection amongst its own peoples. The revolt developed in the fruitful soil of social unrest, so that the Government had not only to fight a war against subversion but also a war against corruption. It achieved victory without destroying the structure of democratic government, but rather by improving it, and without employing foreign troops. American technical, moral and material assistance ensured that the resources of the Government were not overtaxed by the demands of this war on two fronts. A War Damage Commission was set up by the United States Rehabilitation Act of 1946 which spent very large sums of money on economic reconstruction. The harmonious relationship between the Philippines and the United States, the ex-colonial power, prevented the kind of intramural conflicts which occur in South Viet Nam, and which blunt the edge of defence assistance. There were no acute problems of disequilibrium in the Philippines during the Communist revolution there.

[1] Colonel Napoleon D. Valeriano, AFP (Ret.) and Lieutenant Colonel Charles T. R. Bohannan, AUS (Ret.), *Counter-Guerrilla Operations. The Philippine Experience*, Frederick A. Praeger, 1962, p. 29: a book particularly concerned with the XB village level of operations

During the Second World War, the Filipino Communist Party, like the Malayan Communist Party in Malaya, became the only effective local leader of an anti-Japanese resistance movement; the big landowners, industrialists, and most of the Nationalist politicians, flourished under the Japanese. The Filipino Communist Party established the nucleus of its People's Anti-Japanese Resistance Army (Hukbong Bayan Laban Sa Hapon, shortened to Hukbalahap, or Huk), under the command of Luis Taruc, shortly after the Japanese occupation of Manila in March 1942. It was trained by Chinese officers under a veteran of the Communist Eighth Route Army and obtained its weapons from the Bataan battlefields. The Huk devoted more of their attention to murdering their rivals (20,000 victims) than to killing Japanese (5,000 of them), and it came into collision with the American-led guerrilla forces.

The United States granted independence to the Philippines in 1946. The 1946 elections were won with a narrow majority by the 'Liberal' government of President Roxas, a collaborator with the Japanese, by bribery and corruption. The elections to the National Congress of Luis Taruc and another prominent Huk candidate were invalidated by the Electoral Tribunal because of alleged fraud, and the Huk leaders consequently began to prepare for an armed struggle. The Roxas government ineptly claimed that it would destroy the revolt in sixty days. In March, 1948, a month before his death, President Roxas outlawed the Huk movement, but he did not ban the Filipino Communist Party. His successor, President Quirino, at once began negotiations with the Huk, who decided after all that the time was not ripe for an armed struggle, but who insisted, with some justice, on widespread economic reforms, since 3 per cent of the population owned approximately 98 per cent of the land. The Filipino Communist Party made efforts to obtain seats in the legislature in the 1949 elections, which were so corrupt, however, that it decided that a revolutionary situation did exist, and made plans for an armed uprising in 1950. It planned to capture Manila, and establish a Communist government of the Chinese type. Its armed forces were reorganised and their name changed in 1950 to the People's Liberation Army (Hukbong Mapagpalaya Ng Bayan). The Huk developed three types of forces; mobile fighting units under the command of Luis Taruc which operated as a regular military force, seven autonomous regional commands each led by a prominent Communist, and local self-defence groups. The Barrio Units

Self Defence Corps acted as the civilian counterpart of the Huk, provided intelligence and supplied food in areas where the Huk were not in full control. Each guerrilla unit maintained a special terror force. The use of terror to further the revolution was spasmodic after the war, but was resumed in 1946 and intensified in 1949. The Chinese Communist Party of the Philippines, some 3,000 strong, and the Chinese in Manila, apparently gave direct financial support to the insurgents. A special 'expansion force' was created to establish Huk movement outside Luzon.

President Quirino made Ramón Magsaysay the Secretary of National Defence in response to American pressure. Magsaysay fought with the American-led guerrillas during the Japanese occupation. After the war the Americans appointed him military governor of west-central Luzon, and he was returned to the House of Representatives from that district in 1949. In the Philippines, as in South Viet Nam, a nationalist leader emerged under American auspices.

The keynote of the Philippine Government's operations against the Huk insurgents was a programme of reform, economic, political, military, judicial and social, which owed a great deal to the inspiration of Ramón Magsaysay first as Secretary of National Defence (1950) and later as President (1953). The corruption of Philippine public life was exploited successfully by the Huk insurgents in their attempt to build up a mass base in preparation for their eventual seizure of national power in 1952. The rural masses in the Philippines had been alienated from the Government by the monopolisation of political power by rich landowners, by the inequities of the land reform programme, by a tax and judicial system which favoured the wealthy, by the Government's failure to enforce the minimum wage law, by the non-payment of taxes by land-owners, by the interference with statute law by vested interests, and by the bribery, nepotism and corruption which had spread throughout the ranks of the administration. The Huk recruited peasants who were embittered by the Government's failure to put into effect the 70/30 crop share law, which entitled the farmer to 70 per cent of the crop he produced.[1]

From an anti-Japanese Army of 5,000 full-time soldiers in

[1] Enacted by President Roxas in 1947. Before the Second World War the law had restricted the landlord's share of the crop to 40 per cent; traditionally in the Philippines, the landlord received 50 per cent of the crop

1943, the Huk movement developed into an anti-government force of some 12,000 armed guerrillas and 100,000 active members by 1952, at the peak of the insurrection. By 1950, the Huk had set up base areas under their control in 'Huklandia' in central Luzon and headquarters in the Sierra Madre Mountains, and expanded into Panay. The Government's security forces numbered 37,000 in 1950. The regular army was ill-equipped and not entirely free of corruption. It took only a minor part in the counterinsurgency operations before 1950, during the Huk period of preparation for the major assault upon the Government. The brunt of the operations between 1946 and 1950 was borne by the constabulary of the Department of the Interior. The constabulary, whose company-sized units were unable to sustain operations against the Huk, could not check the growth of the revolutionary movement.

In order to maintain its authority and revive the sagging national morale in the face of Huk pressure, the Government had three main tasks. First, it had to contain the military threat of the Huk. It was essential to reform the security forces and develop combat units which were capable of defeating guerrillas in the field. The relationship between the security forces and the populace had to be revised and improved if basic intelligence about Huk movements was to be obtained from the *barrios* (villages). Second, the Augean stables of the administration had to be cleaned out. Government authority at all levels had to be freed from persistent abuses of power, and the Government's effectiveness in the public interest clearly demonstrated. Politically, it was of the first importance that the widespread charges of electoral fraud and of army interference with elections be repudiated, and general confidence in the democratic processes sustained throughout the Philippine islands. Third, it was necessary not only to contain the Huk but to weaken him, to carry an assault against the rural base of the Huk movement by social measures which would provide an alternative outlet to rebellion. These three tasks were tackled vigorously under Magsaysay's direction and with the help of a Joint United States Military Assistance Group and of American loan funds.

One of Magsaysay's first actions when he became Secretary of National Defence was to carry through a reorganisation of the Philippine armed forces. The army was purged of incompetent and unreliable officers, including an army chief of staff. The system of promotion within the services was based upon accomplishments. The reorganised armed services replaced the constabulary as the main counter force. The constabulary was moved from the jurisdiction of the Department of the Interior and placed under the control of Magsaysay's own Department of Defence, its strength was reduced and many of its members transferred to regular units. The army was prepared for counterinsurgency operations by the establishment of 26 battalion combat teams, each consisting of over a thousand officers and men. In addition to the infantry, the battalion combat teams included medical, intelligence and psychological warfare units. Ranger teams were formed to give the counterinsurgency forces greater mobility, for these teams were trained to remain on patrol for a week in the jungle in pursuit of guerrillas. Local defence teams of civilian commandos led by regular army officers released troops for patrol and combat duties.

In an effort to improve the relations between the security forces and the populace, the army carried out programmes of economic reform and civic welfare. Economic reforms at the *barrio* level, results which could be seen by anyone, were given high priority to bear witness to the Government's concern for the humblest community. A special organisation, the Civil Affairs Office of the Secretary of National Defence, was established to co-ordinate these efforts. Civil Affairs Officers were assigned to each echelon of army command down to the battalion level. Their duty was to maintain liaison with military and civilian leaders in the *barrios* and consult with them to make on-the-spot plans for necessary improvements and amenities. A special unit of the army engineers constructed thousands of prefabricated schools to be set up by troops or civilians. The soldiers dug wells, built roads and repaired them, and escorted Department of Agriculture officials into rural areas to instruct the peasants in modern agricultural methods. An attempt was made to stop the unpopular practice of foraging by reorganising the supply of field rations to the troops. The Judge Advocate General's Corps made their legal services available to those peasants who could not pay for legal representation in the courts. A process of education was designed to remove the mutual antagonism between the soldier and the peasant; the soldiers were taught that their mission was to protect the peasant, that they were ambassadors of the Government as well as Huk killers, and the peasants were persuaded that the soldier was a friend. Magsaysay called this policy his Attraction Programme.

The Huk readily enlisted corrupt or apathetic officials in their movement. Indeed, a prime factor in the Huk acquisition of power in Luzon was the support given the insurgents by local officials. In central Luzon, the insurgents established their own administration, their own courts, civil officials and taxation system. In many instances, when Huk forces entered a *barrio* they had no need to replace the existing officials who could be bribed to carry out the insurgents' policies. Municipal authorities in 'liberated areas' were usually Huk sympathisers prepared to inform on government officials and military agents in the area. The counterinsurgency programme showed few signs of success until the Government was able to prevent local officials from helping the Huk. The steps taken to this end by the Government included the suspension of habeas corpus, so that the authorities could detain officials suspected of collaboration with the Huk, trials of officials who had abused their responsibilities, and a massive effort to enlist the support of the public in the campaign against unreliable officials. Magsaysay invited the people to report directly to him, or to his personal staff, any grievances against officials or military personnel. He arranged that telegrams for this purpose could be sent cheaply and made good his promise that each complaint would be acted upon within twenty-four hours and an investigation commenced in that time. This was such a useful device that Magsaysay retained it when he became president, setting up a special agency to deal with complaints.

A major challenge to the Government was to restore faith in the democratic process, not only to justify itself in power but also to justify its title to power. It was necessary to purify the electoral procedures and to demonstrate convincingly that they were purified. The 1949 elections which brought President Quirino to office were fraudulent: 'knowledge of fraud was sufficiently widespread, the protests of the losers were so loud and so persistent, and the propaganda by the Huk so effective, that the people of the Philippines were to some degree persuaded that the chief executive had stolen his office. And the chief executive himself believed that nothing he could say or do, nothing except his re-election, would convince the people of his right to hold office'.[1] The Huk coined the slogan 'Bullets not Ballots' in protest, and their argument that the Government

[1] Valeriano and Bohannan, op. cit., p. 99

had no title to power was effective in creating unrest in central Luzon. Thus the elections of 1951, and to a lesser extent the subsequent elections of 1953 (which brought Magsaysay to the presidency), were crucial points in the relations of the Government and the people.

To prevent the intimidation of voters and frauds at the polls, the Government, in 1951, employed teachers as poll clerks, officer cadets to guard the polling booths and soldiers to protect ballot boxes and polls from interference. These precautions may not in themselves have been sufficient to restore confidence in the integrity of the election, as the army was widely thought to have been a major source of the electoral corruptions of 1949. Further evidence was therefore needed to show that the army had not influenced the result in 1951. This evidence was provided by the guerrilla veterans of the struggle against Japan. The veterans organised a movement, the National Movement for Free Elections (NAMFREL), which inspired confidence and received support throughout the Philippines. The policy of NAMFREL was to act as an independent third force to ensure the honesty of the elections. As impartial poll watchers, the NAMFREL veterans guarded the guardians. The 1951 elections were free of government or military interference, and were seen to be free: most of those elected were opponents of the existing administration. The results convinced the people that the Government was indeed their government, responsive to their will by means of ballots instead of bullets. The Huk leader, Luis Taruc, thought that this electoral service by the security forces broke the back of the Huk rebellion.

Many of the activities of the Attraction Programme were measures to restore the faith of the masses in their government and to erode the mass base of the Huk movement. But one programme was particularly successful in carrying the counter-attack to the Huk. This was the work of the Economic Development Corps (EDCOR) which was initiated in 1950 and became perhaps the greatest civic effort of the security forces on the behalf of the Government. The corps had originally been approved by the Philippine Congress as a means to supply food for the armed forces, by providing farms for discharged and other soldiers. Magsaysay transformed it into a programme for the rehabilitation of Huk prisoners and their dependants, and for inducing other rebels to desert the movement. He regarded land hunger as one of the basic causes of Communism in the Philippines. The Huk campaign to exploit the land hunger of the masses used the slogan 'Land for the Landless' as an effective rallying device, since it reflected a genuine social grievance.

The resettlement programme sponsored by EDCOR was pragsaysay's reply to this Huk campaign, and he used it to Move to the insurgents that it was not necessary to fight for land. By the terms of the programme, each Huk who surrendered received about 15 acres of land, was transported with his family to the site, and given help to build houses and clear the land. Seeds, tools, rations and medical supplies were provided, and the settlers were expected to pay for these services when they had harvested their crops. The first two resettlement communities were established in Mindanao in 1951, when the Huk movement was reaching its height. Two more, in Mindanao and in northern Luzon, were subsequently constructed in 1953 and 1954, during the decline of the movement. Army units built roads and houses before the settlers arrived on the sites and subsequently helped the members of the new communities to build village centres, schools, chapels, dispensaries, sawmills, markets, sanitary and other facilities, and provided legal assistance in connection with land titles. By the end of 1958 the four communities included more than 5,000 settlers. EDCOR reported that by 1959 they were firmly established and becoming independent social units. The communities were economically viable, the settlers were able to start payments for their land, and were politically secure. There had been no evidence of organised dissidence amongst the former rebels.

In addition, EDCOR undertook two other major projects. The first was a Huk rehabilitation centre in army buildings outside Manila for those rebels who had rendered material assistance to the Government. There a vocational school was established and carpentry taught. The workshop produced furniture for army installations and the producers retained the profits. The other project was essentially an essay in psychological warfare. It was too expensive to be repeated in other areas where such assistance as it offered was equally desirable, but Magsaysay believed that the venture was more effective against the Huk than several battalions in the field. A *barrio* in the municipality of San Luis, Pampanga Province, the birthplace of the Huk commander Luis Taruc, was impoverished. The farmers did not own the land they farmed and cultivation had been impossible for some years because of the war. The *barrio* was an example on the small scale of the larger issues and revealed the kind of social deprivation which had been a source of strength of the Huk movement. The inhabitants were resettled on nearby public domain. A battalion of army engineers cleared the ground of the tough cogon grass whose roots defy the plough, drained it, built dykes and raised roads, and finally moved the *barrio* people's houses intact to the site. After a short period the farmers received title to the land.

To judge the results of the EDCOR projects the whole programme must be seen in a broad perspective. The resettlement measures as such did not significantly affect the economic reconstruction of the country after the wartime destruction, or its general social welfare. At the most, perhaps a thousand families were directly benefited and some few thousand more indirectly affected. The land, after all, was made available to those who had fought for it, to the Huk who surrendered in preference to the loyal or neutral peasants.[1] There was no real social engineering involved in this limited attack upon the basic causes of Communism in the Philippines. It was a palliative, not a cure. Nevertheless, the psychological results were profoundly important in the context of the revolt,[2] and the real value of the scheme was the way in which it asserted the good intentions of the Government. It created a new respect for the Government and the security forces and offered the Huk rebels a safe alternative to the hazards of guerrilla warfare. It demonstrated the importance of a good surrender policy in counterinsurgency operations.[3]

The grounds of the Huk protest, 'Bullets not Ballots', were removed by the political reforms and the demonstrably free elections of 1951 and 1953. Magsaysay's resettlement programmes, with all their limitations, made a successful attack upon the social conditions summed up in the slogan, 'Land for the Landless'. These measures by the Government broke the links between the insurgents and the people and relaxed the bonds between the insurgents themselves. The Government succeeded

[1] Thus tempting peasants to join the Huk in order to surrender and obtain land from the Government

[2] The authors of *Counter-Guerrilla Operations. The Philippine Experience* (p. 226) calculated that 'EDCOR could be credited with accomplishing the same effect as 30,000 soldiers'

[3] In Malaya, the British made good use of Surrendered Enemy Personnel who received salaries and took part in political and military operations against their former comrades. By January 1956 1,752 terrorists had surrendered, 1,173 had been captured and 5,933 killed

in offering a strong temptation to individuals to desert the Huk movement, and the security forces were able to obtain from defectors the military intelligence necessary to break the movement. By 1954, two years after the date set for the seizure of power, the Huk revolutionary movement had lost most of its effectiveness.

The lessons of Malaya, 1948–60

The Philippine experience demonstrated the need for counter-insurgency measures to isolate the guerrilla from the people and to strike at the base of his support. In Malaya, Communism has traditionally been largely a Chinese movement. During the Emergency, 1948–60, the civil strife developed along racial lines of division since approximately 95 per cent of the support-ers of terrorism were Chinese, and over 90 per cent of the Communist losses were also Chinese. The Malayan Communist Party, founded in 1930, was closely associated through its history with the Chinese in Malaya, who were second-class citizens,[1] and with China. Until 1939, it was an illegal or-ganisation with an appeal mainly to the Chinese community in Malaya and Singapore. The role of the Malayan Communist Party during the Second World War made it a national symbol of anti-Japanese resistance and broadened its appeal: Ch'en P'ing, a leading Malayan Chinese Communist, was granted the Order of the British Empire for his military services against the Japanese. With the help of the British, the Malayan Communists organised an effective People's Anti-Japanese Army, which was later called the Malayan Races Liberation Army in order to attract recruits from outside the Chinese community.

In 1944–45, the Malayan Communists were planning to use this armed force to seize power after Japan was defeated. The People's Army formed secret units which would remain hidden in the jungle while the formations known to the British authorities remained in the open. During the interregnum between the Japanese withdrawal and the British resumption of control, the Malayan Communists set up their own people's councils and took the opportunity to eliminate their potential rivals in the Dog Extermination Campaign. After the British authorities resumed control, the open units of the People's Army were demobilised (but kept in touch with the party

[1] One-sixth of the Chinese community had citizenship rights in mid-1949

through veterans' associations), while some 4,000 men of the secret formations retained their arms. Arms were also hidden for the day of the general uprising. The Malayan Communist Party adopted a programme of liberal reforms to disguise its Communist objectives and to broaden its support. The Communists employed united front tactics to gain control of the labour movement after the war; their leaders made plans to declare a Communist Republic of Malaya in August 1948. The central committee called for a mass struggle against British 'imperialism' in March 1948, and in the following May the Communists were ordered to go underground. During April and May of 1948, the Communists attempted to disrupt the economy by strikes and a terrorist campaign against the rubber plantations, mines, factories and people of Malaya. The British authorities declared a state of emergency in June 1948, and banned the party in July.

The main Communist forces in the revolt were the People's Army, which originally numbered about 4,000 and never rose above approximately 6,000 men, and a civilian support organisation, known as the *Min Yuen* or Popular Movement. The estimates of the strength of the *Min Yuen* vary from 10,000 to 100,000 active members. Most of the members of the *Min Yuen* were in the first place drawn from those Chinese who had squatted on the fringes of the jungles during the Japanese occupation to avoid Japanese reprisals and harsh measures against Malayan Chinese. Their duties were to provide the Communist fighting units with food and information, to supply couriers for the People's Army and the cells and to maintain contact with the masses. Many of the *Min Yuen* were volunteers, but numbers of them were forced to serve the Communists. A 'Blood and Steel' terrorist corps extorted funds and carried out special punitive tasks for the Malayan Communist Party. The Communist terrorists (as the Government called them, after experimenting with the term 'bandits') attempted to apply Mao Tse-tung's methods of mobilising the rural masses of China to the different conditions of jungle warfare in Malaya. In the first phase, the Communists planned to expand their own forces and to weaken the security forces. In the second phase, irregular warfare would develop into mobile warfare and the Communists planned to drive the security forces from the hinterland of Malaya and confine them to strategic centres. The Communists, in the third phase, would establish 'liberated' bases and from them extend their control over the remaining areas.

Despite the formidable strength at the disposal of the Malayan Communist Party, the revolution did not develop beyond the first phase of irregular warfare. The Communists failed to obtain mass support, to mobilise major striking forces for the phase of mobile warfare, or to secure their jungle retreats. The Chinese associations of the movement limited its appeal to a minority of the Malayan population while, on the other hand, a government programme of political reforms won support for the authorities through organisations like the Malaya Labour Party, the non-Communist Malayan Chinese Association, and the Independence of Malaya Party. A major security measure was the plan devised by Lieutenant General Sir Harold Briggs when he was Director of Operations and instituted in 1950, to resettle the Chinese squatters in villages controlled by the security forces. The plan effectively curtailed the operations of the *Min Yuen*, and forced the Communist terrorists to devote an increasing part of their energies simply to obtaining enough food to stay alive in the jungles. Food shortages caused the People's Army and the *Min Yuen* to reorganise into small groups, and eventually the Communist supply system broke down. The security forces arrayed against the Communist terrorists consisted of regular troops, regular police and special constables, as well as home guards to protect the villages. The British authorities employed 49,000 regular troops and had recruited 25,000 regular police and 50,000 special constables by 1953. A force of 250,000 home guards was raised. The security forces totalled more than 350,000 members and outnumbered the guerrillas and their active supporters by a ratio of more than twenty to one.

The Briggs Plan called for a unified command of the civil and military operations against the Communist terrorists. This object was achieved by the appointment of General Sir Gerald Templer both as High Commissioner (the first military man in that post) and as Director of Operations.[1] General Templer described the campaign to isolate the Communist terrorists from the people as 'securing the base'. The New Villages scheme is the most notable expedient of the campaign. Other measures to isolate the Communists were authorised by the Emergency Regulations of 1948, which provided for the

[1] Some planning techniques used in the Emergency were retained by the Malayan Government after independence. In Kuala Lumpur, the whole economic programme is run from a centre modelled upon Templer's operations room

preventative detention or rehabilitation in special centres of Communist suspects. Detained persons could be repatriated.

To fulfil the Briggs Plan, the Government resettled in New Villages a total of approximately 500,000 Chinese squatters, cr more than 10 per cent of the population of the Federation of Malaya. The New Villages effectively separated the Communist terrorists from their planned sources of supplies and intelligence, by keeping out the *Min Yuen* agents and restraining potential Communist supporters within their bounds, but Communist activities within the settlements did not automatically cease. Strict security measures were instituted in the villages, food was carefully rationed to limit any exportable surplus, and the home guard patrolled the perimeters. Within the New Villages the Government implemented an assistance programme with particular concern for the health and educational needs of the inhabitants, agricultural developments and public works.

Four-fifths of Malaya's total of 50,690 square miles of territory consists of swamps and jungles. The jungle areas of Malaya were an important factor in the strategy of the Malayan Communist Party. Their purpose was to provide the Communist terrorists, during the first phase of the revolution, with safe sanctuaries, analogous to the secure rural retreats of the Communist Army in China. And when the implementation of the Briggs Plan deprived the Communist terrorists of access to supplies from the *Min Yuen* they attempted to grow their own food in jungle clearings which were visible from the air. Deep jungle penetration by the security forces, air reconnaissance and the tactical use of helicopters to increase mobility, all enabled the security forces to deny the Communists their sanctuaries in the jungle, and contributed to the breakup of the Communist regiments into smaller mobile units. These security forces were able to set up their own supply depots in the jungles. Another possible sanctuary for the Communist terrorists lay across the Malayan border, in Thailand. The Communists possibly received arms from China by this route. The security forces were able to curtail the movement of supplies to the Communist terrorists by sea. By controlling both the sea and land borders of Malaya, the security forces made it difficult for outside help to reach the Malayan terrorists. An agreement made in 1949, between the Malayan authorities and the Government of Thailand, permitted the Malayan security forces to pursue Communist terrorists for ten miles inside

Thailand. Both the jungle and the border sanctuaries of the Communist terrorists ceased to be safe. Only a few guerrillas remained in the field by the end of 1958. Since the end of the Emergency, a remnant of the terrorist force continues to maintain itself in the jungles of the border area.

The Communist uprising began with a deliberate campaign of indiscriminate terror, to demonstrate that the party was strong enough to strike when and where it chose, and to attract support by fear when necessary. By October 1951, however, the disadvantages of this policy decided the central committee to adopt more selective forms of terrorism. The Communist lines of communication were so broken at this time that in a number of instances months elapsed before the directive reached particular destinations, and it was increasingly difficult to co-ordinate policy. The *Min Yuen* leaders found that the terror tactics adversely affected their work amongst the masses, and they feared that if indiscriminate terror was allowed to continue it would drive the people into the arms of the Government. Indiscriminate terror attacks upon the centres of rural production in Malaya deprived workers of all races of their livelihood, and damaged the image of the Communists as the champions of the people. At the peak of the revolution, in 1951, the High Commissioner was assassinated. He was replaced in office by General Templer who announced the British Government's policy that Malaya would be a self-governing nation. The central committee's decision to step up its terror campaign in 1952 alienated the Malayan people at a stage in the revolution when the Communists needed at least their sympathy in order to exist as a revolutionary force. Indiscriminate terror weakened the claim of the Communists to champion the interests of the Malayan peoples. As guerrilla warfare failed to achieve the Communist objectives, the Malayan Communist Party turned once more to the indiscriminate use of terror, despite the lessons of 1951; it became 'a prisoner of terrorism'.[1]

In the course of its efforts to influence directly the political behaviour of the people, the party became isolated from the main political developments within Malaya, a factor of considerable importance in the Emergency. In order to build a mass base, the party had to develop a political programme for Malaya that would attract Malays and Indians, as well as

[1] Lucian W. Pye, *Guerrilla Communism in Malaya. Its Social and Political Meaning*, Princeton University Press, 1956, p. 106

Chinese. It needed to show that it was not just an Overseas Chinese movement. This task was complicated by the rivalry between Malay and Chinese nationalisms, and by the party's desire to follow scrupulously the developments of the international Communist line of policy. For example, following the Soviet-German Non-Aggression Pact, the party had decided to adopt an anti-war policy in 1939. In February 1940, it set up an Anti-Imperialist National Front, which was designed to appeal to anti-British sentiment amongst the Indian and Malay communities, to sabotage the British war effort by hampering Malaya's contribution, and to support the Chinese struggle against Japan. The party's Ten Point Interim Programme of 1940 demanded the removal of British 'imperialism' from Malaya and a Malayan Democratic Republic. The Chinese Communist Party intervened in September 1940, and instructed the Malayan Communist Party to stop opposing the British war-effort: this is apparently the first clear instance of the Chinese Communist Party assuming the role of the Comintern in Southeast Asia. The German attack upon the Soviet Union in June 1941, made it respectable for Communists to support the struggle, thus resolving any confusions within the Malayan Communist Party between the Russian and Chinese lines.

The main political objectives of the 1940 programme appear again in the Malayan Communist Party's Nine Point Anti-Japanese Programme of February 1943. The party reaffirmed its 1943 programme when Japan surrendered in August 1945, though there were disagreements within the party whether to achieve its political objectives by a guerrilla struggle against the British or by resuming the pre-war efforts to build a mass base. The mass base policy was chosen as the more orthodox Communist line at the time, and the Malayan Communist Party lost the opportunity to seize power in 1945. The party's Six Demands to the British, issued in September 1945, demanded immediate self-government for Malaya pending the grant of independence. The United Kingdom rejected this demand but tacitly allowed the Malayan Communist Party to operate, for the first time, as a legal political body.

The British Government favoured the development of a Union of Malaya and a Crown Colony of Singapore, which was to be kept separate from Malaya because it was predominantly Chinese, with constitutional arrangements which would grant Malayan citizenship to most Malayan Chinese. The Malay reaction to this proposal revealed the extent of their fears of Chinese influence; and, shortly after the British proposal was made known in 1946, a United Malay National Association was formed. The Association opposed the union plan and supported a federation scheme which would limit Chinese citizenship. The reaction of the Malayan Communist Party was to issue in May 1946, a programme for a Malayan Democratic United Front, and to demand national self-determination for Malaya and a constitution granting electoral rights without racial or other forms of discrimination: provisions designed to attract all the Malayan communities. The party set out to build up a mass base, particularly in the trade union movement, to enable it to dominate a united front organisation and achieve a Malayan Democratic Republic by a policy of peaceful struggle. But a new and aggressive line for international Communism was laid down by Zhdanov at the first meeting of the Cominform, in September 1947 and the implications of the policy for the Communist parties of Southeast Asia were probably made known to the Malayan Communist Party early in 1948, at Communist congresses in London and Calcutta. In May 1948 the Malayan Communist Party rejected the policy of peaceful struggle as right-wing opportunism, and proclaimed a militant policy of mass struggle against the British.

The elements of the Malayan Communists' political programmes which were most likely to appeal to the various Malayan nationalisms, Chinese, Indian and Malay, were those relating to the political evolution of Malaya towards independence. The Communist themes of British 'imperialism' and 'colonialism' lost their effectiveness when it was clear that the United Kingdom was prepared to grant independence to Malaya, after solutions to the communal problems were found. To Malays, the Communist rebellion represented the height of the communal problem, and they regarded the United Kingdom as the defender of their interests against a Chinese armed threat. The Communist revolution in China had the effect of making Malay nationalists aware of the need for compromise with the Chinese and Indian communities, in the interests of Malaya's future as an independent state. Malayan thinking about the communal problem began to crystallise proposals to which the United Kingdom could respond. The 1947 proposals for a Federation of Malaya, which would include Singapore, made provision for Malayan citizenship for all those born in the Federation and for aliens who were prepared to swear their loyalty to the country. The United Kingdom implemented Federation of Malaya proposals in February 1948, though Singapore remained a Crown Colony. Thus, before the Emergency was declared, some principles of the Malayan Communist Party's political struggle had been conceded.

The Malays themselves took steps towards an acceptable solution of the communal problem, which had important results for Malaya's political future. The United Malay National Association and the Malayan Chinese Association made an alliance at the end of 1951. The Alliance formed a committee to deal with communal questions. Malaya held her first election in 1955. For the 1955 elections, the Alliance joined with the Malayan Indian Congress and gained all the elected seats but one in the Legislative Council. Malayan nationalism had come of age and was preparing to secure its political future. Probably because it understood the significance of these developments, and also because it was out of step with the Communist policy of peaceful co-existence, the Malayan Communist Party issued a communiqué in December 1955, which made substantial concessions to Malay nationalism. Point Five of the communiqué recommended that Chinese, Indian and other nationalisms, should unite around Malay nationalism, suggesting in fact exactly what the Alliance was accomplishing and was better able to accomplish than the party itself. Although the party continued fighting after August 1957, when the federation became independent, on the grounds that Malaya's independence was incomplete, the Communists announced that they were willing to renounce armed struggle and take part in the normal constitutional processes. Their leaders sought peace after independence, while the rank and file of the party deserted in large numbers. The Alliance Party, under Tunku Abdul Rahman, became the Government of the new state of Malaya. The elections of 1959, which gave the Alliance Party 74 of the 104 seats in the lower house of Parliament, confirmed its authority. The elections of 1964 were a test of popular acceptance of the new Federation of Malaysia, and the Alliance Party won 80 of the 104 seats in Parliament.

Regarded in its broad historical setting, the Communist revolution which began in Malaya in 1948 was an interruption in the political evolution towards independence of a country under British rule. But, in one respect, the Communist revolu-

INTERNAL DEFENCE 183

tion accelerated the evolutionary process by stimulating the growth of a responsible and politically organised Malay nationalism in the brief span of a decade. At the end of the Second World War, the Malayan Communist Party was the only political organisation in Malaya which demanded self-government; ten years later, the Alliance Party won the first Malayan election by an overwhelming majority. This is the real revolution in Malayan politics since 1945. The United Kingdom was able to work with the Malayan revolution until, in the end, it was the Communists who were isolated from the main streams of Malayan political development. This ensured the political defeat of the Malayan Communist Party and contributed towards its military defeat. The guerrillas' reliance upon bases in the jungles meant that their logistical support must come from civilian sources. The guerrilla sanctuary of the jungle and border areas was invaded by the security forces who prevented outside help reaching the Malayan Communist Party. The resettlement programme enabled the security forces to control the Chinese squatters and break the links between the guerrillas and their civilian support group. The *Min Yuen* could not carry out its essential tasks of winning over the people and supporting the guerrillas, as the New Villages contained its supporters and the Communist terrorist campaign stultified its efforts. The Malayan Communist Party set out to strengthen its influence by fear, but its indiscriminate terrorism caused a general aversion to the party and its methods. The secretary of the party's special committee for Malacca was executed in 1951 for the heretical view that the Communist armed revolt should cease until a mass base was created. Yet, when the central committee directed that the terror tactics be more discriminating, it was found that less terror meant fewer supplies. By the time that the Malayan Communist Party ordered an increase in the armed attacks upon those it called traitors, the United Kingdom had announced her policy of self-government for Malaya, and the United Malay National Association had entered into an alliance with the Malayan Chinese Association, laying the foundations for the future government of independent Malaya.

The Problems of Viet Nam

The guerrilla wars in the Philippines and Malaya are the two classic examples of successful operations against Communist insurgents in Southern Asia since the Second World War. In neither case did the guerrillas receive substantial assistance from outside the country: they were forced to rely upon local resources. The Philippine experience and the lessons of Malaya show how the guerrillas were prevented from drawing their strength from the people, with crucial results, since, as Mao Tse-tung explained, the guerrilla fishes must flourish in the sea of the people. Both governments won positive popular support in their campaigns to isolate the guerrillas. The normal processes of government were retained during the emergencies and in both examples elections were held which rallied national political forces against the guerrillas. Reform movements were set in motion as part of the politico-military offensives against them. The same cannot be said of South Viet Nam.

The problems of Viet Nam are on a much greater scale. In comparison with the 12,000 Huk guerrillas in the Philippines, and the 6,000 Communist terrorists in Malaya, there were an estimated 35,000 Viet Cong guerrillas in South Viet Nam in 1964, strengthened by an irregular force of between 60,000 and 80,000 men. A ratio between the security forces and the guerrillas of twenty to one (roughly the proportion in the Philippines and Malaya) is thought necessary if the security forces are to defeat the guerrillas in the field. In South Viet Nam the ratio of approximately fourteen to one should enable the security forces to break even. Some four-fifths of the terrain in South Viet Nam consists of jungle, bush and swamp areas where the Viet Cong have set up bases and a 'government' of National Liberation. A considerable part of the rural areas has passed under direct or indirect Viet Cong control, where the guerrillas establish their own local administration and recruit their forces. Supplies of men and materials reach them from North Viet Nam by a land route through Laos and by sea; they find safe sanctuaries in Laos and in Cambodia, where they are believed to have training camps and re-groupment centres beyond the reach of the security forces and beyond the power of the Cambodian Government to suppress. The Viet Cong 'Government' has entered into a quasi-diplomatic relationship with the Government of Cambodia, and has close contacts with the Pathet Lao and with Hanoi. The Viet Cong guerrillas are militarily powerful enough to challenge the security forces in battalion-size actions and to attack successfully the settlements established by the Government to isolate them from the people.

In the ten years since the Diem Government was established

in 1954, with American backing, the governments of South
Viet Nam have not developed a strong political foundation
for their campaign against the Viet Cong. General Nguyen
Khanh admitted as much in March 1964. The Government
itself has been divided. Unsuccessful revolts against President
Diem by armed sects in 1955 and by paratroops in November
1960, were followed in November 1963 by a successful coup
which installed General Duong Van Minh as chief of state. A
Military Revolutionary Council was established. General
Khanh ousted General Minh in January 1964. After an up-
heaval in the Military Revolutionary Council in August 1964
General Khanh resigned the presidency, and the leadership
of South Viet Nam devolved upon Generals Khanh, Minh and
Tran Thien Khiem, a key figure in the January revolt. The
three-man military junta was set up to avoid a religious war.
There were reports that a dissident movement had been started
in Central Viet Nam. In November 1964 a civilian, Tran Van
Huong, was installed as premier; Catholic and Buddhist
leaders promptly criticised his efforts to keep religion out of
politics, and student leaders threatened action to force his
dismissal. Later in the month, after the Buddhists had demanded
the dismissal of his government, Mr. Tran Van Huong imposed martial law and declared a state of seige in the capital.

The first Indochina War, 1946–54, was a nationalist struggle
against France, under the leadership of the League for Independence of Viet Nam, the Viet Minh. Founded in 1941, after
the frustration of the Indochinese Communist Party's uprising
against the French which had been planned for the previous
year, the Viet Minh represented various nationalist organisations; but it was dominated from the outset by the Indochinese
Communist Party. By skilful united front tactics, the party
retained its central position in the nationalist movements in
Viet Nam, even when it abolished itself in 1945, in the interests
of national unity. It was represented in the Vietnamese Provisional Government set up in March 1944 to win independence
with Kuomintang support, in the Vietnamese People's Liberation Committee established by Ho Chi Minh in August 1945,
and in the body which replaced it, the Provisional Government
of the Democratic Republic of Viet Nam set up in Hanoi
with Ho Chi Minh as President. The Emperor Bao Dai, who
was ordered by the Japanese to form a Vietnamese government,
abdicated and transferred his authority to the Hanoi Provisional
Government, thus giving it some legal grounds for claiming

to inherit the authority of the Vietnamese Empire. In September 1945 the Provisional Government issued a declaration of independence.

The Viet Minh in turn controlled the National Assembly which met in March 1946 to establish a government of National Union and Resistance. In May 1946 the Hanoi Government formed the United National Front which absorbed the Vietnamese Nationalist Party and other groups. With the National Assembly security in Communist hands in November 1946, a new government was formed with members of the Viet Minh in charge of the important ministries (Foreign Affairs, Defence, Internal Affairs, Finance, Justice, Economics, Education and Agriculture), and a constitution for the Democratic Republic of Viet Nam was adopted. In 1945, France affirmed her intention to reassert her sovereignty in Indochina through an Indochinese Federation within the French Union. By an agreement with the Government of National Union in 1946 France recognised the Republic of Viet Nam as a free state within the Indochinese Federation and the French Union. But the Republic's position in the Federation remained to be settled, and, in an atmosphere of increasing tension, the French authorities sought to limit the Republic of Viet Nam to a minor role. After the French attacked Haiphong in November 1946, the Vietnamese Government withdrew from Hanoi and in the caves of Tongking prepared for guerrilla war.[1]

In the course of the first Indochina War, there were several developments in the Vietnamese Communist Organisation which had a bearing upon the later sequence of events. Before it technically dissolved itself in 1945, the Indochinese Communist Party had looked to the Russian and the French Communist Parties for guidance. This had been a source of tension on the eve of the first Indochina War, before the Cominform had announced the Russian hard line in 1947, and when the French Communist Party advised the Indochinese Communist Party to refrain from overt hostilities against the French authorities until Moscow's permission was obtained. The Indochinese Communist Party re-established itself in 1951 as the Vietnamese Workers' Party (Viet Nam Dang Lao

[1] The Viet Minh organisation for war is described in George K. Tanham, *Communist Revolutionary Warfare. The Vietminh in Indochina*, Frederick A. Praeger, 1961. The war is described from the Viet Minh viewpoint in General Vo Nguyen Giap, *People's War, People's Army*, Foreign Languages Publishing House, Hanoi, 1961

Dong), or Lao Dong. In its new manifestation, the Indo-chinese Communist Party deliberately based itself upon the Chinese Communist Party and turned to China for inspiration.

During the war, the Viet Minh extended its revolutionary influence into neighbouring Cambodia and Laos through the local nationalist movements. The Viet Minh made provisions to aid the Cambodian resistance movement, Khmer Issarak (Free Cambodia), and in 1949 set up a Committee for a Revolutionary Khmer People's party. The founder of the Khmer Issarak movement joined the Viet Minh. The Viet Minh also supported the nationalist movement in Laos led by Prince Souphanouvong, who was made leader of the Free Laotian Government (Pathet Lao) established by the Viet Minh in 1953, in the province of Sam Neua in east Laos. The Viet Minh began to co-ordinate the revolutionary nationalist movements throughout Indochina. A secret order of the Lao Dong in November 1951, stated that 'The Vietnamese Party retains a permanent right of supervision over the activities of the fraternal Cambodian and Laotian Parties', and added that 'Later, when conditions permit, the three Revolutionary Parties of Vietnam, Cambodia, and Laos will unite to form a single Party'. The Viet Minh continued to develop united front tactics during and after the first Indochina war. In 1951 the movement combined into a broad front (Lien Viet) to wage the war more efficiently. The Lien Viet became an even wider Fatherland Front in 1955, with a programme for the unification of Viet Nam, with a single National Assembly and a unified army, but with limited rights of self-government in the north and the south zones to take account of local conditions.

The Geneva Conference of 1954 brought the first Indochina War to a close. The Conference did not effect a political settle-ment of Viet Nam—its prime purpose was to end the hostilities —but it attempted to establish the conditions for one. The Conference did not assume that the 1954 cease-fire division, between the Democratic Republic of Viet Nam and the State of Viet Nam, would necessarily be permanent. The Final Declaration stated that the military demarcation line should not be interpreted in any way as constituting a political or terri-torial boundary. The line was merely an expedient, until such time as the Vietnamese people decided their own political future; and the Conference set a limit on the time for that decision. The national will of the Vietnamese people was to be expressed in 'free general elections by secret ballot', to be held in July 1956, after an interval for consultations between North and South Viet Nam.

Representatives of the two countries, who participated in the Geneva Conference, but did not sign the Final Declaration, also accepted the principle that the Vietnamese people should determine their own political destiny through free elections. The United States declared for free Vietnamese elections under United Nations supervision, to ensure that they were properly conducted, and associated herself with the South Vietnamese protest that the Geneva arrangements for Viet Nam's political future were inadequate. The South Vietnamese delegation considered that the agreement gravely compromised the political future of Viet Nam. They protested against the 'summary rejection' of their proposals for achieving an armistice without dividing the territory of Viet Nam, and for provisional United Nations control over the whole of Viet Nam pending free elections. They protested, as well, that the Geneva agreement 'abandons to the Vietminh territories, many of which are still in the possession of Vietnamese troops and thus essential to the defense of Viet Nam in opposing a larger expansion of Communism and virtually deprives Viet Nam of the imprescriptible right to organise its defense otherwise than by the maintenance of a foreign army on its territory'.

The Indochinese Communist Party emerged from the first Indochina War as an efficient military and political organisation whose influence was felt in Cambodia, Laos and the South. Thirteen years after the Vietnamese refugees in China founded the Viet Minh, the party was the most powerful engine of Vietnamese nationalism, with a battle-hardened People's Army and the great prestige of its guerrilla victory over the French Union forces. In the next phase of its activities, it followed the Communist line of peaceful co-existence in its relations with the state of Viet Nam. To prepare for the 1956 elections, which it had reason to believe would unify Viet Nam under Communist control, the party employed the Fatherland Front to attract support in the South, where French influence remained strong. It set out to capture the remaining forces of Vietnamese nationalism in the divided South from the rival government which had been established there under American protection: 'the U.S.–Diem clique'.

The Government of South Viet Nam, which had been formed during the Geneva Conference, appeared to have no secure foundations. The premier, Ngo Dinh Diem, lacked an organised following. The Binh Xuyen syndicate and the Cao Dai and Hoa Hao sects, with their private armies, threatened the security of the state, and issued the Government with an ultimatum in February 1955. The members of the Viet Minh who remained in the south after the armistice constituted an underground movement (Viet Cong) at the disposal of the Indochinese Communist Party. The political and economic structure of the state of Viet Nam was built with American support, and in the process the United States replaced France as the foreign protective power. Before 1954, the United States was an active supporter of the French military effort in Indochina; but after that date her policy was to remove French influence. France still controlled the army and the administration of the state of Viet Nam, and had considerable interests in the economy after 1954. Considering the French presence to be a political liability, the United States supported Diem's independence in order to form a new basis for policy. American aid was withdrawn from the French forces in South Viet Nam and granted directly to the government of the Republic of Viet Nam. France, whose responsibility it was to implement the Geneva agreement in South Viet Nam, withdrew her military presence from the country by 1956, under American and South Vietnamese pressure.

Diem refused to entertain North Vietnamese proposals for consultations about the elections in July 1956, prescribed by the Geneva Agreement, and, with American backing, maintained his opposition despite North Vietnamese complaints and British and Russian advice to comply with the agreement. In October 1955, after a referendum to decide the issue, South Viet Nam was proclaimed an independent republic with executive power vested in an elected president. Ngo Dinh Diem became the first president. His supporters gained five-sixths of the seats in the National Assembly in the elections of March 1956. (There were no opposition candidates; those who attempted to run were disqualified.) The constitution promulgated by this body in October 1956 defined South Viet Nam as an anti-Communist state. A basic provision of the constitution stated: 'All activities having as their object the direct or indirect propagation or establishment of Communism in whatever form shall be contrary to the principles embodied in the present Constitution.'

Ho Chi Minh announced in July 1956 that his government's policy was to seek normal relations between the two republics, to develop contacts in various fields and to consult with the

Government of South Viet Nam on the question of unification but in the same month the Government of South Viet Nam embarked upon a policy to eradicate dissidents. As the campaign against political dissidents mounted in the south, the Indo-chinese Communist Party changed its tactics. It called in May 1959 for appropriate measures to unify Viet Nam, and shortly afterwards accepted responsibility for the liberation of South Viet Nam. The Third Party Congress, in 1960, directed the Viet Cong to establish a national united front against the Diem Government and its American supporters. A National Liberation Front of South Viet Nam was set up in Cochin China in December 1960 to 'overthrow the camouflaged colon-ial régime of the American imperialists and the dictatorial power of Ngo Dinh Diem, servant of the Americans, and institute a government of national democratic union', and with the probable objective of gaining acceptance for a Laos-type solution in South Viet Nam.[1] The National Liberation Front remains the major Communist organisation for political warfare in South Viet Nam, although a Viet Nam People's Revolutionary Party was established in June 1962 for tactical purposes. By 1964 the National Liberation Front had estab-lished a kind of international position. With European head-quarters in Prague, the National Liberation Front maintained missions bidding for support in Algiers, Cuba, Indonesia and East Berlin (but not in Moscow). The front has received friendly replies to messages sent to Prince Sihanouk of Cambodia, implying a measure of recognition.

Viet Cong attacks upon the political authority of the Govern-ment of South Viet Nam increased after the establishment of the National Liberation Front. The political tactics whereby the Viet Cong seeks to erode the Government's authority in the provinces and at the village level, and establish a Communist administration in its stead, have already been described. In 1957 the Viet Cong directed an offensive against the local officials and village notables who form an essential connection between the Government in Saigon and the people. (A similar campaign against schoolteachers was launched in 1959, and government social and medical workers have been selected targets.) Over 2,000 civil officials were killed by the Viet Cong in 1959–60. Four thousand officials were killed in the period from May 1960 to May 1961, a rate of nearly ten a day. The

[1] Philippe Devillers, 'The Struggle for the Unification of Viet-nam,' *The China Quarterly*, No. 9, January–March 1962, p. 18 ff

result of these Viet Cong activities was to create situations in many provinces where the government authorities rather than the Viet Cong cadres were intruders. This was the position in Kien Phong Province in Cochin China by October 1961, the date of the Viet Cong Report on XB village. By 1961, too, Communist activities in the *montagnard* areas in the strategic plateau of Annam seriously challenged the Government's position; the pressure of Viet Cong control is the reason advanced for the great exodus of 125,000 mountain peoples into the lowlands during 1962. Areas of heavy Viet Cong penetration spread in an arc round Saigon itself late in 1961. The 1962 Viet Cong Report on the Revolutionary Movement in the South claimed that from one-half to three-quarters of the rural areas of South Viet Nam were either liberated or relieved from enemy pressures. According to the Report, the Viet Cong objective 'for the near future is to set up a system of well-organised large, medium, and small bases, all connected, economically, politically and military strong enough to be capable of defense as well as attack; to enable the armed forces to move and to operate from one area to another; and to facilitate the use of communications and transport corridors from one area to another, from mountain and forest areas to the delta'. This, as it turned out, was also the Government's plan.

The response of the Government of South Viet Nam to the Viet Cong challenge to its authority was slow to develop, but grandiose in its conception. The programme, called 'Operation Sunrise', was inaugurated in March 1962 in Binh Duong Province north of Saigon. 'Operation Sunrise'[1] was a campaign to resettle the South Vietnamese people in strategic hamlets where they could be protected from the Viet Cong. A British advisory mission, led by the former Secretary for Defence in Malaya, Mr. R. K. G. Thompson, was instrumental in working out the basic plan. The political role of the strategic hamlets programme was to increase the participation of the Vietnamese people in grass-roots politics, to build democratic habits from below within the framework of the authoritarian state of Viet Nam. As a social experiment, the strategic hamlets were designed to create a new hamlet leadership; to replace

[1] The Vietnamese have a flair for code names. A campaign by government troops to clear the Viet Cong out of their redoubt in the Camau Peninsula was called 'Operation Waves of Love'. It failed

the thousands of murdered officials and to break away from the
conservative system of village elders and develop younger, more
vigorous leaders loyal to the Government.

The strategic hamlets also had a military function. The pilot
hamlet of Bên Tuong near the town of Bên Cat in Binh Duong
Province was selected because the area was a key part of the
guerrilla-infested belt north of Saigon. By means of a network
of strategic hamlets, the Government of South Viet Nam
planned to break through the arc of insurgency around Saigon
and gradually to extend and fortify the areas cleared of guerrillas throughout the country into a vast defensive and offensive
system. The general purpose of the strategic hamlets programme
was deduced very accurately by the Viet Cong. The 1962
Report on the Revolutionary Movement in the South noted
that 'in order to isolate the revolutionary forces from the people
they [the Governments of South Viet Nam and the United
States] hurriedly set up a system of centres to regroup rural
and urban people, under the slogan of "strategic hamlets",
with the purpose of controlling the people, contending with
us for manpower and economic resources, re-occupying rural
areas to isolate us from the people, and concentrating forces
to destroy us. They are intensifying the people's activities
against the revolution. This plan is the combination of experiences in counter-revolutionary activities against the people,
acquired inside and outside the country . . .' It was as important
for the Viet Cong to destroy this programme as for the Government to sustain it. The strategic hamlets therefore became a
focus of the military and political efforts of both antagonists
to control the people of South Viet Nam.

The strategic hamlets programme involved a task of social
engineering far greater than the resettlement programmes in
the Philippines and Malaya. The responsibility developed upon
a powerful special agency, the Inter-Ministerial Committee on
Strategic Hamlets, which was supervised by Diem's brother,
Ngo Dinh Nhu, and included the Chief of the General Staff of
the Armed Forces, and the Secretaries of Defence, Rural
Affairs, Civic Action and Education. The programme moved
apace. In October 1962 Diem announced to the National
Assembly that more than 7 million people had been transferred to 3,074 completed and 2,679 about to be completed
strategic hamlets. The Government planned to finish 600
strategic hamlets each month; and it estimated that more than
9 million people (some two-thirds of the population of South

Viet Nam) would be settled in strategic hamlets by the end of 1962. By the end of 1963, the Government expected to have housed the entire rural population in 12,000 strategic hamlets, while strategic boroughs protected the urban areas. Within a year of its inception, the programme fell behind schedule. In April 1963 less than 6,000 strategic hamlets were built, containing 8,150,187 inhabitants, or more than a million people less than the 1962 target.

Despite government censorship and official rebuttals of criticism, it was clear that during the last year of President Diem's rule the strategic hamlets programme was a spectacular failure. It was badly planned and executed, over-extended, and the guerrillas were not, as in Malaya, being kept from the people behind the stockades. Strategic hamlets were infiltrated by the Viet Cong and betrayed from within. Too frequently, the Government forces did not respond to appeals for help from hamlets under attack, or else help came too late. The prototype strategic hamlet of Bên Tuong was overrun by the Viet Cong in August 1963. Captured strategic hamlets were absorbed into the Viet Cong network of offensive and defensive bases. After Diem's assassination in November 1963 the extent of the difficulties of the programme became clearer, though not all the blame was attributable to his government, since the Viet Cong took the opportunity of the successive coups to step up their campaign against the strategic hamlets. In March 1964 the premier, General Nguyen Khanh, announced that the political economic and social situation in the countryside offered no promising prospect for South Viet Nam. Almost half of the existing 8,000 strategic hamlets were abandoned by their defence units and many were subverted by the Viet Cong.

General Khanh set out to reorganise the strategic hamlets programme, giving high priority to strengthening the hamlet militias, the civil guards and the para-military forces in his 'pacification plan'. Inheriting (as it claimed) the corruption and inefficiency of the Diem régime, the Khanh Government had difficulty in finding efficient civil servants. Early in 1964 General Khanh inaugurated training schemes to provide civil administrators at the district and hamlet levels. Officers were given special training for administrative duties in the districts and hamlets, and special formations were recruited for military and political work in the villages. The pacification plan began in March 1964, in Quang Tri Province on the border with North Viet Nam, and was designed to clear and hold the villages of the province by the following May. Under the guidance of a provincial chief who was imprisoned for six years by the Diem Government, fourteen pacification teams of between 50 and 60 men set out to spend several days in each village. Each team consisted of 30 or so self-defence instructors, whose duty was by day to teach the villagers how to defend themselves and by night to protect the villages, a dozen cadres of the strategic hamlet programme, and civil officials from the Departments of Agriculture, Education and Health, concerned with village development. General Khanh described the main difference between this plan and 'Operation Sunrise' as the extra emphasis which his Government placed on obtaining good will as well as on providing security in the hamlets. The new strategy was to clear areas and to hold them, step by step, province by province, avoiding an over-extension of available resources and always guarding the rear: thus it was intended to avoid the mistakes of the Diem Government. General Khanh claimed that his government had 'the force to clear but we cannot hold. By hold I mean not the military or the terrain but I mean hold the population. The objective is the population.'[1]

The South Vietnamese Governments' political steps to reach that objective have been few, and limited to palliative measures. There has been nothing comparable, in effect, to the Attraction Programme in the Philippines or the development of vigorous local political forces working with the Government in Malaya. Diem's 'Open Arms' programme, suggestive of Magsaysay's policy of 'All-Out Friendship or All-Out Force', was not launched until April 1963, in the seventh year of the struggle with the Viet Cong. The elections conducted in the years of Diem rule were marked by overt government interference, and displayed those very symptoms which the Philippine Government set out to eradicate. Political forces developed in South Viet Nam which had no part in the processes of government. Growing Buddhist opposition to the Diem Government led to bloody repressive measures. Since November 1963 there has been Caesarism without a Caesar. The shifts of power within the military juntas, which replaced the Diem Government, reflect intramural conflicts rather than national movements, though they are affected by external pressures: in August 1964 Minh was restored to power reportedly to placate the Buddhists, and Khanh maintained in power to conciliate the United States.

[1] *Christian Science Monitor*, 25 March 1964

The successive governments have not succeeded in creating amongst the South Vietnamese people a widespread feeling of sharing in the purposes of the Government, whereas a special object of the Viet Cong movement is to inculcate a sense of participation in the revolution. The one government attempt to provide an ideology or national formula for South Viet Nam, President Diem's 'Personalism' (Nhan-Vi), was aptly described as a mixture of papal encyclicals and kindergarten economics.[1] Since then, the Government's objectives have been defined as to defeat Communism finally, to unify the country and build democracy and freedom. According to General Khanh, a drive to the north would fulfil South Viet Nam's destiny; but it would not solve her problems. In 1954, South Viet Nam's objective was to remain separate from North Viet Nam; on the tenth anniversary of the Geneva Agreement, in 1964, General Khanh, speaking of the national shame caused by the *loss* of the north, claimed that Buddhists, Catholics, Nationalist leaders, students and refugees, all advocated a drive north to re-unite the country. It is doubtful if the various groups agree on this, and they agree on little else. Ten years after the establishment of a separate state of South Viet Nam, the narrowed political life of the country is marked by war-weariness, factionalism, fatigue and cynicism. There is a noticeable disposition on the part of the politicians and officials to cast off their identifications with the Saigon Government, for fear of reprisals when the Communists gain power. Where are the forces of cohesion necessary to build a firm political foundation? Neither the deeply-divided religious factions, nor the disunited and ineffectual political groups, appear to provide an answer; and the Viet Minh seems to have pre-empted the active forces of Vietnamese nationalism.

*   *   *

The experience of the Filipino and British operations against insurgents suggests certain lessons which have not been properly learned in South Viet Nam. For example, the Government must have a clear aim, and it must function in accordance with the law, or cease to be a government. Nhan-Vi and a drive to the north do not constitute a useful formula to rally the Vietnamese peasants: the former does not have the virtue of simplicity which the Communists recognise to be essential, and the latter is not

[1] There is a more extensive description by John C. Donnell in *Problems of Freedom, South Vietnam Since Independence*, Chapter 3

'made to fit the feelings of the people' like Viet Cong propaganda. The Government's disregard for the normal processes of the law has bred a lawlessness in the streets which threatens to destroy its authority. There must be effective co-ordination between the different arms of the Government, as in Malaya, but in South Viet Nam, for example, there are ten different intelligence services. The Government must secure its bases and not worry too much about the peripheries; but the strategic hamlets were over-extended and the Viet Cong use the villages to surround the towns, on the Chinese model. It is essential to get the population on the side of the Government. This was accomplished in the Philippines and Malaya by certain economic and political reforms which have not, or cannot, be applied in South Viet Nam, where the Viet Cong control some 5 million people, or about one-third of the population. With American support, South Viet Nam has built up large armed forces consisting of more than 3 per cent of the population. The army has more regular troops than Indonesia, but its activities have emphasised the inadequacies of technological aids like helicopters in counterinsurgency operations against a People's Army.

The American involvement in South Viet Nam has steadily grown during the last decade, but American officials and military personnel are hampered by lack of knowledge of the French and Vietnamese languages, of Vietnamese psychology, and by their own assumptions. Their number has increased to more than 20,000 in 1964, when they were so numerous that they were said to be experiencing difficulty in finding counterparts, since each American is supposed to advise a Vietnamese *alter ego*. American standards of organising, training and equipping armed forces have been uncritically applied to South Viet Nam.[1] In 1954, when the United States decided to withdraw aid from the French Union forces, her military training responsibilities were transferred to the American Military Assistance Advisory Group, under the command of Lieutenant General O'Daniel, an expert trainer of South Korean divisions. The group then consisted of 685 men. Under General O'Daniel, and his successor, Lieutenant General Williams, the army of South Viet Nam was trained for fighting conventional armed forces, in preparation for a direct conflict with the army of North Viet Nam, with the result that it had difficulty in coping with re-

[1] This problem is discussed by Jordan, *Foreign Aid and the Defense of Southeast Asia*, p. 48 ff

volutionary warfare. General Williams was succeeded in 1960 by Lieutenant General McGarr, who inherited an impossible situation when security conditions in South Viet Nam deteriorated in 1961. In February 1962, the Military Assistance Advisory Group was absorbed into an American Military Command, Viet Nam, under the command of General Harkins, Deputy Commander-in-Chief and Chief of Staff, U.S. Army, Pacific. The American military establishment in South Viet Nam was up-graded into a four-star command.

The United States has been deeply involved in the politics as well as the military affairs of South Viet Nam since 1954, but not as a unifying, or even as a united, factor. The various American agencies, including the Central Intelligence Agency, have adopted independent and conflicting policies, and involved themselves in differing degrees with the warring local factions. The Central Intelligence Agency is believed to have had a closer and more private relationship with the Diem régime than the ambassador. This led to serious friction at the highest levels between Americans in South Viet Nam, and between the Americans and the Saigon governments, which amounted to positive distrust when Diem accused the Americans of plotting to overthrow him.[1] The United States welcomed, and may even have encouraged, the November 1963 coup against Diem, as establishing a pro-American activist régime; but within three months it was regretted for its neutralist inclinations. The coup in January 1964 which deposed the Minh junta, was not apparently engineered by any American agency, but the then ambassador, Mr. Lodge, was informed of it at least forty-eight hours in advance, and did nothing to prevent it, only requesting that there be no bloodshed. This suggested, however, that, despite the massive American commitment and presence in South Viet Nam, the State Department knew remarkably little about what goes on in the country. The State Department appeared to have lost control, and it was Mr. McNamara, the Secretary of Defense, not Mr. Rusk, the Secretary of State, who flew repeatedly to Saigon for consultations. (The resignation of Mr. Hilsman from the State Department in 1964 was thought to signify a serious conflict of policy.) In March 1964 Mr. McNamara visited Saigon for consultations with General Khanh, accompanied by General Taylor, chairman of the joint chiefs of staff. General Taylor, an advocate of

[1] During Diem's rule the Government fabricated false intelligence to mislead the Americans

the bombing of selected targets in North Viet Nam, subsequently became ambassador to South Viet Nam, with a quasi-viceregal role.

The acute problems of disequilibrium in the relationship between the United States and South Viet Nam raise general questions about the role of external powers in the internal defence of Southern Asian countries against Communist or other forms of subversion from without. One question concerns the political conditions in which defence assistance is granted. For example, should the external powers come to the assistance of Southern Asian governments which are clearly not masters in their own house? The United States is beginning to realise that she must demand this criterion in her dealings with the countries of Latin America, but it is not applied to Southern Asia, because of overriding strategic considerations, and there are signs that it will not be applied to the Congo.

Since the United States has assumed the responsibility for the defence of South Viet Nam, the American establishment there has proliferated around the unstable centre of the country's alien political life. In one sense at least, the United States is an irrelevant factor in South Vietnamese politics; for, despite American involvement with various factions, the United States is there merely to ensure that a political life may exist. It is not there to determine the character of South Vietnamese politics. But the main criterion of American policy has been whether those whom it supports can wage war effectively against the Viet Cong. The original American choice of Ngo Dinh Diem was made with this in mind. Owing to the stultification of political activities under the Diem régime, and to the inherent weakness of the political groups, this has inevitably meant that the United States has been drawn into a close relationship with the army. Since the army has a vested interest in the war, and since at the time of writing its leaders are opposed to the neutralisation of their country and can make their opposition effective, the United States is supporting an organisation which may grow increasingly out of touch with national aspirations or, less grandly, with the objectives of the small politically-articulate minority of the population. Thus, the United States may be faced with a dilemma if the forces of neutralism increase in strength in South Viet Nam, possibly under Buddhist leadership, and find no legitimate political outlets. Would the United States continue to support the war if a majority of voices in South Viet Nam were raised for a neutral solution and an army minority, holding the reins of power, opposed it?

Future developments may reveal that, in seeking to defend South Viet Nam against Communism and, at the same time, to develop a local democratic political structure, the United States is following divergent policies. There were striking parallels between Diem's régime and the Communist North. The anti-Communism of the Diem Government and the military leaders has been anti-democratic in character; the political factions can hardly govern themselves, let alone the country, well enough to create an anti-Communist Government, and the government which might emerge from a coalition of civilian groups might not be anti-Communist at all. As a protecting power restricted to an advisory military and political role, the United States cannot provide or create political leadership. It would defeat the whole purpose of the war if she were to assume political control in order to wage it more effectively. It would rally the Communists and probably increase the number of their supporters, as well as provide a reason for the intervention of other powers. China would be particularly sensitive to such a development close to her borders. There would also be adverse political repercussions if, as has been suggested, the United States took command of the South Viet Nam armed forces; and it would place American prestige at too great a risk when military set-backs occurred. Differences between the policies of the two countries came to a head on the question of aid. The Diem Government in many cases successfully resisted American pressure for political reforms to make the employment of aid a more effective factor in the war effort. This is a basic problem, for defence assistance is given to a country from above, through the political leadership at the top, to meet a Communist threat of subversion from below.

The problems of Viet Nam raise serious doubts whether a protecting power can take over the security responsibilities of another country, with any prospect of success in a revolutionary war, if, first, it supports a central authority which is divided and lacks the capacity and resolution of the Magsaysay Government in the Philippines, or, second, it does not have control of the political future of the country, as the United Kingdom had in Malaya.

Chapter 6

High Level Violence in Southern Asia[1]

I. Conventional War

AT present China can only wage conventional war against the countries of Southern Asia, or support revolutionary movements inside their territories. Until she achieves a local nuclear capability, the level of violence which she can offer lies below the nuclear threshold. A local nuclear capability is defined here as the ability to strike with nuclear weapons against those countries on China's periphery which do not possess strong air defence systems either of their own or supplied by the Western powers. Until such time as China can develop her own supersonic bombers or medium- and long-range ballistic missiles with thermonuclear warheads, which might take as long as twenty years, or unless she receives them from the Soviet Union after a radical change for the better in their relationship, her ability to deliver a strategic nuclear attack is strictly limited. China has a small force of Russian subsonic light bombers, and within the next decade she could probably develop a rudimentary delivery system, with a few nominal bombs, which would be effective only against weak air defence systems. China will not obtain an advanced nuclear capability until she possesses long-range bombers or inter-continental ballistic missiles.

With her present military capability, China cannot directly threaten the external powers, like the United Kingdom and the United States, who have interests and obligations in Southern Asia; and if she seriously challenged them she would lay herself open to nuclear devastation. But although she is unable to challenge the nuclear-armed powers, China's conventional strength gives her certain advantages over her immediate neighbours. Only the external powers can handle the top ranges of the possible Chinese conventional threats: American strength protects Taiwan.

China has a formidable strength in conventional arms. The

[1] In writing this chapter, I have been greatly assisted by the comments of Mr. A. L. Burns and Mr. Leonard Beaton

People's Liberation Army numbers more than 2 million men in 115 divisions, including 4 armoured divisions and 1 or 2 airborne divisions. There are approximately a quarter of a million armed para-military forces and a civilian militia totalling many millions. The air force has 2,300 aircraft, mainly MiG interceptors but not of the most modern type. It lacks spare parts and has suffered from a fuel shortage. The small navy includes 28 submarines and 500 naval aircraft. China is developing air-to-air, ground-to-air and short range ground-to-ground missiles, and has a missile range in Sinkiang. The People's Liberation Army is adequately equipped with Chinese-built light infantry weapons, automatic rifles, machine guns, mortars, rocket launchers and light and medium artillery. Much of the equipment of the army is obsolescent, of the Second World War vintage, delivered by the Soviet Union before 1960, when supplies ceased, or produced in China from Russian prototypes. The army is tactically mobile.

The infantry are trained to march from 30 to 40 miles a day or night with full equipment. But it has inadequate logistical support and a limited strategic mobility. There is no area defence system in China. The maximum of the Chinese airlift capability has been estimated to be as little as two battalions. China lacks a modern highway system. She is developing her railways, but has few lateral rail communications. There is a great deal to be done to modernise the Chinese armed forces. The levels of radar and tactical electronic equipment are believed to be comparable with those of Western armed forces in 1941. There are major shortages of tanks, heavy artillery, military vehicles, engineering and airfield construction equipment. But these sorts of weaknesses are present in many, if not all, armies, and equipment is always overrated in peacetime estimates. The Chinese army has a very successful record.

The Bulletins of Activities of the General Political Department of the Chinese People's Liberation Army (Kung-tso T'ung-hsun), which were acquired by the United States, contain many comments on the obsolescence of army equipment.[1] The bulletins cover the period from 1 January to 26 August 1960, when army morale was critically low and civilian militiamen and army defectors led an armed uprising in Hunan province. For example, 79 per cent of the army's boats, mainly landing craft, were built before 1949. A proposed increase in the manufacture of spare parts was cut back by 85 per cent in the first

[1] See *New York Times*, 5 August 1963

half of 1961; the construction of barracks was curtailed by 50 to 70 per cent, and steel and timber supplies reduced from 30 to 50 per cent. About two-thirds of the infantry and three-quarters of the artillery troops lacked combat experience. The system of recruitment was reorganised in 1961 and training has improved in recent years.[1] The army's highly disciplined performance against India, in 1962, suggests that most of the difficulties of morale referred to in the bulletins were rapidly overcome, and it would now seem that the Chinese Communist Party can rely completely upon the army.

With her conventional strength, China has a number of options for disturbing the relationships between Southern Asian states, and for exerting military pressure in the Indian sub-continent and the Indochina zone. At present, in the Maphilindo area, the main threat to security comes from Indonesia, until China extends her influence throughout the Indochina zone, or becomes a serious air and naval power, or acquires a local nuclear capability.

In the Indian sub-continent, China is in a position to exert a direct military threat to Pakistan and India, but her policies have shown a remarkable incongruity. To Pakistan, a SEATO member and ostensibly committed to an anti-Communist posture, China has offered her good will; with respect to non-aligned India, China is in a state of undeclared war. The main threats of high-level conventional violence in this zone are the repetition or extension of the Chinese attack upon India, and a conflict between Pakistan and India. The Indian Government must take into account the fact that China may acquire a local nuclear capability in the near future that might threaten Delhi and Calcutta, as well as preparing the Indian army for conventional operations in the Himalayan region and the plains of north India. The problems of Indian defence planning are enhanced by the possibility of conflict between India and Pakistan. China's friendship towards Pakistan and hostility towards India have acerbated the relations between them. The Kashmir question not only diverts Indian resources from the high priority defence against China, it also prevents India and Pakistan from co-operating in the general defence of the zone.

[1] There are no serious staffing problems in the Chinese army according to a recent American report: *Staffing Procedures and Problems in Communist China*, A Study submitted by the Subcommittee on National Security Staffing and Operations to the Committee on Government Operations, United States Senate, 1963, pp. 33–38

A further Chinese attack upon India would not by any existing treaty directly involve the external powers, the United States and the United Kingdom, although they would support India militarily and politically. Therefore, the possibility of a direct confrontation between China and the United States appears to be fairly remote in this context, provided of course that India does not join a defence pact with the United States. There may be a natural role in the defence of India against Chinese aggression for the United Kingdom and other countries, such as Australia, New Zealand and Canada, arising out of the Commonwealth connection and indeed confirming it. The United Kingdom could offer India a nuclear guarantee against China, if it were desired. But a military alliance between India and the United Kingdom might in the long run draw India into conflict with Indonesia, if that country remains hostile to British interests in Southern Asia. The unlikely event of a Chinese attack upon Pakistan would involve the SEATO powers and possibly the Middle Eastern CENTO countries. There is thus no formal defence treaty to cover a major threat of high level conventional violence in this zone. Certain SEATO powers, like Australia, would probably try to stand aside in any conflict between India and Pakistan, since at the time of the Manila Pact, in 1954, the Australian Government indicated that it would not become involved in a war between members of the Commonwealth, and its successors may seek to honour this stipulation. But it is a question how long the Australians wish to keep out of quarrels between her Commonwealth partners can be maintained as world re-alignments develop. Australia might decide to support India if, in the event of a war between Pakistan and India, Pakistan was drawn into closer relations with China in order to offset Russian backing of India.

Although the strategic mobility of her army is very limited, China enhanced her capability to wage conventional warfare against India by developing the road system along India's northern borders, where political conflict between them could easily arise over the Himalayan hill states. She is building a network of roads and airstrips in the frontier areas from the Tadzhik Soviet Republic in the west to Viet Nam in the east. There are roads from Szechwan and Tsinghai provinces through Tibet and over the 'white stone' waste of the Aksai Chin to Sinkiang. South of the Aksai Chin, a road branches through Rudog and Gartok (where there is said to be an airfield), to

Taklakhar, which is near to the Lipu Pass at the north-west border of Nepal. A road following roughly the line of the Tsangpo (Brahmaputra) River on the northern watershed of the Himalayas, connecting with roads to Tsinghai and Sinkiang, and with branches to Katmandu and the Chumbi valley, was mapped by Western cartographers in the 1940s. This road system, traversing extremely difficult terrain, was hastily built and hard to maintain. In the 1950s, however, its main disadvantage to the Chinese was that it ran through areas where the Kham rebels operated in excellent guerrilla country.[1] For these reasons, the alternative route across the Aksai Chin was constructed, providing an ingress from the west through easier and almost uninhabited country, east of the existing road through the Karakoram Pass, north from Rudog. From Taklakhar, a road continues apparently some twenty miles north of the Tibet-Nepal border beyond Sikkim into the Chumbi Valley between Sikkim and Bhutan. A highway from Tibet to Katmandu, the capital of Nepal, has been constructed. Further roads run east in areas bordering Bhutan and the North East Frontier Agency.

It is significant that the additional roads provide easier routes or run closer than previous roads to the boundaries of the states on India's northern borders. The programme of road building is probably connected with the Chinese proposal that a confederation of Himalayan states be formed, to include Nepal, Sikkim, Bhutan, Nagaland, and an Eastern Hills State in what is now the North-East Frontier Agency. The confederation, guaranteed by China, would be independent of India.[2] The proposal is a direct political challenge to India, who claims a special relationship with Nepal, Sikkim and Bhutan, and represents an increase of Chinese activity in this strategic area between the plains watered by the Brahmaputra and Ganges Rivers and the Himalayan watershed. The Chinese proposals for regional autonomy in this area include autonomy for Darjeeling-Dooars District, a federation of Sikkim and Bhutan, and Gurkhastan, which would include the Nepalis in north Bengal and Assam. These suggestions are part of an effort to replace India's authority in the region, and there has been an en-

[1] Leo E. Rose, 'Conflict in the Himalayas', *Military Review*, February 1963, p. 5. See, also, the first map in *Chinese Aggression in Maps*, Government of India, 1962

[2] G. F. Hudson, 'What does China want in the Himalayas?', *Financial Times*, 18 February 1963

couraging response to them, from the Chinese point of view. The president of the Sikkim National Congress Party, the state's strongest political group, stated that 'in this proposal lay Sikkim's only hope'. The Chinese political courtship of Bhutan includes the offer to recognize her sovereignty and provide technical aid.[1]

At the time of the Chinese attack on India, the borders of Nepal, Sikkim and Bhutan with India were delimited (that is, defined in a document) and demarcated (that is, marked on the ground). On the north, the boundary between Nepal and Tibet was both delimited and demarcated; the boundary between Sikkim and Tibet, although delimited, was not demarcated; the boundary between Bhutan and Tibet was neither delimited nor demarcated. The situation appears to invite an outbreak of cartographic warfare, but at present these borders seem generally acceptable. However, in view of her special relationships, India claimed the right to include the northern boundaries of Sikkim and Bhutan in any Sino-Indian agreement. In 1960, Chinese delegates refused to discuss with India the Tibetan borders of Sikkim and Bhutan, on the grounds that the hill states were not part of India. This attitude suggests that the dispute between India and China over the hill states is about the special relationships claimed by India, and the nature of their political affiliation. Are they to remain the northern boundary of India or become the southern boundary of China?

Mr. Nehru once described India's policy towards Nepal as not interfering with her independence and not favouring any interference with it. In 1950, after the entry of Chinese troops into Tibet, he drew attention to the strategic importance of Nepal: 'The Himalayas lie mostly on the northern borders of Nepal. We cannot allow that barrier to be penetrated because it is the principal barrier to India. Therefore, much as we appreciate the independence of Nepal, we cannot allow anything to go wrong in Nepal ... because that would be a risk to our own security.' Indian security required some surveillance of Nepalese internal affairs, and the Chinese penetration of Tibet sharpened the logic of the argument. Nepal has been internationally recognised as an independent state by the United Kingdom in 1923, the United States in 1947, and France

[1] George N. Patterson, 'Recent Chinese Policies in Tibet and towards the Himalayan Border States,' *The China Quarterly*, October–December 1962, pp. 191–202

in 1950. In 1950 the reactionary Rana dynasty fell and the subsequent politics of Nepal have been subject to a pull from the north as well as the south. Neither direct nor constitutional rule has worked well; and whilst the elected members of Parliament tended to look to India, the dispossessed nobles turned towards China. This pattern was complicated by developments in Nepal's democracy during 1963, after the lifting of the ban on all political parties and activities. The new constitution, inaugurated in April, strengthened the pro-Communist element. The Parliament which King Mahrenda suspended was replaced by the advisory National Panchayat, a continuous assembly, one-third of whose members retire every two years. Although Nepal's small, disciplined Communist Party has been banned, one in seven of the National Panchayat members were said to be Communist, and their political influence has been increased by the absence (in jail or exile) of the strong anti-Communist leaders. Nepal receives aid from India and China. The 1955 agreement providing for the establishment of diplomatic relations between China and Nepal was followed by the Sino-Nepalese treaty on Tibet (1956), a border demarcation protocol, and a peace and friendship treaty (1960). China built a 'Road of Friendship' from Lhasa to Katmandu.

The small Buddhist state of Sikkim lies on the shortest and main trade route between the Tibetan plateau and the plains of India.[1] A British protectorate from 1890 to 1947, Sikkim became an Indian protectorate in 1949; a 1950 treaty confirmed the arrangement. India acquired control of Sikkim's external relations, the right to construct and control her communications, and the responsibility for her defence which included the right to station troops there. In November 1962, a state of emergency was declared in Sikkim because of the border hostilities, and the Indian Government has accused China of several violations of Sikkim's frontier. The Chumbi Valley, which is occupied by about 80,000 Chinese troops, is a wedge between Sikkim in the west and Bhutan in the east.[2] Chinese maps have depicted parts of north-western and eastern Bhutan within China, a claim which broadens the base of the

[1] Sikkim and Bhutan are the subject of an interesting study by Werner Levi in *The World Today*, January–December 1959, pp. 492–500

[2] George N. Patterson, 'The Himalayan Frontier', *The Journal of the Royal United Service Institution*, May 1963, reprinted in *Survival*, September–October 1963

wedge pointing south to the narrow corridor linking India with Assam.

The Buddhist kingdom of Bhutan, the Land of the Thunder Dragon, is part of the traditional route from central Tibet to India. The United Kingdom relinquished control of Bhutan's foreign policy and India assumed it in 1949; but there is an unresolved conflict between the two countries about the extent of India's responsibilities. In January 1961 it was revealed that China had unofficially suggested border talks with Bhutan and offered economic aid, measures which implicitly rejected India's authority. Bhutan's sovereignty, unlike that of Nepal, has not been internationally recognised; unlike Sikkim, her internal affairs are her own responsibility. The palace politics were disturbed during 1964, when the prime minister was assassinated, several leading officials fled the country, and what appeared to be an attempted coup was reported in November. There has been an influx of Chinese agents into Bhutan. The 'Government', which in 1963 consisted of 130 illiterate headmen, has been reluctant to allow Indian troops in the country, but in 1959 the prime minister visited New Delhi to obtain assurances of help against aggression.

Bhutan must placate both her powerful neighbours. East of Bhutan, at the western end of the disputed boundary of the North-East Frontier Agency, there was an impressive display of Chinese conventional strength, and the lesson of the rout of the Indian Central Army in 1962 was not lost on Bhutan. The increase of Chinese influence in this area threatens India's main oil supplies in north-east Assam, once thought by the Indian Government to be an objective of the Chinese attack. A narrow 30-mile strip of territory separates Bhutan from East Pakistan; and a Chinese occupation of the country would greatly increase the difficulties of the Indian defence of Assam and the North-East Frontier Agency, particularly if Pakistan remained neutral in a conflict between India and China. If Nepal also remained neutral, Indian forces, holding Sikkim and covering the narrow corridor into India, could be outflanked by a Chinese advance through Bhutan, and their position made indefensible. Bhutan is a vulnerable link in the Himalayan chain, and a likely victim of Chinese intimidation. The strategic balance in the area would be markedly altered if, as a result of a Chinese military success and political pressure, Bhutan lost confidence in India's ability to defend her, and did not resist a Chinese demand for preventative occupation.

Because of the difficulties of the mountain and jungle terrain, there is little India could do to defend Bhutan once the Chinese had invaded from the north.

Communist propaganda anthropomorphises these territories. Tibet is the palm of China's hand, and Ladakh, Nepal, Sikkim, Bhutan and the North-East Frontier Agency are its fingers. Ladakh, Nepal, Sikkim and Bhutan are also the four teeth with which China will grind her way to the Bay of Bengal. China's irredentist claims are based on the fact that historically Nepal, like its neighbour Tibet, once paid tribute to China, and both Sikkim and Bhutan were tributaries of Tibet. Sikkim's status within the Indian political system is questioned by China, who has also challenged India's interests in Bhutan. Peking would regard as a *casus belli* any Indian move into Bhutan to forestall China, and Mr. Nehru declared that a Chinese entrance into Sikkim and Bhutan would be regarded by India as an act of war.

The threats of high level violence in the Indochina zone stem directly from China and North Viet Nam. The decline of Russian influence, and the apparent lack of interest on the problems of the area (particularly of Laos) displayed by Mr. Khrushchev, have made the Soviet Union a less direct threat. But she maintains some leverage, which the Russian leaders may attempt to use or increase, amongst the revolutionary forces in the area. As shown by her relationships with Indonesia, India and Pakistan, the Soviet Union has not lost the desire to assert an influence in Southern Asia. But she is not aggressive in terms of territory.

A Chinese outflanking movement against India through Burma would activate SEATO for the defence of Thailand, where the western as well as the eastern frontier would be directly exposed to Communist pressures. There seems little immediate likelihood that Cambodia will be invaded by China or North Viet Nam; they would have first to extend their holding in Laos, but they already use the country as a sanctuary and base for attacks upon South Viet Nam and may in the future use it in a similar fashion against the south-east of Thailand. This would raise the prospect of a war on Cambodian territory against Communist forces by a Thai–South Vietnamese–United States (and probably SEATO) coalition. Laos occupies a strategic position from which Communist thrusts can be made against Thailand and South Viet Nam, and an extension of Communist control in the country would have serious strategic consequences. The line that must be held in Southeast Asia runs through the waist of Laos.[1]

China and North Viet Nam have incorporated northern Laos in a road system which enables them to launch a conventional attack or revolutionary war against Thailand. In Paris, in April 1963, SEATO officials stated that China was quietly developing a network of strategic roads to Laos, Thailand and as far as Burma. China was evidently taking full advantage of the agreements, announced on 13 January 1962, giving her road building rights in the Communist sections of Laos. Few details of these roads have been released, but a general impression can be obtained of a road system which provides access routes to the Southeast Asian peninsula, and which SEATO officials compared to the Chinese road building programme before the invasion of India.

Two roads from Yunnan penetrate the mountains and jungles of Laos. One enters Laos at the border village of Muong Sing and runs south-east to Nam Tha, where it joins with a road to Ban Houei Sai, on the Thai frontier not far from the roads running south into Thailand. The other reaches the northern Laotian town of Phong Saly and may be continued to Dienbienphu, in the mountains of North Viet Nam. From Vinh, the starting point of the Ho Chi Minh trail in North Viet Nam, a road passes south-west into the narrow waist of Laos at Lak Sao, and thence to Tchepone, a depot on the Ho Chi Minh trail into South Viet Nam. Another road runs from North Viet Nam to Thakhek, a road junction on the Thai–Laotian border from which roads pass deep into Thailand. The SEATO report of April 1963 mentioned a road which skirts the Laotian border towards Burma. Another report stated that construction by North Viet Nam of two strategic roads was announced on 10 December 1962 by the official Lao Presse news agency, and that a few days later Radio Hanoi announced the completion of the roads before the scheduled date.[2] The first road leaves Dienbienphu and traverses difficult country as far as Sop Nau, in Phong Saly province of Laos. The second road links Sam Neua in Laos, which is some 120 miles from Hanoi, with the North Vietnamese communications system. Two other roads were also mentioned, running down into Kammouene province. These roads increase the opportunities for Pathet

[1] See Denis Warner 'A Line in S.E. Asia?', *The Reporter*, 10 September 1964, reprinted in *Survival*, November–December 1964

[2] *Christian Science Monitor*, 10 January 1963

Lao and North Vietnamese military activities in areas where Communist infiltration is already a serious problem. A guerrilla war in the north-east of Thailand is a likely contingency.

The new roads are significant additions to the existing network of communications in the peninsula. For example, Dienbienphu is also linked to Hanoi, and the road to Sop Nau follows the previous Viet Minh invasion route used by the foot soldiers in the first Indochina war, when they approached within a few miles of Luang Prabang, the royal Lao capital. (The Pathet Lao have demanded that the administrative capital of Laos be moved north from Vientiane into an area they control.) According to Vientiane sources, the roads across the mountain passes into Kammouene province could curtail by as much as 90 per cent the travel time of troops from North Viet Nam to the valley of the Mekong, a river which Mr. Rusk described as 'the main artery of Southeast Asia'. This increases the strategic significance of the parts of Laos under Pathet Lao control, which are linked by road communications to China and North Viet Nam, whilst the Pathet Lao is controlled from Hanoi. Intelligence sources indicate that arms and ammunition has been stockpiled in this region. The roads also consolidate the Viet Cong supply routes from North Viet Nam via Laos to the guerrilla areas of the high plateau in west central Viet Nam and zone D north of Saigon. From zone D, the Viet Cong can interrupt Saigon's northward communications on the ground and establish bases supplied via Cambodia or from the high plateau via Laos. From their strongholds in the Plain of Reeds on the Cambodian border, the Viet Cong thrust at the vital delta region of South Viet Nam.

There is a strong possibility of a direct conflict between the United States and China in the Indochina zone. It could occur, for example, either as a result of the war in South Viet Nam, through a stage of escalation involving North Viet Nam in the first instance, or in Laos arising out of a Pathet Lao and North Vietnamese advance across the Mekong River, or as the outcome of a Communist attack upon Thailand by conventional or guerrilla war. American policy in Southeast Asia and the Far East might be clarified when China demonstrates that she has even a minimum nuclear capability; the United States might take the opportunity to draw a line in the Indochina zone, indicating to the Chinese just how far they can go. As suggested below, there is a sense in which a non-nuclear country loses its immunity when it becomes a nuclear power. A

Chinese threat to use, or the use of, nuclear weapons, would give the United States the best possible grounds for a nuclear attack upon China, and remove American inhibitions on counter threats. But the Western powers are inhibited by political constraints from countering with nuclear force a Chinese conventional attack. The threat from China's conventional forces will increase as she modernises and develops her armed forces; and it is possible that China could saturate the defences of the Indochina countries in the event of a full scale conventional war.

Malaysia is the only mainland country in the Maphilindo zone. Her security would be threatened by the extension of Chinese and North Vietnamese influence down the Indochina peninsula. If Thailand were to come to terms with China and North Viet Nam and move out of the western orbit, hostile elements could penetrate as far south as the Thai–Malaysian border, and link up with the surviving Communist terrorists in the jungles. Indonesian guerrillas have tried to make contact with the Malayan terrorists, presumably in order to start a guerrilla war in northern Malaya.

If, in the course of an Indonesian–Malaysian War, Indonesia attacked Australian territory (and the proposed air and naval base in Timor would facilitate this), the aggression would take place within the 'treaty area' as defined in the Manila Pact. But unless, or until, Indonesia becomes a Communist state, the Manila Pact is of doubtful application, since the United States declared her intention only to recognise Communist aggression, and the indigenous members of SEATO could not be expected to support a war against Indonesia without American backing, even if they recognised a treaty obligation to do so. The ANZUS treaty, on the other hand, is not restricted to a Communist threat or to attack on its members' 'territories'; it also covers attacks upon the members' forces. During 1964, Australian troops engaged in operations against Indonesian guerrillas in Malaya. Before his resignation as Australia's Minister for External Affairs in April 1964 Sir Garfield Barwick was quoted as stating that any Indonesian attacks upon Australian troops which might occur in Borneo during the Malaysian crisis would lead to action in support of Australia by the United States under the ANZUS treaty. The United States has accepted this interpretation, although it is not clear how she would respond if and when the situation arises. In certain circumstances, it is conceivable that Indonesia would be at war with Malaysia, Australia, New Zealand, the United Kingdom and the United States.[1]

The chance that the policy of confrontation (on which the major parties agree) might lead Indonesia into a war with nuclear-armed Western powers must prompt their leaders to seek powerful allies; and the choice of alliance might depend upon the outcome of the internal struggles for political power in Indonesia. For example, there is the prospect of a military alliance with China based upon the ascendancy of the Peking-oriented Indonesian Communist Party. If this happened, Thailand, South Viet Nam, Malaysia and the Philippines would be flanked by the most powerful indigenous military combination in Southeast Asia. Thailand might seek accommodation with China and Indonesia, weakening the whole Western position in Southeast Asia. Malaysia would be critically exposed, and Australia's security menaced. On the other hand, if the Indonesian Communist Party achieved control of the state, Indonesia might disintegrate into a number of warring islands, with the Communists in control of West Java, but unable to pose a significant threat to the security of the region unless China were to provide more substantial military assistance than she is capable of at present.

An alliance between China and Indonesia would change the strategic balance of forces in Southern Asia. For example, a SEATO combination against China and North Viet Nam, which had been joined by a pro-Chinese Indonesia, could result from a Communist attack upon Thailand. A British, American and Commonwealth pact with India against China could become an anti-Chinese–Indonesian coalition, if the Communist Party of Indonesia aligned Djakarta with Peking. A war between Pakistan and India could lead eventually to a line up of India, the United Kingdom and Commonwealth countries, the United States (and even the Soviet Union) against Pakistan, China, North Viet Nam and Indonesia. A Sino-Japanese *rapprochement* might produce a military agreement which included Indonesia.

Alternatively, Indonesia might enter into a military alliance with the Soviet Union, probably through the army and against the inclinations of the pro-Chinese Communist Party. It is possible that a closer Russian–Indonesian agreement will

[1] A similar contingency was envisaged in the *Report of the Special Study Mission to Southeast Asia of the Committee on Foreign Affairs*, Washington 1963, p. 21

develop out of the existing arms arrangements between them. The Indonesian armed forces rely heavily upon Russian weapons which are not, and are unlikely to be in the near future, manufactured in Indonesia. For example, the striking power of the air force consists mainly of Russian bombers, and all the interceptors are Russian-made. The military build up adds to Indonesia's budget deficit, which increased by 800 per cent between 1960 and 1962, while her Malaysian policy has caused the International Monetary Fund and other sources to curtail their aid. Indonesia's military power, the basis of her policy of confrontation, is dependent upon further Russian supplies; and if the conflict with Malaysia escalates, Indonesia's dependence upon the Soviet Union will increase.

Indonesia's potential makes her a difficult country to accommodate to a regional system, which she might dominate, and raises the question of the nature of her participation in world alignments. The Soviet Union, for example, can play a significant part in Southern Asia in the near future. As Indonesia is potentially a very important power, the Soviet Union may wish to prevent it joining China in an alliance which could swing the balance within the Communist world towards China. Russian influence in Indonesia would also give the Soviet Union a bargaining position with the United States in Asian affairs. A military alliance between Indonesia and the Soviet Union (and conceivably supported by China, if her relations with the Soviet Union were mended), in a conflict over Malaysia would face SEATO or an ANZUS plus the United Kingdom combination. An overriding consideration of Russian policy, however, may be her conflict with China, and by establishing their power in Indonesian waters the Russians might hope to contain China southwards as well as northwards.

A military alliance with Indonesia would enable the Soviet Union to operate nuclear submarines from Indonesian bases. It is at present uncertain whether the suggestion for an Anglo-American base in the Indian Ocean was designed to forestall a Russian deployment, and whether the project would, if it took place, induce a Russian move into an area where there could be 'just the sort of vacuum of power China would abhor to leave unfilled'.[1] It might be in Russian interests to have

[1] 'Indian Ocean Base?', *The Economist*, 5 September 1964, reprinted in *Survival*, November–December 1964. In any case, it might be unnecessary; the Americans may acquire stronger base facilities in Singapore as a result of supplying military assistance to Malaysia

British and American forces opposing Chinese expansion in Thailand, Malaysia and the Philippines. Both the Russian and Indonesian apprehensions of China might facilitate the development of a SEATO, Soviet Union and Indonesian combination in Southern Asia against China. One essential point about all three zones, however, is that by far the greatest military power, the United States, is not indigenous; neither are the United Kingdom and the Soviet Union (even if she takes up her Indonesian option). For the future, China, also an external power, has a great capacity for conventional ground-force threats to the security of the Indian sub-continent and the Indochina zone, while Indonesia is a major threat in the Maphilindo area.

II. China and Her Nuclear Capability

In considering the range of possibilities of high level violence in Southern Asia, we can attempt to project the various threats to the security of the area into the foreseeable future. The evolution of the Chinese threat to Southern Asia is related to China's progress in modernising her armed forces and in her nuclear technology. We can follow some of the implications of this relationship by setting existing threats in the framework of a timetable extending over the next decade and estimating their duration.

The pace of the development of Chinese nuclear weapons is central to the issues of future high level violence in Southern Asia, and for the purposes of this exercise certain guesses must be made about China's progress in nuclear technology and advanced delivery systems. In recent years, Western estimates of the date at which China would detonate a nuclear device shifted from 1961–63 to 1963–65. The explosion of a Chinese nuclear device in Sinkiang in October 1964 revealed that China's nuclear technology was more advanced than was thought in the West. The triggering method was unexpectedly sophisticated, and the fissile material (the nature of which can be deduced from the fallout) was uranium-235. It was thought that the advanced separating processes required to produce uranium-235 existed only in the United States, the United Kingdom and the Soviet Union; and the means by which China procured uranium-235 were something of a mystery at first. One possibility was that it came from the Soviet Union before 1960; but it is now thought that China succeeded in building a gaseous diffusion plant, perhaps on the basis of a project which had substantial Russian aid in its early stages. The length of time China will take to develop thermo-nuclear weapons, and it is not known at present whether she is developing them, depends upon the state of her fusion techno-logy. The state of China's rocket technology was an unknown quantity at the time of the explosion.

China is considered to be technologically advanced enough to have acquired a local nuclear capability with nominal bombs and a rudimentary delivery system within a few years of her nuclear detonation: let us say '1970–75'. A longer period must elapse before China develops by her own efforts an advanced nuclear system with missiles capable of carrying thermo-nuclear warheads: let us say '1984', since the date has appro-priate connotations. In terms of a solitary effort to develop her nuclear technology, the timetable is as follows.

1964. China detonates a nuclear device. During this first period, the main threat to the security of the region comes from Indonesia (and her connection with the Soviet Union) with a major subsidiary threat from China's conventional power. There is the prospect of SEATO—China wars if China risks conventional operations in the Indochina zone, of a war between China and India and between Indonesia and Malaysia, and the possibility of a conflict between India and Pakistan. Faced with a Chinese advance into Southern Asia, Indonesia might attempt to achieve her territorial ambitions in a hurry before China is in a position to curtail her. In this phase China will probably attempt to exploit her nuclear potential by ex-tracting political concessions from her neighbours.

1970–75. China acquires a local nuclear capability and begins to join Indonesia—plus—Russia as the prime military threat. The Chinese threat to the Indian sub-continent and the Indochina zone increases, and with it the further possibility of an escalation of the war in South Viet Nam.

If by '1984' (or its actual equivalent), China were to possess an advanced nuclear capability, she would present a for-midable threat to the security of Southern Asia; but the possibilities of Chinese technology and economic growth, and of future arms control agreements, make the '1984' situation a remote contingency. A balance of prudence might be estab-lished in Asia before '1984', and the Chinese threat neutralised. There may never be a nuclear war in Southern Asia, but the consequences of China's nuclear development upon war and

peace in the region will be profound; they may come to dominate the political and strategic problems of the area for the
foreseeable future. Several issues stand out in importance
amongst the range of problems that can be selected for comment. First, there are the political problems brought into existence by the threat of China's nuclear weapons. What, for
example, is likely to be the effect of this development upon the
relations between China and the Soviet Union and how will it
modify their respective policies in Southern Asia? Second, how
will the Southern Asian countries react to the threat? At present,
only three Asian countries (China, India and Japan) could if
they chose embark successfully upon a nuclear weapons
programme. Technically, Australia is the only other contender
in the area. Three types of reaction are possible; they will rely
more heavily upon the deterrent power of the United States
and seek firm alliances with her; they will become neutral
under the shadow of China; and they will become protec-
torates of China. Third, and arising from this, is the specially
important question of the future of the alliance structure in
Southern Asia. Will the nuclear threat from China paralyse the
resolution of the committed Asian countries to defend themselves individually and jointly against Chinese aggression? In
other words, has the notion of collective defence any future in
Southern Asia?

There are also a number of strategic problems which bear a
close relation to these political problems. It will remain to be
seen whether China's leaders, once they are in possession of a
nuclear capability, will adopt policies entailing a high degree
of risk, and whether they are capable at that juncture of
estimating the risks correctly. (They might be tempted, for
example, to embark upon the risky policy of nuclear blackmail
of their weaker neighbours.) An analogy with the nuclear
development of the Soviet Union has sometimes been made in
this connection, and the conclusion drawn that when the
Chinese Government has understood nuclear technology and
the destructiveness of nuclear weapons they will become
cautious and, like the Russians before them, seek some understanding with the Western nuclear powers. Is this a useful
analogy for setting out guide lines to Chinese nuclear policy?
Above all, what strategic doctrine is China likely to evolve? In
the broader context of Sino-American strategies, there is the
problem of the nuclear threshold—the point in an escalating
conflict when the use of nuclear weapons becomes a real

possibility. Will China's nuclear capability, and the doctrines that guide it, raise or lower the nuclear threshold?

There are a number of imponderables involved in any analysis of Chinese strategic doctrine—the degree of Chinese miscalculation of the implications of a thrust and the response of the opponent, for example—but there are also certain assumptions about the course of China's policies that can be made with some confidence. One of these assumptions is that China will make political use of her nuclear detonation with the object of gaining certain advantages *vis-à-vis* the United States. There is no good reason to suppose that her measures will be consistent. In addition to threatening or blackmailing her neighbours, China might renew her suggestions for a de-nuclearised zone in Southern Asia. This is a policy which offers China particular advantages as a weaker nuclear power than the United States, but its main purpose would probably be to organise Asian opinion against the United States and perhaps to stimulate the growth of neutralism in Asian countries. The second assumption is that the general objectives of China's policy in the future will probably be the same as those which she has tried to gain with her conventional strength. They are: first, to remove American bases from her periphery and eject the United States' military presence from Southern Asia; second, to win hegemony in Southern Asia; and third, to gain international recognition of her great power status.

China's acquisition of even a local nuclear capability by '1970-75' will effect Sino-Soviet relationships at several sensitive points, and it will probably have the result in the long run of widening the breach between China and the Soviet Union. The Soviet Union has suggested that China's determination to obtain nuclear weapons raised doubts about the objectives of Chinese foreign policy, and intimated that China had 'special aims and interests that the socialist camp cannot support with its military force'.[1] If their past form is any guidance, the Chinese leaders will try to employ their technological success as a political and diplomatic gambit against the Soviet Union. They will endeavour to extract the utmost political capital from the event—and at the expense of Russian influence in Southern Asia. A Chinese assertion of independence in nuclear matters might therefore exacerbate Sino-Soviet

[1] See the discussion, 'Sino-Soviet Nuclear Dialogue', by Alice Langley Hsieh, reprinted in *Survival*, September–October 1964, from *The Journal of Conflict Resolution*, June 1964

relations. In view of the split between China and the Soviet Union, the trend of Chinese comment upon their nuclear achievement will very probably take on an anti-Russian character, stressing China's ability to develop sophisticated modern weapons despite the Russians' unwillingness to offer more than a token assistance. Peking is fairly certain to represent the progress of China's nuclear technology solely as a Chinese achievement. The limited but indispensable Russian assistance during the initial stages of China's nuclear weapons programme is likely to be minimised or even ignored in the Chinese propaganda, which will show the nuclear device as the first manufactured by an Asian power. It will be presented as a triumph of Asian Communism in a field previously dominated by 'white' technology. The implications of this Chinese and Communist achievement will be iterated at length for the benefit of a susceptible Asian audience. For, in spite of Japan's advanced industry, in spite of India's capacity for nuclear development, China was the first Asian power to achieve the breakthrough and join the 'white' nuclear powers. One can expect that the Chinese will make a special effort to convince those Asians who are unfamiliar with nuclear technology, and unable to differentiate between weapons systems, that China's nuclear device brings her to a nuclear parity with the Soviet Union, the United States, and the European nuclear powers.

This type of propaganda might be effective in Asia in persuading China's neighbours that the Soviet Union has ceased to be the supreme source of strength in the Communist world, and that China has replaced her as the revolutionary centre of that world. When China has a nuclear capability, her leaders will be less likely than ever before to accept a role subordinate to the Soviet Union in Communist activities. If the Chinese leaders choose subsequently to make a strenuous bid for the leadership of the Communist countries, they might make the split with the Soviet Union irrevocable and force the Soviet leaders to make a public renunciation of the Sino-Soviet Pact.

In seeking to exploit their nuclear achievement against the Soviet Union, China will have a number of options to follow. The choice of a time for the original detonation of a Chinese nuclear device may have been influenced by such considerations as its effect on Sino-Soviet relations, the struggle for Communist leadership and for the control of the Communist

Left Wing, and the particular situation at the time in Southern Asia. Even before the Chinese nuclear explosion, the Soviet leaders made it clear that they were reluctant to allow themselves to be committed to courses of action in Southern Asia as a result of Chinese chauvinism. Their apprehensions are likely to be increased by it. Consequently, an aggressive stance in Southern Asia by a nuclear-armed China could prove to be an acute embarrassment to the Soviet Union, whose influence in the area has declined. Unable to influence Chinese policy towards moderation and co-existence, and unwilling to become involved in Southern Asia at China's instigation, the Soviet Union may hasten the process of her disengagement in Southern Asia, leaving the field to China, or seek to contain China by an alliance with Indonesia and other powers.

An alternative view is that China will eventually moderate her harshness towards the Soviet Union when she acquires a nuclear capability and realises the importance to her own security of a Russian nuclear deterrent that will remain technologically more advanced than her own for a very long time to come. This is a prediction based upon the debatable assumption that the present Chinese leaders are relatively ignorant of the implications of nuclear warfare and that in their ignorance they have underestimated the consequences of a nuclear attack upon China. The conclusion is that once they have acquired nuclear experience from their own weapons programme, China's leaders will patch up their quarrel with the Soviet Union, follow the Russian precedent, and seek to co-exist with the West. American analysts of China's nuclear development do not attribute much weight to this line of reasoning, arguing that it starts from a false premise. Their view is, on the contrary, that the Chinese military experts are already sensitive to the threat of the United States nuclear capability and are gaining the necessary skills to make analyses of weapons systems. If their view is correct, there appears to be little reason to expect that the Chinese Government will experience a change of outlook when they obtain in their own hands a weapon of whose destructive power in the hands of others they are aware. References to a possible nuclear attack on China in the 1961 Bulletins of Activities of the General Political Department of the Chinese People's Liberation Army support this military appreciation. In other words, it would seem more reasonable to suppose that Chinese hostility to the Soviet Union, notwithstanding China's nuclear inferiority, would not abate simply because China had completed a nuclear weapons programme.

China has offered a direct challenge to India's position in Southern Asia and has conducted a brief military campaign on Indian territory. The fighting which took place on India's northern borders was confined to operations on the ground; but in any future warfare in this area there is no guarantee that either side will refrain from the use of air strikes. Construction by the Chinese of air strips along the line of the Himalayas implies China's intentions to threaten India from the air, and the Indian Government must take appropriate precautions. In this condition of undeclared and likely-to-be-renewed war, India has embarked with Western assistance upon a rearmament programme in order to build up her defences against a Chinese attack by land or from the air. In particular, the Indian Government has given priority to the construction of an effective air defence and warning system to the north. Strategic targets on Indian soil (like the oilfields of Assam) are within an accessible striking distance of air bases in China. China's tactical bomber force poses a considerable threat to India's national security, although it consists mainly of older aircraft like the turbojet Il-28s. The prospect that in the near future China will acquire a local nuclear capability increases India's security and defence problems and forces the Indian Government to take difficult policy decisions to meet the conditions of the '1970–75' era of threats. Basic questions concern the defence of India against Chinese nuclear attack or the threat of a strike after '1970–75'. A conventional Indian air defence could not be relied upon to limit the damage that China could inflict to an acceptable level. The problem, in any case, is not merely one of defence, it is also one of deterrence. In what manner might the Chinese leaders be deterred from a nuclear attack upon India if they determine to launch one? How can the Indian Government obtain the necessary strength, both political and military, to deter China by the threat of retaliation in kind?

These are questions which present the Indian planners with several types of policy choices. Whatever alternative is finally selected, the subsequent policies will be a distinct break with political traditions which were affirmed in the manner of dogmas during the years of Mr. Nehru's leadership. They must firmly repudiate the courses of action which he laid down for India and establish new foundations of policy. In the first place, the Government could choose to remain non-aligned and yet decide to embark upon a crash programme to transform India's potential for peaceful atomic development into a war machine to manufacture nuclear weapons. India's capacity to produce plutonium gives her Government an option on nuclear weapons. The reactor at Trombay, built with Canadian assistance, produces enough plutonium each year to make two atom bombs. India has also commenced to manufacture her own uranium fuel. With her own source of plutonium and the means to extract it, India has the foundation of a nuclear weapons programme, and the Director General of the Indian Atomic Energy Commission has stated that she could if necessary explode a nuclear device within two years. But this seems an unlikely contingency in the near future, as Mr. Shastri reaffirmed in November 1964 that India had no intention of making nuclear weapons. There are good political reasons for this decision. The use of plutonium from the Canada–India reactor for weapons would be a breach of the agreement between the two countries that the reactor would only be employed for peaceful purposes. The agreement has no enforcement or inspection, but it is a serious undertaking. Moreover, in order to manufacture nuclear weapons, India would have to withdraw from the Test-Ban Treaty, an act which would damage her standing in the Afro-Asian world.

If, in spite of these political inhibitions, India developed a nuclear weapons programme, she could raise the cost of any aggression against her and place the Chinese Government under pressure by involving it in a process of nuclear bargaining, the macabre strategic equivalent of an eye for an eye and a tooth for a tooth. But it would also be necessary to acquire the means to deliver Indian atom bombs on Chinese targets. India has no existing or planned delivery system that could reach any important group of Chinese strategic targets; and she could not acquire one without Western or Russian help. If India bought or was given long-range bombers, such as the American B-47s, she would have a much better delivery capability than anything that China could build during the next decade. An Indian nuclear deterrent against China would only become effective at the stage when India possessed, *vis-à-vis* China, a delivery system secure against Chinese counter attacks and a supply of nuclear weapons adequate for all target requirements. India would have to enter the '1970–75' era with the nuclear capability to inflict unacceptable damage upon China. That is to say, India would be drawn into, and have to commit herself to, a nuclear confrontation with China,[1] or rely upon external powers to provide a deterrent.

A strategic policy which leads to a nuclear arms race with China, even if it is within India's power to sustain, would probably encounter strenuous domestic opposition in India. It is, of course, totally opposed to the Nehru tradition of eschewing the military application of nuclear power and to the deeply-rooted Indian belief that India's authority in world affairs should rest upon a moral and not upon a military foundation. It is, moreover, a policy that could give rise to increased difficulties with Pakistan. Pakistan's sensitivity to India's superior strength is so great, and her people's suspicions of 'Hindu imperialism' so profound, that if it became known that India was engaged in the production of nuclear weapons the Pakistani reaction might pass the bounds of rational appraisal. A special effort would be required to adjust Indo-Pakistan relations. The price that India might be asked to pay in order to reassure Pakistan of her good intentions could well be a settlement of the Kashmir dispute on more favourable terms than India has been prepared to consider. Certainly, Pakistan as a SEATO member would expect a great deal of understanding from her allies for her anxieties about India's nuclear weapons and would test the value of the alliance by the sympathy and diplomatic support which she received.

Finally, there are strategic disadvantages to an Indian 'go it alone' nuclear programme which could threaten the basis of Indian strategy. In the event that the Soviet Union intervened at any stage of the arms race between India and China and cast the weight of her nuclear power in the balance on China's behalf, the Indian Government might have in reply to adopt its second choice and seek military alliances with the West. Non-alignment would have to be sacrificed in the interests of national security. Or, if the situation arose that China achieved a nuclear capability before India did, the Indian Government would face the possibility that China might engage in a preemptive strike against the sources of Indian nuclear strength.

[1] It was probably in 1954, or later, that China began with Russian assistance to create the base for her nuclear weapons programme. The Indian Atomic Energy Commission celebrated its tenth anniversary in 1964. Russian assistance to China ended in 1960. India has had continuous American, British and Canadian technical assistance

India could seek insurance against this contingency by appealing for guarantees from the United Kingdom and the United States. In return for any available guarantees, these powers would require certain assurances from India about the conditions in which she would employ her nuclear weapons against China in the future. India would thereby lose to some extent the control over her own nuclear options against China and Indian strategy would have in this manner to accommodate itself to the broader priorities of the deterrent posture of the United States. As a consequence, the Indian Government would not retain the freedoms of a purely national use of its nuclear capability. In addition to destroying the non-aligned base of Indian policy, such a choice would cost India her highly-valued relationship with the Soviet Union. An Indian alliance with two major NATO powers could precipitate a Russian intervention in the arms race between India and China, a contingency already alluded to, unless the Soviet Union tacitly supported a British–American–Indian combination against China. In any event, the innocence of Indian non-alignment would be finally compromised after '1970–75'.

In the light of these diplomatic and strategical possibilities, and of the economic and social sacrifices entailed by an arms race with China, India might make a third choice; namely, to rely upon allies rather than her own nuclear strength to deter China. This decision not to manufacture nuclear weapons but to enter an alliance would also require significant re-orientations of Indian diplomacy, which has previously been most reluctant to entertain the concept of collective security. As a participant of a collective security structure, seeking protection against high level violence, India might in return be required to make her contribution to the general battle order in the form of a major support role in situations of low level violence, conventional and revolutionary wars and police actions. Although India might in this way hope to increase her security by adding to the number of her official friends and allies, it is conceivable that she might multiply the number of her official enemies as well. She might, for example, be drawn in the wake of her allies into a conflict with a militant power like Indonesia. In a major support role, the Indian Government might be asked to make available bases upon Indian soil, to allow India to become an arsenal of the alliance, or to provide troops and services for actions outside India in crisis situations involving other members of the alliance more directly than

India herself. The demands of the alliance would be for a more general application of India's military power than was possible under the policy of non-alignment; and in order to fulfil these demands certain adjustments might prove to be necessary in the Indian military machine, in the training, organisation and deployment of troops, in her weapons and logistical services. The influence which Mr. Nehru hoped to exercise upon international developments by moral authority and principles of good conduct would instead have to be exerted through the consultative bodies of a military coalition designed to prevent Chinese expansion into Southern Asia, including the Indian sub-continent: unless India decided to accept Chinese hegemony in Asia on suitably generous terms.

Japan will most probably become a major target of the Chinese political, psychological and propaganda offensive that may be expected to follow upon China's first detonation of a nuclear device. The propaganda offensive is likely to be the least effective, since the Japanese authorities are well aware of the distinction between a detonation and a capability; but the psychological and political pressures will probably be fruitful from China's point of view, particularly if China played upon the Japanese sensitivity with regard to nuclear weapons. It does not seem at all probable that Japan's reaction will be to develop her own nuclear weapons in the near future. She would not in the circumstances face the same threat as India and would have less incentive to transform her nuclear development programme into a weapons industry. The reaction is likely to be most significant in the realm of Japanese internal politics, where there already exist divisions that the Chinese offensive would endeavour to exploit, and which it might successfully accentuate. A pronounced feature of Japanese thinking has been that there is little Japan has to fear, in a military sense, from China. Those who hold this comfortable belief may be shocked by Chinese efforts to bring pressure upon Japan by virtue of China's nuclear superiority, for this type of pressure implies (however remotely) a nuclear threat to Japan's security. A fairly certain objective of the Chinese pressure would be to influence Japan's foreign policy along lines determined in advance by Peking. The main outlines of this objective can be identified as first, that China would attempt to persuade the Japanese Government, whether of the Right or the Left, to abolish its diplomatic relations with Taiwan and enter into closer relations with China, and second, that Japan should cease to provide base facilities at Yokusuka on the Japanese mainland and at Okinawa in the Ryukus, from which American forces are deployed to threaten China's national security.

There are powerful bodies on the Left in Japan who accept at least the second of these lines of policy, and the result of the Chinese efforts is likely to be a further polarisation of Japanese internal politics. China could play upon the strong anti-American sentiments of many Japanese in the hope that they would produce tangible political results, such as an increased agitation for Japan to declare her neutrality. The Socialists, who advocate 'positive neutrality', will probably agitate for closer ties with China at the cost of the existing ties with the United States. The Japanese Right, on the other hand, is likely to take the view that Japan should make efforts to ensure her national security by entering into a closer relationship with the United States, as the protective power, and to react sharply to the implied threat from China by seeking to strengthen Japan's national defence forces, in spite of constitutional obstacles.

The choice of Japan's foreign policy and alignments will ultimately be a matter for the decision of whatever government is in power when China brings pressure to bear upon Japanese politics. Japan's difficulties in establishing bipartisan foreign and defence policies since the Second World War may be increased in the future; and one can only speculate about the manner in which Japan will assert her influence in world affairs, and the influence of other powers, such as the Soviet Union, on her policies. But any combination between Japan and China would disturb the balance of power in Southern Asia, since Japan is potentially the leading Asian nuclear-military power. The development of close ties between China and Japan could lead to some agreement between them concerning their respective spheres of influence in Asia.

Alternatively, a Japan which felt threatened by Chinese and Russian nuclear power might join with the ANZUS treaty members in an Asian-Pacific multilateral force. Japan's economic prosperity might provide a clue to the direction her policy will take in the immediate future. Without a down-swing in prosperity, the forces of the Right appear likely to retain their political majority, and their policy is to retain the connection with the United States. A recession could bring the Left to power, and there could follow a period of great development of Japan's relations with China.

The political reactions of the other Southern Asian states to China's token nuclear capability will be diverse but not necessarily unpredictable. It is possible to suggest tentative answers to some general questions about their future behaviour. A central question is what will happen to formal alliances in Southern Asia? In the first place, they are not likely to expand their membership. The policies of a small neutral country like Burma will if anything move farther away from the West towards a closer accommodation with China. The problem is rather whether the urge for accommodation will be confined to neutral and uncommitted states, or whether the members of anti-Communist defence pacts will in their turn also opt for a neutral position? Will Thailand stand the strain? Or, more generally, will the bonds of SEATO dissolve and with them the notion of collective security in the region?

One thing is clear at the start. It is that the allies of the United States in Southern Asia are the least likely countries to mistake the shadow of the Chinese detonation for the substance of a Chinese nuclear capability. They will probably not change their stance as a result of Chinese propaganda, or panic, or feel that their situation has become hopeless; though some of them may be attracted by Chinese proposals for a nuclear-free zone. They can expect the impact of Chinese pressure to withdraw from their collective security arrangements before they are actually threatened by China's nuclear power. Whether or not they will bow to this pressure will depend in large measure upon their confidence in American policy at the relevant time.

The Philippines has an unequivocal American guarantee (which President Eisenhower reaffirmed in June 1960),[1] as well as her membership of SEATO. Her claim to part of North Borneo reflected the desire to reassert her independent Asian dignity; but in spite of this, the Philippines is not likely to break her Western associations or oppose the agreement for bases. The Philippines has become more mature and responsible as her relations with Indonesia and Malaysia have developed. Whilst the underlying mood is towards a strong sense of independence, there is no wish to see the British and American presence removed from the area or an extension of Communist influence in Southeast Asia.

The Thai Government is concerned about Chinese nuclear capability, and will probably require intensive education in

[1] *New York Times*, 18 June 1960

the effectiveness of active defences against any attack China could launch, as well as reassurances about the certainty of an American response against China, and China's knowledge of that certainty. These are reasonable apprehensions, since the chief danger from China for the next decade might be a Chinese calculation that, since they could retaliate against the Southern Asian countries protected by the United States, the United States would be unwilling to use nuclear weapons against China, even in the face of a massive conventional invasion of Indochina by Chinese and North Vietnamese armies. The Australian Government, already deeply aware of its dependence upon American power, may become more amenable to requests from the United States to place missiles directed against China on Australian soil, provided that it had some control over their use. But it can expect bitter opposition in the country until it was clear that China could (and might) attack Australian cities. Australia fears a Russian–Indonesian combination and would be concerned that the American missiles would give the Soviet Union an excuse to place missiles in Indonesia. If a Cuban-type Russian relationship with Indonesia develops in the future, there is some possibility that the Soviet Union would hand over nuclear weapons to the Indonesian Government. New Zealand's commitment should remain firm. Assuming that Malaysia endures the Indonesian confrontation, her Government (particularly if the Alliance Party remains in power) might ask for and receive nuclear guarantees from the United States and the United Kingdom.

The driving force of China's policies for more than a decade has been to achieve international recognition of her great power status, and universal acceptance of Peking as the sole voice and authority of modern China. One of China's aims in developing nuclear weapons, a reason why she has accepted all the difficulties involved, is generally conceded to be the wish of her leaders to obtain one of the most potent outward and visible signs of great power status. As Marshal Chen Yi, the Deputy Prime Minister and Foreign Minister, explained, 'Whatever the leading powers in the world can do, Whatever level of technology they have reached, we want to catch up and arrive at the same level. We may be unable to catch up with a few very advanced powers in 10, 20 or 30 years, but we will never give up trying to catch up.'[1] It is also agreed that this type of symbolism is of great importance to them, and fulfils deep-seated

[1] *The Times*, 4 May 1964

needs in the Chinese national temperament. By exploiting the threat of her nuclear power in a vigorous political warfare, or by advancing suggestions about limitations on nuclear weapons, China will aim at extracting, principally from the United States, but also from the Soviet Union, what she regards as an appropriate recognition of her position in world affairs. For example, China could create situations where a prudent American government might acknowledge the benefit of discussions and negotiations directly with Peking, in order to take the steps necessary to resolve crises in Sino-American relations. Chinese moves or threats against Taiwan or South Viet Nam would entail risks, but would provide opportunities for this type of political exaction. France might be employed as an intermediary in the initial stages of Sino-American contacts, to establish the terms of reference for direct negotiations. The possibility should at least be mentioned of French assistance to China's aircraft or missile programmes—many of China's nuclear scientists were trained in France—which might arise if France broke with the United States and allowed her anti-American sentiments full play.

China could build up a form of political pressure against the United States by making proposals for the control of nuclear weapons. This would be very difficult for the United States wholly to ignore, particularly if the Chinese initiative were backed by a volume of Asian opinion. The official Chinese announcement of the nuclear detonation proposed that 'a summit conference of all the countries of the world be convened to discuss the question of the complete prohibition and thorough destruction of nuclear weapons, and that, as a first step, the summit conference should reach an agreement to the effect that the nuclear powers and those countries which will soon become nuclear powers undertake not to use nuclear weapons, neither to use them against non-nuclear countries and nuclear-free zones nor against each other'.[1] An initial American reaction was that the United States was ready to discuss these questions with China whenever Peking had anything constructive to say. It is self-evident that any plans for a denuclearised zone in Southern Asia could be carried out only with China's consent. As a member of the nuclear club, China would require important political or strategic concessions from her adversaries as the price of taking part in schemes to control nuclear weapons; on the other hand, she would have to accept the

[1] The Times, 17 October 1964

inspection of her nuclear resources. Chinese co-operation in measures to control nuclear weapons might begin, but could not remain, on an *ad hoc* basis: China would have to occupy a regular place in world counsels. The question of China's admittance to the United Nations would be unavoidable.

The problem of getting to the heart of Chinese thinking on nuclear doctrine is made more complicated by the statements of the Chinese leaders on nuclear war. They are perhaps the only people in the world who regard the atom bomb as a paper tiger. Mao Tse-tung's remark that men not materials count is well known. Propaganda which has disparaged the effects of nuclear destruction and asserted that a nuclear war would mean the end of the imperialist system, not of man, has lent substance to the thesis that China's leaders do not really understand what they are talking about when they discuss nuclear war in such terms. The thesis seemed to be strengthened by the polemics directed against the Chinese by prominent Communists like Khrushchev and Togliatti who affirmed (in 1960 and 1962 respectively) that the leaders of China knew nothing about modern war. There is perhaps truth in the argument that during the 1950s Chinese judgements about nuclear technology were uncertain, that the Chinese leaders had an imperfect understanding of nuclear war at the time of the Korean War, and that they appeared to miscalculate the gains that they could make as a result of the Russian missile and Sputnik achievements of 1957.

However, it would be a mistake to attach much significance to Communist propaganda of the Sino-Soviet dispute, and miss its significance, or to underestimate the Chinese capacity to learn from their own nuclear programme. In 1960, Chinese leaders argued that any exaggeration of the destructiveness of nuclear weapons (a Russian sin) lowered 'socialist' morale, paralysed the revolutionary spirit, and merely played into the hands of American nuclear blackmail. (The Chinese announcement of their nuclear detonation stated, consistently with this, that it was a major step in the struggle to 'oppose the United States imperialist policy of nuclear blackmail and nuclear threats'.) The crucial point was, as the Chinese Government pointed out in September 1963, what should be the Communist policy in the face of American nuclear blackmail—resistance or capitulation? The Chinese chose resistance. They argued, moreover, that in wars of national liberation, 'where the lines zigzag' as in South Viet Nam, nuclear weapons would inflict damage on both belligerents and have a limited use; and they noted the political constraints upon the American use of nuclear power in Asia.

There has been a wide gulf between Chinese bellicosity in words and deeds. The history of several post-Korean War crises in Indochina and Quemoy strongly suggests that China has been restrained by American power, and has sought to avoid a direct clash with a nuclear armed United States. There has been no confrontation; instead caution, not recklessness, has been the keynote of Chinese employment of military force in situations likely to involve American national interests. There is a powerful school of thought amongst American analysts of Chinese military doctrine which believes that caution will predominate in Chinese policy when China acquires nuclear weapons. Mrs. Hsieh, who has written about this problem, has concluded that 'the Chinese do understand the significance of nuclear warfare and are not inclined to be reckless.'[1] The writings of Chinese military experts are amongst the evidence brought forward to support this conclusion. In striking contrast to the official pabulum for public consumption, Chinese analyses of military doctrine and modern war reveal an awareness of the destructive capacity of nuclear weapons, of China's vulnerability to nuclear strikes, and a lively concern for the possibilities of a surprise nuclear attack. There is a familiar, even comforting, rationality about all this which goes far to dispel the assertions of Chinese ignorance and recklessness in the nuclear age. As if to confirm this, Marshal Chen Yi has denied that China will become aggressive when she acquires nuclear weapons.[2] The implication is not that China will repudiate her foreign policy objectives but that she will be cautious in the pursuit of them in the nuclear age.

Assuming that the Chinese leaders do understand the significance of nuclear warfare, there are four factors which would caution them against recklessness. They are: first, the ability of Chinese military experts to understand the implications of

[1] Alice Langley Hsieh, *Communist China and Nuclear Force*, The Rand Corporation, 1963 (Paper P-2719), p. 13. See also her *Communist China's Strategy in the Nuclear Era*, Prentice Hall, 1962, passim. I have drawn on Mrs. Hsieh's studies and on Harold C. Hinton's 'The Implications of Communist China's Emergence as a Nuclear Power', Institute for Defense Analyses, Washington (ronoed, n.d.), a paper delivered in 1962 to a Columbia University seminar

[2] *The Times*, 4 May 1964

various nuclear weapons systems. What is sometimes called 'weapons differentation' is not, or will shortly not be, beyond their capabilities. Thus they can calculate the relative strength of Chinese weapons. This is supported by the Kung-tso T'ung-hsun material of 1961. Second, Chinese military experts understand the significance of their own nuclear capability in the balance against the immensely superior capabilities of the United States and the Soviet Union. As a result, they are likely to realise the extent of their military dependence upon the Soviet Union in situations of high level violence. Third, on the basis of their previous experience of Russian assistance, and as a result of the Sino-Soviet split, the Chinese leaders would presumably remain uncertain of the character of the Soviet Union's military commitment to China. Thus, they recognise China's nuclear inferiority and seek, by their policy of military 'self-dependence', to deter American attack without the benefit of Russian nuclear protection.[1] Fourth, the Chinese leaders cannot but be aware of the vulnerability of Chinese cities, ports, industrial complexes and communication systems even to American conventional attack. There are a limited number of economic and industrial centres in China—some 51 according to an estimate published in 1962[2]—and it is well within the capability of the United States to destroy them all. Knowledge of this has a bearing on Chinese calculations of what they could regard as acceptable risks in a challenge to American interests. The Chinese nuclear industry itself remains extremely vulnerable during the years of fissile accumulation to American conventional or nuclear attack. The United States could find a 'Tonking pretext' to destroy the gaseous diffusion plant and with it the Chinese nuclear weapons programme for several years.

Is there any reason, then, for presuming that when China acquires a local nuclear capability, the point—the threshold—at which the United States will be prepared to introduce nuclear power of her own against China will be affected? Since the time of the Korean War, that is for a number of years before China detonated a nuclear device, the threshold has been at a fairly high level of violence. During this period there have been major constraints and serious limitations upon the

[1] Davis B. Bobrow, 'Peking's Military Calculus', *World Politics*, January 1964, reprinted in *Survival*, May–June 1964
[2] See Alice Langley Hsieh, *Communist China and Nuclear Force*, fn. pp. 14–15

availability of American nuclear power in Asia; political limitations and the very real constraints imposed by the American commitments in other areas. Will the advent of Chinese nuclear power imply that the United States is prepared to introduce nuclear power at lower or higher levels of violence than she would otherwise have been?

China will remain in a position of nuclear inferiority to the United States until the time when she achieves the nuclear capability to deter the United States from a strike by the ability to inflict unacceptable damage upon the United States after being herself damaged; until, that is, she develops a relatively invulnerable long-range strategic deterrent. Meanwhile, a considerable period must elapse before China acquires the nuclear capability to strike directly against the United States. In the circumstances, caution is warranted, and the Chinese leaders may be assumed to be sufficiently rational to see it. In the circumstances, too, some of the strategic options which analysts have thought China might use appear to involve a high level of risk which might prove to be unacceptable. There is, for example, the concept of a 'catalytic War', according to which China contrives to bring the United States and the Soviet Union to a nuclear conflict in order that she might gain from the devastation of the two nuclear giants. Even if she engages in operations at a low level of violence, China will have reason to fear the prospect of the escalation of the conflict out of the range of her possible nuclear responses. She might attempt to insure herself against American nuclear action by threatening the smaller Asian allies of the United States with nuclear weapons. The effects of this hostage strategy are difficult to calculate at long range, but they have a bearing upon the question of whether the threshold is raised or lowered in the future.

The deterrent value of the nuclear weapons which they will acquire has probably been an important element in the Chinese determination of policy options. Presumably, they have calculated that Chinese nuclear weapons would deter an American nuclear counter blow in response to some non-nuclear aggression by China. If this is the case, they have assumed that China's nuclear capability will actually raise the threshold of violence before the United States would retaliate with nuclear power. This would be the point of a hostage strategy against Thailand, for example, designed to make the Thais so fearful of involvement in a nuclear exchange that they would not wish the United States to protect them with nuclear weapons. The possibility that the Soviet Union might be drawn into a conflict between China and the United States would also tend to raise the threshold. It might be lowered if the Soviet Union made it clear that she would not defend China.

A reason generally taken as the motive for nuclear diffusion is the fear of vulnerability on the part of the non-nuclear countries. In the development of strategic doctrine there has been an interesting implication that when a minor nuclear power emerges it loses the immunity which it might obtain by remaining without nuclear weapons. There are risks as well as privileges involved in joining the circle of nuclear powers. In other words, the way for a country to become vulnerable is to acquire nuclear weapons. Now, until the time that China develops a nuclear capability to counter-attack the United States, her nuclear power can only be employed in actions in Asia. The deterrent value of China's nuclear weapons would be local, confined to the region. There would seem, then, to be no logical reason why the threshold should rise. For a country may possess nuclear weapons without retaining its nuclear capability under all circumstances of attack. This is the position of China for the foreseeable future: she is still a long way from acquiring a nuclear capability which will survive an American nuclear attack. On purely military grounds, there would be good reason for the United States to use her nuclear power against China at a lower level of violence. China can have few illusions that, in the event of a war with the United States, the types of restraint which had characterised American policy in the Korean War would be observed. In this sense, the nuclear threshold would be lowered by a Chinese nuclear capability.

Chapter 7

An Indigenous Defence System

A N indigenous defence system for Southern Asia should be able to deal with local aggression, including subversion directed from without, against its members, as SEATO was designed to do. It must also contemplate a problem which appeared to be fairly remote in 1954, when SEATO was established. In the ten-year interval China has moved closer to the stage where she acquires a local nuclear capability with which to menace her neighbours and assert her authority in the area; she might choose to increase her conventional threats to Southern Asia under cover of it. The prospect of aggression from a nuclear-armed China confirms the need for some form of continuing Western military presence as the basis of an indigenous defence system. As a form of that Western presence, SEATO is not particularly effective against subversion in the treaty area, its value as a deterrent to aggressors is debatable, and its general usefulness after China acquires a local nuclear capability is open to question. A Western presence is only one ingredient of a collective security system; there must also be a sense of common responsibility for the security of the area amongst the Southern Asian countries themselves. There is little evidence of a growth of this sense in Southern Asia. Apparently it was not induced by the obvious and varied threats of subversion in Southern Asia, nor by the plain examples of Chinese and Indonesian military pressure. It is indeed as likely that the response of the Southern Asian countries to a nuclear-armed China might be an acceptance of neutrality under Chinese hegemony as that it would be a stiffening of their collective will to resist aggression. Is there, then, much scope at all for a collective security system in Southern Asia?

The members of SEATO have made notable efforts to give the treaty organisation a social and economic content. Altogether, the SEATO projects to promote the general welfare of the member countries are designed to complement the work of the other aid organisations and not to compete with them. It is therefore in the political and military fields that SEATO'S distinctive contribution to collective security in Southern Asia is most appropriately judged. SEATO, a collective security organisation with three Asian members, has been described throughout its career as inadequate. It is regarded by its critics as a political liability, dividing its Asian members from their neighbours and increasing the general tensions of the area. If SEATO really has this result, it is clearly defeating its own purposes, and one may ask whether this alleged effect is peculiar to SEATO itself or is likely to follow any attempt to establish a system of collective security for a region as weak and divided as Southern Asia.

Perhaps the most damaging criticism of SEATO is that because of its divisive effect it inadvertently serves Communist purposes in two ways: 'It tends to isolate internationally, and particularly from the rest of Asia, the Southeast Asian governments associated with it'; and 'The SEATO approach has pushed various nonaligned countries towards the Communist bloc'.[1] But have the three Asian members of SEATO—Pakistan, Thailand and the Philippines—been isolated in any significant manner by their membership? They are not members of a bloc which walls them off from their neighbours. Their subscription to the Manila Pact has not noticeably isolated them internationally or, except perhaps in the case of Pakistan, from the Asian countries who refused to join SEATO. After 1954, Pakistan fell away from the 'Hindic group' of Colombo Powers, India, Burma, Indonesia and Cambodia, 'the modern equivalents of the Hinduized states of the pre-European era.'[2] Trade and cultural exchanges between Pakistan and the Soviet Union have shown a marked development in recent years. China's relationships with Pakistan have broadened since 1954 on diplomatic foundations laid down before the establishment of SEATO. It might even be suggested that Pakistan's membership of SEATO provided the two great Communist powers with an extra incentive to develop friendly relations with her in order to weaken the treaty organisation. The political barriers between Pakistan and India are not of SEATO's making. Pakistan joined SEATO to gain an advantage over India, and her criticisms of the treaty organisation show that she does not think this has been achieved. India's strong criticisms of SEATO

[1] Oliver E. Clubb, Jr., *The United States and the Sino-Soviet Bloc in Southeast Asia*, The Brookings Institution, 1962, p. 99

[2] J. H. Brimmell, *Communism in South East Asia. A Political Analysis*, Oxford University Press, 1959, pp. 286–87

were directed at the Western powers for interfering in the affairs of the region rather than at the Asian powers for joining the treaty organisation. Her attitude towards receiving military assistance from external powers has mellowed considerably after the experience of Chinese aggression. Both Thailand and the Philippines played a useful role as mediators in the early stages of the dispute between Indonesia and Malaysia. Japan's policy in Southern Asia is to promote closer ties with SEATO and non-aligned countries alike.

Few of the various non-aligned countries of Southern Asia appear to have been pushed by the SEATO approach towards the Communist bloc. India's policy of cultivating friendly relations with the Soviet Union and with China was not caused by her unfavourable reaction to SEATO. In 1949 India and Burma were the first two non-Communist countries to recognise the new government of China. Indonesia established diplomatic relations with China in 1953. The foreign policies of these three countries were based upon their rejection of cold war diplomacy, and their attitudes towards SEATO were part of that general context. India and Indonesia both modified their hostility towards SEATO after their respective difficulties with China. The Government of Malaysia is anti-Communist and in sympathy with the purposes of SEATO, although it is not a member of the organisation. Cambodia's decision to move towards the Chinese sphere of influence may have been partly the result of a calculation of SEATO's ineffectiveness in Indochina, but for years she was content to receive aid from SEATO sources. There seems on balance to be little of substance in the criticisms about SEATO'S divisive effects in Southern Asia. Such criticisms would appear to exaggerate the political significance of SEATO as a factor in the relations between the countries of Southern Asia. The real faults of SEATO lie elsewhere.

The Manila Pact publicly declared the members' 'sense of unity', so that any potential aggressor would appreciate that the parties 'stand together in the area'. But the parties clearly do not stand closely together in the area, and the SEATO consultative processes have not had a conspicuous success in developing common viewpoints. During the early years of SEATO the organisation was not an effective forum for consultations between its members on important matters occurring within the treaty area, such as the Indonesian rebellion of 1958. The crisis in Laos between 1960 and 1962 caused strains within the alliance; not all the members were satisfied with the rather vague SEATO viewpoint on an appropriate course of action which was adopted after the seventh annual meeting of the Council of Foreign Ministers in 1961. Greater agreement was reached on a policy which resulted in SEATO members (apart from France and Pakistan) sending forces to Thailand in response to a Pathet Lao advance towards the Thai border in May 1962. But it cannot be said that anything like a SEATO viewpoint or a SEATO bloc has been achieved in Southern Asia. A SEATO viewpoint is no longer necessary before certain actions can be taken in SEATO's name. In March 1962 the United States assured the Thai Government that her obligation under SEATO to help Thailand resist aggression by Communist armed attack was individual as well as collective, and did not depend upon the prior agreement of all the other Manila Pact signatories. In other words, the use of American military power to deter Communist armed attack does not require SEATO agreement or a sense of unity amongst the members of the treaty. SEATO has the appearance of a cover for an American–Thai bilateral pact.

SEATO's value as a deterrent to armed attack within the treaty area, and specifically to armed attack by China, has been assumed rather than demonstrated. It is difficult to arrive at a firm conclusion about whether SEATO has in fact deterred armed attacks by China upon its members, because of the nature of the evidence required about the workings of Chinese policy. There have, of course, been no external, armed Communist attacks upon Pakistan, Thailand and the Philippines during SEATO's existence. But to draw from this the conclusion that SEATO deterred China is to make the very large assumption that China intended to attack those countries after 1954, that she had the capability to attack them, and that she was inhibited from attacking them by the threat of a collective SEATO response. SEATO is not a collective defence system like NATO, with a command structure and a system of permanently assigned forces; it is a body for making military plans and conducting annual exercises with forces loaned for the purpose. It has an annual budget of less than $1 million. The deterrent aspect of SEATO is American military power, which is in any case deployed in the treaty area and which is not significantly increased by the contributions of other members of SEATO. This is recognized by the United States who urges her allies to contribute token forces or assistance,

as in South Viet Nam, in order to demonstrate the political
solidarity of SEATO.

Measured against its original objectives with regard to
subversion, SEATO has had a limited success. It has not
prevented subversion directed from without and its counter-
subversion activities are restricted to analysis and advice. By
these means, SEATO hopes to facilitate counter-subversion
arrangements between the member governments, but it has no
power to compel those governments to make arrangements or
accept its advice. It tends, that is, to *légiférer dans le vide*. The
task of countering subversion is, by its very nature, the responsibility of each member government, and as a SEATO
official explained to the author the SEATO authorities must
proceed tactfully with their advice in order to avoid the
impression of seeking to exercise too much influence over the
internal affairs of the member governments. Many SEATO
recommendations in the field of counter subversion have been
rejected by sensitive member governments, who have interpreted them as criticism of their policies. Other recommendations have been accepted, for example, by the Thai
Government, as useful contributions to the task of countering
subversion. In doing so, SEATO ought to be able to operate on
Interpol lines, but the Asian countries lack their own Scotland
Yards or FBIs and have a backward concept of police functions
and civil intelligence. Moreover, SEATO's usefulness as a
counter subversion organisation within the treaty area is
limited by the extent of its Asian membership. There seems to
be no immediate threat to Pakistan or to the Philippines from
subversion directed from without. SEATO's efforts appear to be
concentrated on the subversive threat to Thailand. SEATO is
not much use with regard to Malaysia and the problems of
subversion directed from Indonesia. In this respect, SEATO is
a regional pact without responsibility for the region.

The prospects for a system of collective security in Southern
Asia which has a broader Asian participation than SEATO
depend ultimately upon the degree to which Asian countries
feel collectively responsible for their own security. Developments in Asia since 1954 have increased the concern of individual countries for their own security in the face of a clearer
threat from China and Indonesia, but it is less certain that any
sense of common responsibility has been evolving. The major
Asian powers have not taken a definite lead in this respect.
Although Japan is reluctant to undertake military commit-

ments outside her borders, her diplomatic and economic interests in the area may lead her in the future to a position of greater political responsibility, as suggested by the Prime Minister, Mr. Sato, in November 1964. India is too pre-occupied with her own defence problems to express much general concern for Asian security. After the Chinese attack upon her borders and the death of Mr. Nehru, she has played a more subdued role in Asian affairs and is engaged in formu-lating new approaches. The efforts of her foreign policy, how-ever, are directed towards improving her position with her immediate neighbours. A similar trend of individual rather than of collective concern is apparent amongst the lesser Asian countries. None of the Asian countries has joined SEATO after 1954. Part of their reluctance to become involved in a collective defence system may be their calculation that their security is better served by bilateral arrangements with the great powers, but it is also attributable to the unresolved conflicts throughout the area.

In each of the three strategic zones of Southern Asia there are conflicts and antagonisms which inhibit the opportunities for military collaboration between the indigenous countries for mutual defence. The Kashmir imbroglio prevents a common approach in the Indo-Pakistan zone, although it has not prevented the co-operative venture of the Indus Basin project. In the Indochina zone (including Burma and Thailand), border issues divide the several states, though the riparian countries have given their support to the Mekong Basin programme. (This has certain disadvantages for the Govern-ment of South Viet Nam, as the Mekong River forms one of the most important Viet Cong supply routes from China via Cambodia).[1] The Indonesian hostilities against Malaysia have split the Malay countries in the Maphilindo zone and damaged the usefulness of regional co-operative groups, such as the Association of Southeast Asia inaugurated in 1961 to advance the social and economic progress of the region. Impulses towards regional co-operation clearly exist in each zone, but they remain weak in comparison with the divisive factors. It is uncertain whether the movement towards regional co-opera-tion in Southern Asia will increase after China acquires a local nuclear capability. In all probability, smaller countries like Burma and Cambodia, who have embarked upon a course of

[1] Robert R. Brunn, ' "Red Trails" Traced In Cambodia', *Christian Science Monitor*, 9 September 1964

anti-Western neutrality, will be confirmed in their policy. On a broader scale, much will depend upon the Indian and Japanese reactions to the Chinese development of nuclear weapons, and whether they seek guarantees from the Western nuclear powers for their own security.

In view of the absence of a strong movement for regional co-operation in Southern Asia, plus the need for a continuing Western presence and the problem of disequilibrium associated with it, what are the prospects of developing over the next decade or so an indigenous system of collective defence for the Southern Asian countries, with the United States and the United Kingdom (or some wider European grouping) as its residual guarantors, but no longer providing its front line troops? If the question is considered in relation to the three possible levels of violence—first, subversion directed from without; second, local aggression and conventional wars; and third, high level violence where the conflicts approach the nuclear threshold—it is apparent that an indigenous system of collective defence can reasonably be expected to deal only with situations in the first two levels of violence. Situations of high level violence will directly involve the interests of the external guarantor powers. If nuclear weapons are deployed throughout Southern Asia, the nuclear threshold may be lowered as a deliberate strategy of the nuclear powers or as the result of miscalculations. It is very improbable that China would distribute nuclear weapons, and the possibility of nuclear diffusion in Southern Asia seems fairly distant, since it is not the policy of the existing nuclear powers to encourage it. The main problems of aggression during the next ten years will most likely be concerned with subversion and local wars; that is, with conflicts that are conceivably within the capacity of an indigenous defence system to control.

We may also surmise that future conflict in Southern Asia will be more difficult to justify after the end of the colonial era. Both Malaysia and South Viet Nam became independent countries on the withdrawal of a Western colonial power, and the governments which oppose those countries argue with some plausibility that they are merely disguised forms of colonialism in Asia. Indonesia and North Viet Nam publicly explain their policies to an Afro-Asian audience by the nationalist claim to be righting a colonialist wrong. The defence of Malaysia and South Viet Nam poses serious problems for their external supporters, not the least of which are the political constraints upon direct action against the aggressors. It is not very likely that the Western powers will be faced in Southern Asia with new situations of the Malaysian and South Vietnamese types; that is, where they defend states whose right to a separate existence is denied by the aggressors. There are virtually no more colonial situations to be liquidated in Southern Asia which could provide additional opportunities for aggression to be disguised as anti-colonialism. Apart from Brunei, the remaining Portuguese footholds in Asia, part of New Guinea and some Pacific dependencies, the colonial map of Southern Asia has been redrawn.

As a consequence, future Asian aggression will be directed against independent Asian countries. It will be aggression un-disguised by the anti-colonial arguments which apparently carry so much weight in the Afro-Asian world. North Viet Nam makes out a case for the unification of Viet Nam to justify its methods to achieve that end. To rationalise her policy of confrontation against Malaysia, Indonesia offers arguments about Borneo which are not universally held to be worthless. China's arguments about her borders with India have been sympathetically received in a number of countries, Pakistan, Taiwan and elsewhere in Asia. In each instance, there has been an effort to justify an aggressive policy by arguments which relate to the colonial period, in order to create political con-straints against the use of countervailing power and to win general acceptance for the policy. Future aggressors in Asia, whether they be Communist or nationalist, will not find 'colonial' arguments as ready to hand. One can only speculate about the long-term effects this situation might have upon world opinion and the development of political constraints against the defending powers. A result might be that it will be easier to marshal, or even to formulate, world opinion against Asian aggressors. It might remove some of the existing political constraints upon intervention by external powers on the behalf of the victim of aggression. Perhaps it would have a favourable effect upon the movements towards regional co-operation in Southern Asia.

One function of an indigenous defence system in Southern Asia would be to deal with subversion and local aggression if possible without allowing the particular conflicts to escalate beyond its military capacity to the point where external powers were obliged to intervene. The members of the system would therefore have to possess the will as well as the resources to fight long wars, if necessary, on the lower levels of violence. Counter-insurgency operations are protracted affairs. It took nearly ten years to put down the threat of the Huk revolt in the Philip-pines, and the Malayan Emergency lasted from 1948 to 1960. During 1964 it was estimated that the effort to defeat the Viet Cong guerrillas in South Viet Nam could take at least another ten years with American assistance, and the director of opera-tions in the North Borneo states said that the Indonesian guerrilla war against Malaysia could drag on for a similar period.[1] Neither the South Vietnamese nor the Malaysian Government possesses the resources to sustain such struggles unaided for years on end. If the United States and the United Kingdom are to withdraw from a front line role in those countries and become the residual guarantors of an indigenous defence system, military assistance to South Viet Nam and Malaysia, at least comparable with American and British support, must be forthcoming from the other Asian powers in the region. But it is an unlikely contingency that Asian coun-tries, unless they are directly attacked, will involve themselves militarily in South Viet Nam and Malaysia, or indeed else-where, in wars of 'Asians against Asians'. On this showing, the United States and the United Kingdom will probably be involved in a front line role in Southern Asia for a decade or more, as a result of their respective obligations to defend South Viet Nam and Malaysia, assuming that the Governments of South Viet Nam and Malaysia do not collapse under pressure in the meantime. In order that the United States and the United Kingdom might assume, over the next ten years, less a front line and more a guarantor role in relation to the free countries of the area, there must be, first, an indigenous defence system capable of dealing with aggression by subversion and local attacks, and, second, a credible deterrent to aggression in Southern Asia.

In the first place, no such system exists. It can be constructed around the collective strength of the major Asian powers, like Indonesia, India and Japan, only when their governments are willing or able to change their traditional policies and enter into military commitments with the weaker Asian countries. In the case of Indonesia, this policy would require a fundamental alteration in her foreign relations from an aggressive to a de-fensive outlook, which was an objective of American policy, but probably only a serious threat to Indonesian security by China

[1] *The Times*, 13 April 1964

would cause such a major reversal of attitude. There are strong political forces in India and Japan opposed to those countries assuming military commitments in Southern Asia. In Japan's case, there are constitutional impediments as well which preclude any Japanese participation in an indigenous system of collective defence. The ninth article of the Japanese Constitution states that Japan shall not possess any war potential. This prohibitive clause has been interpreted by the Government to mean military capabilities over and above the minimum necessary for the defence of Japan itself. Moreover, the Cabinet Legislative Bureau views the right of self-defence in such a manner as to exclude collective self-defence. Under the present constitutional arrangements, it is not thought possible to employ Japanese troops outside Japan. The revision of the Constitution to enable Japan to develop her military strength and to take part in the collective defence of Asia is not practicable in the present political climate. (By 1964, ten years after the Japanese Parliament passed the Self Defence Forces Law and established the Self Defence Agency, the Supreme Court had not made a definite pronouncement of the constitutionality of the Self Defence Forces.)

There would have to be very strong inducements for India and Japan to shift their diplomatic positions to the extent that they became the focal points of a regional defence system; for it would mean that they accepted the front line role of the United States and the United Kingdom in the area, with all its responsibilities, frustrations and expenditure of military resources, as well as raising the possibility of conflict with China which they might otherwise avoid. If the threats to the weaker Southern Asian countries are confined to subversion and local aggression from militant states like China, Indonesia and North Viet Nam, then India and Japan would presumably lack a strong enough incentive to intervene in a front line capacity against the aggressors, particularly since the Western powers will probably offer their support to the victims in any case. If India and Japan are themselves threatened by subversion and local attacks, their governments may not feel that they have sufficient resources to spare for assisting weaker Asian countries, and may seek to concentrate their efforts upon handling the threats to their own integrity. It is hard to see what inducements the external powers can offer India and Japan to persuade them to accept the risks of military responsibilities in Southern Asia, or what actions they can take to bring about an increased Asian involvement in the problems of collective defence.

In the second place, there is the problem of deterring aggression in Southern Asia: this is basically a matter of preventing direct or indirect aggression by the three main candidates—China, North Viet Nam and Indonesia. The Southern Asian countries (including Australia) do not have the military power necessary to deter high level violence; that power is possessed by the external countries, and specifically by the United States. It may be true to say that China and North Viet Nam are deterred from committing major aggression by American power. It is also true that Western military strength has not so far deterred those countries, or Indonesia, from supporting subversion. Subversion is a form of aggression which is difficult, perhaps impossible, to deter. It is a technique designed to offer few risks to the external sponsors, for example by taking advantage of local conflicts under the cover of national movements. The resumption of Viet Cong activities in South Viet Nam in 1964, after the American air strike against bases in Tongking, showed the difficulty of deterring the Hanoi Government from its policy of unifying Viet Nam by armed force. (In this case, there are also the related questions of how self-sufficient the Viet Cong would be in a situation where they received no support from North Viet Nam, and whether the revolutionary movement in the South would stop its armed efforts on orders from Hanoi.) It is proving extremely difficult to arrive at ways of deterring aggression-by-proxy in Southern Asia, and elsewhere.

Part of this difficulty is knowing exactly where to place the emphasis of the threat to make deterrence credible. Take the fairly straightforward case of Indonesian hostilities against Malaysia: how does the United Kingdom deter the Indonesian Government from its policy of confrontation? The Malaysian Government does not possess the military strength to deter the Indonesian leaders. The Indonesian military leaders probably take the threat of a British counter-blow more seriously, or more rationally, than does the President. The military leaders are capable of estimating the effects of possible counter-blows, but the degree to which they can exercise a moderating influence upon the Government is limited by a number of considerations. They, too, have to be fervent nationalists in competition with the Indonesian Communist Party. It is the party which might benefit most of all from a conflict which broke up the existing government of Indonesia and weakened the armed forces. Western strategic thinking places reliance upon the rationality of a Russian reaction to a deterrent threat, and is placing some reliance upon the rationality of a Chinese reaction. But it does seem that little reliance can be placed upon the rationality of an Indonesian reaction, at least under the existing government.

To sum up this stage: the Southern Asian countries lack the power to deter aggression by the three main aggressors, and only the external powers can maintain convincing deterrent policies (though there are qualifications with regard to certain forms of conflict, such as subversion). The question, in terms of collective security, is whether aggression can best be deterred by a system of alliances or associations, which makes clear to potential aggressors the stages at which countervailing power would be employed? Or whether such a system would be likely to increase the range of conflicts below the force levels at which that countervailing power could be most effectively and acceptably employed? The discussion so far has assumed that an increased Asian participation is desirable, and that it would contribute towards the desired goal of a greater collective security in Southern Asia. But would it have this effect? The question is worth raising, since implicit in the assumption itself is the notion that an objective of Western policy should be to bring about a greater involvement of Asian countries in other Asian countries' troubles. If this objective were to be achieved in any degree, despite the many difficulties, would it follow that there was an increased deterrent to aggression? Or would a likely result be that aggression in Southern Asia involved extra countries in conflicts which might escalate more rapidly? This is a rather abstract way of putting the question, but it does suggest one of the basic problems of collective defence in Southern Asia. An indigenous collective security system which does not deter aggression, but which multiplies the number of countries obliged to deal with it, might provide the conditions for great power intervention and increase the scope of the conflict. The description of Southern Asia as a balkanised region seems particularly appropriate in this context.

The question poses interesting issues about what kinds of power in Southern Asia will deter aggressors, and in what circumstances. But the immediate point is that for there to be a credible Western deterrent in Southern Asia, a Western military presence in the area is desirable for political as well as military reasons. It is clear that some more satisfactory manner of linking the deterrent power of the interested Western countries to the security requirements of the Southern Asian countries must be found, if aggression is to be deterred as well as dealt with in the future. This problem may become easier to solve if the forms of aggression become less ambiguous in ways already suggested. Even so, the presumption here is that it is the Western and not the Asian view of the threats to the countries of the area that will have to prevail before a satisfactory military solution is reached. The plain fact is that the power to deter aggression in Southern Asia will only be made available when the external countries who possess that power regard it as in their own interests to use it. It may be, as some Southern Asian statesmen have feared, that there is no way of guaranteeing that Western power will be used in the defence of their countries, particularly if the stakes are high enough. Yet it is a paradox of some Asian (and specifically Indian) thinking that Western power will, in any case, be used in their defence, if the stakes are high enough.

This latter opinion about the role of the Western great powers in Southern Asia may prove in the event to be an imprudent assumption, to say the least, but its effect is to reinforce the tendency of Southern Asian countries to rely for their defence in certain contingencies on *ad hoc* assistance, rather than upon collective security systems which would involve them in their neighbours' troubles. (Neither of the SEATO members on the Asian mainland appear to have much faith in SEATO as a deterrent, as is indicated by Pakistan's continued fear of Indian aggression and Thailand's desire for additional guarantees within the SEATO framework.) It may be imprudent, that is, for non-aligned statesmen to assume that the Western powers will continue to underwrite the state system in Southern Asia and go on accepting front line responsibilities for perhaps an indefinite period. There are signs that the British Government would prefer to scale down its responsibilities in Southern Asia, even within the SEATO alliance, and that the American administration is becoming more selective and discriminating with its assistance to non-aligned countries. Of the Western SEATO powers, France has moved furthest in the direction of disengagement in Southern Asia. There is a general tendency amongst the interested Western powers to re-examine their positions in Southern Asia and to review the assumptions of the containment strategy of the

1950s in the light of the developments since SEATO was established.

One significant aspect of this re-thinking process is a realisation of the subordinate role played by SEATO in the Southern Asian state system, either as a defensive coalition or as a diplomatic grouping. The influence of the Western powers in Southern Asia, as exercised through the treaty organisation, does not bear directly upon main military developments in the region or upon the major challenges by aggressive Asian countries. (The fact that the aggressors have not challenged the SEATO countries may be a tribute of a sort to the effectiveness of SEATO as a deterrent.) The development of adequate collective security measures to meet the evolving aggressive threats in Southern Asia is complicated by the need to find a *modus vivendi* between the two currents of Western and Asian policy which differ in their proposed solutions to the defence problems of the area. The Western policy whose object is to ensure a greater Asian participation in the burden of defence runs counter to the Asian policy which relies upon an increased Western effort to defend both allied and non-aligned countries.

Neither the United Kingdom nor the United States wishes to remain in the front line in Southern Asia. Both governments are prepared to do so to honour their existing commitments through SEATO, ANZUS and their respective bilateral responsibilities such as in Malaysia and South Viet Nam. But this situation is regarded in London and in Washington as essentially a temporary state of affairs; and it is a long-term objective of American and British policy in Southern Asia to withdraw from a front line to a guarantor position when a viable defence system can be constructed by the indigenous countries. It seems improbable, however, that this condition will be met in the immediate future, and in the United Kingdom and the United States there is a sense of disillusionment with the efforts of their Southern Asian allies and associates to build up their defence capabilities and assume more substantial responsibilities for the collective security of the area.

Conclusion

The Security of Southern Asia

THE problems of the security of Southern Asia require a co-ordinated rather than a collective approach. A central problem is that of building viable nations, in some cases out of unpromising and divided elements, which are capable of some measure of self-defence common effort, in a sensitive area close to China where the Chinese have special interests. This involves the Western powers in the task of propping up individual countries whilst attempting to establish with their help a stable combination of states. If the West is to provide an intelligent focus for the national efforts of the indigenous countries, it may have to adopt new approaches. There may be a case for more informal arrangements rather than pacts, for the use of diplomacy rather than of central organisations like SEATO, in order to steer the countries of the area towards sensible objectives and make the best use of the assistance granted to them. The Western objective, to help build a stable international society in Southern Asia, is counter to the Communist interest in creating instability and sponsoring revolutionary movements throughout the area.

Chinese influence at present casts a longer shadow than Chinese power over the remarkably confused set of national relations emerging in Southern Asia. The encouragement of violence and chaos in the region, probably by indirect means, presents greater opportunities for China, at least in the foreseeable future, than a direct challenge to the United States. Chinese investment in subversion will pay large dividends. The economic and political conditions of nearly all Southern Asian countries provide excellent conditions for subversion directed from without by Communist or other forces; the only exceptions are perhaps Australia and New Zealand.

The tensions of multi-racial societies, as in Malaysia, the Overseas Chinese communities in Singapore, Thailand and elsewhere, and the ubiquitous Communist Parties, are all sources of subversive activities built in to the structure of individual Southern Asian countries. Some governments in the area are not masters in their own houses. Laos is virtually partitioned, with the Pathet Lao controlling the length of the frontier with South Viet Nam, and is governed by factions. In South Viet Nam, the Government has lost control over much of the countryside, and a rival government flourishes in the guerrilla areas, conducting its own diplomacy with neighbouring governments. In Burma and Thailand, the central government has tenuous control over the remoter areas, where Communist subversive activities can develop amongst the racial minorities indifferent or hostile to Rangoon and Bangkok. In north-east Thailand, there is being waged against Communist subversion from Laos 'a vital war in which the survival of the Thai nation as it is today is at stake'.[1] There is a strong pro-Chinese group in the divided Indian Communist Party. The pro-Chinese Communist Party of Indonesia could possibly come to power in the near future.

The internal weaknesses which facilitate Communist penetration in Southern Asian countries increase the difficulties of the West's relationship with them. Communist assistance to individual countries, such as Russian aid to Indonesia, has on the whole been more successful than Western aid as a means of acquiring political influence. American aid has in some cases not only failed to win friends for the United States but also helped to lose them. Burma, Cambodia and Indonesia have rejected it and turned to Communist sources for assistance. This shift in the outlook of the three Colombo Powers is significant. Prince Sihanouk of Cambodia requested Chinese, Russian and French weapons to replace the American equipment for his army and air force, and all American military advisers have been withdrawn from the country. In 1964 he commented of American aid: 'Sous prétexte de nous aider à défendre la liberté, elle nous desservait, en nous corrompant. Ils avaient trouvé un moyen de pousser à la concussion: c'était de louer les maisons à des prix exorbitants';[2] and irrespective of the logic of his reasoning, his conclusion is important. This is an example of a failure of a relationship between an external donor and an indigenous recipient which is crucial for the defence of Southern Asia.

Even in those countries which continue to rely upon American aid, such as South Viet Nam and Pakistan, there have been

[1] Theh Chongkhadikij, 'The Battle for the North-East', SEATO Press Release, Bangkok, June 1963

[2] *Le Monde*, 24 June 1964, reprinted in *Survival*, September–October 1964

problems of disequilibrium in the relationship. The United States is the main support of the Saigon Government, but American influence upon it has been a limited and even dis-unifying factor. Pakistan's friendship with China is regarded in Washington as a breach of alliance solidarity. The problems of disequilibrium will be increased if the Chinese attempt to subvert the opposition parties and members of the governments in the Southern Asian countries, as they are attempting to do (not without success) in East Africa, and increase their influence amongst the economically powerful and politically articulate sections of Asian communities. This contingency cannot be ignored in the case of Pakistan, the recipient of large sums of American assistance, where the Chinese connection has been greeted with enthusiasm. Pakistanis regard American defence assistance to India as endangering their security (and clearly do not think that SEATO restores the balance), just as Sihanouk believes Cambodia to be threatened by American aid to Thailand and South Viet Nam. It is quite possible that American military equipment obtained by Indonesia will be employed against Malaysia (and even against Americans, if the ANZUS treaty is invoked and acted on). Thus, American defence assistance designed to promote the stability and security of Southern Asia has produced tensions within countries and between states. In this sense, it can be said to have defeated its own ends, and adversely affected the relations of some countries with the United States whilst promoting them with China.

The antagonisms of the Southern Asian countries, and the lack of a strong tradition of co-operation between them, are additional factors which favour the pursuit of Communist rather than Western objectives in the area. The difficulties of defending the Indochina zone against Chinese and North Vietnamese Communism are greatly increased by Thai-Cambodian–South Vietnamese hostility. Guerrilla sanctuaries in Cambodia and Laos add immeasurably to the military capabilities of the Viet Cong. Whilst the United States and the SEATO powers are unable to develop a common defence policy with these countries because of their mutual hostility, the Viet Minh and its local instruments, the Viet Cong and the Pathet Lao, can co-ordinate their plans for the entire Southeast Asian peninsula.

Similar problems of collective security in the Indian sub-continent and the Maphilindo zone are caused by Indo-Pakistani conflict and Indonesia's confrontation of Malaysia.

The defence of these zones against external aggression would be strengthened if there were a usable tradition of co-operation in Asia. Without it, the Indochina peninsula is particularly vulnerable to low level aggression. The Indo-Pakistani conflict prevents a common approach in a vital area along China's southern borders. An association with other indigenous states, such as the proposed Maphilindo grouping, or something like it, might be a better way in the long run of strengthening Malaysia's security than increasing her armed forces. But smaller Asian countries, such as Cambodia, Pakistan and Malaysia, fear their more powerful neighbours, in some instances apparently more than they fear China; and this reduces the chances of developing an indigenous defence system. The larger Asian powers have in any case been reluctant to take part in collective security pacts with their weaker neighbours, and to accept military responsibilities which might bring them into conflict with China. The shadow of China falls over their relationships. Consequently, it is extremely improbable that the United States and the United Kingdom can in the foreseeable future withdraw from a front line to a guarantor role in the defence of Southern Asia.

The development of a collective approach to this problem has been inhibited by Asian reactions to the very concept of formal regional security pacts. Non-aligned countries rejected it when the idea was sounded in 1954, after being accepted by the United States. India, Indonesia, Burma and Ceylon refused to participate in the Manila Conference, believing that a military pact with external powers would jeopardise their independence. Indians regarded SEATO as a *pis aller*, an American device to exert diplomatic pressure on the Colombo Powers. India's official attitude to formal collective arrangements had not changed by 1964, despite the Chinese attack in 1962, but she had made informal arrangements for her defence with Western powers.

There has been a decided preference for bilateral security pacts with the United States on the part of some aligned Southern Asian countries. The Philippines is the only state with a mutual defence pact with the United States which has joined SEATO; but, before the Manila Conference in 1954, she received an unequivocal guarantee of American assistance under the mutual defence pact of 1951 in case of attack. She has tended to place more reliance upon the 1951 arrangement than upon SEATO. Thailand has sought (and received) what amounts to a bilateral pact with the United States under the cover of SEATO. Pakistan joined SEATO as an insurance against Indian aggression rather than in the interests of the defence of the region. The sense of collective responsibility for Southern Asian security appears to be relatively undeveloped amongst the Asian members of SEATO as well as the non-aligned countries.

The political restraints which prevent a collective approach to the problems of Southern Asian security raise the important question whether defence co-operation could most easily grow out of political co-operation, or vice versa as to some extent occurred in Europe in the course of NATO's development. This involves a broader approach than an attempt to extend the membership of SEATO, which would be unlikely to succeed, or to establish new bilateral relationships with the West throughout Southern Asia. It is a problem of defence diplomacy and informal arrangements designed to make the best use of existing political capital, indigenous resources and defence assistance. It also concerns the extent to which militarily useful collaboration in Southern Asian conditions is better achieved in terms of large, formal organisations and treaties, or on a more moderate and *ad hoc* basis.

It is clear from the example of SEATO that for the foreseeable future it will not be possible to achieve an Asian NATO, an overall organisation with permanently assigned forces and a central planning headquarters. But new arrangements must be made which would overlap with SEATO (which in spite of its name is really concerned with the Indochina peninsula), just as to some extent it overlaps with CENTO, in order to co-ordinate defence measures on an area basis. NATO has both guarantees and an elaborate organisation; SEATO has guarantees but, on the whole, a weak organisation, partly as a result of American and British reluctance to develop it or to tie down permanent conventional forces in an Asian strategic reserve. The Southern Asian collective security system has become a series of multilateral and bilateral guarantees (which cannot be made specific for all future contingencies), without a structure of forces. This is a reason why the Chinese have described SEATO as a paper tiger.

Multilateral pacts often have inherent weaknesses which limit their political and military usefulness. They are generally negotiated under the shadow of an active threat (as SEATO was, in 1954, to meet a cold war situation that had changed), and have to evolve to meet new conditions. Change may cause political disagreements, or bring them to a focus. In recent years there have been disputes within NATO about the best formula for defence and deterrence in Europe, and within SEATO over the crises in Laos. The problems of nuclear strategy and deterrence which concern the NATO powers at present will be increasingly significant for SEATO as China's nuclear weapons programme advances. The conventional attacks that NATO and SEATO were designed to meet have not occurred. SEATO was slow to adopt itself to meet the increased threat of subversion in the treaty area, and continues to be relatively ineffective in the face of it. Formal defence arrangements make common interests explicit, but do not create them; they also establish a situation in which divergences of interests can be made plain. Some members of SEATO have criticised the allocation of responsibilities and resources of the organisation, and may come to believe that their military and political interests in it cease to be compatible. These are real problems in Southern Asia where national policies are in a state of change and governments have a limited ability to meet their formal obligations.

Active external threats to national security can not only stimulate the development of multilateral defence arrangements, but also help to bind the members of them together in a common military effort. (It is possible that had the aggression which SEATO was formed to meet ever eventuated, more countries would have joined it.) The development of NATO was affected in this way by the Korean War. But, at the time of writing, hostilities against India, Malaysia and South Viet Nam have not had this effect amongst the countries of Southern Asia, or even persuaded the victims that their security lies in multilateral defence pacts. They continue to rely upon bilateral agreements or informal arrangements with the Great Powers. Would a flare up of high level violence between India and Pakistan over Kashmir, or a Communist government in Indonesia, or a Viet Cong victory in South Viet Nam, have a different result? It is probable that it would. Some possible outcomes of developments like these have been discussed in Chapter 6, where, it is argued, a major long-term threat would be an aggressive China possessed of an advanced nuclear capability. Some of the changes described in Chapter 6 would radically alter the structure of alliances and power alignments in Southern Asia, but many of them might only occur after a considerable lapse of time, in the '1984' era when China may have a sophisticated delivery system and fusion bombs, and are extremely conjectural, to say the least. Meanwhile, in Southern Asia, where a basic problem of security is concerned with nation building, there is no virtue in waiting for an external danger, however obvious it may appear, to produce a common political approach amongst the threatened indigenous countries and with the West.

There are more immediate threats in Southern Asia than the nuclear one. Without Russian assistance, no Asian country can at present launch a nuclear attack upon its neighbours; but many of them are already able to carry out high level conventional violence and are increasing their capabilities. For some years to come, hostile pressures against Southern Asian countries will most probably take the form of subversion and conventional attack, and the problem is to find means of co-ordinating their existing and potential military resources in defence of the region. Political difficulties should not be allowed to inhibit the search for a solution, and elaborate organisational methods may not be necessary. For example, in the case of subversion, the security of Thailand's north-east concerns SEATO; but if Viet Cong-type movements develop in other areas, such as in Burma, it is doubtful if SEATO would be invoked, and the West might have to rely upon informal assistance. The existing multilateral approach to this problem is inadequate, though SEATO can play a useful part as a clearing house for information about subversive activities. But there is no need for the Western powers to have a SEATO organisation or relationship with the indigenous countries in order to transfer their experience and techniques of counter subversion operations to the local authorities: a man or an advisory mission (like the Thompson Mission to South Viet Nam) may suffice.

A marked feature of the military situation in Southern Asia in recent years has been the spectacular expansion in conventional forces, and in one instance at least this has led to a significant development in defence co-operation between the donor countries and the recipient. The following are some examples of the increases in Asian armed forces between 1963 and 1965.[1] First, in the Indian sub-continent: The Indian army increased from 550,000, plus at least 250,000 reserves, to 825,000, plus 47,000 reserves; and it is estimated that it will

---

[1] The details are taken from *The Military Balance 1963–1964* and *1964–1965*, published by The Institute for Strategic Studies

not reach its full strength for several years. The Indian air force grew from 18,000 to 28,000 men. In the last year, the Indian armed forces have expanded by more than 50 per cent. Pakistan's army did not increase, but her air force was raised from 15,000 to 17,000 —25,000 men. Second, in the Indochina zone: The People's Army of North Viet Nam has remained at about 250,000 men, but there has been a significant increase in its anti-aircraft capability. The Pathet Lao forces have expanded by some 6,000 men, and are thought to be supported by several thousand regular North Vietnamese troops. (The Thai Army has shrunk from 90,000 to 50,000 men.)

Third, in the Maphilindo area: There has been a substantial increase in the size of the Philippine armed forces. The Indonesian Army remained at about 350,000 men, including reservists, but the para-military and police forces expanded by more than 100,000 men. Indonesian defence spending is estimated to have more than doubled. In November 1964, the Australian Government announced that it proposed to introduce selective compulsory service for the regular army, which will be increased by more than 10,000 men by the end of 1966.[1] Expenditure on the three armed services will increase by more than 20 per cent in the three financial years ending 1967–68, following substantial recent increases. In announcing the programme, the Prime Minister, Sir Robert Menzies, spoke of the real risk of war as a result of Indonesian policies (which have caused Australia to prepare for the future defence of the frontier between Papua and New Guinea and West Irian), and Communist activity in Laos and South Viet Nam.

This Asian rearmament provides one of the most significant recent developments in joint military planning in Southern Asia; namely, the co-operation between the United Kingdom, the United States and non-aligned India, which has taken place without any formal treaty arrangements. There are several military and political lessons to be drawn from this example, which raises basic questions concerning the political machinery of formal or informal collective security measures in Asia. It shows how defence co-operation can be effected in Asia with a country whose political inhibitions regarding military pacts remain of profound importance in her national life. This kind of arrangement has political significance; for it is concerned with contingencies of Chinese aggression which would, of their own nature, clear away many existing political obstacles to

[1] *The Times*, 11 November 1964

collective defence, if they were ever to materialise. At the same time, however, it enables provision to be made against future Chinese aggression in a manner which is not likely to create new political difficulties in India's relationship with the West. As already suggested, there are conceivable situations in which India will join in defence pacts with the West, but meanwhile it is necessary to develop a tradition of military co-operation before those situations arise. A firm basis for such planning already exists in the numerous military training and exchange ventures between Asian and Western powers.

The air defence of India against possible Chinese attacks is an example of the wider problem of Western conventional and nuclear support, and military guarantees of such support, for Southern Asian countries without a formal commitment between them. Most of the estimated Chinese air threat to India at present could be met by the modernisation, with Western assistance, of India's Air Force. In the event of high level conventional violence between China and India, there might be Chinese targets which would have to be neutralised by the Western powers. There is a real political problem of what kind of guarantee can be given to India by the Western powers to meet this sort of contingency, which would be acceptable to all the parties. It will be increased when China can pose a nuclear threat to India, unless the threat itself changes the Indian outlook. In the case of India, the military exigencies cannot wait for the development of a climate of opinion which favoured formal arrangements with Western powers; the military decisions, some of them dependent upon weapons technology, must precede the large questions of national policy. This is an example of the need in Southern Asia to make provision for crises which, if they occur, will probably remove the political restraints upon defence collaboration with the West; for if provision is not made in advance the victim of aggression may not be able to offer an adequate defence.

There are substantial military grounds why informal approaches will have to be adopted, rather than treaty arrangements. There are, for example, certain forms of defence assistance which, for technological reasons, can only be provided on an area basis. During the '1970–75' era, the development of China's conventional air and nuclear striking power might make it necessary for the Western powers to provide active air defences for the major Asian cities, which would be vulnerable to Chinese hostage strategy and nuclear blackmail. But this would depend upon the establishment of an effective early warning system which would involve the co-operation of all the Southern Asian countries, irrespective of their political alignments.

The defence requirements for the future in Southern Asia seem to demand co-ordinated efforts on a broader scale than the existing multilateral and bilateral pacts will allow. But, in present conditions, it is not likely that the system of formal alliances will be expanded to enable the security of the region to be planned on a regional basis. The growing cost and complexity of modern weapons systems places them beyond the capacity of most of the Southern Asian countries to produce, or to pay for. The disparity in the military power of the Western Great Powers and the indigenous countries will not grow less as new weapons systems are developed, and for many situations of high level violence in Southern Asia obsolescent Western weapons will not be sufficient to counter aggression. The increased range of threats which China will be able to make during the '1970–75' and '1984' eras increases the dependence of the Southern Asian countries upon the striking and deterrent capabilities of the United States, and, perhaps, the United Kingdom as well.

These considerations pose the question whether multilateral defence or security arrangements for Southern Asian countries are not obsolete in the nuclear age, or becoming irrelevant to major questions of defence policy. If militarily useful defence co-operation between the Western Great Powers and the Asian countries can generally be established without entering into formal pacts of the old type, multilateral pacts might come to have a less central significance in the area. Individual countries can be given a guarantee of protection without the necessity of bilateral reassurances. Great Power guarantees could be general. One of the characteristics of nuclear deterrence is that it should create uncertainty in the mind of a potential aggressor. The United States and the United Kingdom could create this uncertainty in the minds of China's leaders by making clear that they will react to any threat to the security of the free Asian states, aligned or non-aligned, without specifying how they will do so.

This strategy involves the provision of facilities for rapid military action in threatened areas, and it could not be implemented without standby bases or other arrangements in the countries concerned; for example, bomber bases in north India.

It could not all be done from the sea; although a major deterrent effect could be achieved by a missile force in the Australian desert. Local military facilities would have to be improved, along lines already undertaken in India and Thailand. These are possible arrangements which need not raise insurmountable problems of formal commitment in the initial stages of planning and construction.

There would be the familiar complications of dual control, sharing of targeting responsibilities and whose finger was on the trigger; but there is no reason to expect that they would be as grave as they would be in a centralised alliance system which kept permanently assigned forces in forward areas. (There was a broad bipartisan approach, though disagreements about details, on the part of the Australian political parties in the case of the American communications facilities recently established in the north-west of Australia. It is important to emphasise these developments because of their significance for further changes in defence policy.) The proposed force, such as American bombers in India, would only be deployed when the host country requested it, either to deter or counter active threats of aggression; that is, at a stage when internal opposition to it would be readily overcome by the governments concerned. But there would still be anxieties on the part of the local powers about the validity of the Great Power commitment. In Europe, for example, the United States has had to maintain 6 divisions because of the similar anxieties of her Western allies. In Southern Asia, the Great Powers must either demonstrate their commitment or give the associated countries a share in the control of their forces.

The trend of political and military developments in Southern Asia is blurring the cold war divisions between aligned and non-aligned countries. Non-alignment has come to mean very different things in India, Indonesia and Burma; whilst the alignment of Pakistan, Thailand and the Philippines involves widely varying approaches to China. Political alignments and military connections are foreshadowed which bear little relation to the formal labels and official postures of the Southern Asian countries. A new set of relationships with the Western powers is emerging, which is leading in turn to some re-thinking about American and British attitudes and their defence responsibilities. There are signs, for example, that the implicit division of the Indian and Pacific Ocean areas into British and American spheres of influence, where each country has its own military obligations, is evolving into a wider concept of area defence. One sign is the proposal for an Anglo-American base in the Indian Ocean. Another is the principle laid down at the American discussions about the Southeast Asian situation, at Honolulu in June 1964, 'that no country in the area could be seen in isolation, and that the defence of the region was indivisible'.[1]

This process of reappraisal is being accelerated by the development of Communist and nationalist threats to the area, which also relate the situation in South Viet Nam to the security of Thailand and Malaysia. The growing Indonesian *rapprochement* with the Communist powers, exemplified by Sukarno's sense of solidarity with the aspirations of North Korea and North Viet Nam to unify their respective countries, is creating a nexus of political sympathies which may come to have military significance, just as Western sympathy for India led to the granting of military assistance. (Sukarno sees 'outside imperialist forces' as 'disturbing the security of Viet-Nam, Laos, Cambodia and the so-called "Federation of Malaysia" and surrounding areas'.)[2] In response to this and similar contingencies, there might emerge a subtle Anglo-American division of labour in the Indian and Pacific Oceans areas, (though the American share would be very much larger than the British), which would have many strategic advantages. It would strengthen the position of India and the pro-Western Southeast Asian countries and protect the non-aligned states. Coupled with the deterrent threat, it could create problems for aggressors, whether they be Chinese, Russian or Indonesian.

There are limitations on what can be done at present to defend Southern Asia on a regional basis. The possibilities of Asian military co-operation are restricted, and for the foreseeable future the Asian countries can be expected to be concerned only with their own and not the region's security. Thus military interdependence can in the circumstances arise only out of Western assistance, and perhaps Western insistence. It is very much in the West's interests that the underdeveloped countries do not spend too much on defence and weaken their prospects of economic growth, since their security rests ultimately on an economic basis. Western economic support as a

[1] *The Times*, 22 June 1964
[2] See his address to the Second Conference of Non-Aligned Countries at Cairo on 6 October 1964: *The Guardian*, 20 November 1964

whole remains an essential factor in the security of Southern Asia, because the indigenous countries cannot afford to develop their economies at the same time as they maintain large military forces. The United States, who has carried the major burden of direct economic assistance, welcomes the trend towards spreading the responsibility through the World Bank and other loan sources, as well as the increased participation of other European powers in the economic development of the Southern Asian countries. The developed countries increasingly recognise that economic assistance to underdeveloped states is a moral obligation as well as sound politics.

The recent increases of the armaments of the Southern Asian countries could threaten the economic and political stability of the region, and arms control agreements for Southern Asia are politically desirable as well as necessary to prevent the indigenous countries acquiring burdensome military establishments. As a first step, the Soviet Union might be persuaded to join the Western powers in arrangements for limiting the amount of sophisticated weapons which are supplied to the indigenous countries, and which, for the most part, they do not need for their own defence. Without American and Russian arms, Indonesia would be much less of a danger to her neighbours. Second, a positive Western response could be made to the Chinese proposals for a conference on limiting nuclear weapons and for a denuclearised zone in Southern Asia. The Chinese have an interest in arms control measures which would make American complex weapons inapplicable and help prevent American escalation of conflicts,[1] and discussions could begin even on this basis. It is possible that China might find it politically inexpedient to withdraw from arms control negotiations once she had commenced them.

Some of the important factors which make it practically impossible to have a nuclear-free zone in Europe are not present in Southern Asia. For example, tactical nuclear weapons are not an integral part of SEATO, as they are of NATO; and the peculiarities of the German situation have no parallels in Southern Asia. A denuclearised zone in Europe would probably mean a permanent *de facto* division of Germany, and the end of Bonn's hopes of reunifying the country. But most of the indigenous countries, except perhaps Taiwan, would support efforts to develop a nuclear-free zone in Southern Asia. One way in

[1] See Davis B. Bobrow, 'Peking's Military Calculus', *World Politics*, January 1964, reprinted in *Survival*, May–June 1964

which the United States could demonstrate her sincerity to China in arms control negotiations would be to withdraw her nuclear force from its forward positions in Asia. China could still be threatened, if necessary, with Polaris submarines and Minutemen missiles in the United States, but the presence of strong American forces close to China's borders confirms the Chinese suspicions of American intentions and helps to perpetuate her hostility to the United States.

The hostility between China and the United States, and the relations of both countries with the Soviet Union, basically affect the problems of the security of Southern Asia. Relations between the Soviet Union and the United States have developed to a stage where a balance of prudence is established in Europe, and they might conceivably reach the point where a joint Russian–American guarantee against aggression could be given to the Southern Asian countries, to deter middle power intransigence in the region. But there seems to be little hope of a stable settlement with China for a long time to come. The United States has made it clear that her policies towards China could evolve when the Chinese for their part show their willingness to abandon aggressive designs, and China has said that there could be a thaw in Sino–American relations when the American threat is removed. If any basis of Sino–American understanding can be reached, the conflicts between the Southern Asian countries could be controlled and kept to low levels of violence; without such an understanding, they could produce the occasion for major conflicts involving the Great Powers.

Appendix 1

The Armed Forces of the External Powers and the Indigenous Countries

The following details, except for Burma, are taken from *The Military Balance 1964–65*, published by the Institute for Strategic Studies, which is an estimate of 'the military balance as it existed at the end of October 1964 and as it will, on present indications, change during the ensuing year'. The material concerning the external powers has been edited and includes only the parts that may be relevant to Southern Asia; the sections on the indigenous countries are reprinted *in toto*. The information about the Burmese armed forces is taken from *The Statesman's Year-Book 1964–65* (Macmillan, 1964), *Jane's Fighting Ships 1963–64* (Sampson Low, 1963), and sources in Burma. The section on China has been slightly edited in the light of subsequent knowledge of how the Chinese produced their nuclear device.

The Communist Powers

CHINA

Estimated Population: 750,000,000.
Military Service: 3 years (selective).

The Chinese military forces, like those of the Soviet Union under Stalin, adhere closely in their military doctrine and training to Mao Tse-tung's own pronouncements on military strategy. Nevertheless, if the inheritance of Mao's doctrines appears restrictive, it is also reasonably well suited to the current military preparedness and posture of the country. China's greatest asset is its manpower, and in every other respect it is quite unable to claim the status of a great, or even a medium, military power despite the quality of its native scientists. Indeed China is probably the only country in the world which is totally deprived of access to the sophisticated equipment and expertise which the world's leading military nations continue to make available to a host of lesser countries. In these circumstances, Mao's doctrines of the ultimate decisiveness of the human element and the supreme importance of revolutionary and political indoctrination make a certain sense for the kind of wars that China could contemplate fighting. They also imply an avoidance of serious conflict with either the United States or the Soviet Union and a deliberate isolation of China from those areas of conflict which could lead to a world war. The Chinese can thus contemplate, or abet, limited wars in South Asia precisely because there is little likelihood at present that their current posture could lead to the introduction of nuclear weapons, and because they can therefore claim to be free of the 'nuclear fetishism' of which they have until recently accused Mr. Khrushchev.

The explosion at Lop Nor in Sinkiang of a Chinese nuclear device in October 1964 has shown not only that the régime is anxious to claim a nuclear status, but also that Chinese nuclear technology is apparently considerably more advanced than it was generally given credit for. Not only was the triggering technique of implosion more sophisticated than had been expected, but the fissile material was uranium-235, not plutonium. Other nuclear powers have not previously succeeded in producing uranium-235 without a gaseous diffusion plant: it is considered that China has constructed one of these. Some partially-enriched uranium must have been supplied to China by the Soviet Union as fuel for the research reactors which it had built.

It is to be supposed that missiles have been fired on the range that has been developed in Sinkiang. There is no sign of a Chinese designed bomber. China is unlikely to have an advanced indigenous capability in delivery systems in the foreseeable future, though it is possible that the Government may decide to be content with cruder instruments than those available to the United States or the Soviet Union. Even so, the régime appears to recognise the effective limitations of its nuclear capability: recent statements have emphasised that China still regards the nuclear bomb as a 'paper tiger'.

There is no sign today of disagreement on policy between the Communist Party and the military hierarchy in China. The selection of conscripts is more rigorous than in the past decade (only one in seven or eight young men of military age is conscripted into the People's Liberation Army, most of the rest are trained in the militia) and it would appear that the Party can rely completely on the PLA. Training and leadership at the middle and lower levels have also improved considerably in recent years.

For all this, the Chinese Army still suffers greatly from inadequate logistic support and obsolescent equipment. It has a high standard of tactical mobility but is restricted at the strategic level. Chinese forces can be moved from area to area, but there is no area defence system, and the effective defence of any one area would leave many others open to attack. In general, mobility is restricted by a shortage of motor-transport and petrol, by the obsolescence of the armoured equipment, and by an inadequate range of specialised (e.g. reconnaissance and troop-carrying) vehicles. It is best over bad terrain, where the endurance of the Chinese soldiers enables them to move comparatively fast.

The equipment of the army is largely Soviet, of the generation of the Second World War, delivered before supplies were stopped in 1960, or else manufactured in China from Soviet, or Chinese-modified, blue-prints. But it should, again, be noted that this kind of equipment, robust and simple to operate, is in many respects highly suitable for the PLA. It includes a range of Soviet artillery up to 152-mm. calibre, and 160-mm. mortars, and the JS-2 heavy tank. The T-54 is also probably replacing the T-34.

It is impossible to estimate how much China spends on defence, but there is some evidence that in spite of rapidly obsolescent equipment and a comparative deterioration of China's military position, the proportion of the GNP which is allotted to conventional defence may be declining.

ARMY

Total Strength: 2,250,000.

115 divisions. There are now 4 armoured divisions, and 1 or 2 airborne divisions, supporting troops and desert cavalry. There are some well-equipped mountain divisions in Tibet.

The greater part of the manpower is divided among some 30 field armies. They are adequately equipped with infantry weapons, light and medium mortars, rocket launchers, recoilless rifles and light and medium artillery, and in some cases tanks, all of which are produced in China. There are grave shortages of heavy and self-propelled artillery as well as transport, and there is only primitive radar and electronic communications equipment. The Chinese airlift capability could only be measured in terms of battalions.

NAVY
    Total Strength: 136,000, including Naval Infantry.
        28 submarines.
        4 destroyer escorts.
        800 other vessels.
        500 naval aircraft.
    There are some high-speed MTBs. The rest are mainly coastal vessels and patrol boats. The Chinese amphibious capability is primitive.

AIR FORCE
    Total Strength: 90,000.
        2,300 aircraft.

    Most of these are MiG interceptors, mainly MiG-15s and 17s with a small number of MiG-19s. There is a force of light bombers, mainly Il-28s, and a small number of transports, including a few recently acquired Il-18s. The Civil Air Bureau has about 350 aircraft, which could be used to supplement the Air Force transport capabilities.
    The training of pilots is still inhibited, by lack of spare parts, though there may have been some progress in producing aviation spirit. The average flying-time for a pilot may be no more than ten hours a month.

PARA-MILITARY FORCES
There are perhaps a quarter of a million armed para-military forces, backed up by a civilian militia of many millions.

THE SOVIET UNION

Population: 228,000,000.
Basic Military Service: Army 2 years, Air Force 4 years, Navy 5 years.
Defence Budget: 13,289m. roubles.
    At the official exchange rate, this figure would be approximately $14,725 million. It is thought that in real terms total Soviet military expenditure represents something between 30,000 and 35,000 million dollars a year.

The total size of the Soviet forces is now estimated to be about 2,450,000 men, a figure which represents a considerable reduction from last year's estimate. The para-military forces, the security and border troops, have also been reduced by about 10 per cent in spite of some reinforcements in the Chinese border areas, and now total about 270,000 men.

STRATEGIC ROCKET FORCES

Operational ICBMs now total about 200. (This figure might increase substantially during 1965.) Perhaps a third of these are of the second generation ICBM, which has a storable liquid fuel and is somewhat easier to conceal than the first generation launcher.

The number of MRBMs and IRBMs appears to be between 700 and 750. These can cover most strategic and semi-tactical targets such as fighter airfields in Western Europe, and much of the Far East. There are two types of MRBM, with ranges of 700 and 1,100 statute miles respectively. The IRBM, with a two-stage, liquid-fuelled engine has a range of 2,100 miles. Some of the MRBMs are mobile-based and can be transported on lorries. The majority of MRBMs and IRBMs are based near the western, southern and eastern borders of the Soviet Union, on the Pacific coast and in Siberia.

AIR FORCES

The Air Force comprises 10,500–11,500 operational aircraft. (There are in addition about 800 aircraft of the Naval Air Force.) The total strength of the Air Force, excluding the Naval Air Force, is 510,000 men.

The Air Force is organised into five major components:

(1) The Long-Range Air Force (strategic bombers);
(2) The tactical or front-line force which includes fighters and tactical bombers;
(3) Air Defence Command (fighter interceptors);
(4) The land-based Naval Air Force (medium bombers);
(5) The Air Transport Force.

There is also an independent transport force for the airborne divisions.

The Long-Range Air Force has been very active in recent months. Exercises over long distances in the North Atlantic and North Pacific have been observed this year but this may indicate a change in the role of the *Bear* to naval reconnaissance missions. It is grouped in three main areas: Western Russia, the Central Ukraine and the Far East, and in addition has staging and dispersal points in the Arctic. Its strength in intercontinental bombers remains considerably below that of SAC, but there is still a very strong force of medium bombers for operations in the Eurasian theatre.

(a) Strategic Striking Power

(i) About 70 Turbo-prop *Bears* (Tu-95), able to carry one large winged missile.

120 4-jet *Bisons*, also able to carry a winged missile.

(ii) About 1,000 twin-jet medium-bomber *Badgers* (Tu-16). The Naval Air Force also contains a strike force of some 400 *Badgers* with winged missiles for ship attack.

(b) Tactical Air Power

The strength of the Soviet Tactical Air Force has remained fairly constant for the last four years or so. There are at present nearly 4,000 aircraft altogether. These include: light bombers, ground attack and interceptor fighters, transport aircraft, helicopters and reconnaissance units.

There are probably over 6,000 fighters in service.

Land Forces

The total size of the Soviet Army (including the Home Air Defence Force) is estimated at 1,480,000 men. It is thought to be organised in 140 divisions.[1] There are three degrees of combat-readiness in the Soviet Army (as was stated in the book *Military Strategy* published last year in the Soviet Union under the editorship of Marshal Sokolovsky), but about half the 140 divisions are at or near full combat-strength. The remainder could be brought up to strength at short notice, although about a quarter of the total, i.e., some 35 divisions, at the lowest degree of readiness, would require major reinforcement.

The geographical distribution of the Army is as follows:

75 divisions in European Russia.
22 divisions in Central Russia.
17 divisions in the Far East.

[1] Ten less than estimated in the 1963–64 edition of the *Military Balance*. But this represents a re-assessment on the part of Western scholars, not necessarily a reduction of forces.

26 divisions in Eastern Europe. (20 in East Germany, 2 in Poland, 4 in Hungary.)

At least 12 of the divisions in the Far East are maintained at combat strength; the other 5 divisions there are thought to be in the second category of readiness: below combat strength, but not requiring major reinforcement in the event of war. The 75 divisions in European Russia are of varying degrees of strength, but the majority of the remaining 32 combat-ready divisions are probably among them. The 22 divisions in Central Russia would require major reinforcement.

The airborne forces total some 70,000 men in 9 divisions. The transport fleet could lift 2 divisions and supporting elements simultaneously over short or medium ranges.

Tactical nuclear weapons units are now organic to Soviet formations whether inside or outside the Soviet Union, and the conventional firepower of a Soviet division is as great as that of most divisions in NATO. The Soviet Army is also well equipped for offensive and defensive chemical warfare.

SEA POWER

The total strength of the Soviet Navy and naval air force is 460,000 men. In total tonnage, it is the second biggest navy in the world, but its main strength still lies in the submarine fleet. There are indications that the Naval Air Force and the missile-bearing submarines have an increasingly important role in Soviet strategy.

(a) *Submarines*

There are some 400 conventionally-powered and 30 nuclear-powered submarines. (Nuclear submarine production appears to have settled down to the rate of ten a year.) At least 40 can fire ballistic missiles, and carry an average of three each. Over 300 are ocean-going. The four submarine fleets are distributed as follows: 70 in the Baltic fleet, 150 in the Arctic, 50 in the Black Sea, and about 120 in the Far East. The 40 missile-carrying submarines are divided between the Arctic and Far East fleets.

(b) *Sea-to-ground Missiles*

A very large naval missile has been shown in Moscow parades, and it is probable that the Soviet Union has successfully developed the true submarine-launched ballistic missile, which Mr. Khrushchev claimed. But it does not appear to have been generally introduced into service yet, or to have the range of the American Polaris missiles. Of the 40 missile-firing submarines, however, some do have a limited capability for submerged firing. A ballistic missile with a range of 400 miles is deployed on G and Z class submarines for surface firing.

(c) Tactical Missiles

Some ships and submarines are known to be fitted with cruise missiles for anti-ship use. Submarines would have to fire such missiles from the surface.

(d) Naval Air Force

There are no aircraft-carriers in the Soviet Navy. The land-based Naval Air Force comprises about 400 bomber and 400 other aircraft. Most of the bombers are based on the north-western and south-western shores of the Soviet Union. They comprise:

(a) The Tu-16 *Badger* with a range of 3,500 miles. The partial replacement of this aircraft with a version of the *Blinder* may begin soon.

(b) The torpedo-carrying Il-28 *Beagle* with a range of 1,500–1,800 miles.

(e) Surface Ships

The surface-ships of the Soviet Navy consist of:
20 cruisers (of which 2 are missile-firing).
90 destroyers.
15 missile-firing destroyers.
400 fast patrol boats, many with surface-to-surface missiles.
1,900 other vessels.

(A number of adapted trawlers are used for radar and reconnaissance purposes.)

A proportion of the destroyers and smaller vessels may not be fully manned.

The cruisers are of three different types. *Sverdlov*, one or two have been re-equipped with medium-range surface-to-air missile launchers, perhaps as an experiment; *Chapayev* and *Kirov*. New destroyers include: *Kynda* class, *Kashin* class, *Krupny* class, *Kildin* class and *Ketlin* class.

Soviet press articles in the summer of 1964 suggest that the Russians have re-established a small Marine Corps, units of which are said to have been stationed in the Baltic and Pacific Fleets.

PARA-MILITARY FORCES

The security and border troops now number some 270,000. There are also perhaps about 1½ million DOSAAF members who participate actively in para-military training.

The SEATO Powers

UNITED STATES

GENERAL

Population: 192,070,000.
Length of Military Service: selective service for 2 years.
Total Armed Forces: 2,690,000.
Defence Estimates (new expenditure authority) 1964–65: $50,450,000,000.

STRATEGIC NUCLEAR FORCES

The official objective of the United States Administration is that the strategic retaliatory forces should be 'large enough to ensure the destruction, singly or in combination, of the Soviet Union, Communist China, and the Communist satellites as national societies, under the worst possible circumstances of war outbreak that can reasonably be postulated, and, in addition, to destroy their warmaking capability so as to limit to the extent practicable, damage to this country and to our Allies'.

(a) Bombers

The American strategic bomber force now has about 1,100 aircraft. The main element of the bomber force is 630 B-52s organised into 14 wings and based in the United States.

(b) Land-based Strategic Missiles

American land-based strategic missile forces have been growing rapidly for the last two years. The figure has risen from 400 to over 800 in the last year. *Atlas*, the first intercontinental ballistic missile to go into service, has completed its build-up with 126 organised into 13 squadrons at 11 bases.

The full planned force of 108 *Titan* intercontinental ballistic missiles was completed at the end of 1963. There are 6 squadrons of HGM-25B *Titan I* missiles and 6 squadrons of LGM-25C *Titan II* missiles. Each squadron has 9 missiles. It is planned to phase out the 54 *Titan Is* though the date has not been announced.

The build-up of the solid-fuel *Minuteman* intercontinental ballistic missile is continuing. By the middle of 1964, about 600 had been mounted in hardened silos, and 800 are planned for the middle of 1965. Thereafter, however, the build-up will be slower than originally planned. As LGM-30F *Minuteman 2* missiles are produced, they are in many cases replacing LGM-30A and B *Minuteman 1* missiles rather than being given new silos. *Minuteman 2* has either a longer range or a larger pay-load. It is also more accurate and can be launched by radio from an airborne command post.

(c) Seaborne Strategic Missiles

The United States Navy has now embarked fully on its programme for 41 submarines each carrying 16 *Polaris* missiles. This total of 656 weapons is due to be completed by the middle of 1967. 26 of the 41 submarines are now in service. The first 5 are equipped with the UGM-27A *Polaris* A-1 missile of 1,200-mile range and the next 13 are equipped with the UGM-27B *Polaris* A-2 of 1,500-mile range. The remaining submarines will be equipped with the UGM-27C *Polaris* A-3 of 2,500-mile range. This weapon will also be fitted into the original 5 *Polaris* submarines, making a force of 28 boats equipped with A-3 missiles and 13 with A-2 missiles.

ARMY

Total Strength: 972,000.

The regular army is organised into 16 operational divisions.

A 17th division is a provisional air-assault division being used to test new techniques of air mobility for troops and their equipment. The 16 operational divisions are divided into 6 infantry, 4 mechanised, 4 armoured and 2 airborne. All divisions have now been reorganised on the ROAD concept with considerably increased conventional fire-power and tactical mobility.

With the 3 divisions of the Marine Corps (see below), the United States maintains 3 divisions in the Western Pacific area and 10 divisions in the continent of the United States. Special forces committed in South Viet Nam number 20,000. The Eighth Army in South Korea has 2 divisions, the 1st Cavalry and 7th Infantry. A divisional headquarters, the 25th, is in Hawaii and an airborne brigade in Okinawa. The eight army divisions in the United States are divided into III Corps and XVIII Airborne corps which together are known as the Strategic Arms Corps (STRAC). III Corps has the 1st and 2nd Armoured, 4th Infantry and 5th Mechanised Divisions and XVIII Corps has the 1st and 2nd Infantry and 82nd and 101st Airborne Divisions.

NAVY

Total Strength: 668,500.
The General Purposes Forces navy consists of 840 ships. The fleets are the first in the Eastern Pacific, the second in the Atlantic, the sixth in the Mediterranean and the seventh in the Western Pacific. The main units of the active fleet are:

15 attack carriers—one (USS *Enterprise*) nuclear-powered, six of the *Forrestal* class, three of the *Midway* class and five of the *Essex* class. One *Essex* class ship is being replaced by an additional *Forrestal* class ship. Heavy attack aircraft are being sharply reduced in the fleet as the end of the carriers' strategic alert nuclear mission approaches. All but a few A-5 *Vigilantes* will become RA-5C reconnaissance aircraft. A-3B *Skywarriors* are being kept only to provide long-range nuclear striking power for the *Essex* and *Midway* class carriers. New subsonic light attack aircraft are being procured—the A-4E *Skyhawk* and A-6A *Intruder*. A new aircraft, the VAL, is being developed to replace the *Skyhawks*. Interception is carried out by F-4B aircraft except in the *Essex* class carriers, which retain F-8E *Crusaders*.
9 anti-submarine carriers: these are all of the *Essex* class. They are being equipped with S-2E long-range search aircraft and SH-3A helicopters.
103 submarines (excluding *Polaris* and *Regulus*: see seaborne strategic missiles) of which 23 are nuclear-powered.
23 destroyer escorts.
195 other destroyer types, including multi-purpose and anti-submarine ships.

160 logistic and operational support ships.
14 guided missile cruisers.
6 light and heavy cruisers.

In addition, there are over 400 escorts and about 16 cruisers in reserve. The active fleet and reserves include about 250 amphibious ships, 200 minesweepers and 850 service, patrol and other craft.

MARINE CORPS

The Marine Corps maintains 190,000 men organised into three divisions and three air wings. A fourth division/wing can be provided on mobilisation by the Organised Marine Corps Reserve. *Honest John* missiles have proved too unwieldy for the types of missions assigned to the Corps and the three batteries of them have been returned to the Army. The three Marine Air Wings have about 1,155 combat and support aircraft and the number of helicopters is being steadily increased with the acquisition of large numbers of CH-46A types which carry 17 men. The 15 fighter squadrons are being equipped entirely with F-4 *Phantoms* armed with *Sidewinder* and *Sparrow* missiles.

AIR FORCE

Total Strength: 840,000.

The General Purpose Forces of the Air Force have been built up in recent years so that they could engage in a sustained non-nuclear conflict in support of the Army. The tactical fighter force is being increased from 21 wings to 24 wings with increasing emphasis on the ground attack role. It is equipped with F-100, F-102, F-104 and F-105 fighter-bombers and one wing is now equipped with F-4C *Phantom* aircraft. Three squadrons of F-102 interceptors are being withdrawn from Europe and Japan this year and the rest will follow. B-57 tactical bombers have now all been transferred to the Air National Guard. Tactical air forces in the United States have been organised around the new Tactical Air Warfare Center at Eglin Air Force Base, Florida. The ninth Air Force (Shaw AFB, South Carolina) and twelfth Air Force (Waco, Texas) are now kept ready for immediate deployment and action, in addition to the nineteenth Air Force (Seymour Johnson AFB, North Carolina). United States Air Forces in Europe—(USAFE), with headquarters in Wiesbaden, have an inventory of more than 1,000 tactical aircraft. Their strike aircraft are F-100 *Supersabres*, F-101 *Voodoos* and F-105 *Thunderchiefs* and reconnaissance RB-66s and RF-101s. They also have five squadrons of the *Mace*-A and one of the *Mace*-B tactical bombardment missiles. Pacific Air Forces (PACAF) with headquarters in Hawaii, control the fifth Air Force in Japan, Korea and Okinawa (F-105 and F-100 tactical fighters, RF-101 reconnaissance and KB-50 aerial refuelling tankers and two *Mace*-B squadrons in Okinawa), the thirteenth Air Force in the Philippines (which has F-100s and F-102s in the Philippines) and task forces in Formosa and Viet Nam. For the future, large orders have been placed for F-4 *Phantoms* and the first procurement of the F-111A is scheduled for 1965.

Tactical reconnaissance forces are being increased substantially over the present 14 squadrons of RF-101s and RB-66s.

The Military Air Transport Service operates about 1,000 aircraft, about 500 of which are the airlift force of C-135 Jet *Stratolifters*, C-133 *Cargomasters*, C-130 *Hercules*, C-124 *Globemasters* and C-118 *Liftmasters*. First deliveries of the C-141 *Starlifter*, which will replace the piston-engined transports by 1970, began in 1964.

The Special Air Warfare Forces include a substantial number of B-26, T-28, A-1E, C-46 and U-10 aircraft.

UNITED KINGDOM

GENERAL

Population: 53,812,000.
Voluntary Military Service.
Total Armed Forces: 425,000.
Defence Budget (1964–65): £1,998,540,000 ($5,596,000,000)

ARMY

Total Strength: 190,000.

The Army is organised into 65 infantry battalions, of which 57 are British and 8 Gurkha; 3 parachute battalions; 22 tank and armoured car regiments; 31 artillery regiments; and engineer and signal regiments. The British Army of the Rhine, based in Germany, has 53,000 men in 18 battalions. About 14 battalions are normally maintained in the United Kingdom garrison, in addition to 6 battalions in the Strategic Reserve. The basic Middle East strength is 4–5 battalions and that in

Southeast Asia and Hong Kong 12–15 battalions, including the 8 Gurkha battalions. Other garrisons include 3,000 men in Berlin and troops in Libya, Malta, Gibraltar and the Caribbean.

NAVY

Total Strength: 100,000.
- 4 aircraft carriers.
- 2 Commando ships (carriers).
- 2 Cruisers.
- 4 guided missile destroyers.
- 10 other destroyers.
- 4 fleet pickets.
- 14 general purpose frigates.
- 3 anti-aircraft frigates.
- 3 aircraft direction frigates.
- 33 anti-submarine frigates.
- 1 nuclear submarine.
- 38 conventional submarines.
- 61 minesweepers.
- 7 patrol and dispatch vessels.
- 8 landing vessels.
- 93 fleet support ships.

The Fleet Air Arm has a nuclear and conventional strike capacity with the *Buccaneer* Mark I which, together with its *Scimitar* and *Sea Vixen* aircraft, can be fitted with *Bullpup* air-to-surface missiles. The *Sea Vixen* Mark II is now in service with the *Red Top* air-to-air guided missile.

The Commando carriers carry troops in *Wessex* Mark I and *Whirlwind* 7 helicopters.

Orders worth £200 million have been placed in connection with the programme for 5 *Polaris*-firing nuclear submarines (80 missiles) for the 1970s.

The Royal Marines are organised into 5 Commandos of 600 men each.

There are 9,683 men in the naval and marine reserves.

AIR FORCE

Total Strength: 134,000.

Bomber Command provides the United Kingdom strategic nuclear force and is also integrated into the war organisation of the NATO European headquarters. It is equipped with about

180 medium bombers of which the central force is the Mark II *Vulcan* and Mark II *Victor* bombers, which will all be equipped with the *Blue Steel* air-to-ground strategic missile by the end of 1964. A force of *Valiant* air-refuelling tankers is also maintained and a substantial photographic reconnaissance force of *Valiants*, *Victors* and *Canberras*.

Transport Command has 23 *Britannia* and 11 *Comet* airliners for strategic airlift. In addition, it is acquiring 14 long-range jet *VC-10*s for passengers and freight and 10 long-range *Belfasts* for heavy equipment. 56 medium-range *Argosy* freighters, 48 *Hastings* and 12 *Valettas* are now in service and a freighter version of the *H.S.* 748 airliner will be acquired in 1965 for short-range transport in addition to the present force of 28 *Beverleys*. Helicopter transport is provided by *Belvederes*, *Whirlwinds*, and *Wessex* Mark IIs.

Far East Air Force provides tactical air support to Borneo, particularly with helicopters and *Pioneer* aircraft. The command is equipped with *Shackletons*, *Canberras*, and *Hunter FGA*s.

FRANCE

GENERAL

Population: 48,250,000.
Length of Military Service: 18 months.
Total Armed Forces: 620,000 including 400,000 conscripts. The Government is proposing to halve the number of conscripts over the next few years by the introduction of a system of selective service.
Defence Estimates (1965): NF 20,806,000,000 (= $4,270 million).

ARMY

Total Strength: 415,000.
6 divisions stationed in Europe (*forces de manoeuvre*).

These include 1 mechanised and 1 armoured division assigned to NATO in Germany equipped with *Honest John* and *Lacrosse* launchers, and 3 light divisions and 1 air transportable division under national command in France. The air transportable division, based on parachute troops, together with an amphibious group and supporting arms and services, makes up the permanent element of a French strategic reserve (*force d'intervention*).

The remaining troops are stationed in metropolitan France for local defence (*forces du territoire*).

NAVY

Total Strength: 72,500.

2 22,000-ton aircraft carriers.
1 14,000-ton aircraft carrier.
1 10,000-ton helicopter carrier.
2 anti-aircraft cruisers.
1 experimental guided missile ship.
60 destroyers, frigates, other escort ships.
22 submarines, of which 6 are ocean-going.
102 minesweepers.
8 landing craft.
225 other ships.

Naval aviation comprises approximately 500 aircraft, including 4 fighter squadrons with 80 *Etendard* IV aircraft, 2 *Alizé* ASW squadrons, 5 *Neptune* maritime reconnaissance squadrons, and 3 helicopter squadrons. Deliveries of 47 F-8E *Crusaders* are due to begin in October 1964.

AIR FORCE

Total Strength: 125,000.

(a) *The Strategic Air Command*

In September 1964 this had 8 *Mirage* IVs in service; 3 undergoing trials and others scheduled to come off the assembly lines at a rate of 2 a month up to a total of 50.

12 KC-135 tankers have been purchased from the USA to permit in-flight re-fuelling.

(b) *COTAM (Transport Command)*

6 *Noratlas* squadrons.
2 DC6 and Breguet *Deux Ponts* squadrons.
4 miscellaneous squadrons.

The 12 KC-135 tankers (see Strategic Air Command, above) may also be used for troop transport.

The Indian Sub-continent

INDIA

GENERAL

Population: 470 million.
Voluntary Military Service.
Total Armed Forces: 867,000.
Defence Estimates (1964–65): 8,937,700,000 rupees (=$1,970 million).

ARMY

Total sanction strength: 825,000 plus 47,000 in a volunteer reserve Territorial Army organised on a battalion and technical unit basis.

16 divisions including 9 recently formed mountain divisions. In addition 4 infantry divisions on a reduced establishment have been sanctioned. It will take three years to bring the army up to its full strength. Ready forces include:

    1 armoured division equipped with *Centurions*.
    1 armoured brigade with *Shermans*.
    2 light tank regiments with AMX-13.
    2 light tank regiments with *Stuarts*.

NAVY[1]

Total Strength: 16,000.

    1 16,000-ton carrier.
    2 cruisers.
    3 destroyers.
    5 anti-submarine frigates.
    3 anti-aircraft frigates.
    5 other escort ships.
    6 minesweepers.
    13 light coastal vessels.
    2 amphibious warfare ships.
    5 survey vessels, training ships.

[1] India is also endeavouring to obtain submarines from the United Kingdom and possibly from the Soviet Union. See *The Guardian*, 27 November 1964

Naval aircraft include 24 *Sea Hawk* strike/interceptor planes and 15 *Alizé* ASW planes.

AIR FORCE

Total Strength: 28,000 (strength sanctioned—45 squadrons).
    4 HF-24 *Marut* fighter-bombers.
    4 interceptor squadrons with 25 *Mystère* IVs each.
    4 interceptor squadrons with 25 *Gnats* each.
    4 bomber squadrons with 20 *Canberras* each.
    6 fighter-bomber squadrons with 25 *Hunters* each.
    Several *Ouragan* and *Vampire* fighter-bomber squadrons.
    1 reconnaissance squadron with 8 *Canberras*.
    The transport force includes 80 C-119s, 24 *Antonov* 12s, and about 50 C-47s.
    2 *Ilyushin* 14s, some *DH Otters* and *Viscounts* 723 and 730.
    Avro 748s and *Caribous* are being acquired. The Auxiliary Air Force squadrons chiefly fly *Harvard* and *Vampire* trainers.

PAKISTAN

GENERAL

Population: 98,570,000.
Voluntary Military Service.
Total Armed Forces: 253,000.
Defence Estimates (1964–65): 1,290 million rupees (=$269 million).

ARMY

Strength: 230,000.
    8 divisions organised on a triangular basis and equipped with M-47 tanks.
    250,000 lightly armed militia and about 30,000 Azad Kashmir troops.

NAVY

Total Strength: 7,700.
    1 light cruiser (cadet training ship).
    5 destroyers.
    2 ASW frigates.
    8 minesweepers.
    10 other ships.

Air Force
Total Strength: 17,000–25,000.
 200 aircraft. These include 30 B-57 *Canberras* in two
  squadrons.
 1 F-104 A *Starfighter* squadron (a second is to be formed).
 4 F-86 F *Sabre* squadrons.
RT-33As are used for tactical reconnaissance. The transport
force includes 4 C-130 B *Hercules*.

The Indochina Zone

NORTH VIET NAM

Population: 17,000,000.
 The North Vietnamese armed forces still receive aid from
both China and the Soviet Union though the Chinese proportion is probably increasing. A few MiG-15s and 17s arrived
in North Viet Nam in August 1964.
 The Regular Army numbers about 250,000. There is also a
regionally organised militia of about 200,000. The Frontier and
Coastal Security troops, and the People's Armed Security
Force total another 40,000. (Assessments of the size of this force
have been considerably reduced.)
 The Regular Army is thought to have about 100 miscellaneous armoured vehicles, which probably include some
Soviet PT-76 tanks, made available to the anti-government
forces in Laos in 1961. There has been a significant increase in
the army's anti-aircraft capability, and it appears to have
Soviet 85-mm. guns in quantity. It has otherwise no heavy
equipment, and meagre transport and logistic support. There
are about 2,500 men in the North Vietnamese Navy. It has
about 80 ships, mainly patrol vessels.
 North Viet Nam provides help to both the Pathet Lao (in
Laos) and Viet Cong (in South Viet Nam) guerrillas. The
full-time Viet Cong forces total about 30,000 men.

The Protocol States

(a) SOUTH VIET NAM

GENERAL

Population: 15,000,000.
Length of Military Service: all men between ages 25–33 liable
for mobilisation.
Total Armed Forces: 500,000, including auxiliaries.
(U.S. aid is $500,000,000 a year.)

ARMY

Total Strength: 210,000 (regular), 186,000 (auxiliary forces—
establishment strength).

The regular army is organised on the basis of 4 Army Corps
Areas: the First Corps in the northern mountain region, Second
Corps in the central highlands region, Third Corps in the
northern Mekong area (including Saigon), Fourth Corps in the
southern half of the delta.

There are also two auxiliary forces, the Civil Guard and the
Self-Defence Corps. These forces have establishments of
83,000 and 103,000 men respectively, but it is believed that
effective strength is far below these levels, due to poor recruiting
and desertions.

In general, a static defence role (villages, bridges, supply
dumps, etc.) is given to the auxiliary forces, and the regular
troops are kept back for mobile, counter-guerrilla operations.
The building of 'strategic hamlets' is proceeding at a slower
rate than originally planned and these have been renamed
'new-life hamlets'.

The 6,000 Special Security Troops, formerly responsible for
political security, have been reconstituted since the overthrow
of the Diem régime. The Americans now plan to raise a force
of Special Troops (a) for special operations against Viet Cong
in South Viet Nam, (b) for guerrilla warfare in North Viet
Nam.

There are about 17,000 American military personnel, of
which 3,000 take part in combat actions. Some American
officers are in command of Vietnamese Rangers recruited from
the ethnic minorities.

NAVY

Total Strength: 15,350, including a Marine Brigade of about 5,000 men.

5 escorts (including 1 submarine chaser).
14 motor gunboats, coastal patrol vessels.
5 coastal minesweepers.
25 landing craft.
500 other small vessels (including motorised junks).

AIR FORCE

Total Strength: 20,000.

(500 strike aircraft by end of 1964).
30 A-1 H *Skyraider* piston-engined aircraft.
70 T-28 trainers in ground support role.
32 C-47 transports, H-19 and H-34 helicopters.
25 F-84 *Bearcats*.
B-26 light bombers.
1 squadron AD-6 fighter-bombers.

(*b*) CAMBODIA

GENERAL

Population: 6,000,000.
Total Armed Forces: 29,500.

ARMY

Total Strength: 27,300.

The Cambodian Army is organised along two main lines: the static defence system of the villages, with a militia officered by small groups of officers and NCOs: and the mobile detachments where a popular militia is equally heavily represented. A considerable proportion of the Army is engaged on economic and social services.

The country is divided into 5 military regions. In command terms, it is organised into 28 infantry battalions, 2 parachute battalions and 1 armoured regiment. There are 6 batteries of 105-mm. artillery and a company of light tanks. 24 pre-war AA guns have been supplied by the Soviet Union.

There is a small French training mission, but all American military advisers have been withdrawn.

NAVY

Total Strength: 1,200 (plus Marine Corps of 150).
4 patrol vessels.
1 support gunboat.
3 seaward patrol craft.
11 landing craft.
50 small craft.

AIR FORCE

Total Strength: 1,000. Chiefly concerned with internal police and transport duties.
5 MiG-17 interceptors.
2 *Fouga Magister*, some MS 733 *Alcyon* light attack aircraft.
C-47 *Beaver* and 2 Il-14 transport.
Cessna L-19 observation and *Alouette* helicopters.

(*c*) LAOS

GENERAL

Population: 2,500,000.

(*a*) *Royal Lao Forces*
Total: 50,000–70,000.

ARMY

About 50,000 men, including the 3,000 to 5,000 strong neutralist army of General Kong Le with whom they are now allied. The neutralist forces suffered severe casualties in the Pathet-Lao advance of May 1964 which gained control of the whole Plain of Jars.

NAVY

4 river squadrons small gunboats.

AIR FORCE

7 T-28 and some *Texan* piston-engined trainers in ground-support role.
C-47 transports.
The Government are supported by about 5,000 Meo tribes-

men harassing the Pathet-Lao in the mountains around the Plain of Jars.

(b) Pathet-Lao Forces

Strength: about 26,000 men.

These are now believed to be supported by up to 3,000 regular North Vietnamese forces operating in the northern provinces. They have received a large supply of arms and ammunition of Soviet and Chinese origin but no troops from these countries.

The Pathet-Lao now control all the eastern half of Laos, including the Plain of Jars and the complete frontier with Viet Nam.

THAILAND

GENERAL

Population: 31,000,000.
Length of Military Service: 2 years plus 7 years in first reserve, 10 years in second reserve, 6 years in third reserve).
Total Armed Forces: 84,500.
Defence Budget (1964-65): 1,919,810,000 bahts (= $92 million).

ARMY

Total Strength: 50,000.
  3 infantry divisions (nominally with 3 brigades each).
  1 composite division with armour.
  There are about 3,000 U.S. military personnel at present in Thailand, and supply dumps have been established for the accommodation of a force of 5,000 men within forty-eight hours.

NAVY

Total Strength: 18,000 (plus 3,500 Marines).
  6 frigates, other escorts.
  6 minelayers and minesweepers.
  9 submarine chasers.
  13 armoured gunboats, patrol boats.
  13 landing craft, landing ships.
  16 other ships.

Air Force

Total Strength: 13,000.
  1 wing of 40 F-86 F fighter-bombers.
  1 wing of 30 F-84 G *Thunderjet* fighter-bombers.
  1 wing of 30 T-6 and T-38 light close support aircraft.
  About 100 training and transport aircraft including C-54,
  C-47 and C-45.

BURMA

General

Population: 23,735,000.
Total Armed Services: approximately 104,200.

Army

Total Strength: approximately 100,000, including 25 battalions
of constabulary which were incorporated into the regular army
in 1962. The Army is organised in 5 major commands, one
infantry brigade and the Arakan force. The commands deal
directly with the units; the divisional and brigade system was
disbanded in 1961. Equipment is mixed, but British weapons
predominate.

Navy

Total Strength: 3,300 officers and ratings, including reservists.
(Jane's figure is 3,030.)
  1 frigate.
  1 escort minesweeper.
  5 motor torpedo boats.
  4 support gunboats.
  21 river gunboats.
  13 gunboats, 1 transport and 1 tug.

Air Force

Total Strength: approximately 900.
  2 *Sea Fury* fighter-bomber squadrons.
  Transport aircraft, including Bristol Freighter, C-47,
    Otter and *Beech* D-18 aircraft, *Alouette* 111, Japanese-
    built *Bell* 47, and American-built *Huskie* helicopters.
  Training in piston-engined *Provosts* and *Vampire* jets which
    are fitted to carry light armament for security operations.

The Air Force is basically for internal security duties, and most of the equipment is British-built.

The Haphilindo Area

INDONESIA

GENERAL

Population: 101,000,000.
Total Armed Forces: 412,000.
Defence Budget: equivalent $980,000,000 (latest estimate available).

ARMY

Total Strength: 350,000 (regular 200,000) (reservists 150,000).

The Army is basically organised into sixteen territorial regions, but detailed organisation only exists at the battalion level and above, including the provision of artillery, engineer and technical support. The emphasis in training and combat experience alike has been on guerrilla and anti-guerrilla fighting.

The infantry battalions are equipped with American and some Russian small arms. The Army also has 57-mm. Soviet AA guns and associated radar equipment, and at least one battery of Soviet 105-mm. howitzers. There are very few armoured formations. There is a paratroop force of about 30,000 men.

Para-military forces and police number about 130,000.

NAVY

Total Strength: 35,000 (25,000 regular navy plus naval air forces, a commando corps and a 3,550 strong Marine Corps).
2 heavy cruisers (ex-Soviet *Sverdlov* class).
4 destroyers (ex-Soviet *Skoryi* class).
6 frigates.
18 submarine chasers.
6 submarine (plus 3 submarine parent ships).
19 motor torpedo boats.

[1] The Army was reported to have launched some Indonesian-made rockets. *The Observer*, 15 November 1964

30 motor gunboats (including 12 *Komar* class with guided missiles).
21 minesweepers.
17 landing ships, landing craft.
25 seaward defence craft.
66 other vessels.

Naval aircraft includes 1 ASW squadron equipped with *Gannets* and helicopters.

AIR FORCE

Total Strength: 27,000 (plus 30,000 parachute troops).

The Indonesian Air Force is organised into 7 main air areas, each with one main base, and some auxiliary bases and combining the separate commands. There are about 450 aircraft.

Interceptor

Over 100 MiG, including 18 MiG-21s.

Strike

30 Tu-16 *Badger*, some with an air-to-air guided missile.
25 Il-28 *Beagle*.
18 B-25 *Mitchell*.

Transport

About 60 Il-4 and C-130B *Hercules*.
About 25 Soviet and Japanese helicopters.
There are up to 125 light aircraft, trainers, etc.
There is at least 1 surface-to-air missile unit, which is claimed to be equipped with an advanced missile.

MALAYSIA

GENERAL

Population: 10,810,000.
Military Service: all persons between 21 and 29 are liable for conscription into armed forces or civil defence work.
Total Armed Forces (regular): 22,000; (Volunteer): 27,700.
Defence Budget (1964): £10,700,000 (= $92,000,000) of which one-third for expenditure on ships and naval bases.

ARMY

Total Strength: 19,000 (regular).
  8 infantry battalions.
  1 reconnaissance battalion.
  Artillery, engineer and administrative units. These will
    later be brought up to 20 battalions, with supporting
    arms, so as to form 5 mobile brigade groups. Of these 2
    brigades will be used in the Borneo territories.
  (Reserve) Territorial Army which it is planned to increase
    up to 27,000 men. The first reservists were mobilised
    during March 1964.
  (Police) 24 companies para-military field police (23,000
    men).

NAVY

Total Strength: 2,100.
  1 frigate.
  1 coastal, 6 inshore minesweepers.
  6 seaward patrol vessels (2 squadrons).
  A landing craft and 16 *Vosper* patrol craft are on order
    from Britain.

AIR FORCE

Total 57 aircraft.
  Tactical transport planes only.
  14 Twin *Pioneer*, 5 *Pioneer*.
  8 *Dart Heralds*.
  Some *Alouette* helicopters.

PHILIPPINE REPUBLIC

GENERAL

Population: 30,500,000.
Voluntary Military Service.
Total Armed Forces: 57,000 including 15,500 officers and men
of the Philippine Constabulary.
Defence Estimates (1964–65): 285,500,000 pesos = ($72,900,000).

ARMY

Total Strength: 25,500.
  1 combat division.
  4 training divisions.
  There is a reserve of 120,000 men.

NAVY

Total Strength: 6,500.
  6 escort patrol vessels.
  2 command ships.
  6 submarine chasers.
  2 coastal minesweepers.
  9 landing craft.
  19 patrol boats.
  25 other ships.

AIR FORCE

Total Strength: 9,500.
  3 F-86F day fighter squadrons.
  1 F-86D all-weather fighter squadron.
  Transport, observation, air/sea rescue and training units.

The Offshore Powers

AUSTRALIA

GENERAL

Population: 11,000,000.
Voluntary Military Service.[1]

Total Armed Forces: 52,000.
Defence Estimates (1964–65): £A296,000,000
(=$660,000,000).

ARMY

Total Strength: 23,400 (plus 28,500 citizen military forces
(CMF) with an authorised ceiling of 31,700).
  1 infantry battalion with artillery and engineer support in
    Malaya.
  1 *Centurion* tank regiment.

  [1] In November 1964 the Government announced that it would
introduce selective compulsory service for the regular army

2 battle groups (large infantry battalions reinforced with supporting arms).
1 battle group (on restricted establishment).
1 Pacific Island Regiment. Additional battalions will be raised over next 5 years.
1 Logistic Support Force.
8 CMF battle groups (similar to those of Regular Army).

NAVY

Total Strength: 12,500.
1 light fleet carrier (used for ASW).
1 light fleet carrier (fast troop transport).
4 destroyers (including 1 on loan).
4 frigates.
6 minesweepers.
8 other ships.
1 *Sea Venom* all-weather fighter squadron.
1 *Gannet* ASW squadron.
1 helicopter squadron with *Wessex* MK 31s.

AIR FORCE

Total Strength: 16,100 (plus a Citizens' Air Force of 1,080).
4 fighter squadrons of Australian *Sabres* (F-86). The *Mirage III* will enter service during 1964–65.
3 *Canberra* bomber squadrons.
2 *Neptune* maritime reconnaissance squadrons.
2 transport squadrons (1 C-130 *Hercules*, 1 C-47 *Dakota*). (The Caribou is entering service).
2 *Iroquois* helicopter squadrons.
1 *Bloodhound* Mk 1 surface-to-air missile squadron.

NEW ZEALAND

GENERAL

Population: 2,550,000.
Voluntary Military Service (supplemented by Selective National Service for 2,100 recruits annually for the Army Territorial Force).
Total Armed Forces: 12,500.
Defence Estimates (1964–65): £NZ36,400,000 (= $100,500,000).

ARMY

Total Strength: 5,600 regulars (plus 6,000) Territorials and 34,000 in Army Reserve.
The Army has recently been reorganised to include the following:
  1 infantry battalion to Commonwealth Strategic Reserve in Malaysia.
  A Combat Brigade Group incorporating both Regulars and Territorials.
  A Logistic Support Force—both Regulars and Territorials.
  A Combat Reserve Group—both Regulars and Territorials.
  A Static Support Force—Regulars.

NAVY

Total Strength: 2,900 regulars (plus 4,000 reservists).
  1 light cruiser.
  4 ASW frigates.
  4 escort minesweepers.
  1 Antarctic support ship.
  12 other ships.

AIR FORCE

Total Strength: 4,000.
  1 *Canberra* light bomber squadron.
  1 day fighter ground attack squadron with *Vampire* and *Canberra* trainers.
  1 *Sunderland* maritime reconnaissance squadron.
  3 transport squadrons (*DC-6B, Hastings, Dakota, Bristol, Devon*).
  1 transport squadron is based in Singapore as part of Commonwealth Strategic Reserve.

JAPAN

GENERAL

Population: 97,000,000.
Voluntary Military Service.
Total Armed Forces: 245,103.
Defence Estimates (1964–65): 275,100,000 million yen (= $754,000,000).

ARMY

Total Strength: 171,500 (planned expansion to 180,000 with 30,000 reserves by 1965).
    13 divisions of 7,000–9,000 men, each organised into 3–4 battle groups. 1 division, based on Hokaido, is mechanised.
    The Army has 255 light aircraft and helicopters and 870 American-built tanks. By 1964 40 of 100 Japanese type-61 tanks will be in service.
    2 *Hawk* battalions.

NAVY

Total Strength: 35,000.
    19 destroyers (including 1 guided missile type due for completion early 1965).
    28 frigates, other escorts.
    9 submarines.
    17 submarine chasers.
    44 minesweepers and minelayers.
    52 landing craft.
    52 other ships.
    140 anti-submarine aircraft.
    The naval air component has about 250 aircraft including helicopters.

AIR FORCE

Total Strength: 39,500.
    1 tactical squadron.
    7 fighter wings.
    200 80 F-104Js will be accepted by mid-1965, they will partially replace 90 F-86Ds and 245 F-86Fs in service. The F-104Js and some of the F-68Fs have *Sidewinders*.
    2 wings of 72 *Nike-Ajax* missiles each.

TAIWAN

GENERAL

Population: 12,000,000.
Length of Military Service: 2 years and reserve liability.
Total Armed Forces: 600,000.
Defence Budget: 5,875,000,000 Taiwan $. (=$147,250,000).

ARMY

Total Strength: 400,000, including 80,000 on Quemoy and Matsu.
 21 infantry divisions.
 2 armoured divisions.
 1 *Nike-Hercules* battalion.

NAVY

Total Strength: 35,000 (plus 27,000 marines).
 5 destroyers.
 11 frigates, other escorts.
 27 submarine chasers.
 20 minesweepers and minelayers.
 57 gunboats, coastal craft.
 71 landing craft.
 83 other ships.

AIR FORCE

Total Strength: 82,000.
 3 F-86 and F-104 interceptor wings.
 1 F-100 fighter-bomber wing.

Appendix II

Viet Cong Reports

(A) The *Report on the Revolutionary Movement in the South*, dated 25 September 1962, was captured during the following October by South Vietnamese forces in Kien Giang Province, near the Cambodian border. It is a long document of some 30 foolscap pages in mimeo, which discusses the status of the revolutionary movement, its present characteristics and the enemy's plan of activity. The following extracts are taken from section IV, entitled: 'Plans and Specific Activities for the Immediate Future.'

*　　*　　*

1. OPPOSING AND DESTROYING STRATEGIC HAMLETS AND REGROUPMENT CENTERS

The enemy is mobilising military and civilian personnel to conduct terrorist and mopping up operations and to set up strategic hamlets and regroupment centers so as to isolate our armed forces, our cadres and Party members, for the purpose of destroying the revolutionary movement in the South, and resuming control over the people through a combination of military, political, economic and cultural schemes . . .

With his present military superiority, the enemy can set up a number of strategic hamlets, set up a white belt in certain areas and harass our bases. He will increase activities to destroy production, to plunder property and to make further difficulties for the people. He will intensify terrorism to upset the people.

This scheme is so important to the enemy that he calls it 'unique national policy' because in the Staley plan, it is considered as the one most essential factor that will determine victory.[1] Thus, as far as we are concerned, *our counteraction of the enemy's plan of strategic hamlets and regroupment centers will make*

---

[1] Dr. Eugene Staley led a mission to South Viet Nam in 1961. The mission's recommendations included the construction of strategic hamlets

it possible for us to preserve and develop our movement. This will be a most important struggle to be carried out by various echelons in various areas, by political and military forces and by different branches of the Party; this will be a prolonged and stubborn struggle and it is only when there is a big change in the relativity of strength between the enemy and us that we can completely defeat this scheme.

The various echelons should fully appreciate the importance of this struggle; the leading echelons should concentrate all forces, all branches to oppose and counteract the enemy's plan of strategic hamlets and regroupment centers; all forces will be combined and will assist one another in mountain and forest areas; in the delta; in cities; in the zones; provinces, districts, and villages; . . .

2. Some Important Problems

Although the people and the cells have pretty good morale and have acquired enough experience, they should not be subjective because this stubborn and prolonged struggle to oppose strategic hamlets and regroupment centers required better moral preparation, a more comprehensive and stronger movement, and better and more flexible leadership. It will be very important to set up and preserve covert structures so as to maintain the movement and the strength of the people in order to oppose and defeat the enemy's schemes. We should realise that our structures in weak and contended areas are still inadequate and overt and we should try to remedy this shortcoming. In base areas and in areas adjacent to our bases, we should prevent the enemy from regrouping the population and delimiting boundaries by carrying out various forms of struggle. We should have two types of members; legal and illegal ones (their numbers will vary depending on the area); when the enemy rounds up the people, we will introduce covertly those people who are capable of production and of protecting the bases; when the situation is tense, we will exhort the regrouped people to struggle and return and we will withdraw the covert people; we will thus 'tug back and forth' with the enemy.

With regard to military activities, we should urgently intensify the people's movement; set up combat villages and extend guerrilla warfare. In areas where strategic hamlets have been or are being set up, we should have the guerrillas harass the enemy, and organise secret self-defense corps members to create disturbances, to chastise resolutely the evil-doers and paralyse them completely. We will concentrate our armed forces to carry out military operations in a very large area, fight continuously, and penetrate deeply into the enemy's rear to destroy the lines of communication.

In providing leadership, the cells and the district committees should concentrate on the struggle against strategic hamlets and regroupment centers. At the zone and provincial levels, we should assign committee members and cadres who already have assumed direct leadership in areas where there are many strategic hamlets.

3. SETTING UP BASES

The setting up of revolutionary bases is more and more important to our prolonged struggle against the enemy. Bases will ensure our safety in case of difficulty; will enable us to build up forces, to extend the movement and to carry out military offensives . . .

We already have a very large base area, but there are still many weaknesses with regard to the organisation and concentration of forces. Bases should be set up quickly, particularly in mountain and forest areas, and the major effort should be to build up armed forces in order to have strong rear echelons; delta bases should be set up, expanded, and connected with one another by safe communications corridors. We should intensify further our guerrilla movement, our movement of 'secrecy preservation', our movement of production and self-sufficiency, and the cultural and social movement among the people. We should study and carry out a series of agrarian, handicraft, and cooperative policies to encourage agricultural production, handicraft and trade.

Because a base is not a temporary station for the troops and various organisations, nor a retreat, but a place to build up and develop revolutionary forces in every respect to attack enemy areas, and because it is like 'a flag representing the revolution and the new system', the various echelons should understand that it is their responsibility to consolidate the forces and the facilities to set up bases.

With regard to the method of setting up bases in each zone, and in each province, specific rules and instructions will be prescribed . . .

5. Intensifying the Political Struggle

(a) *In Rural Areas*

The main goal of the struggle movement in rural areas at present is to lessen enemy pressure; to oppose operations and terrorism; to oppose strategic hamlets; and to oppose extortion, expropriation of land, compulsory labor, and the army draft.

In areas where enemy pressure has been lessened, struggle activities are no longer carried out routinely; but struggle movements on the spot should be maintained to oppose military operations and terrorism; political forces should still be sent to urban areas and posts and forts for struggles, not on a routine basis, but only when deemed necessary for practical purpose. Thus we will not waste the people's time and effort.

In 'inside' and base areas, we should adjust the military struggle to our possibilities and to circumstances; in areas near the base, where the enemy carries out operations and rounds up the people, we should be very active and take the initiative of shifting the people to an illegal status when the situation becomes tense. Our main concern will be to save the people from being rounded up, but we should not shift the people immediately to an illegal status position when it is of no avail, because it will make additional difficulties for the people.

In rural areas, the number of people with illegal status will increase, particularly draft dodgers, who should be given protection and guidance, and assigned to the self defence corps to evade the enemy. They should not participate in 'face to face' struggle.

Leadership of the political movement in rural areas at present should be resolute and flexible to cope with the enemy; we should be realistic and avoid mobilizing the people in large groups for the struggle just for form, as this would only be a waste of the people's time and effort. On the other hand, we should stir up the people's resentment against the enemy; maintain their fighting spirit, and promote solidarity and mutual assistance in the event that the enemy increases terrorism.

(b) *In Urban Areas*

There will be no basic changes in goals, mottoes, and forms of political struggle in urban areas. But because the U.S. is furthering military intervention; because Diem is increasing pressure, intently mobilizing manpower and resources in urban areas to extend the war, interfering with the nationalist feeling and the everyday life of the various strata of the population, it will be necessary to extend further the movement in urban areas and particularly to intensify the struggle for economic and democratic rights and the struggle against U.S. aggression to demand peace and neutrality.

In providing leadership in urban areas, we should also give attention to the motto that 'this is a long political struggle' in order to preserve and develop the revolutionary forces; we should combat the tendency to subjectiveness and impulsiveness which may lead us to using rural mottoes for urban activities, which hinder the movement in urban areas.

We should continue to lead the people in their struggle; utilise the overt and legal economic, cultural and social organisations as a means to gather forces to struggle against the enemy.

In rural communities which are somewhat similar to urban communities, like land development centers, plantations, etc., the mottoes for organisational methods and struggle activities will be similar to the mottoes for urban areas.

7. Activities in Connection with the Front . . .

(a) *Working upon the upper strata; and taking advantage of the internal differences in the government.*

Vis-à-vis the upper strata and Government employees in the South, our policies are not practical enough; our propaganda and education activities are still inadequate, whereas the enemy is making efforts to corrupt their minds and to urge them to fight us. Sometimes our attitudes and actions toward them are not even consistent with our policies. The capitalists in the South are politically weak, but they are more or less inclined towards neutrality. We should gain influence over proprietors of small shops, intellectuals, Government employees and military officers, so that we can be made aware of the importance of gaining their support, and of the role they may play in the Front. We should give them propaganda on the Front's policies; we should also devise suitable forms of organisation and activity for them and educate them in order to stimulate their anti-U.S. feelings.

Among Government employees, we should develop cadres and sympathisers, and increase propaganda activities; but secret organisations should not be set up as yet.

With regard to dignitaries of religious groups, we should work upon those who are anti-U.S.-Diem. Good dignitaries will be educated and guided to carry out activities to gain influence over the people. Reactionary ones will be unmasked and isolated.

With regard to pro-French elements, even if they are against the revolution, we should still work upon them and win their cooperation in opposing Diem. However, we should understand that we do so just to turn to account the enemy's internal difference and that it is not the same as working upon the upper strata. We should extend the revolutionary movement and not yield our controlled areas to them; and we should try every means of neutralising their influence in areas such as those occupied by the religious sects. We should try by every means to establish relations with them and to secure their cooperation in certain places and at certain moments. Some may even be invited to join the Front, but approval by higher echelons should be obtained.

With regard to organisations such as the National Revolutionary Movement, the Republican Youth, the Women's Solidarity Movement, in areas where we cannot yet carry out subversive activities, such as the cities, we will use the boycott method and will use infiltration to limit their reactionary activities and to disorganise them.

(b) Extending and consolidating the people's organisations

In general the number of people recruited in revolutionary groups is still limited, even in areas where the enemy pressure has been weakened. These groups are often inadequately organised and their activities are not properly planned so that efforts should be made to provide closer leadership to make these organisations more efficient in encouraging the rural population to participate in revolutionary activities and in rural administration.

The Farmer's Association is the most essential organisation for the revolutionary activities in rural areas and our various echelons should make a point of developing and consolidating them. Meanwhile, attention should also be given to youth and women's associations. Young members and female members of the Farmer's Association may join youth or women's associations if they wish, but it is not compulsory. The important thing is to coordinate the activities of the three associations, Farmers, Youth, and Women, in order to avoid overlapping. A person does not have to belong to several groups if it is not practical.

The people's organisations in weak areas and in cities will be set up methodically and secretly. Further efforts would be made to train cadres for the organisations. . .

8. ACTION AGAINST THE ARMY

Action against the army is a strategic task because it has to be carried out from the beginning until the end of the revolutionary struggle in all areas from the rear areas to the enemy's controlled zones; because it not only supports the present struggle so that it can gain advantages step by step, but it also helps in giving strategic orientation for the movement to progress and to achieve complete victory.

New developments are taking place within Diem's army. U.S. Imperialists are gradually turning it into an army of mercenaries. The troops and officers are directly under U.S. control and are beginning to be more or less conscious of nationalsim and dependence. On the other hand, the U.S. is utilising the army in SVN to fight a bloody war, to shoot and kill, so that the fear of the war and the craving for peace are beginning to develop among the troops and officers.

In view of the general trend in the world and in our country, and of the potentialities of the movement under the leadership of the Party, we can see that it is necessary and possible to stimulate nationalism, anti-U.S. feelings, the longing for peace and the aversion to war in the minds of the troops in SVN, with the exception of the feudalists and evil-doers. The slogan, 'coalition between workers, farmers and the troops', is not only used for propaganda to demoralise enemy troops, but under the conditions of a strong political and military struggle movement, it is also capable of inducing enemy units to oppose the war and to rebel. In order for the slogan to be more specific and more effective, it can be worded as follows; 'the people, the troops, and officers in the SVN army should get together to oppose U.S. aggression'. In addition, there will be other slogans aimed at the troops and officers, to stimulate their nationalism, to urge them to oppose the U.S. and the war, to demand peace, and to oppose U.S. commanders.

At present, the people's movement for action against the army is fairly extensive on the surface, but activities such as organising and developing revolutionary structures should be carried out deeper within the enemy's army. Generally speaking, we should continue to rely upon the people, the troops' families, the captured and surrendered troops, to intensify action against the army, but should provide closer leadership and make use of more realistic methods.

Because most officers come from the upper strata of the population, our methods should be nearly the same as those used to work upon the upper strata. We should extend the range of their expectations to induce them to side with the revolution.

Organisations for action against the army should be used properly for immediate and long-range purposes; plans will be made to instigate rebellions and to turn rebel troops into opposition forces to fight the U.S.-Diem clique.[1]

More realistic policies *vis-à-vis* enemy troops and officers should be devised.

At the provincial level and above, councils for action against the army, including representatives of various committees and groups, should be set up under the permanent committee, with cadres specialising in action against officers. . .

*   *   *

(B) *Experiences in turning XB village in Kien Phong Province into a Combattant Village*

The report summed up the lessons to be learned from XB village as follows:

The people are all powerful. It remains only for us to harness ourselves to serving the people. With the people following us,

[1] After a secret meeting with senior officials of the National Liberation Front, Dennis Bloodworth disclosed some of the Viet Cong plans for the subversion of the South Vietnamese Army. The Viet Cong claimed that 40,000 men of the army and its auxiliary defence forces joined them during 1963. They also claimed that they are organised to pull a complete Vietnamese division out of the war, that they are in contact with senior army officers who want to end the war, and that their inside knowledge from men in the Vietnamese units enabled them to make detailed plans for the attack upon the Bien Hoa air base, in which they destroyed six B-57 jet bombers (together with three Skyraider attack bombers and a helicopter), and severely damaged eight more – more than $10 million worth of American equipment, all within 30 minutes: *The Observer*, 29 November 1964

if we have initiative and use tested Party techniques, all operations will succeed.

In the simplest terms, the Party's political line must be based on the needs and interests and rights of the people, the most vital ones. These are concrete and plain to see. On these needs and interests we must build, educating the people, mobilising them to rise and join the revolution.

In any operation we must carefully make specific plans, well in advance. This is particularly true in the launching the organisation of a mass movement. People are not eager to join such movements unless they have carefully been made aware of its objectives and thus are enlightened. In leadership tasks assigned should be graded from the easy to the difficult, and should be assigned with consideration of the person to execute them, that is from capable to less capable persons. In XB, the Party made careful advance preparations; the people were well educated and mobilised prior to the launching of the mass movement and the start of the building of the combat village. Once started everything progressed quickly and smoothly. The day after it was started the people were in a position to repulse an enemy attack. This is the way it should be done elsewhere.

Properly containing security agents and informers depends on uniting the rural people against these enemies. This is done by showing how these agents would deny the people's rights, showing how they do damage, telling about the crimes they commit using specific examples from the local area. This is also done by promoting the spirit of secrecy among the rural people as well as getting them to commit themselves in fighting with the self-defence forces against the enemy. We must also maintain firm leadership of the various civic organisations, and set up special revolutionary groups if necessary—only then can we prevent security agents, local informers and spies from penetrating our area.

We must maintain a spirit of the offense. In order to motivate people to attack our enemies we must make them understand the validity of the Revolution's policies, and must also set up rules and working methods for them. They will not be active unless we carefully show them what they must do. Most of these efforts are political and the poor people must learn how to advance the revolution through political means thus avoiding the risks of regrettable losses which hurt the revolution and discourage the people. Above all, we must keep the masses from becoming passive.

We must better our movement, that is the calibre of Party members, the cadres and all organisations working with us. Highly motivated people will show initiative in carrying out various tasks, making propaganda, etc. In truth, there is a tendency for the Party members to study documents in a mechanical fashion and for form's sake only. As a result the Party members and cadre are not well aware of rules and working methods. In this situation they fail to carry out plans eagerly and as a consequence the movement goes astray. Further, in some places, local policy runs counter, unintentionally to Party policy. Further there are cadres with erroneous thoughts, bureaucrats whose working methods are wrong and these affect the organisation very much. Our internal ranks, therefore, take top priority in training work.

We must increase our spirit of dedication, and be determined properly to carry out Party policy, always serving the people's needs. We need to develop better methods, as was done by the Party at XB. We must rid ourselves of any strong desire for peace, eliminate our fear of the enemy. We must resist adopting irresponsible attitudes. We must develop discipline. We must avoid becoming too optimistic. We must remain always vigilant. We must eliminate bureaucratic attitudes. These things still exist in the Party.

Finally, we must develop a great spirit of offense, determined to attack our enemies ever more fiercely. In this way victory over our enemies finally will be accomplished.

Index

Acheson, Dean, 30, 88
Afghanistan, 38, 65, 69
Aid, external, 196–7, 249–50
Aksai Chin, 203–4
Anglo-Malayan Defence Agreement (1957), 49
Anglo-Malaysian Defence Agreement, 49, 107, 159–60
ANZUS, 18, 115, 116, 211, 213, 225, 247, 250
Association of Southeast Asia, 111, 239
Aung Gyi, Brigadier, 93–4
Australia, xi, 2, 5, 11, 13, 15, 18, 48–9, 51, 57, 59, 86–7, 91, 102, 107, 110, 113–19, 120, 124, 128, 135, 160, 211–12, 244, 248, 258; and nuclear bases, 227; armed forces, 255, 289–90; Asian economic relations, 118; Commonwealth commitments, 203; defence policy, 115–18; foreign policy, 48, 113–15; Labour Party, 114–15; national interests, 118–19; nuclear policy, 116–17
Azahari revolt, 99, 103, 106

Bagdad Pact, 68
Bandung Conference (1955), viii, 23, 24, 29, 64, 107
Bao Dai, Emperor, 185
Bhutan, 31, 43, 60, 203 f., 205–8
Boon Oum, Prince, 87, 88
Borneo, 100 f., 105 ff., 109, 121, 157, 160, 241 f., 276; Commission of Enquiry (1962), 105
Brezhner, Mr., 38, 41
Briggs, Lieut.-General Sir Harold, 177 ff
Briggs Plan, 177–8
Britain, passim; armed forces, 274–7; economic interests in Malaysia, 107; policy in Southern Asia, 46–51; responsibilities of, 18, 26, 28 f., 48–9
Brunei, 47, 103; Partai Rakyat, 105; Sultan of, 105
Burma, 2, 18, 38, 43, 45, 57, 65, 89, 93–8, 135, 138 f., 141 f., 156, 208 f., 235 f., 239–40, 249, 251, 258; Anti-Fascist People's Freedom League, 93, 137; armed forces, 285–6; and Chinese nuclear capability, 226; Chinese policy on, 31–3; Communist Party, 137; Kuomintang troops in, 95–6; Mon National Defence Organisation, 95; National

United Front, 137; nationalisation in, 96–7; Red Flag Communists, 94–5, 97, 137; security problems, 156–8; Socialist Programme Party, 93; White Flag Communists, 94–5, 97, 137

Camau Peninsula, 148, 191
Cambodia, 2, 18, 29, 38, 43 f., 51, 55, 56, 73, 77–82, 88 f., 128, 135 ff., 149 f., 158 f., 184, 187, 208, 210, 222 n., 235, 239–40, 249, 259, 282–3; Chinese policy on, 31–3; Nationalist Party, 138; People's Socialist Community, 138; Viet Cong in, 156
Canada, 11; and Indo-Chinese conflict, 203
CENTO, 18, 26, 68 f., 203, 252
Ceylon, 63, 135, 251
Chiang Kai-shek, 7, 125 n., 127, 128
Che Boestamam, 106
Ch'en Yi, Marshal, 133, 227, 230
Chih Kung Party, 142
China, passim; and conventional war, 200–14; and the Asian balance, 1–27; armed forces, 200–2, 262–5; Communist Party, 180, 187, 202; foreign policy of, 31–6; hostilities against India, see India; national interests of, 28 f., 30–8; nuclear capability of, 17, 36–8, 214–33; 239–40, 253–4, 263; objectives in Southern Asia, 32; Pakistan's recognition of, 68; plans for Himalayan states, 204–5; political objectives, 21–2; U.S. views on policy of, 42–3
Chou En-lai, 68
Clandestine Communist Organisations, 106–7
Cobbold Commission Report, 105, 106
Cobbold, Lord, 105, 106
Collective security, viii–ix, 2–3, 5 f., 10, 17–21, 159–61, 196–7, 216, 223–4, 225 f., 234–47, 251–4; problems of, 248–61
Colombo Powers, 235, 249, 251
Cominform, 186
Confrontation, 3–4, 8, 15–16, 25–6, 99–104, 106, 108 f., 157, 160, 211–12, 213, 234, 236, 241, 244, 250–1
Counter-Guerrilla Operations. The Philippine Experience, 166 n., 171, 174

Counter-insurgency, 162, 164, 166–99, 238, 242–3
Counter-subversion, 161 ff., 238, 244–5, 147–8
Czechoslovakia, 73

Darlac Province, 149 ff.
Darjeeling-Dooars District, 204
de Gaulle, President, 29, 51, 53, 55, 56, 73
Defence aid, external, 159–200
Dhanarajata, 52, 91–2
Dich-Van propaganda units, 146
Diem, President Ngo Dinh, 51, 75–7, 141, 143, 153, 162 f., 185, 188–9, 193, 194, 197, 199, 281, 299, 300 f.; assassination of, 193; 'Personalism', 195
Dienbienphu, Battle of, 24, 28, 45, 53, 162
Douglas-Home, Sir Alec, 108
Dulles, John Foster, 8 f., 74 f.; on Battle of Dienbienphu, 45; on SEATO, 12, 19; on Southeast Asia, 30

East Bengal, 66
East Germany, 260, 268
EDCOR, 172–5
Eisenhower, President, 74, 226; on loss of Indonesia, 24
European Community, 49, 57

Fall, Bernard, 53, 146, 148
Fatherland Front, 187, 188
Formosa, *see* Taiwan
France, 11, 18, 46, 73, 79, 84 f., 87 f., 185, 188 f., 205–6, 237, 246, 249; and SEATO, 13; armed forces, 276–7; Communist Party, 186; national interests of, 38–9, 51–7; policy of, 51–7; proposals for neutral Viet Nam, 54–7; responsibilities, 26, 28 f.
Free Cambodia Movement, 78
Fulbright programme, 97

Geneva Agreement (1954), 6, 38, 40, 55, 83, 85, 189; Conference (1954), 28, 29, 41–2, 74, 79, 80, 187–8
Guam, 13
Gurkhastan, 204

Harkins, General, 197
Harriman, W. Averell, 131
Himalayas, 60 ff., 204, 205
Ho Chi Minh, 38, 71, 72, 73, 185, 189–90; trail, 82, 209
Hoan, Dr. Nguyen Ton, 77

Holyoake, Keith, 119, 121
Hong Kong, 26, 47, 126, 275
Hou Hao sect, 189
Huk, 167–75, 184; revolt, 242
Hukbong Bayan Laban Sa Hapon, 167
'Huklandia', 169
Hunan, 201
Huong, Tran Van, 77, 185

Ikeda, Hayato, 123, 124
India, vii, viii, x, 2 f., 7 f., 10, 18, 20, 29, 44, 57, 66–9, 96, 107, 122, 126, 128, 131, 137, 205 ff., 212, 215 220–4, 235–6, 242–4, 252, 255–6, 258; and Chinese nuclear capability, 220–4; armed forces, 254–5, 278–9; Atomic Energy Commission, 221, 222n.; Chinese hostilities against, x, 20, 23–5, 40, 49, 58–65, 67, 68–9, 93, 129, 202–9, 220, 241, 251, 253; Communist Party, 40, 68, 249; non-alignment of, 24–5; policies and potentials, 59–65; relations with Pakistan, 59, 60, 62 ff.
Indian Ocean, 258–9
Indochina, 4, 21, 24, 30, 38, 49, 53, 55 f., 65, 71–98, 128, 143, 156, 157, 183–9, 208, 210–11, 215, 227, 230, 239, 251, 255, 280; Communist Party, 185–9; French cultural influence in, 26; War, 28, 29, 41, 45, 147 n., 148, 156, 185–7, 210
Indonesia, x, 2, 3, 18, 21, 29, 44, 47, 50, 57, 62, 65, 98–103, 105 f., 109, 111–13, 116, 121 f., 128, 135, 137, 139, 141 f., 211–15, 226, 234–6, 240, 242–5, 249, 250–1, 258 ff.; and Maphilindo, 20–1; armed forces, 255; as threat to Southern Asian security, 25–6; Chinese policy on, 31–3; Communist Party, 45, 100 ff., 135–6, 138, 212, 244, 249; instability of, 45; Nationalist Party, 45; rebellion (1958), 236. *See also* Malaysia
Insurgency, 130 ff., 139 ff., 143–58
Israel, 97

Japan, viii, 2 ff., 11, 18, 30, 37, 57 ff., 61, 89, 96, 118, 135, 160, 167 ff., 175, 212, 218, 238–40, 242–4, 274; and Chinese nuclear capability, 224–5; armed forces, 291–2; defence policy, 243; foreign policy, 121–5; Liberal Democratic Party, 122–3
Jars, Plain of, 82, 283–4
Java, 101 f., 212
Johnson, President, 72, 87, 108, 109, 164; on North Viet Nam, 44–5
Johore, Straits of, 50

Kachins, 95
Kalimantan, 107
Kamchatka Peninsula, 41
Kammouene Province, 209, 210
Karakoram Pass, 204
Karens, 95
Kashmir dispute, 60, 62, 128, 202, 222, 239, 250–1, 253; Security Council on, 66–8
Kashmir National Conference Party, 67
Keidenren, 123
Kennedy, Senator Robert, 108
Khams, 204
Khanh, General Nguyen, 76, 185, 195, 197–8; 'pacification plan', 193–4
Khiem, General Tran Thien, 185
Khmer Issarak, 187
Khmer Serai, 78
Khomen, Thanat, 43
Khrushchev, Nikita, 40, 41, 69, 75, 130–1, 136, 208, 229, 263, 269; fall of, 38, 101
Kien Giang Province, 294
Kien Phong Province, 151
Kong Le, General, 51, 82, 283
Korea, 4, 12. See also North Korea; South Korea
Korean War, 12, 29, 31, 41 f., 123, 230 ff., 253
Kosygin, A., 38, 41
Kris Srivara, 93
Krishnamachari, T. T., 61–2
Kuomintang, 127, 140, 142, 185
Kurile Islands, 41

Lansdowne Committee Report (1963), 105–6
Lao Dong, 186–7; Youth, 152
Laos, ix, 2, 6, 18, 23, 38, 43, 55–6, 73, 78, 80–9, 91 f., 111, 120, 131, 135, 137–9, 141 f., 145, 149, 156, 157, 159, 164 f., 184, 187, 208–10, 236–7, 248–50, 255, 259, 280; armed forces, 283–4; Chinese policy on, 31–3; Communist Party, 137–8; International Control Commission, 84
Lee Kuan Yew, 104, 105 n., 107, 108, 139
Lodge, Henry Cabot, 76, 197
Luzon, 110, 168; subversion in, 159

Macapagal, President, 110, 111, 112
McCarthy Line, 97
McMahon Line, 97
McNamara, Robert S., 58, 75, 76, 197–8; on nuclear defence, 14
Magsaysay, President Ramón, 110, 162, 166, 168 ff., 194, 199

Mahrenda, King, 206
Malaya, 47, 49, 100, 139 f., 179 ff., 191 ff., 196, 199, 211; Anti-Imperialist National Front, 180; Communist Party, 167, 175–83; counter-insurgency in, 175–83; Emergency, 106, 139, 157, 163, 175–84, 242; Labour Party, 177; New Villages scheme, 177–8, 183; People's Anti-Japanese Army, 175 ff.; People's Progressive Party, 103; Socialist Front, 103–4; subversion in, 175 ff.
Malayan Chinese Association, 177, 182, 183
Malayan Races Liberation Army, 175 ff.
Malaysia, x, 2, 18, 26, 45, 47, 57, 64 f., 99 ff., 101, 103–9, 111–13, 116, 121, 128, 135, 137, 156, 158–60, 181–2, 211–15, 226, 240–1, 247 f., 259, 275; Agreement (1963), 106; Alliance Party, 227; armed forces, 287–8; British commitments in, 49; Chinese policy on, 31–3; Commonwealth troops in, 13; Communist Party, 138–9; confrontation by Indonesia, 25–6, 28, 45, 99 ff., 104, 106, 108, 109, 157, 160, 211–13, 227, 236, 239, 241–2, 244, 250–1, 253; fears of Chinese chauvinism, 139–40; internal security problems, 109, 156–8; Socialist Front, 106; U.S. attitude towards, 107–8
Manila Conference (1954), 65, 251; Treaty (1954), viii, 18, 30, 53, 74, 88, 160–1, 203, 205–7
Mansfield Report, 3–5, 11, 19, 42, 54, 78, 164
Mansfield, Senator Mike. See Mansfield Report
Mao Tse-tung, 7, 165, 176, 229, 262–3; on China's nuclear aims, 36
Maphilindo Zone, 20–1, 25, 65, 98–113, 211, 239, 250, 251, 255; armed forces, 286–9; U.S. decisions on, 45
Mekong Basin programme, 239
Mekong River, 82, 85, 89 ff., 151, 210, 239
Menon, V. K. Krishna, 64
Menzies, Sir Robert, 118, 255
Meo guerrillas, 83
Min Yuen, 176–83
Minh, General Duong Dan, 185
Montagnards, 148–55

National Liberation Front, 153, 190, 301 n.
Nationalism, 28–30, 45, 103, 111, 182
NATO, 3, 12, 41, 46, 58, 223, 237, 252,

253, 260, 268, 275–6; compared with SEATO, 12–20

Ne Win, General, 93, 94, 95, 96, 137

Nehru, Pandit Jawaharlal, 8, 37, 64, 65, 205, 208, 220, 222, 239; death of, 59, 60

Nepal, 43, 57 f., 60, 63, 203 ff., 207 f.; Communist Party, 206; National Panchayat, 206; Rana dynasty, 206

Netherlands, 58, 99, 103; interests in Indonesia, 57

New Guinea, 112, 116, 241, 255, Trust Territory, 113, 116

New Zealand, 2, 5, 13, 18, 51, 59, 87, 107, 110, 135, 160, 227, 248; aid to Malaysia, 49; and Indo-Chinese conflict, 203; armed forces, 290–1; defence and foreign policies, 119–21

Nguyen Chi Thanh, 73

Nol, General Lon, 77–8, 80

Non-alignment, 1–2, 20, 63–5, 67, 222, 251, 255; vulnerability of, 24

North-East Frontier Agency, 204, 207, 208

North Borneo, 105, 109. *See also* Borneo

North Korea, 38, 135, 259

North Viet Nam, *passim*; armed forces, 255, 280; as main source of subversion, 137–8

Okinawa, 13, 225, 274

'Open Arms' policy, 162, 194

'Operation Sunrise', 191–4

Overseas Chinese, 22, 43, 89, 98, 100–1, 138–42, 168, 175 ff., 178, 180, 248

Pacific Ocean, 41, 258–9

Pakistan, 2, 18 f., 30, 37, 44, 60, 62, 128, 159, 202, 208, 212, 222, 235–7, 241, 246, 249–50, 252 f.; armed forces, 255, 279–80; *entente* with China, 68–9; policies and potentials, 65–8

Pampanga Province, 110, 173

Pan-Malayan Islamic Party, 103–4

Papua, 116, 255

Pathet Lao, 55–6, 81 ff., 87 f., 90 ff., 131, 137, 156, 184, 187, 209–10, 237, 249–50, 280, 283–4; strength of, 255

People's Anti-Japanese Resistance Army, 167

Philippines, the, 2, 5, 13, 18 f., 25, 29, 30, 57 f., 64, 92, 109–13, 122, 124, 126, 136, 137, 141, 162, 167, 192, 194 ff., 199, 212, 214, 235–7, 242, 251, 258, 274; and Chinese nuclear capability, 226; and Maphilindo,

20–1; armed forces, 255, 288–9; Attraction Programme, 194; Chinese Communist Party, 168; Communist Party, 159, 167; counter-insurgency in (1946–54), 166–75; insurrection in, 110, 159, 167 ff., 184; People's Liberation Party, 167

Phoumi Novasam, General, 82, 84, 87, 88

Poland, 73, 268

Portugal, 7, 241; national interests in Southern Asia, 57

Pracheachon Party, 138

Praphet Charusathien, General, 92–3

Quang Tri Province, 193–4

Quemoy, 230, 293

Quirino, President Elpidio, 110, 167–8, 171–2

Rahman, Tunku Abdul, 47, 104, 107, 109, 111, 182

Reeds, Plain of, 148, 151, 210

Republican Youth, 299

Rhade, 148–55; revolt in, 151

Roosevelt, President F. D., 53

Roxas, President, 167

Royal Khmer Army, 78

Rusk, Dean, 58, 88, 197, 210; on South Viet Nam, 24 n.; on Thai independence, 43

Ryuku Islands, 30, 125, 225

Sabah, 103, 105, 109, 116, 140; Philippine claim to, 111, 112, 113

Sakhalin, 41

Sarawak, 47, 103, 105, 109, 112, 116, 140; People's Party, 107

Sarit Thanarat, Field-Marshal, 87–9, 91 f.

Sato, Eisaku, 125, 239

Savannakhet Province, 83

SEATO, ix, 3, 5, 12, 19, 23, 26, 29, 30, 32, 37, 41–57, 65–9, 75, 79, 86–93, 102, 107, 109, 110–11, 113, 116, 119, 142, 148–55, 158–61, 202 f., 208–9, 211 ff., 222, 234–9, 246–8, 249 n.; 250–4, 260, 270–7; and Chinese nuclear capability, 226; compared with NATO, 12–20; criticism of Britain in, 48; nuclear ambiguities of, 14–15

Shan states, 89, 95

Shastri, Mr., 59

Sihanouk, Prince Norodom, 56, 77–9, 138; on American aid, 249, 250; ultimatum of, 80–1

Sikkim, 31, 43, 60, 203 f., 206–8; National Congress Party, 205

Singapore, 101, 103 f., 107, 109, 139–41, 175, 180 f., 213; Barisan Socialis Party, 103, 104, 106; base, 47, 49–50, 107; People's Action Party, 103, 104–5, 139
Sinkeang, 36, 203, 204, 215, 263
Sino-Nepalese Treaty (1956), 206
Sino-Soviet dispute, 33–4, 35–6, 38, 39–40, 49, 73, 101, 131, 132–5, 217–19, 229–30
Sino-Soviet Treaty (1950), 39, 218
Smith, General Walter Bedell, 74, 80
Souphanouvong, Prince, ix, 83, 84, 85, 187
South China Sea, 159
South Korea, 5, 18, 164, 272, 274
South Viet Nam, *passim*; armed forces, 281–2; counter-insurgency in, 183–99; Military Revolutionary Council, 185; neutralism in, 198–9; subversion in, 183–99; U.S. Commitment in, 43–4
Souvanna Phouma, Prince, 55–6, 81–2
Soviet Union, *passim*; armed forces, 265–70; military power in Asia, 41; national interests, 28 f., 38–41; political objectives, 21–2; position taken in Sino-Zudian dispute, 25. *See also* Sino-Soviet
Strategic hamlets, 191–4, 196, 294, 295
Subversion, viii, 90, 112, 130–58, 160 ff., 166–99, 241, 244–5, 294–303; reasons for, 143; techniques of, 143–58
Sukarno, President, xi, 29, 40–1, 45, 65, 98–100, 101, 102, 108, 112, 136, 138, 259

Tadzhik Soviet Republic, 203
Taiwan, 2, 7, 13, 18, 37–8, 42, 59, 122, 125–8, 141, 224, 241, 260, 274; armed forces, 292–3
Takla Makan Desert, 36
Taruc, Luis, 110, 167, 172–3
Taylor, General, 197–8
Teheran Conference, 53
Templar, General Sir Gerald, 177 ff.
Terrorism, 145–6
Thailand, 2, 5, 18, 38, 43 f., 46, 51–3, 56 f., 64, 78 ff., 86–93, 95, 111, 135 ff., 140, 141, 143, 156 ff., 178–9, 208 ff., 214, 232, 235–7, 239, 246, 249, 251–2, 258 f.; and Chinese nuclear capability, 226–7; armed forces, 255, 284–5; Chinese Communist Party, 138–9; Chinese policy on, 31–3; Communist Party, 138–9; King of, 90; Queen of, 90; Regional

Community Development Centre, 86; U.S. support for, 30
Thei-Meo Autonomous Zone, 151
Thompson Mission, 254
Thompson, R. K. G., 191
Tibet, 63, 203 ff., 208
Timor, 57, 116
Tin Pe, Brigadier, 93, 94
Togliatti, 32, 229
Tongking, 244

U Thant, 117
United Kingdom. *See* Britain
United Malay National Association, 181 ff.
U.N.O., 5, 64, 67–8, 80, 112 n., 117, 128, 165, 188, 229; Good Offices Committee, 114; Trusteeship Council, 116
U.S.A., *passim*; armed forces, 270–4; Asian fear of power of, 45–6; involvement in Southern Asia, 28 f.; Military Assistance Advisory Group, 150, 196–7; national interests, 29–30, 41–6; nuclear policy of, 14; nuclear power of, 7; policy of, 8; political involvement in South Viet Nam, 197–9; relations with China, 4–12; responsibilities of, 18; Senate Report on Foreign Aid (1957), 164–5; strategy, 14; suspicion about British policy, 48
U.S.S.R. *See* Soviet Union

Viet Cong, 54, 72, 76 f., 82, 85, 88, 143–59, 161, 165, 184–99, 210, 239, 242, 244, 250, 253, 280, 281; and minorities, 148–55; 'Government', 184; reports, 294–303
Viet Minh, 85, 90, 138, 145–8, 150, 185–90, 195, 210, 250
Vietnamese People's Liberation Committee, 185
Vietnamese Provisional Government, 185
Vo Nguyen Giap, 73

Warsaw Pact, 3, 12, 15, 17
West Bengal, 136
West Germany, 97, 110–11, 260, 274; Asian interests, 57–8
West Iran, 26, 57, 99, 100, 116, 255

XB village, subversion of, 144 n., 147, 152–5, 165, 301–3
Xieng Khouang Province, 82

Yalta Conference, 53
Yunnan, 209